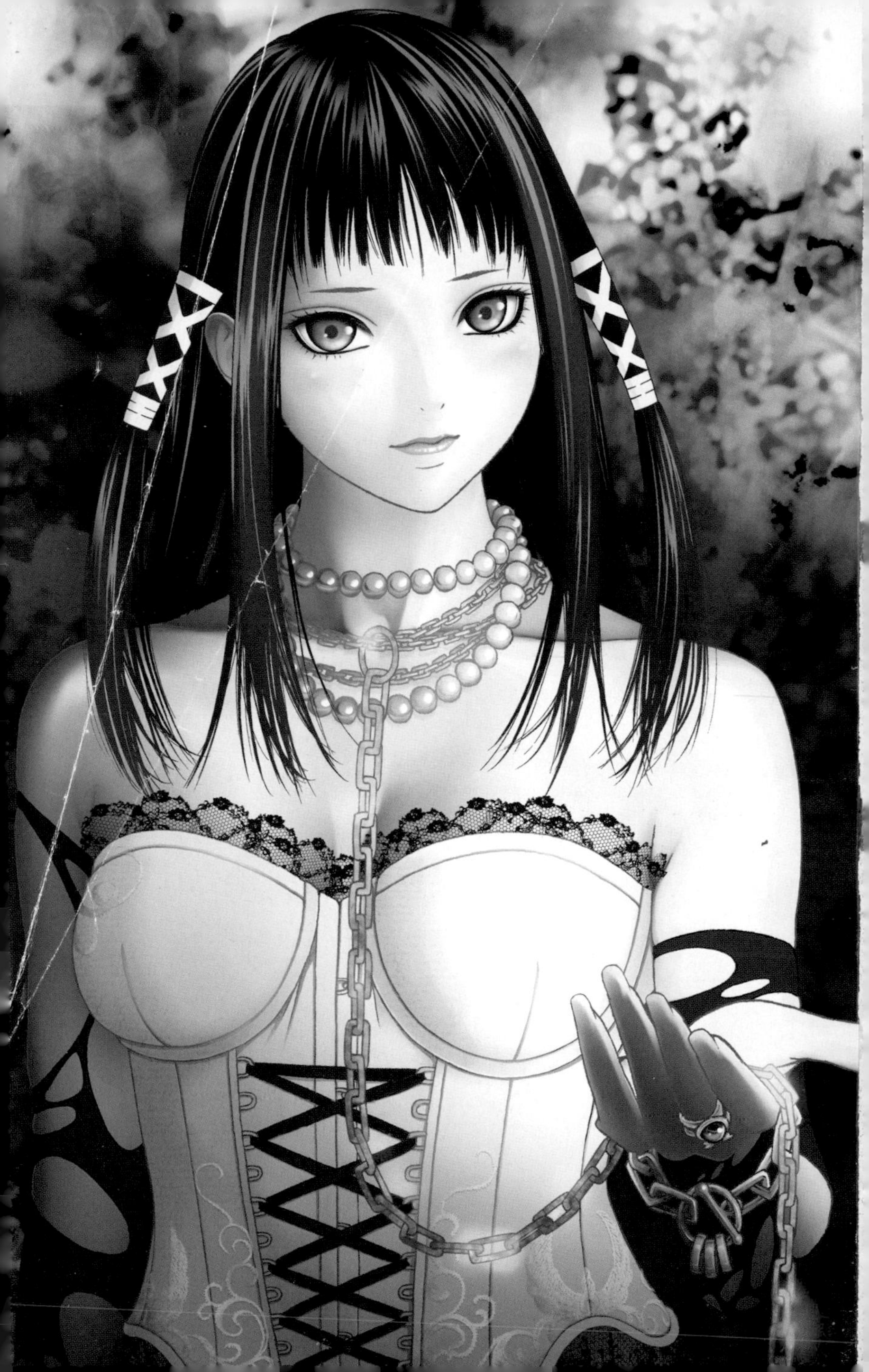

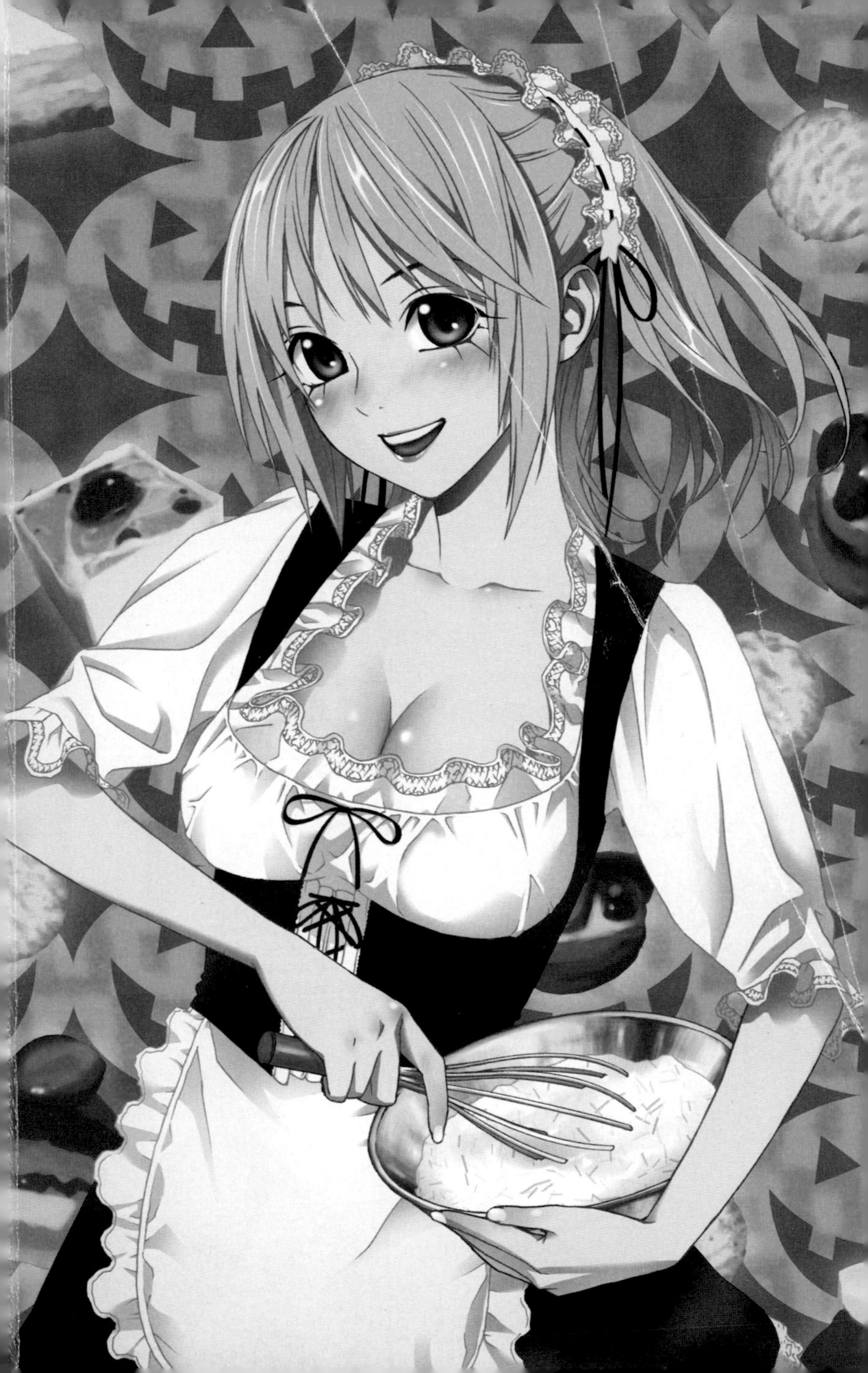

ROSARIO+VAMPIRE

Season II

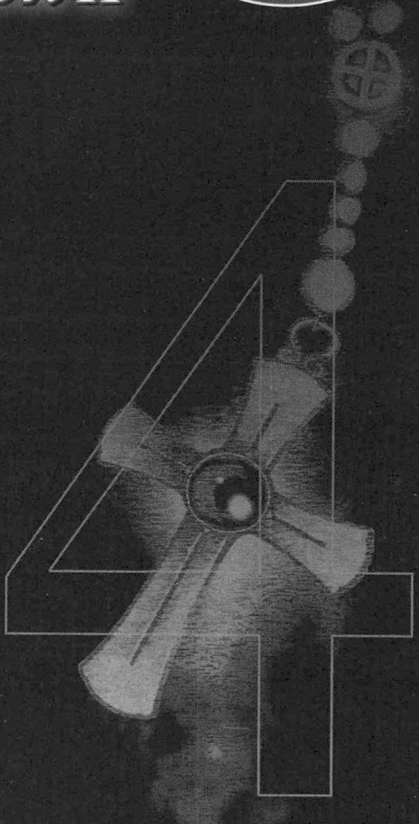

AKIHISA IKEDA

Horror Story Thus Far

Tsukune Aono accidentally enrolls in Yokai Academy, a high school for monsters! After befriending the school's cutest girl, Moka Akashiya, he decides to stay...even though Yokai has a zero-tolerance policy toward humans. (A *fatal* policy.) Tsukune has to hide his true identity while fending off attacks by monster gangs. He survives with the help of his News Club friends—Moka, Kurumu, Yukari and Mizore.

But then a student riot nearly destroys the school, and classes are canceled for half a year for "remodeling." It's already spring by the time the gang (now sophomores) return... and meet Moka's rowdy little sister, Koko, who has enrolled as a freshman.

Then Mizore invites the News Club to her home, the Land of the Snow Fairies...only to be promptly kidnapped! Tsukune and friends sneak into the local Flower Offering Ceremony to save Mizore, but find themselves face-to-face with an unexpected foe...

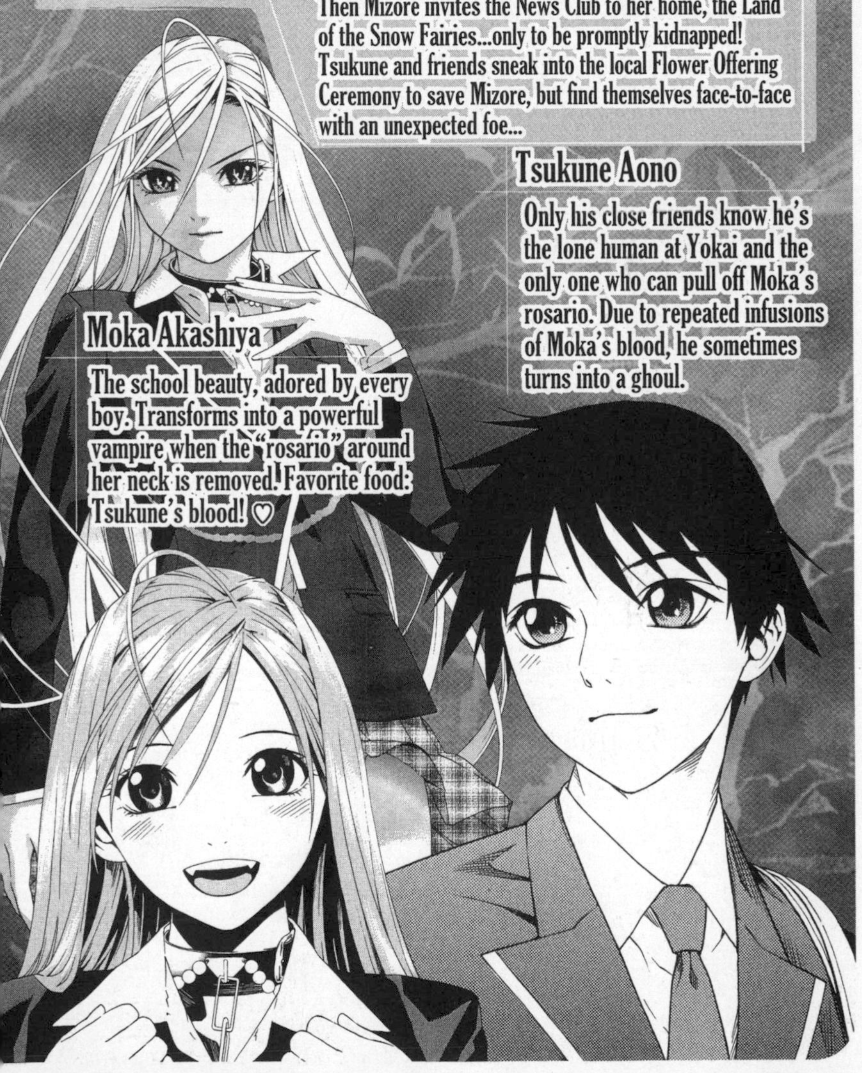
Tsukune Aono
Only his close friends know he's the lone human at Yokai and the only one who can pull off Moka's rosario. Due to repeated infusions of Moka's blood, he sometimes turns into a ghoul.
Moka Akashiya
The school beauty, adored by every boy. Transforms into a powerful vampire when the "rosario" around her neck is removed. Favorite food: Tsukune's blood! ♡

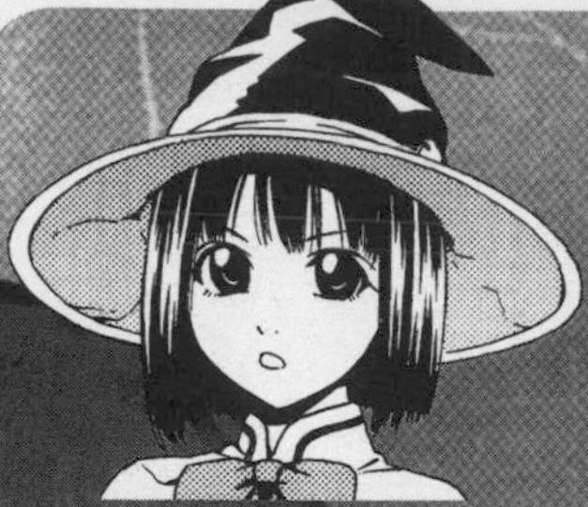

Yukari Sendo

A mischievous witch. Much younger than the others. A genius who skipped several grades.

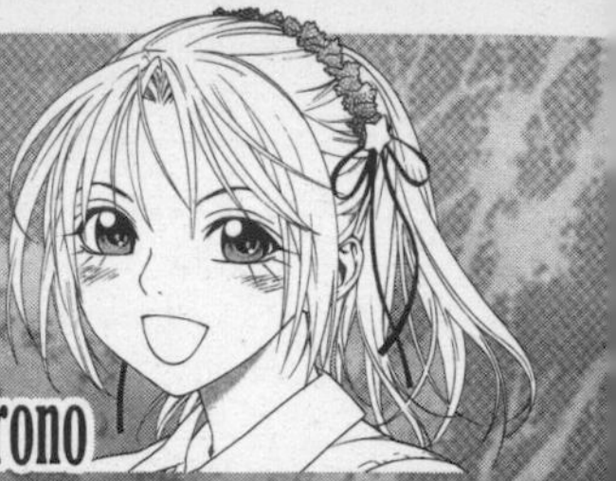

Kurumu Kurono

A succubus. Also adored by all the boys—for two obvious reasons. Fights with Moka over Tsukune.

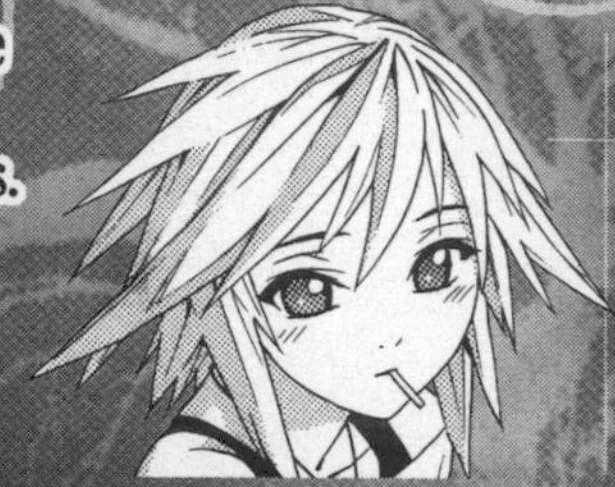

Mizore Shirayuki

A snow fairy who manipulates ice. She fell in love with Tsukune after reading his newspaper articles.

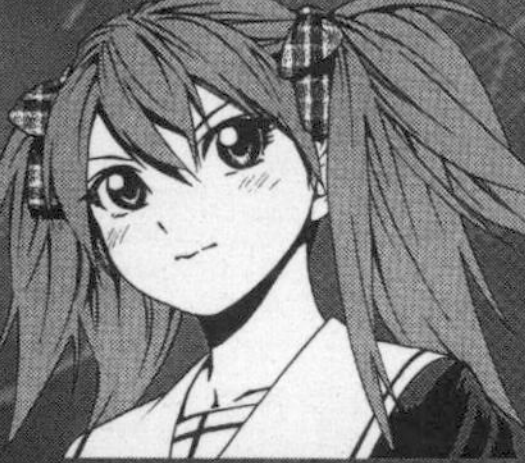

Koko Shuzen

Moka's stubborn little sister. Koko worships Moka's inner vampiric self but hates her sweet exterior. Koko's pet bat transforms into a weapon.

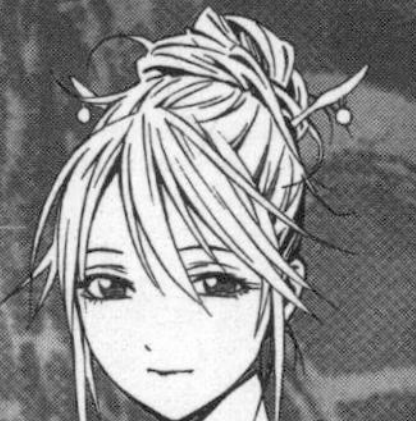

Tsurara Shirayuki

Mizore's mother. She dreams of the day that Tsukune will wake up to her daughter's charms and give her some grandchildren.

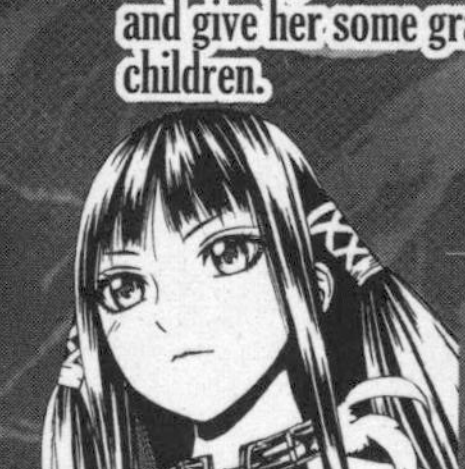

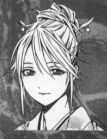

Ruby Tojo

A witch who only learned to trust humans after meeting Tsukune. Now employed as Yokai's headmaster's assistant.

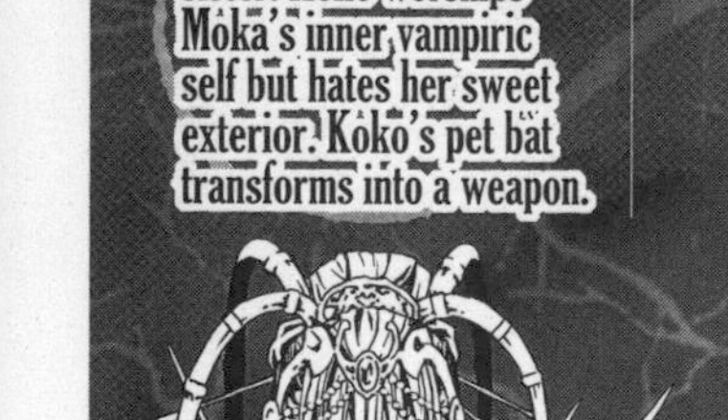

Snow Oracle

The leader of the Land of the Snow Fairies. Clairvoyant, especially in such matters as who the local Snow Fairies are destined to marry.

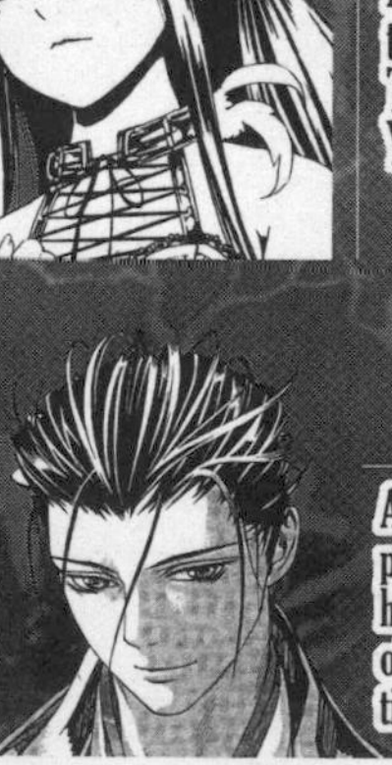

Miyabi Fujisaki

According to the Snow Oracle's prophecy, he is Mizore's husband-to-be. Also an executive of an as-yet mysterious organization from the human world.

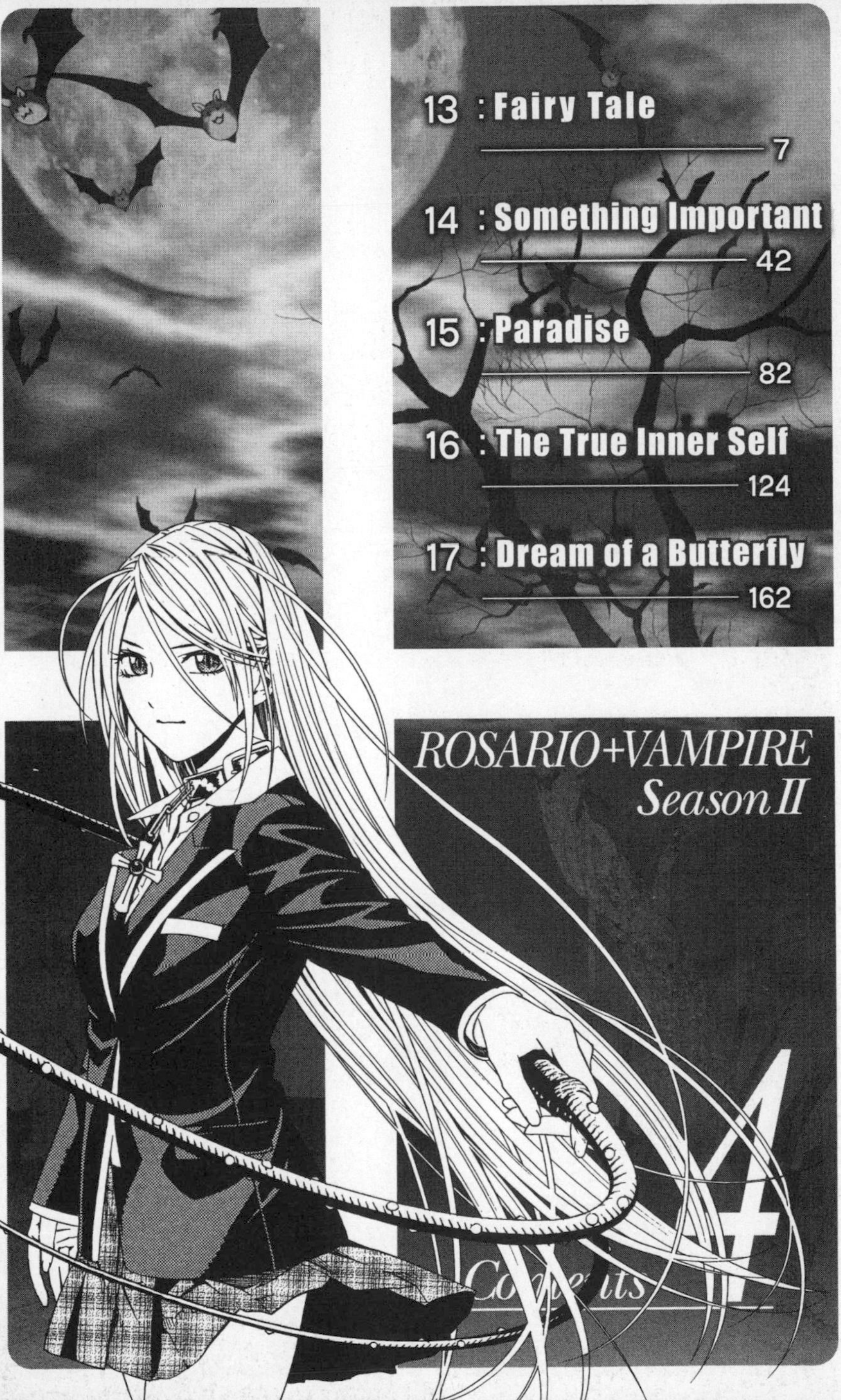

ROSARIO+VAMPIRE Season II 4

Contents

13: Fairy Tale

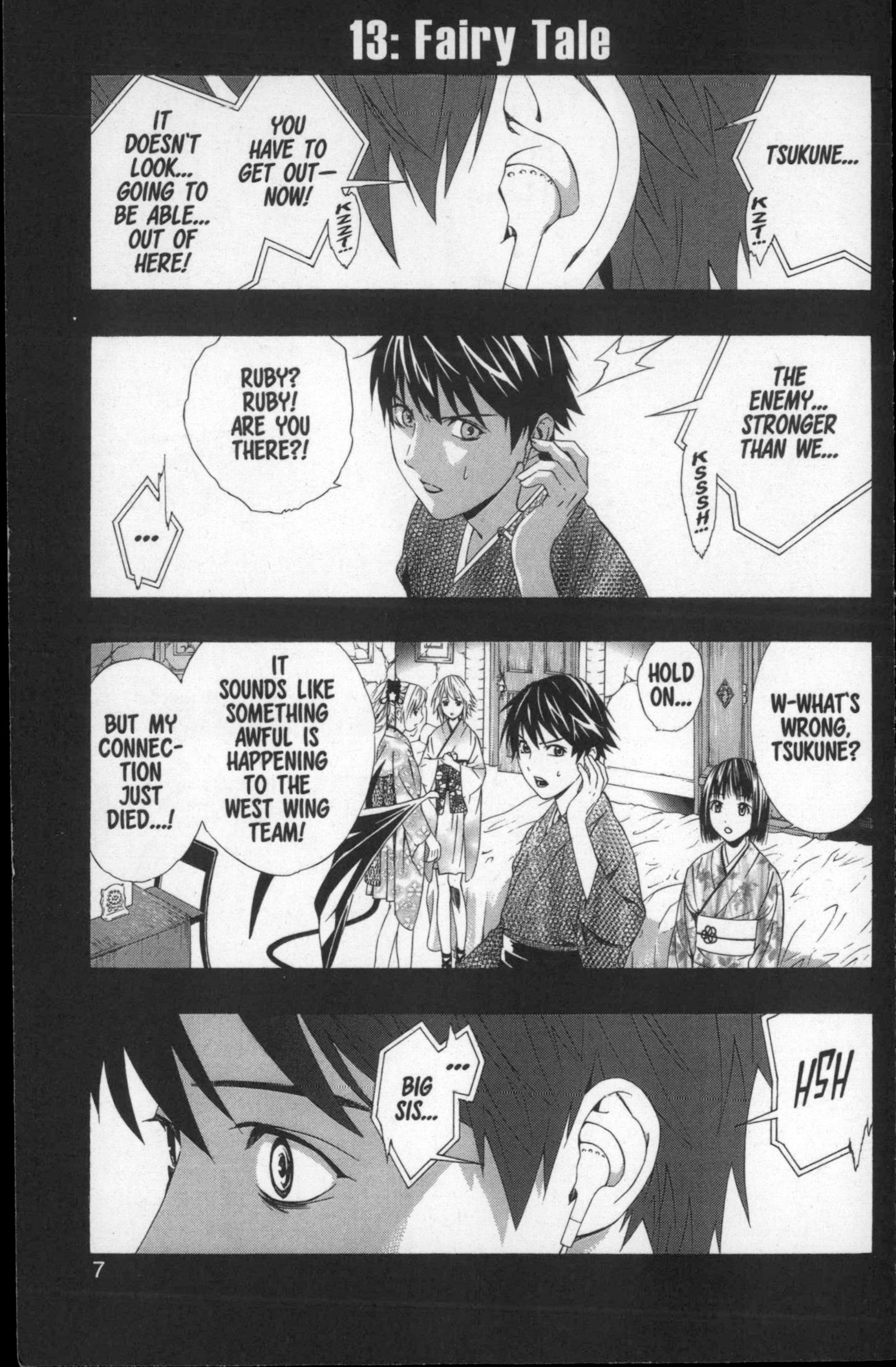
TSUKUNE...
KZT...
YOU HAVE TO GET OUT— NOW!
KZZT!!
IT DOESN'T LOOK... GOING TO BE ABLE... OUT OF HERE!
THE ENEMY... STRONGER THAN WE...
KSSSH...
RUBY? RUBY! ARE YOU THERE?!
...
W-WHAT'S WRONG, TSUKUNE?
HOLD ON...
IT SOUNDS LIKE SOMETHING AWFUL IS HAPPENING TO THE WEST WING TEAM!
BUT MY CONNEC-TION JUST DIED...!
HSH
... BIG SIS...

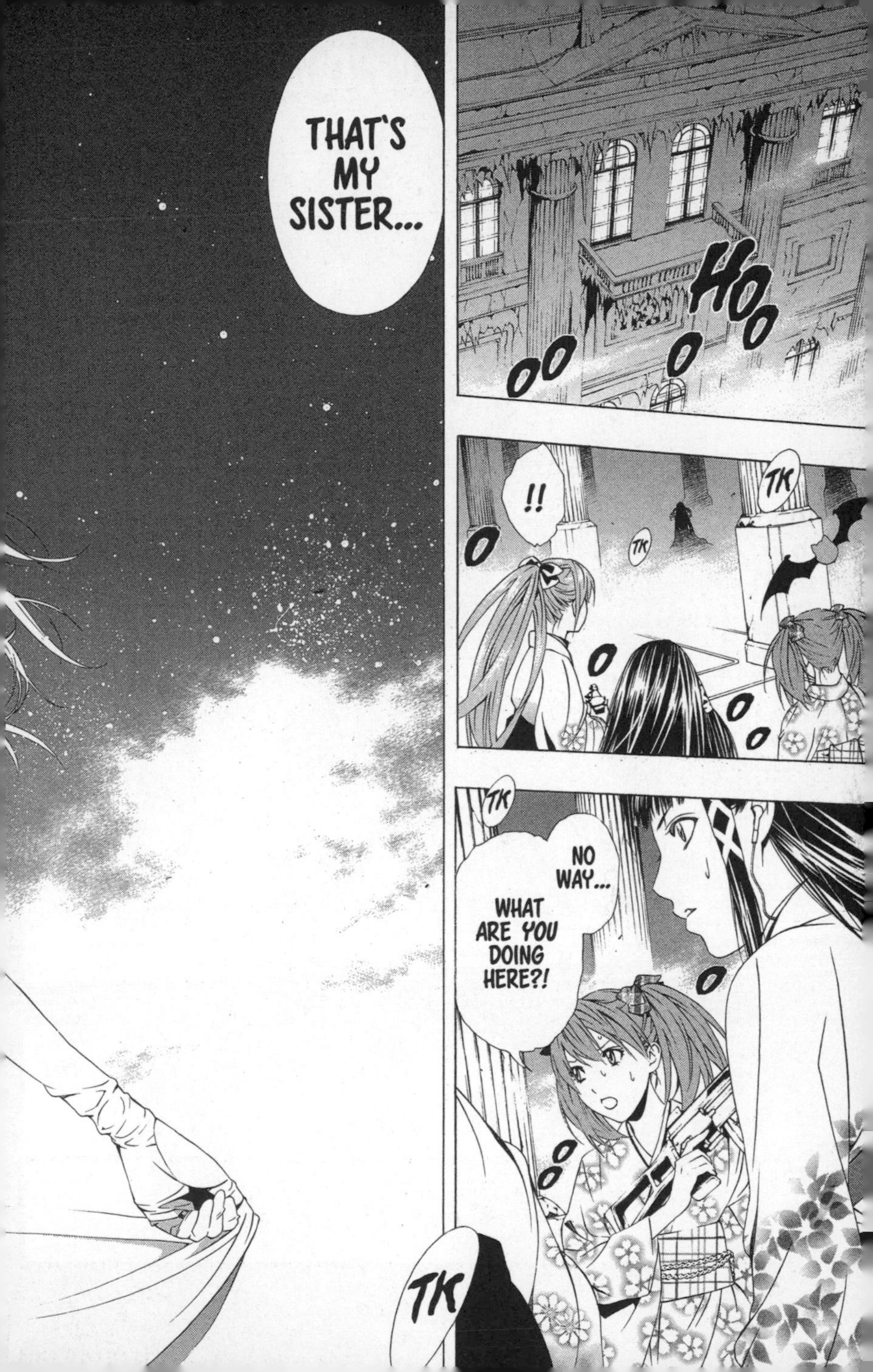
HOOOOO
!!
TK
TK
OOOO
TK
NO WAY...
WHAT ARE YOU DOING HERE?!
OOO
TK
THAT'S MY SISTER...

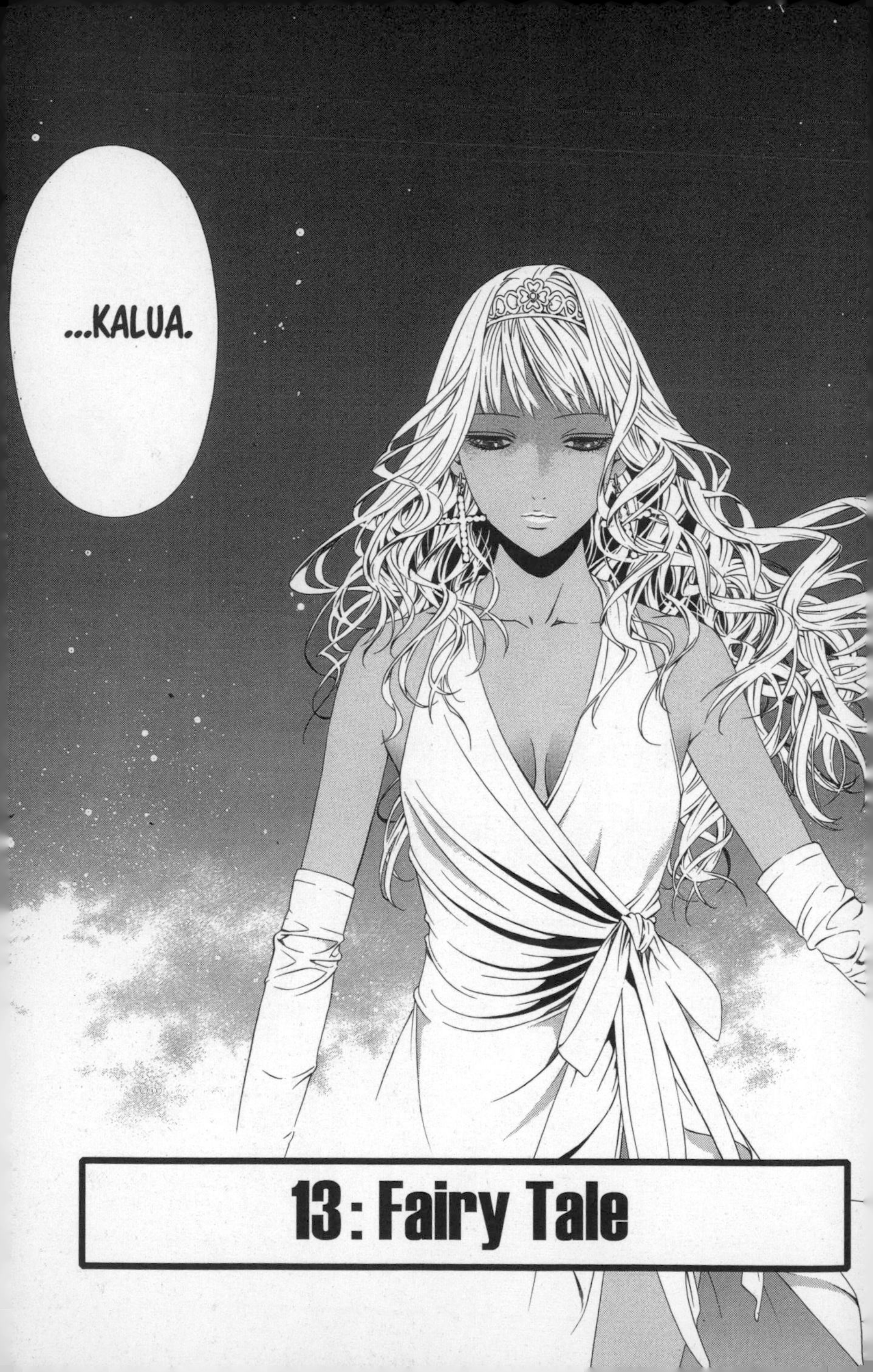
...KALUA.
13 : Fairy Tale

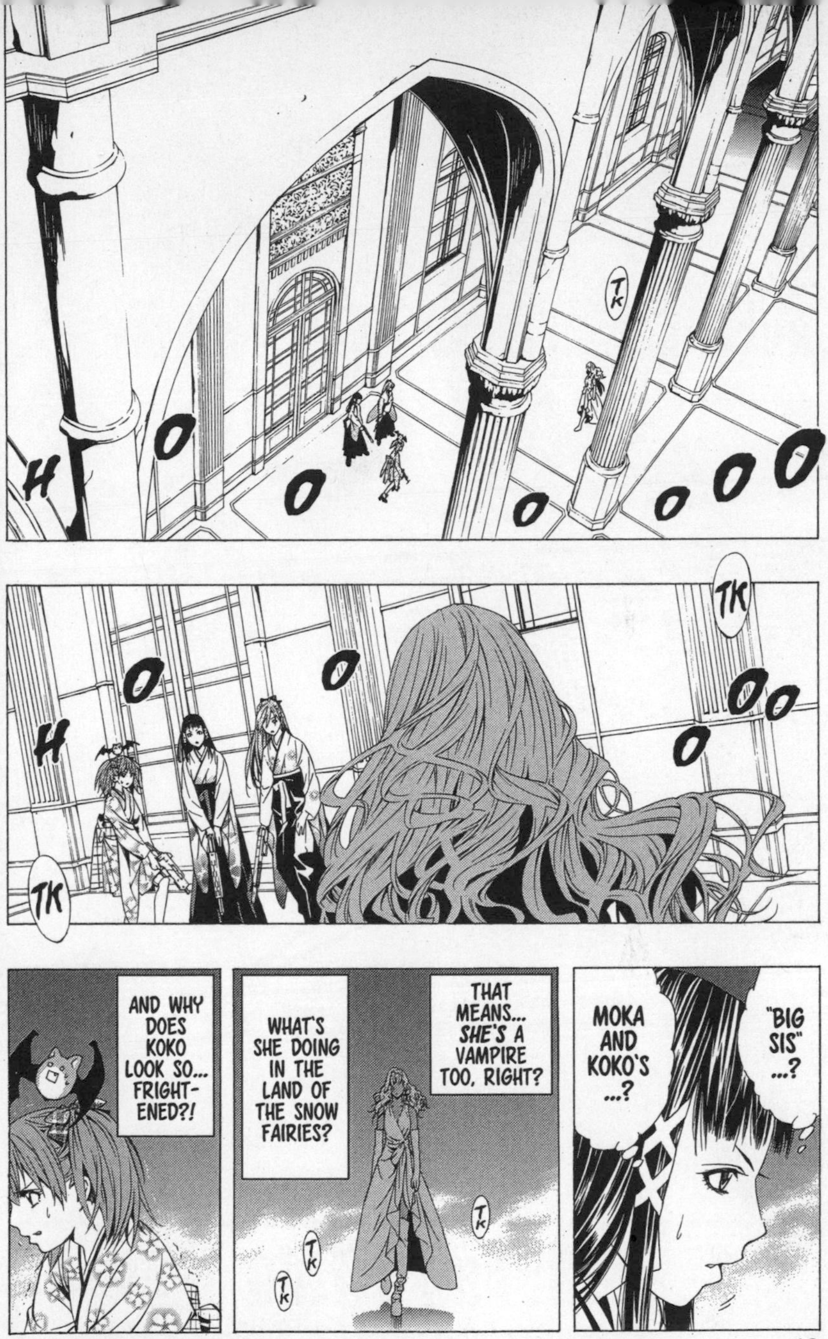
TK
HOOOOOO
TK
HOOOOOO
TK
"BIG SIS" ...?
MOKA AND KOKO'S ...?
THAT MEANS... SHE'S A VAMPIRE TOO, RIGHT?
WHAT'S SHE DOING IN THE LAND OF THE SNOW FAIRIES?
TK
TK
TK
AND WHY DOES KOKO LOOK SO... FRIGHTENED?!

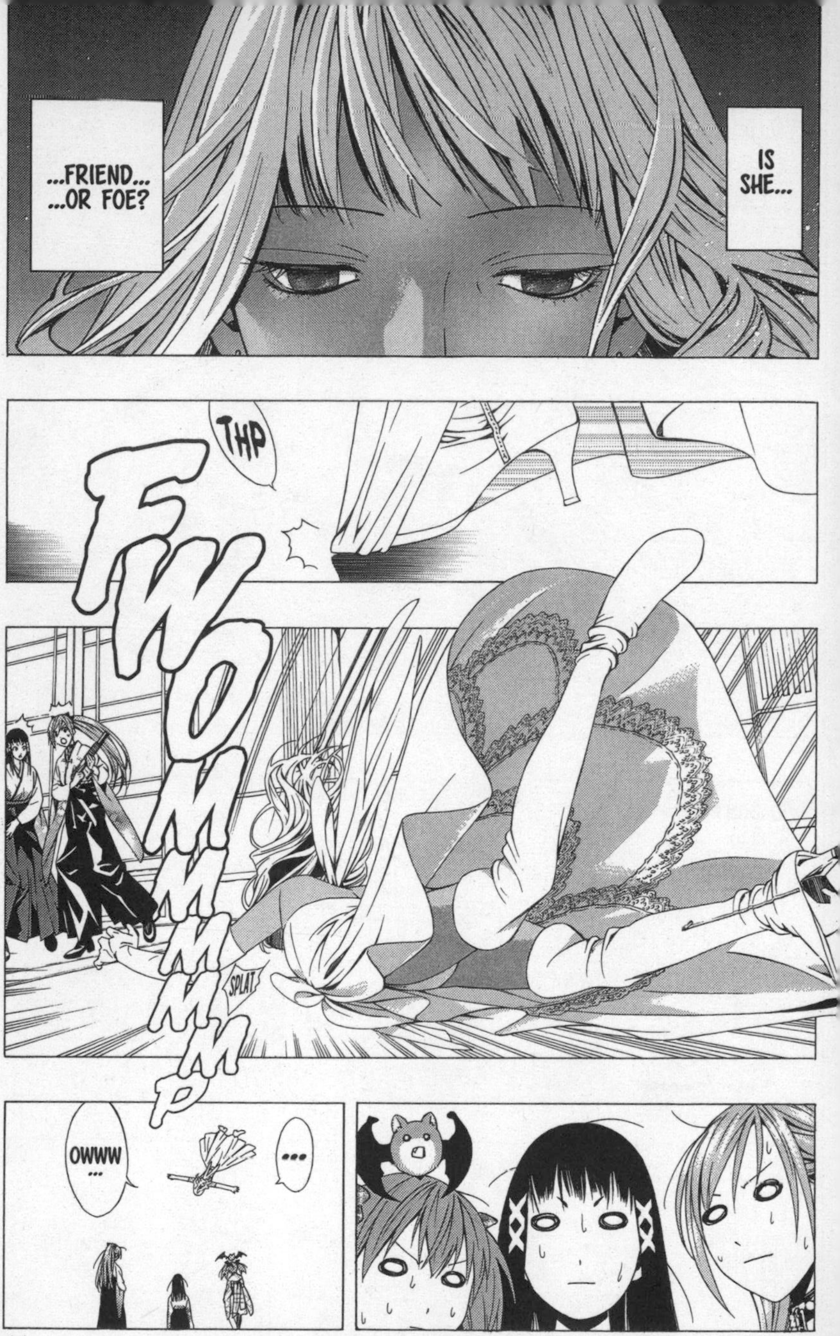
IS SHE...
...FRIEND... ...OR FOE?
THP
FWOMMMMMP
SPLAT
...
OWWW ...

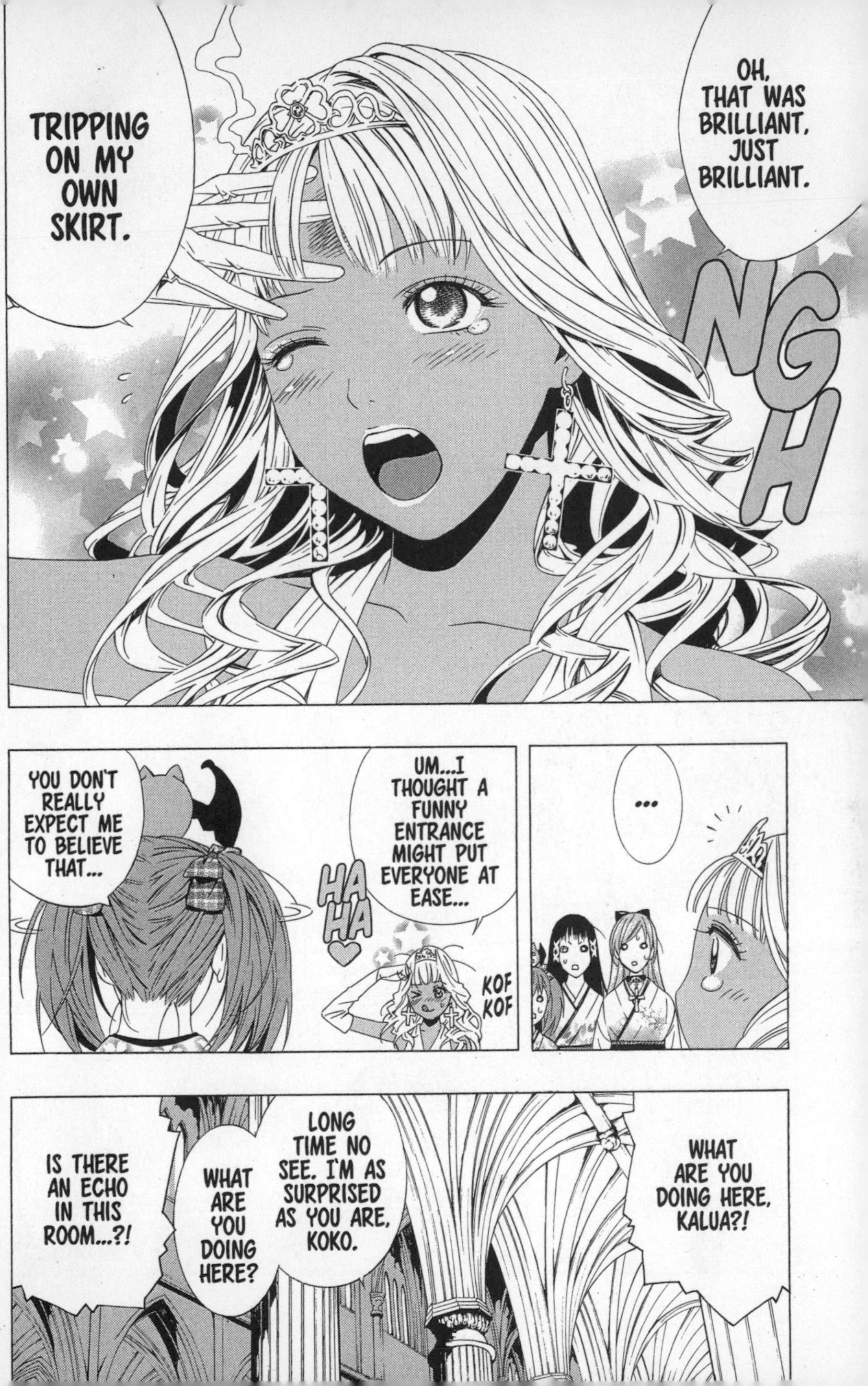
OH, THAT WAS BRILLIANT, JUST BRILLIANT.
NGH
TRIPPING ON MY OWN SKIRT.
...
UM...I THOUGHT A FUNNY ENTRANCE MIGHT PUT EVERYONE AT EASE...
KOF KOF
HA HA
YOU DON'T REALLY EXPECT ME TO BELIEVE THAT...
WHAT ARE YOU DOING HERE, KALUA?!
LONG TIME NO SEE. I'M AS SURPRISED AS YOU ARE, KOKO.
WHAT ARE YOU DOING HERE?
IS THERE AN ECHO IN THIS ROOM...?!

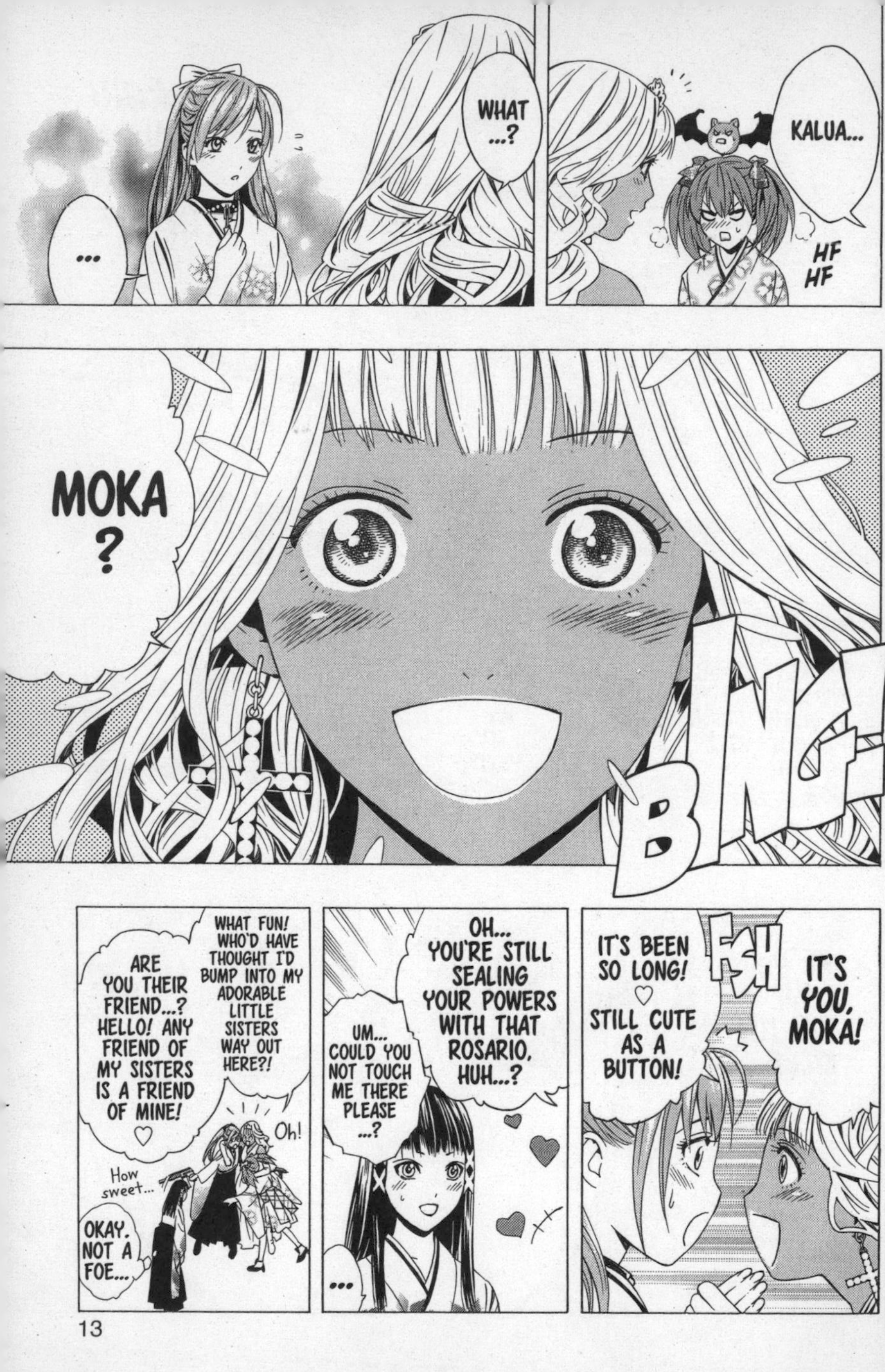
KALUA...
HF HF
WHAT ...?
...
MOKA ?
BING!
IT'S YOU, MOKA!
FSH
IT'S BEEN SO LONG! ♡ STILL CUTE AS A BUTTON!
OH... YOU'RE STILL SEALING YOUR POWERS WITH THAT ROSARIO, HUH...?
UM... COULD YOU NOT TOUCH ME THERE PLEASE ...?
...
WHAT FUN! WHO'D HAVE THOUGHT I'D BUMP INTO MY ADORABLE LITTLE SISTERS WAY OUT HERE?!
ARE YOU THEIR FRIEND...? HELLO! ANY FRIEND OF MY SISTERS IS A FRIEND OF MINE! ♡
Oh!
How sweet...
OKAY. NOT A FOE...

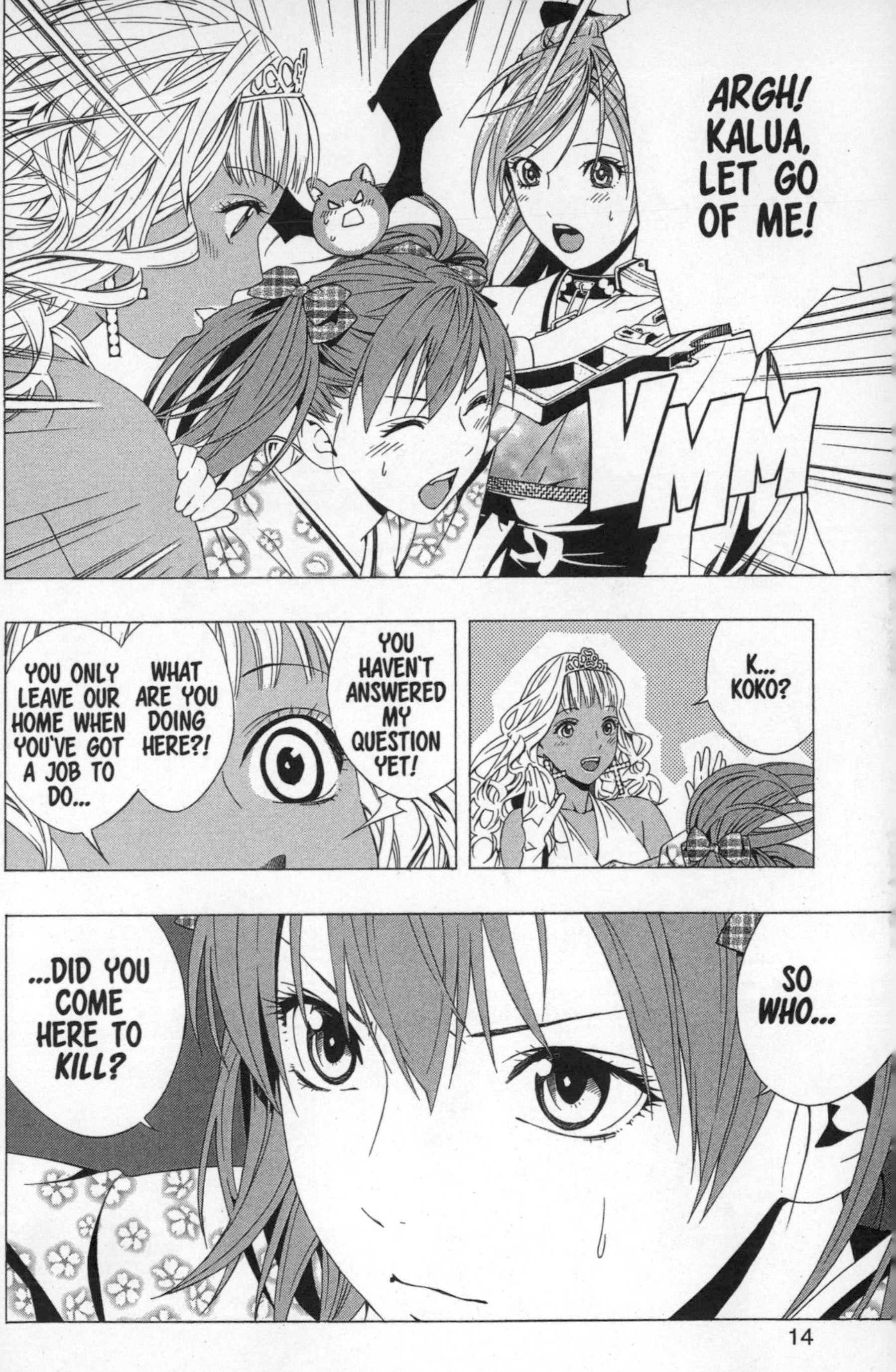
ARGH! KALUA, LET GO OF ME!
VMM
K... KOKO?
YOU HAVEN'T ANSWERED MY QUESTION YET!
WHAT ARE YOU DOING HERE?!
YOU ONLY LEAVE OUR HOME WHEN YOU'VE GOT A JOB TO DO...
SO WHO...
...DID YOU COME HERE TO KILL?

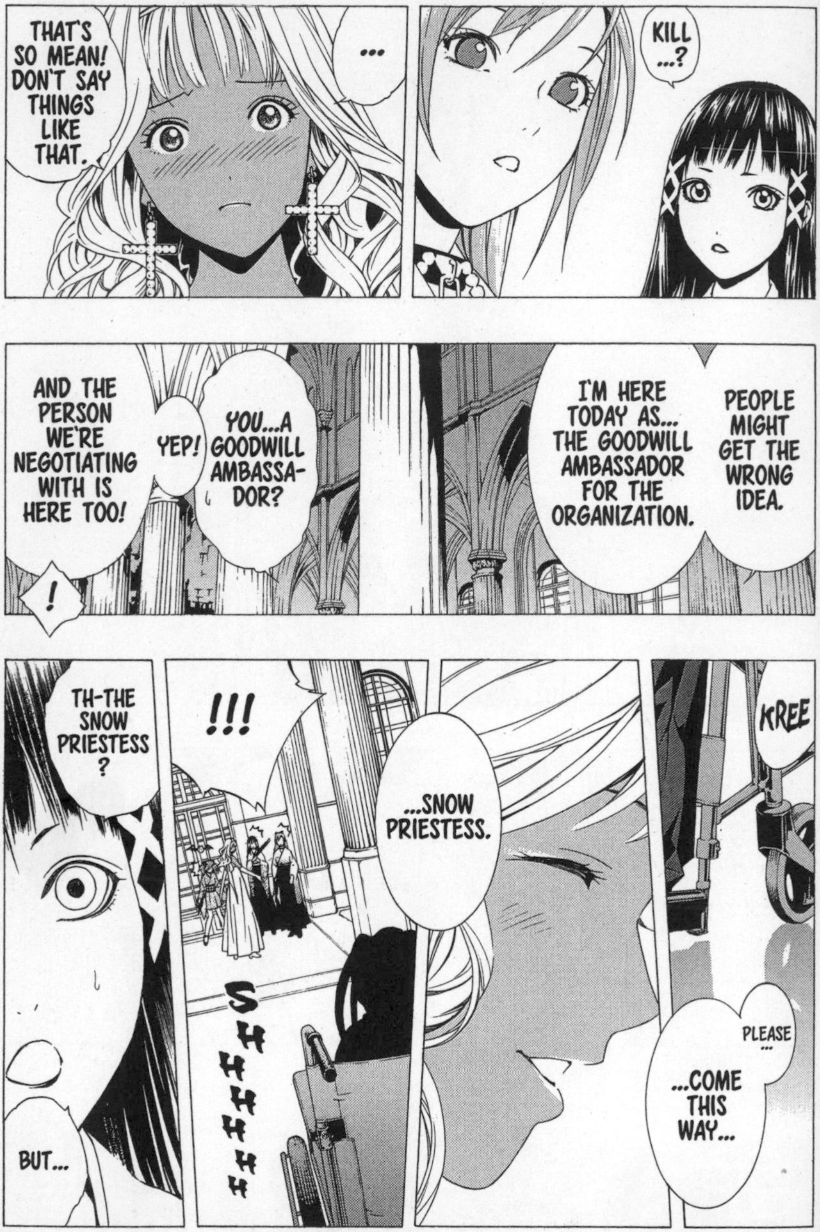
KILL ...?
...
THAT'S SO MEAN! DON'T SAY THINGS LIKE THAT.
PEOPLE MIGHT GET THE WRONG IDEA.
I'M HERE TODAY AS... THE GOODWILL AMBASSADOR FOR THE ORGANIZATION.
YOU...A GOODWILL AMBASSA-DOR?
YEP!
AND THE PERSON WE'RE NEGOTIATING WITH IS HERE TOO!
!
KREE
PLEASE ...
...COME THIS WAY...
...SNOW PRIESTESS.
!!!
SHHHHHH
TH-THE SNOW PRIESTESS ?
BUT...

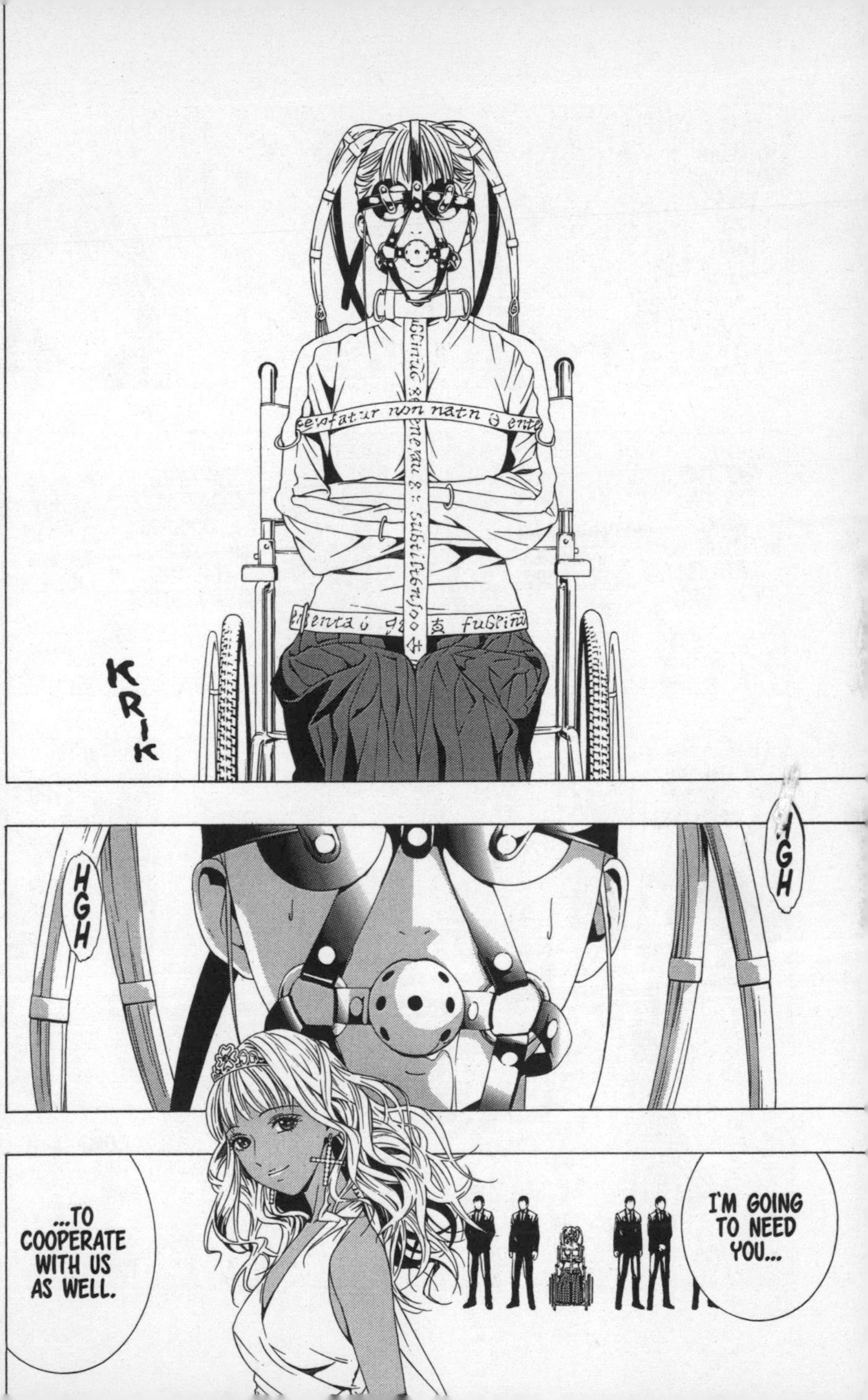
KRIK
HGH
HGH
I'M GOING TO NEED YOU...
...TO COOPERATE WITH US AS WELL.

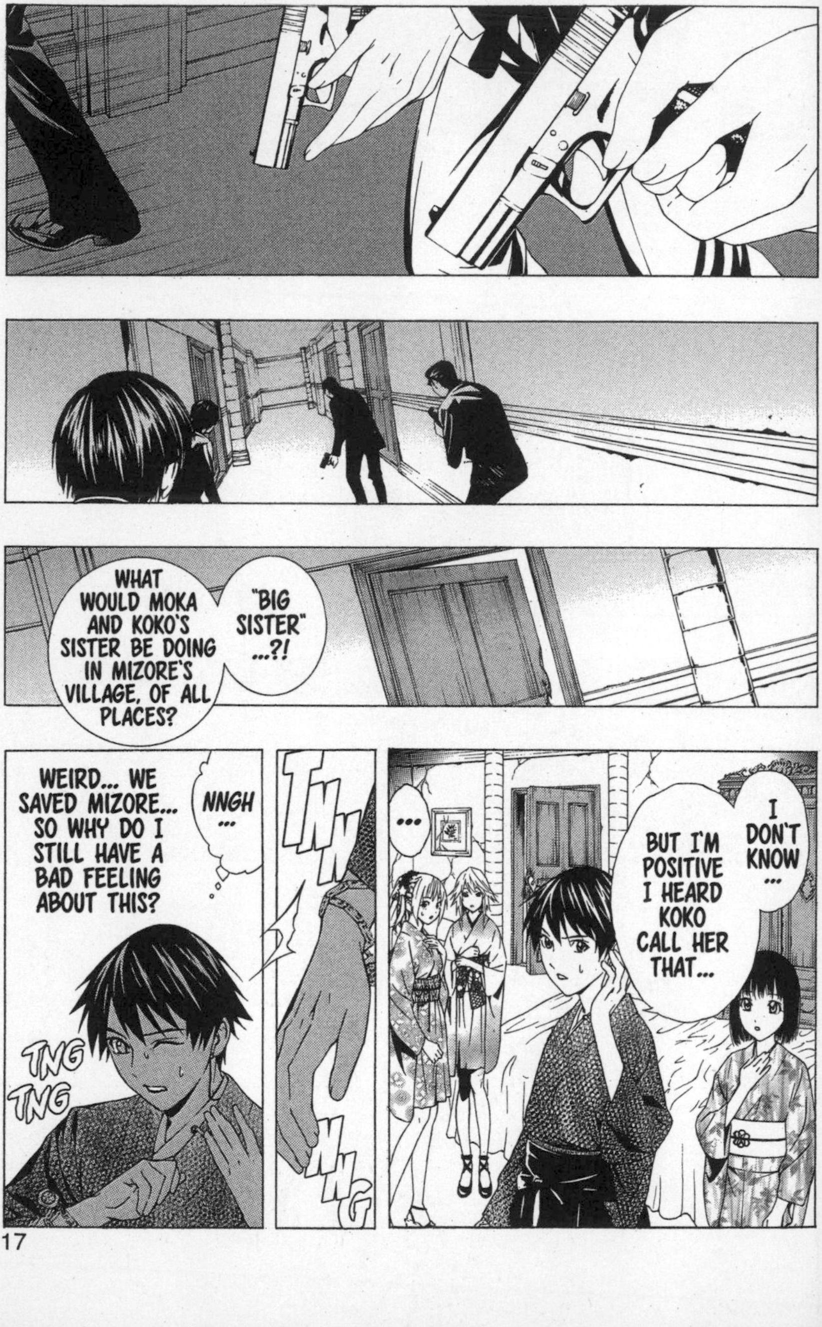

"BIG SISTER" ...?!
WHAT WOULD MOKA AND KOKO'S SISTER BE DOING IN MIZORE'S VILLAGE, OF ALL PLACES?
I DON'T KNOW ...
BUT I'M POSITIVE I HEARD KOKO CALL HER THAT...
...
TNN
NNG
NNGH ...
WEIRD... WE SAVED MIZORE... SO WHY DO I STILL HAVE A BAD FEELING ABOUT THIS?
TNG TNG

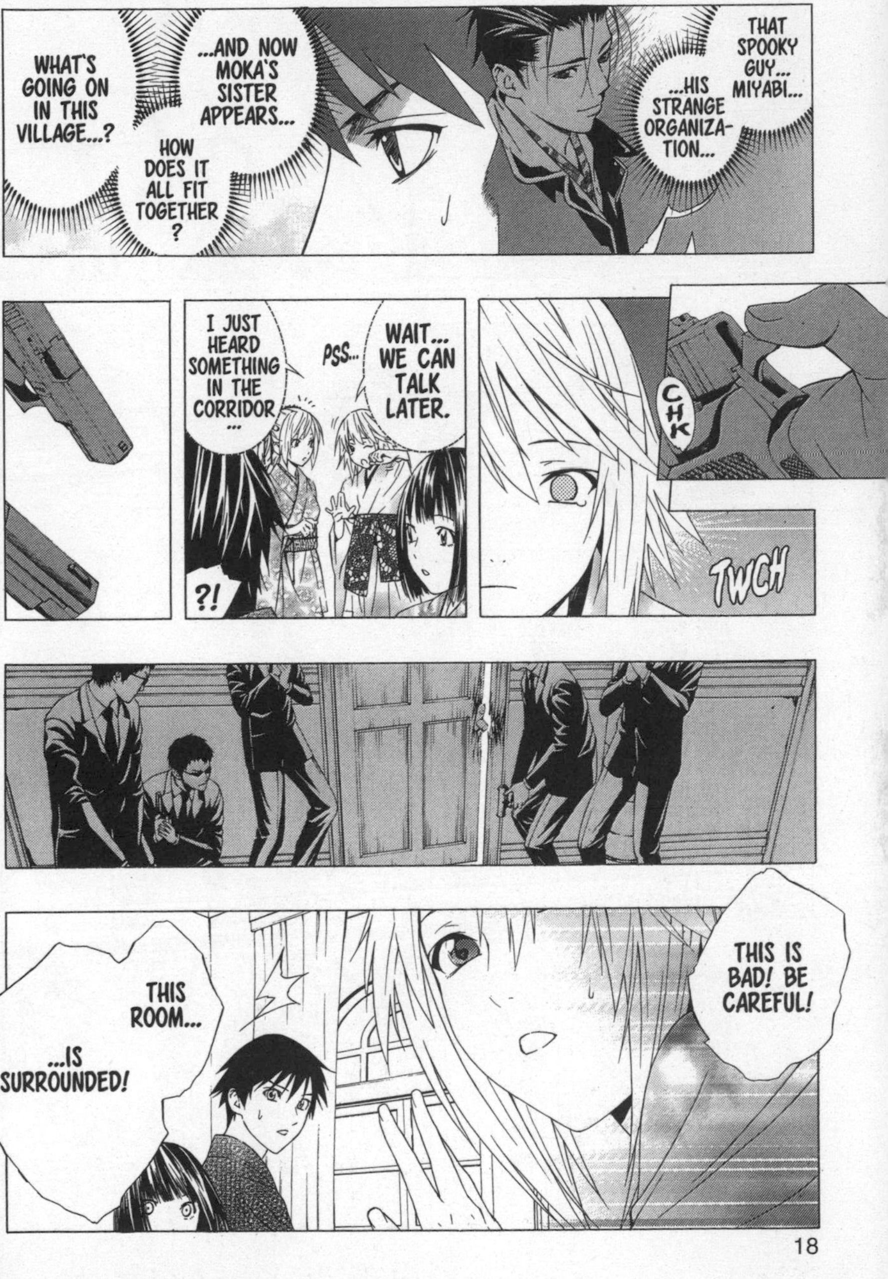
THAT SPOOKY GUY... MIYABI...
...HIS STRANGE ORGANIZATION...
...AND NOW MOKA'S SISTER APPEARS...
HOW DOES IT ALL FIT TOGETHER?
WHAT'S GOING ON IN THIS VILLAGE...?
CHK
TWCH
WAIT... WE CAN TALK LATER.
PSS...
I JUST HEARD SOMETHING IN THE CORRIDOR...
?!
THIS IS BAD! BE CAREFUL!
THIS ROOM...
...IS SURROUNDED!

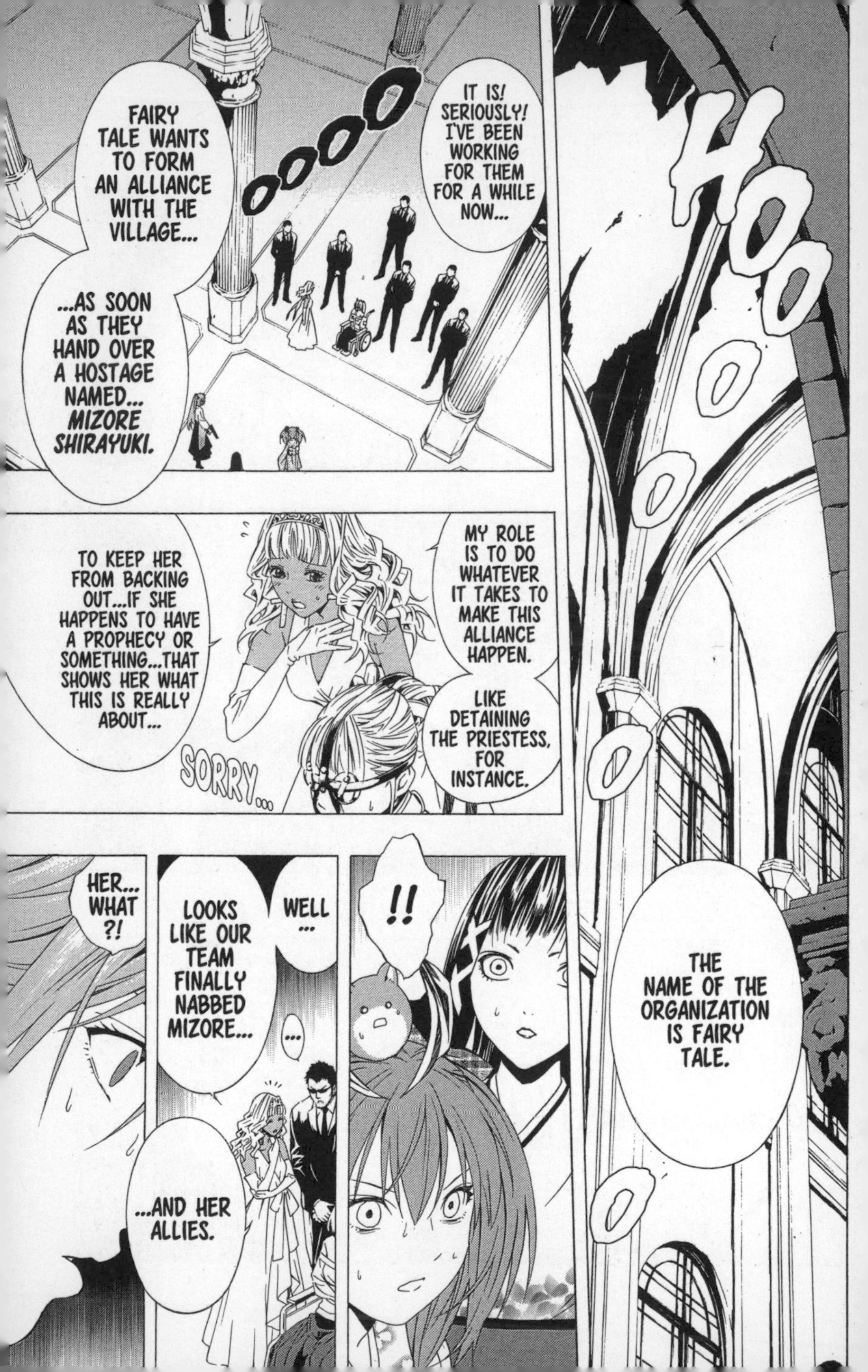
HOOOOOOO
THE NAME OF THE ORGANIZATION IS FAIRY TALE.
OOOOO
IT IS! SERIOUSLY! I'VE BEEN WORKING FOR THEM FOR A WHILE NOW...
FAIRY TALE WANTS TO FORM AN ALLIANCE WITH THE VILLAGE...
...AS SOON AS THEY HAND OVER A HOSTAGE NAMED... *MIZORE SHIRAYUKI.*
MY ROLE IS TO DO WHATEVER IT TAKES TO MAKE THIS ALLIANCE HAPPEN.
LIKE DETAINING THE PRIESTESS, FOR INSTANCE.
TO KEEP HER FROM BACKING OUT...IF SHE HAPPENS TO HAVE A PROPHECY OR SOMETHING...THAT SHOWS HER WHAT THIS IS REALLY ABOUT...
SORRY...
!!
WELL...
LOOKS LIKE OUR TEAM FINALLY NABBED MIZORE...
...
...AND HER ALLIES.
HER... WHAT?!

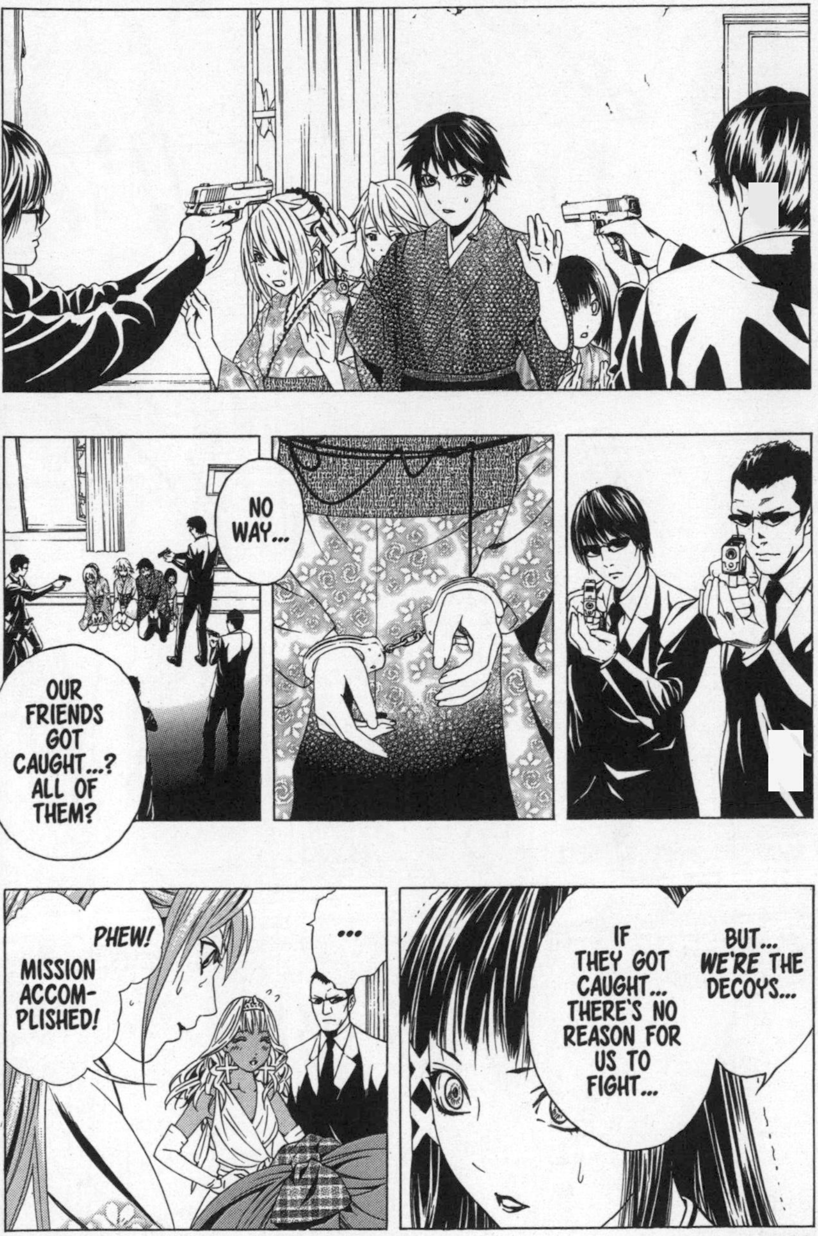
NO WAY...
OUR FRIENDS GOT CAUGHT...? ALL OF THEM?
BUT... WE'RE THE DECOYS...
IF THEY GOT CAUGHT... THERE'S NO REASON FOR US TO FIGHT...
...
PHEW!
MISSION ACCOM-PLISHED!

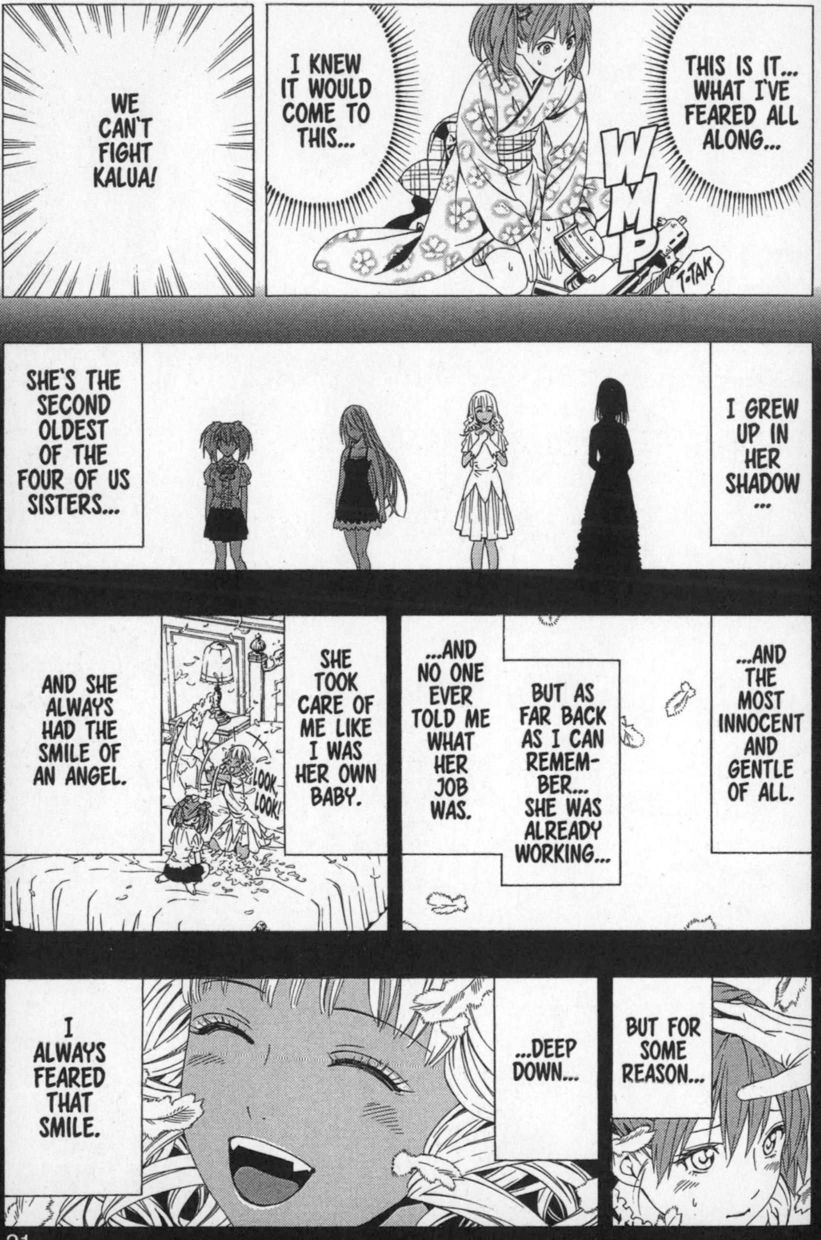
THIS IS IT... WHAT I'VE FEARED ALL ALONG...
WMP
T-TAK
I KNEW IT WOULD COME TO THIS...
WE CAN'T FIGHT KALUA!
I GREW UP IN HER SHADOW ...
SHE'S THE SECOND OLDEST OF THE FOUR OF US SISTERS...
...AND THE MOST INNOCENT AND GENTLE OF ALL.
BUT AS FAR BACK AS I CAN REMEMBER... SHE WAS ALREADY WORKING...
...AND NO ONE EVER TOLD ME WHAT HER JOB WAS.
SHE TOOK CARE OF ME LIKE I WAS HER OWN BABY.
LOOK, LOOK!
AND SHE ALWAYS HAD THE SMILE OF AN ANGEL.
BUT FOR SOME REASON...
...DEEP DOWN...
I ALWAYS FEARED THAT SMILE.

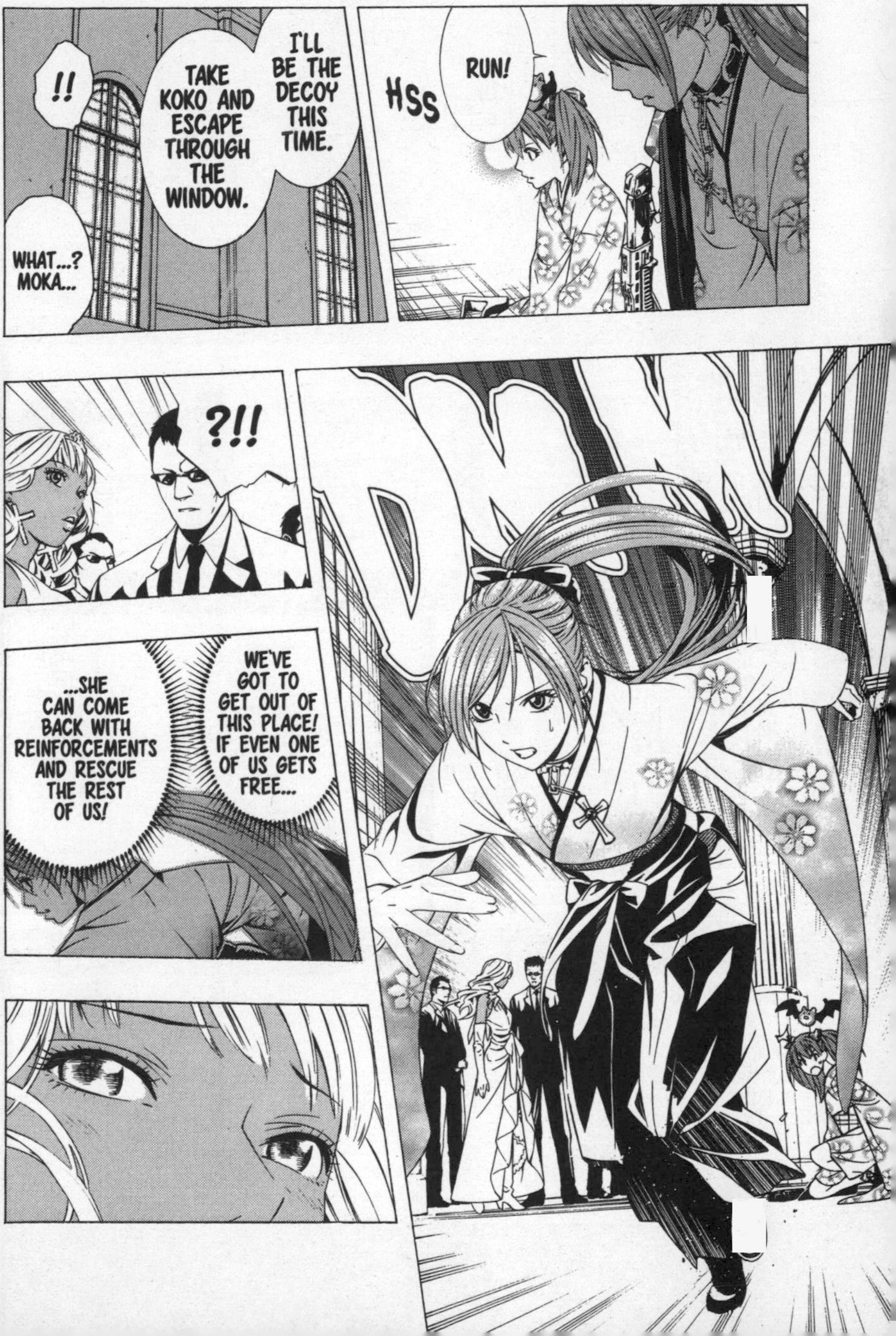
RUN!
HSS
I'LL BE THE DECOY THIS TIME.
TAKE KOKO AND ESCAPE THROUGH THE WINDOW.
!!
WHAT...? MOKA...
?!!
WE'VE GOT TO GET OUT OF THIS PLACE! IF EVEN ONE OF US GETS FREE...
...SHE CAN COME BACK WITH REINFORCEMENTS AND RESCUE THE REST OF US!

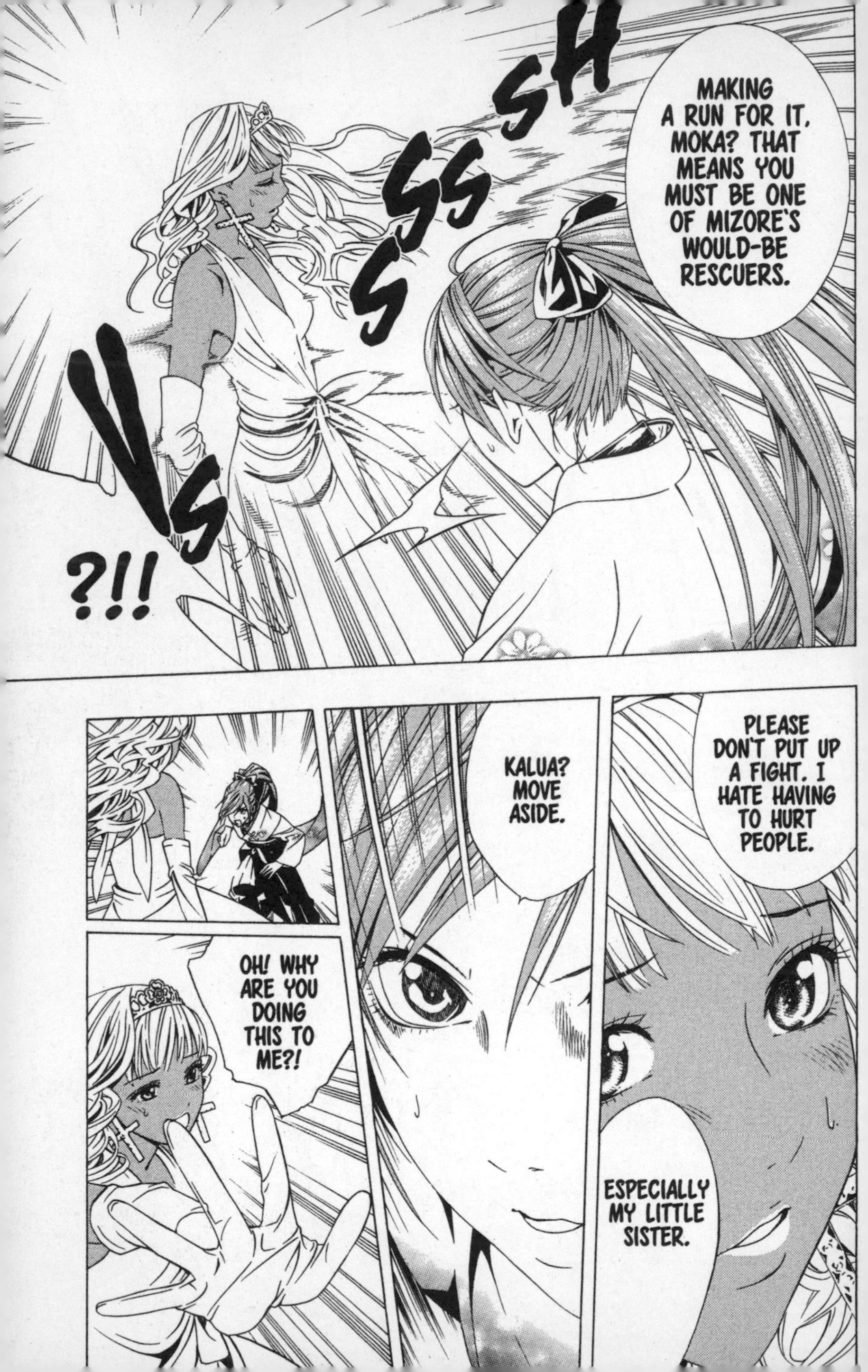
MAKING A RUN FOR IT, MOKA? THAT MEANS YOU MUST BE ONE OF MIZORE'S WOULD-BE RESCUERS.
SSSSH
?!!
PLEASE DON'T PUT UP A FIGHT. I HATE HAVING TO HURT PEOPLE.
ESPECIALLY MY LITTLE SISTER.
KALUA? MOVE ASIDE.
OH! WHY ARE YOU DOING THIS TO ME?!

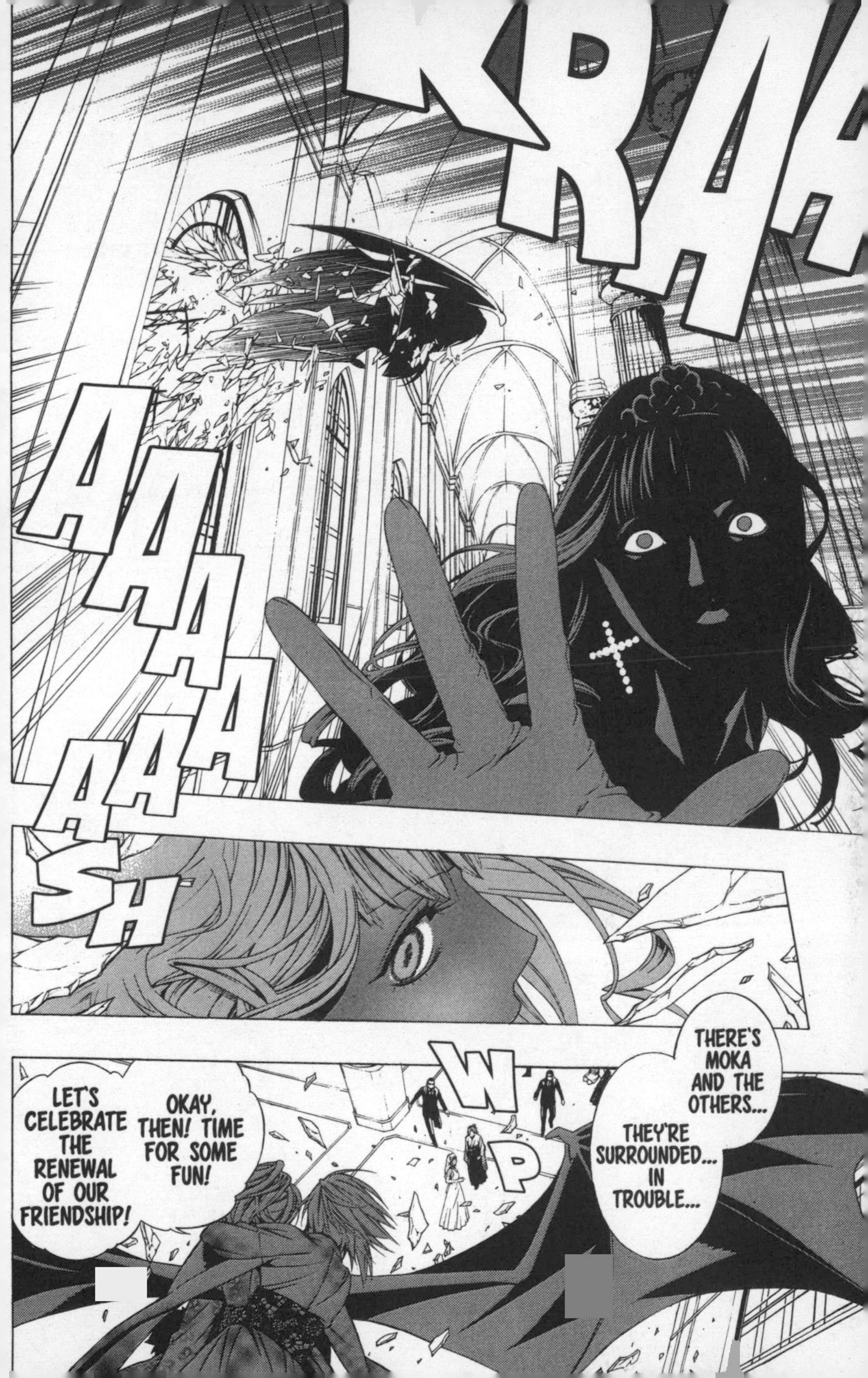
KRA
AAAAAAA
SH
THERE'S MOKA AND THE OTHERS...
THEY'RE SURROUNDED... IN TROUBLE...
WP
OKAY, THEN! TIME FOR SOME FUN!
LET'S CELEBRATE THE RENEWAL OF OUR FRIENDSHIP!

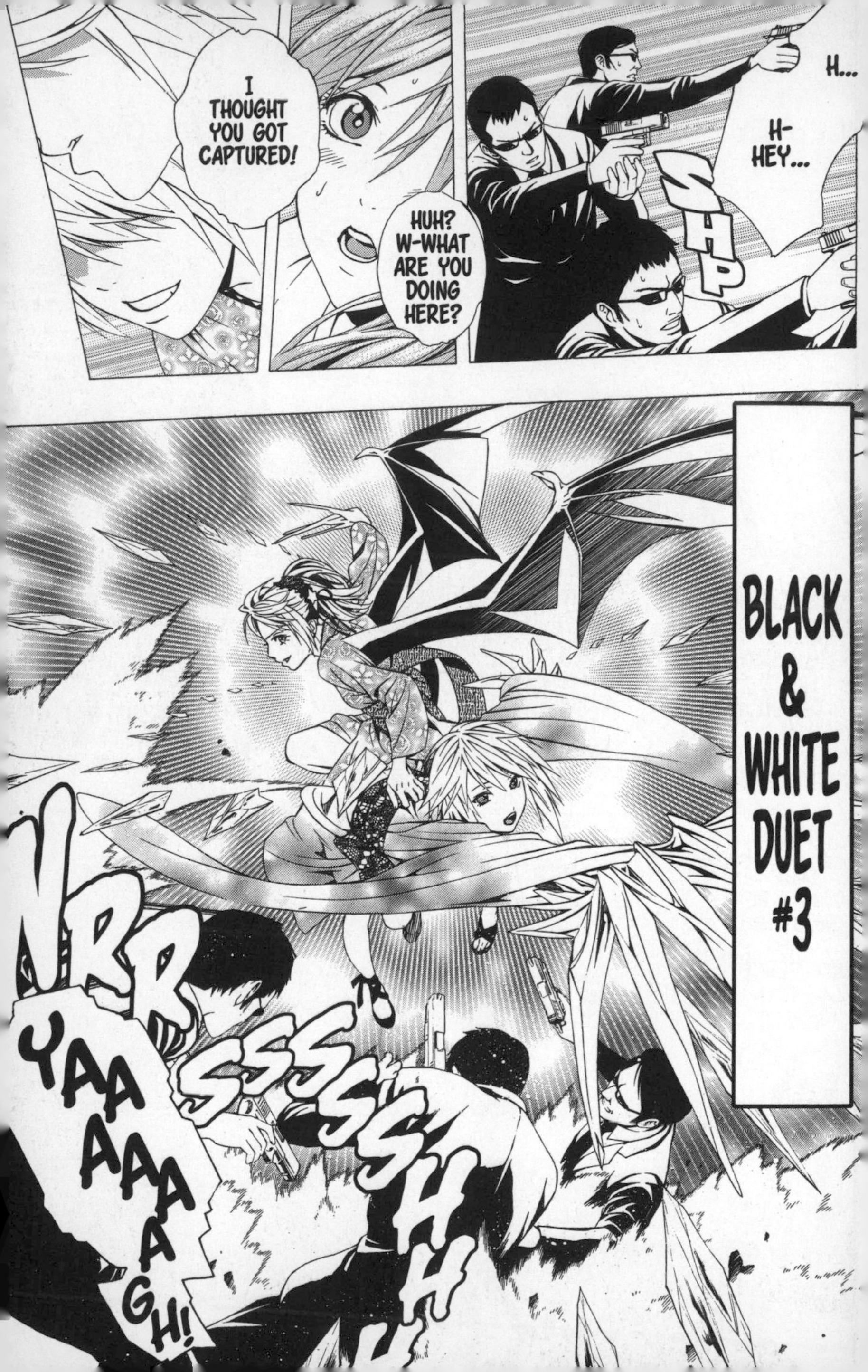
H...
H-
HEY...
SHP
HUH? W-WHAT ARE YOU DOING HERE?
I THOUGHT YOU GOT CAPTURED!
BLACK & WHITE DUET #3
VRR
SSSSSSH
YAAAAAAGH!

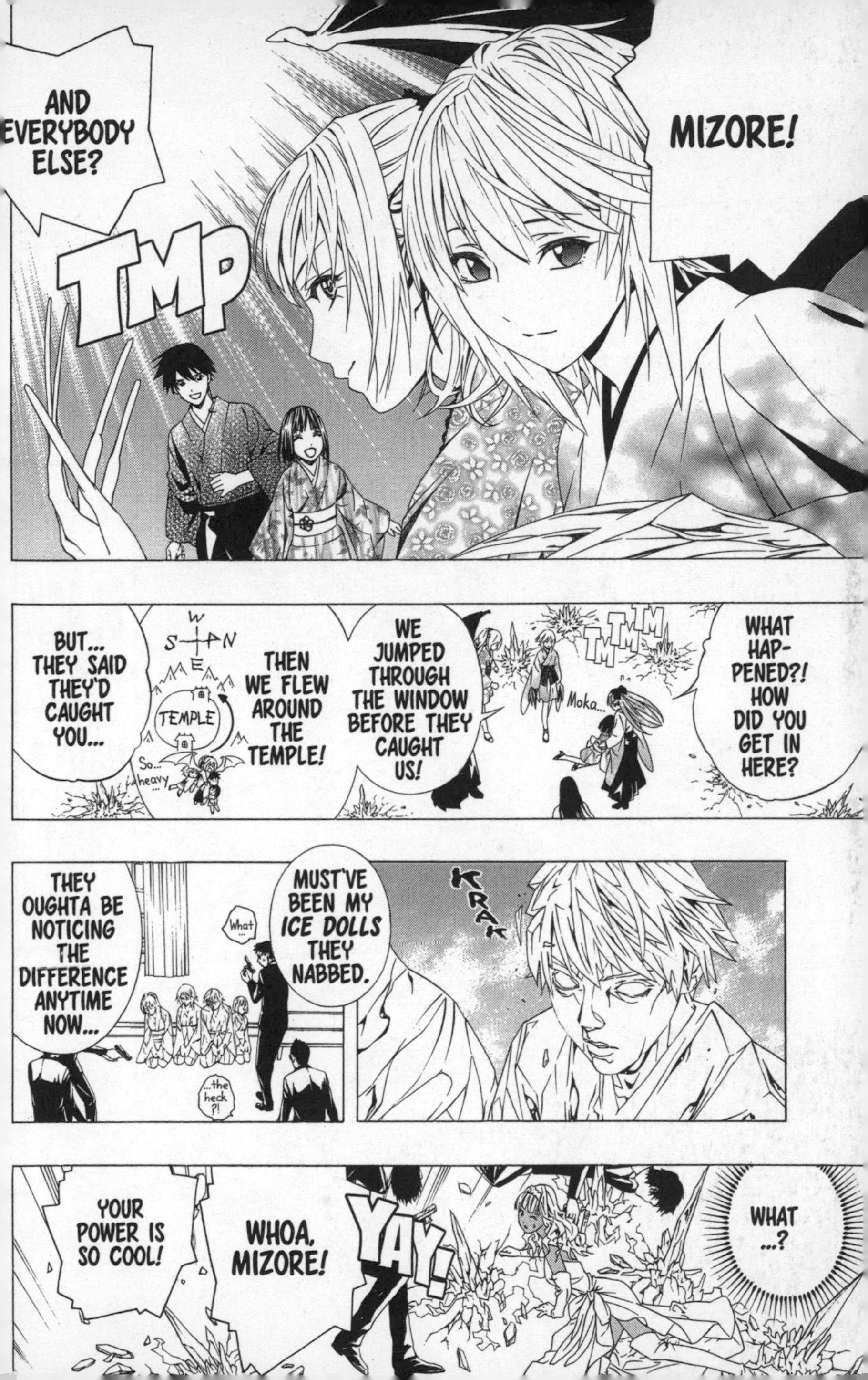

MIZORE!
AND EVERYBODY ELSE?
TMP
WHAT HAP-PENED?! HOW DID YOU GET IN HERE?
TM TM TM TM
Moka...
WE JUMPED THROUGH THE WINDOW BEFORE THEY CAUGHT US!
THEN WE FLEW AROUND THE TEMPLE!
W
S
N
E
TEMPLE
So... heavy...
BUT... THEY SAID THEY'D CAUGHT YOU...
KRAK
MUST'VE BEEN MY ICE DOLLS THEY NABBED.
What...
...the heck?!
THEY OUGHTA BE NOTICING THE DIFFERENCE ANYTIME NOW...
WHAT...?
YAY!
WHOA, MIZORE!
YOUR POWER IS SO COOL!

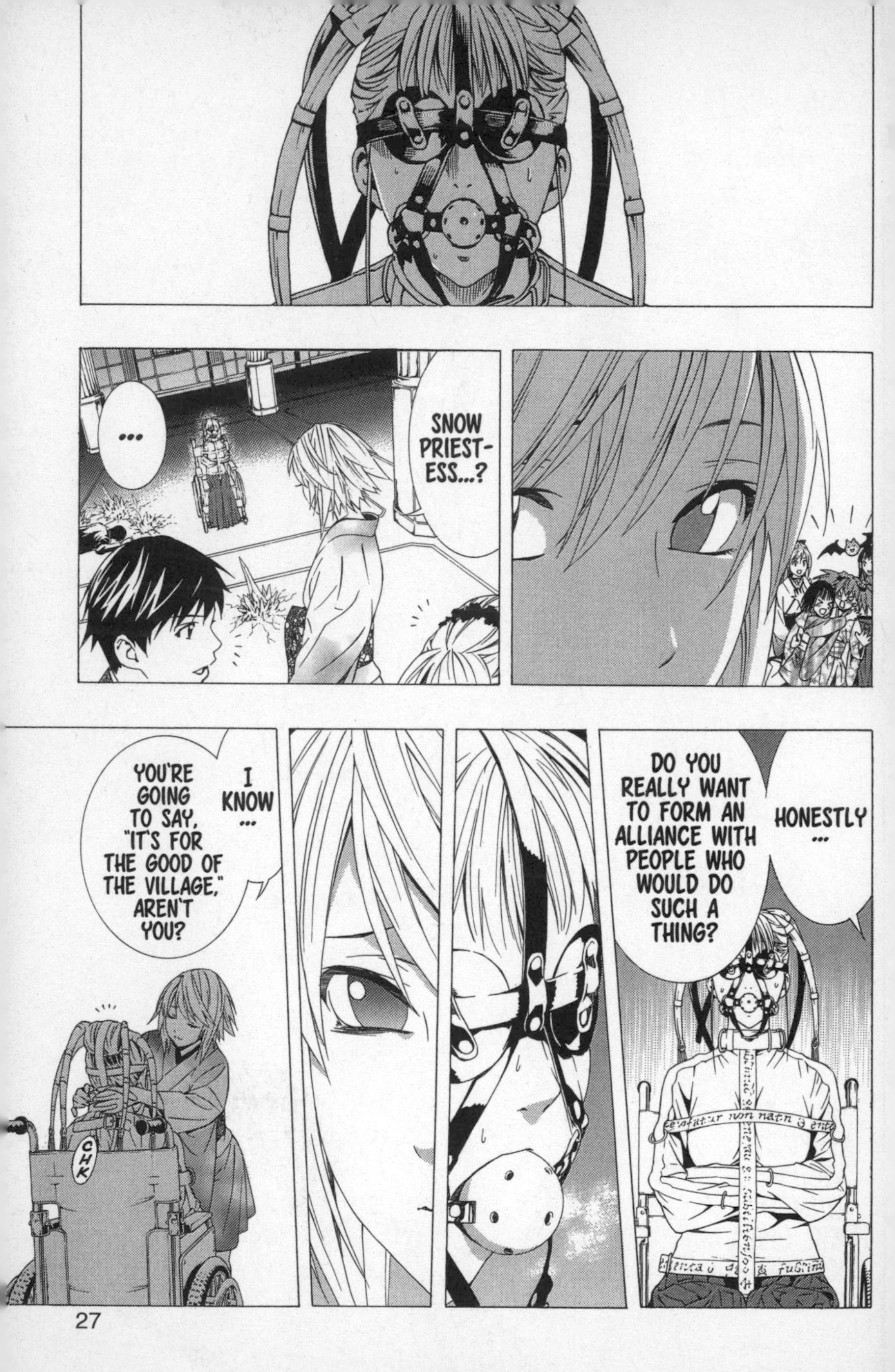
SNOW PRIEST-ESS...?
...
HONESTLY ...
DO YOU REALLY WANT TO FORM AN ALLIANCE WITH PEOPLE WHO WOULD DO SUCH A THING?
I KNOW ...
YOU'RE GOING TO SAY, "IT'S FOR THE GOOD OF THE VILLAGE," AREN'T YOU?
CHK

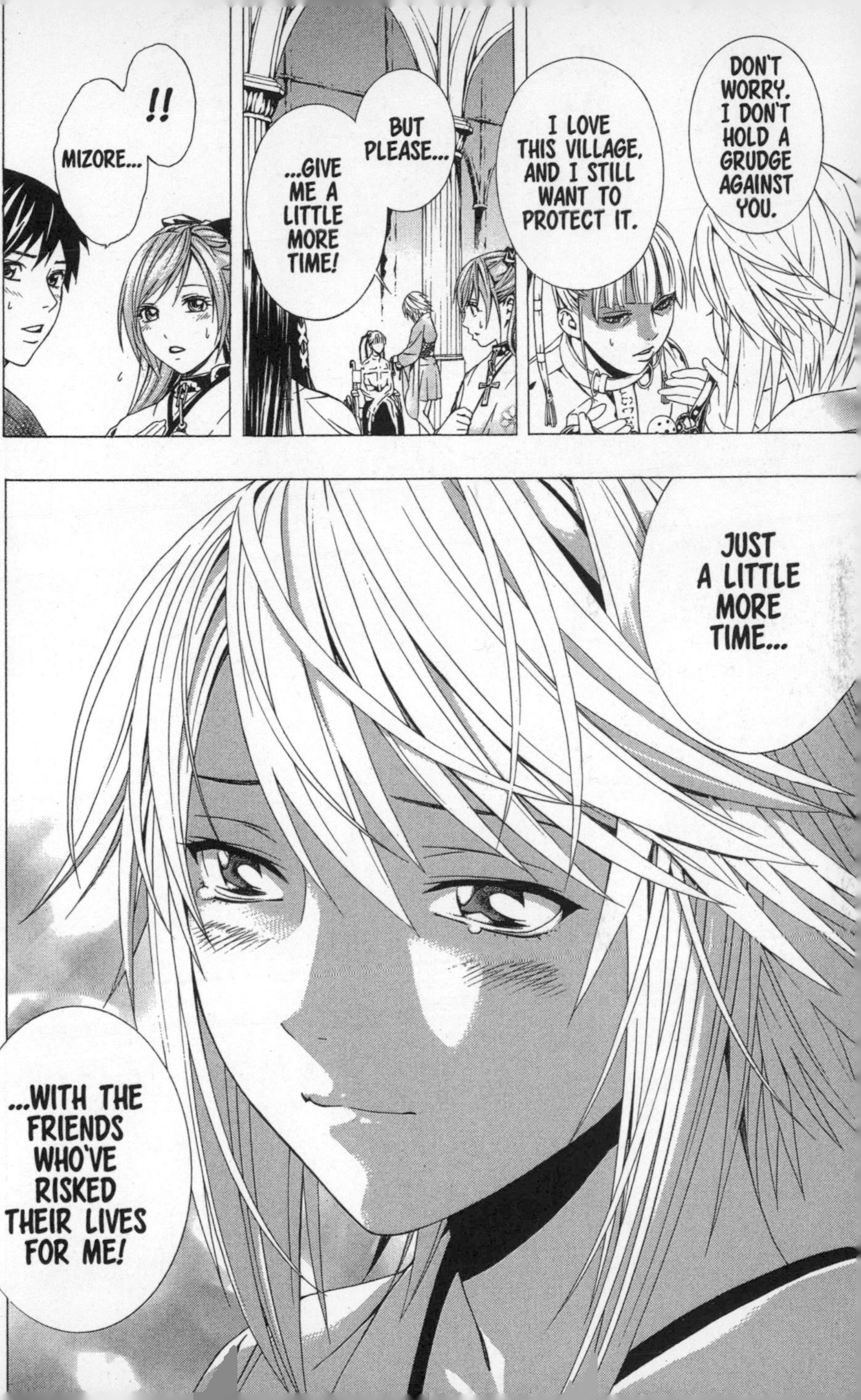
DON'T WORRY. I DON'T HOLD A GRUDGE AGAINST YOU.
I LOVE THIS VILLAGE, AND I STILL WANT TO PROTECT IT.
BUT PLEASE...
...GIVE ME A LITTLE MORE TIME!
!!
MIZORE...
JUST A LITTLE MORE TIME...
...WITH THE FRIENDS WHO'VE RISKED THEIR LIVES FOR ME!

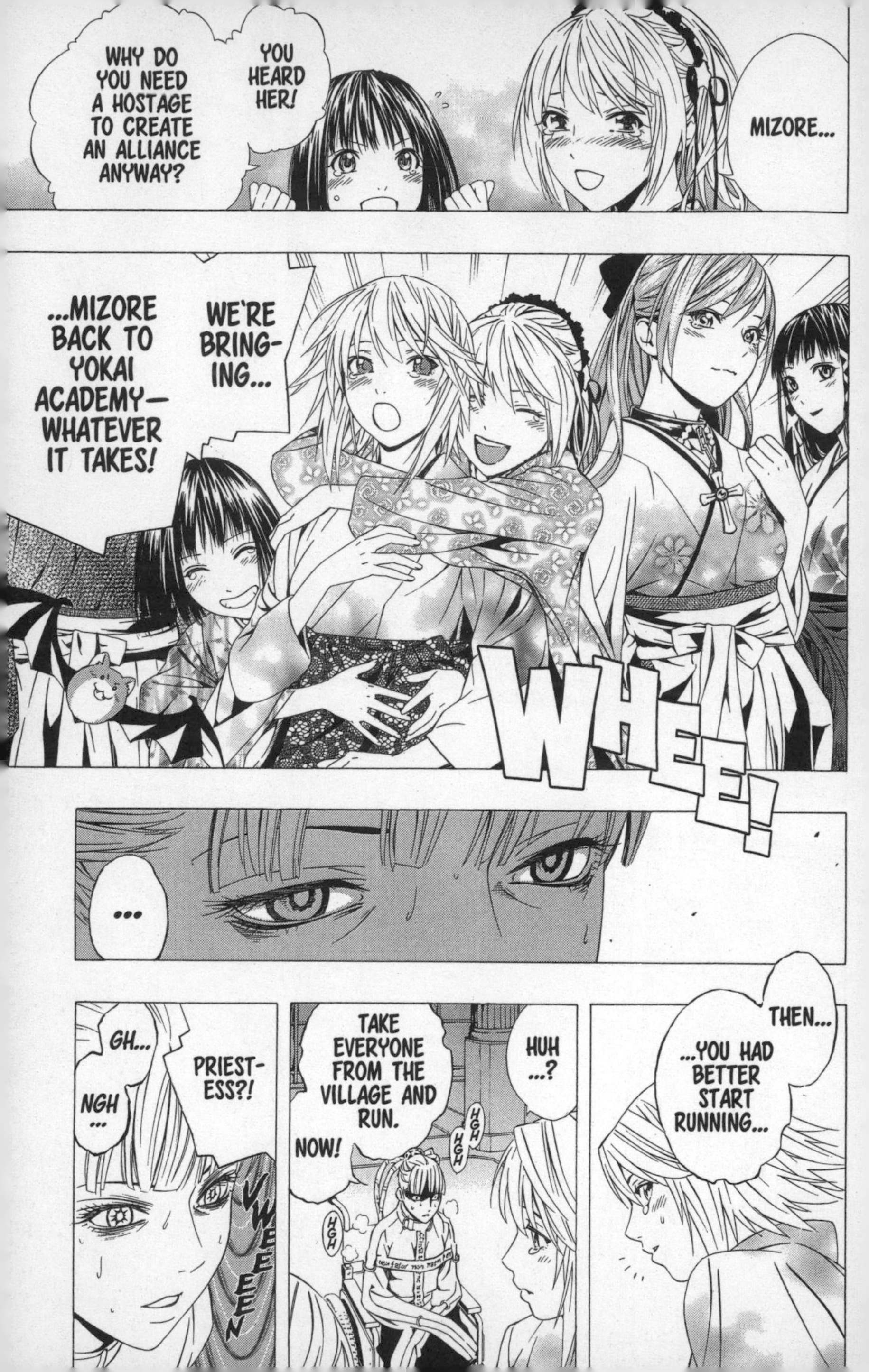
MIZORE...
YOU HEARD HER!
WHY DO YOU NEED A HOSTAGE TO CREATE AN ALLIANCE ANYWAY?
WE'RE BRING-ING...
...MIZORE BACK TO YOKAI ACADEMY—WHATEVER IT TAKES!
WHEE!!
...
THEN...
...YOU HAD BETTER START RUNNING...
HUH ...?
TAKE EVERYONE FROM THE VILLAGE AND RUN.
NOW!
HGH HGH
HGH
PRIEST-ESS?!
GH...
NGH ...
VWEEEEEN

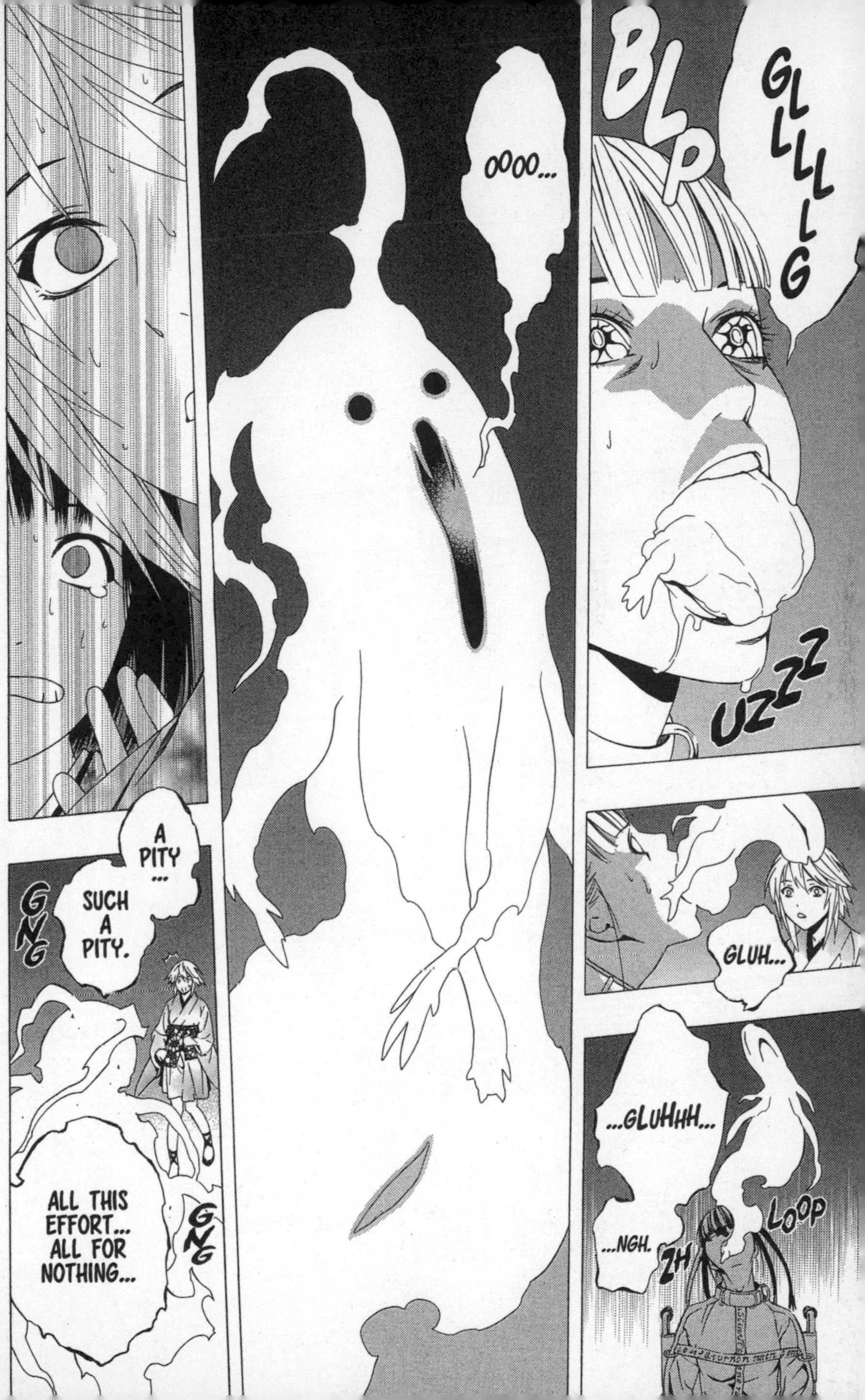
GLLLLLG
BLP
UZZZ
GLUH...
...GLUHHH...
LOOP
...NGH.
ZH
OOOO...
A PITY...
SUCH A PITY.
GNG
ALL THIS EFFORT... ALL FOR NOTHING...
GNG

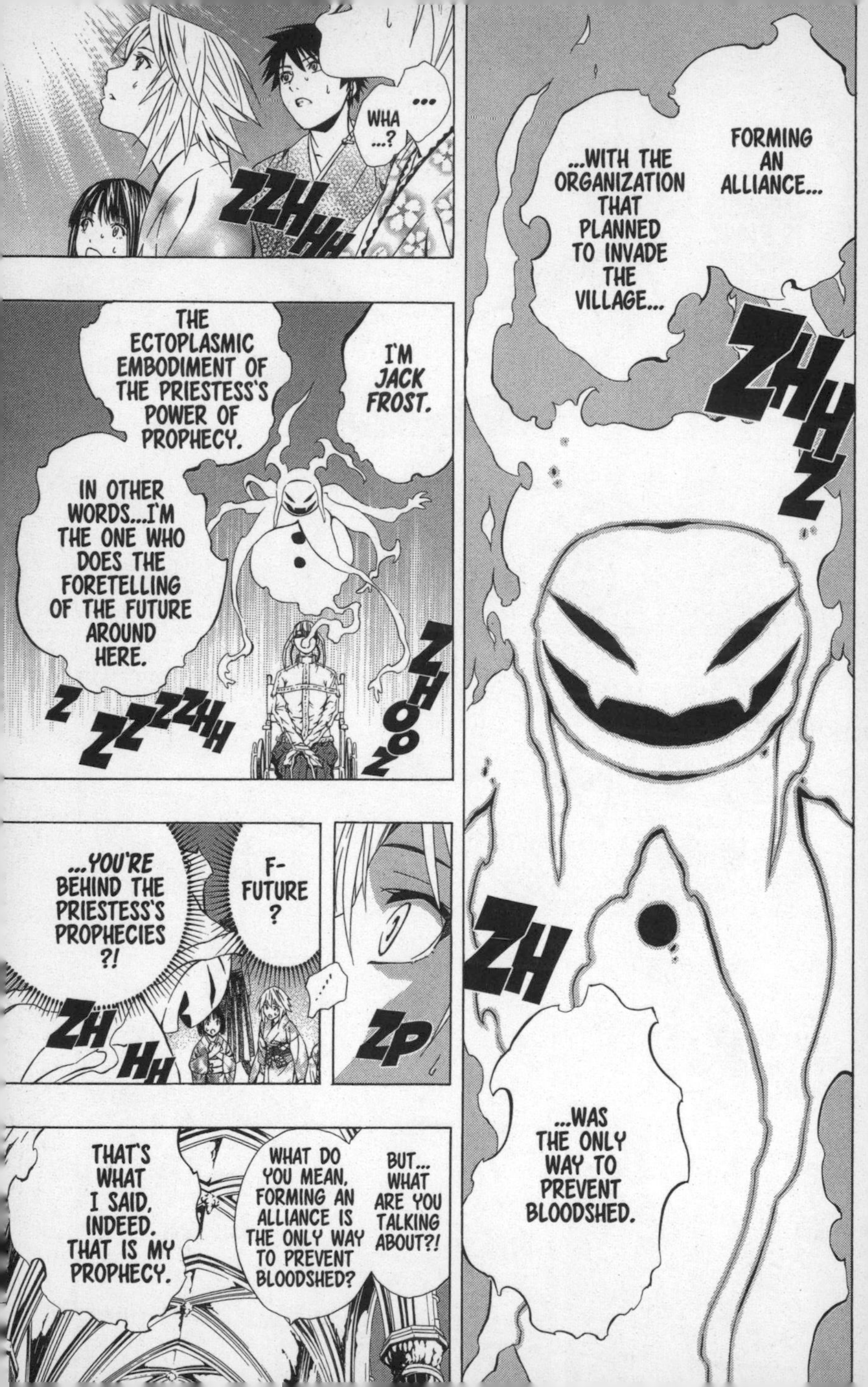

FORMING AN ALLIANCE...
...WITH THE ORGANIZATION THAT PLANNED TO INVADE THE VILLAGE...
ZHHZ
ZH
...WAS THE ONLY WAY TO PREVENT BLOODSHED.
...
WHA ...?
ZZHHHH
I'M JACK FROST.
THE ECTOPLASMIC EMBODIMENT OF THE PRIESTESS'S POWER OF PROPHECY.
IN OTHER WORDS...I'M THE ONE WHO DOES THE FORETELLING OF THE FUTURE AROUND HERE.
ZHOOZ
Z ZZZZHH
ZP
F- FUTURE?
...YOU'RE BEHIND THE PRIESTESS'S PROPHECIES ?!
ZH HH
BUT... WHAT ARE YOU TALKING ABOUT?!
WHAT DO YOU MEAN, FORMING AN ALLIANCE IS THE ONLY WAY TO PREVENT BLOODSHED?
THAT'S WHAT I SAID, INDEED. THAT IS MY PROPHECY.

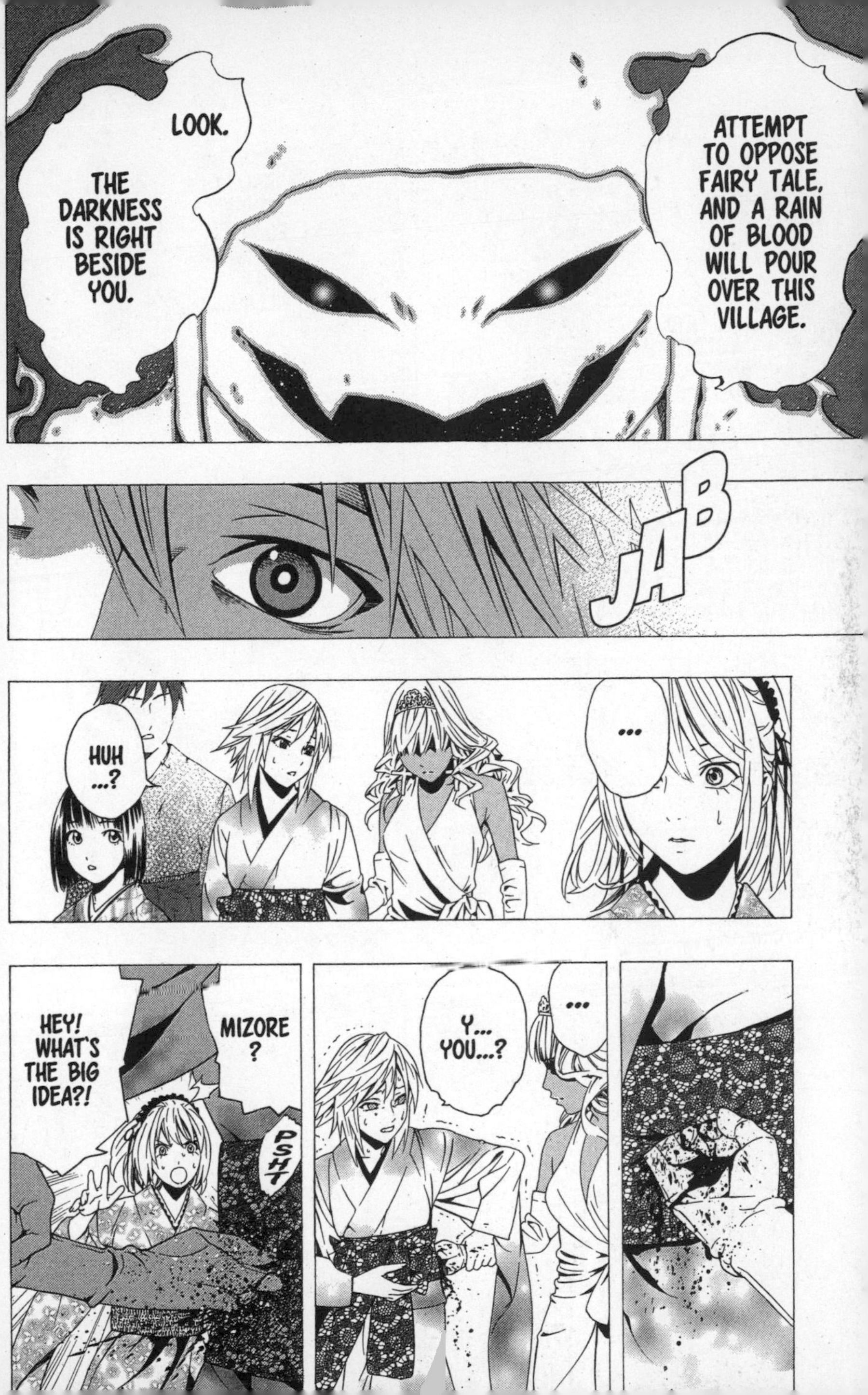
ATTEMPT TO OPPOSE FAIRY TALE, AND A RAIN OF BLOOD WILL POUR OVER THIS VILLAGE.
LOOK.
THE DARKNESS IS RIGHT BESIDE YOU.
JAB
...
HUH ...?
...
Y... YOU...?
MIZORE ?
HEY! WHAT'S THE BIG IDEA?!
PSHT

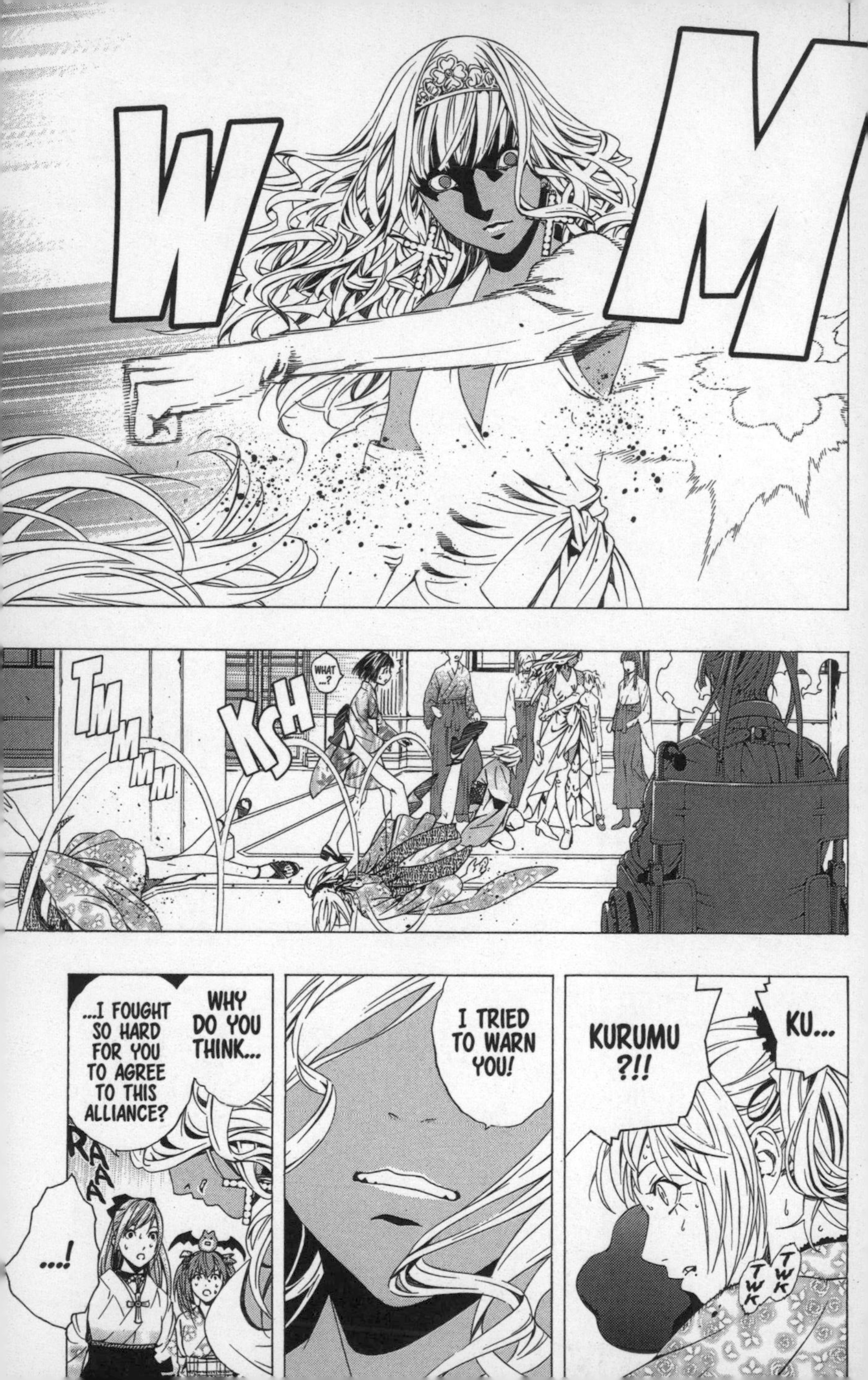
W M
WHAT ...?
KSH
TMMMMM
KU...
KURUMU ?!!
TWK
TWK
I TRIED TO WARN YOU!
WHY DO YOU THINK...
...I FOUGHT SO HARD FOR YOU TO AGREE TO THIS ALLIANCE?
RAAAA
...!

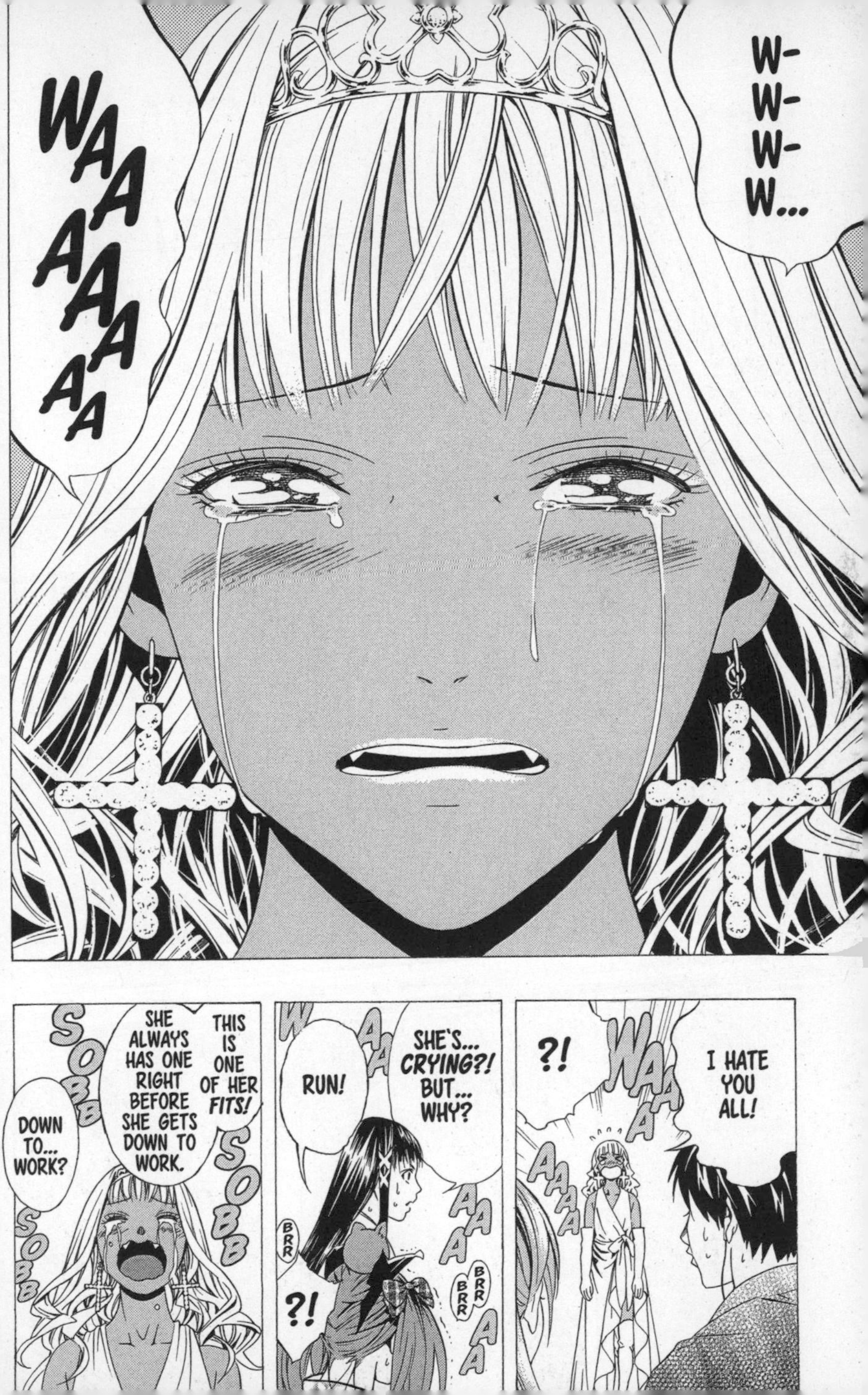
W-W-W-W...
WAAAAAAAAA
I HATE YOU ALL!
WAA
?!
AAAAA
SHE'S... CRYING?! BUT... WHY?
AA
W
RUN!
AAAAA
BRR BRR
BRR
?!
THIS IS ONE OF HER FITS!
SHE ALWAYS HAS ONE RIGHT BEFORE SHE GETS DOWN TO WORK.
SOBB
DOWN TO... WORK?
SOBB
SOBB

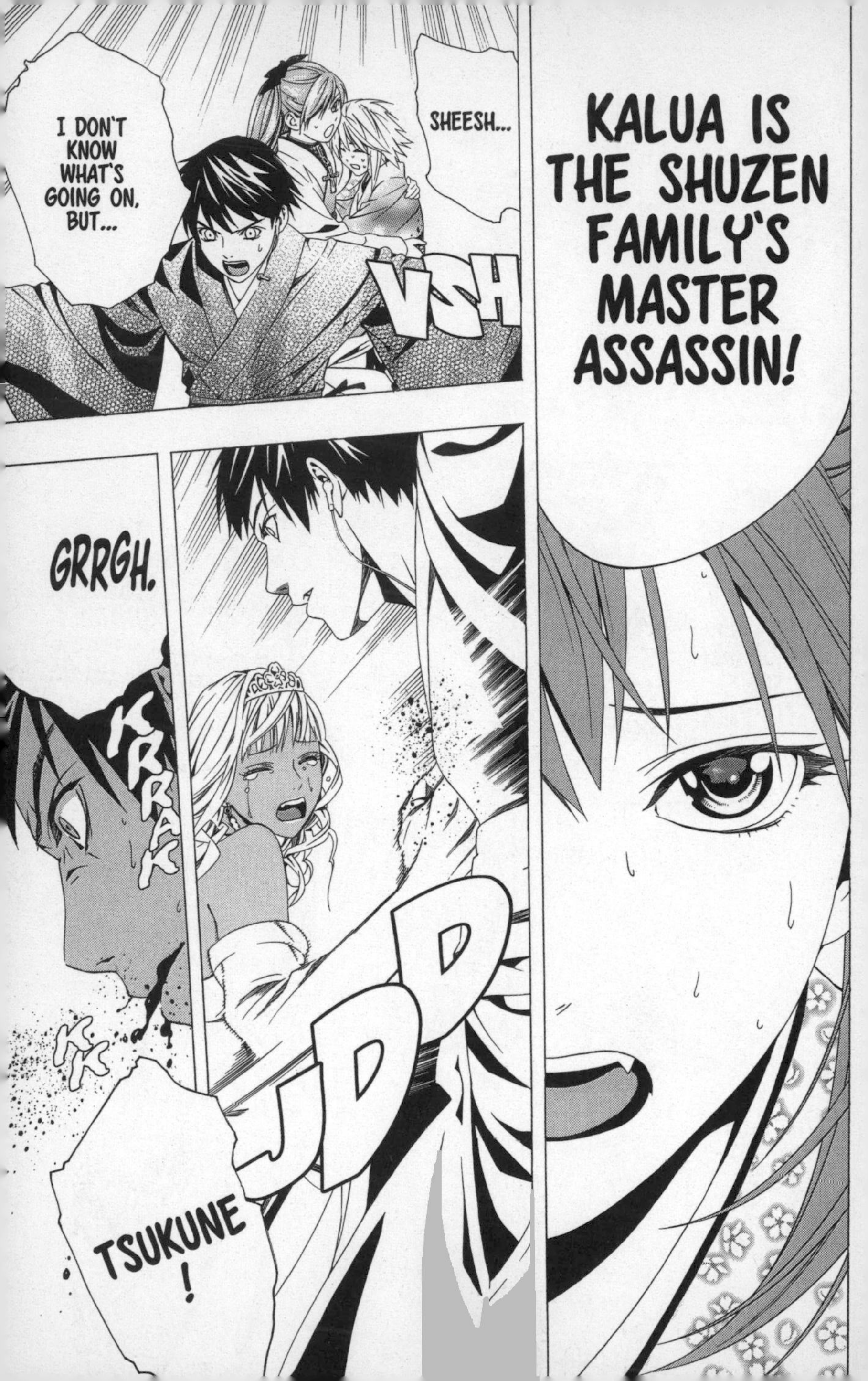
KALUA IS THE SHUZEN FAMILY'S MASTER ASSASSIN!
SHEESH...
I DON'T KNOW WHAT'S GOING ON, BUT...
VSH
GRRGH.
KRRAK
TSUKUNE!

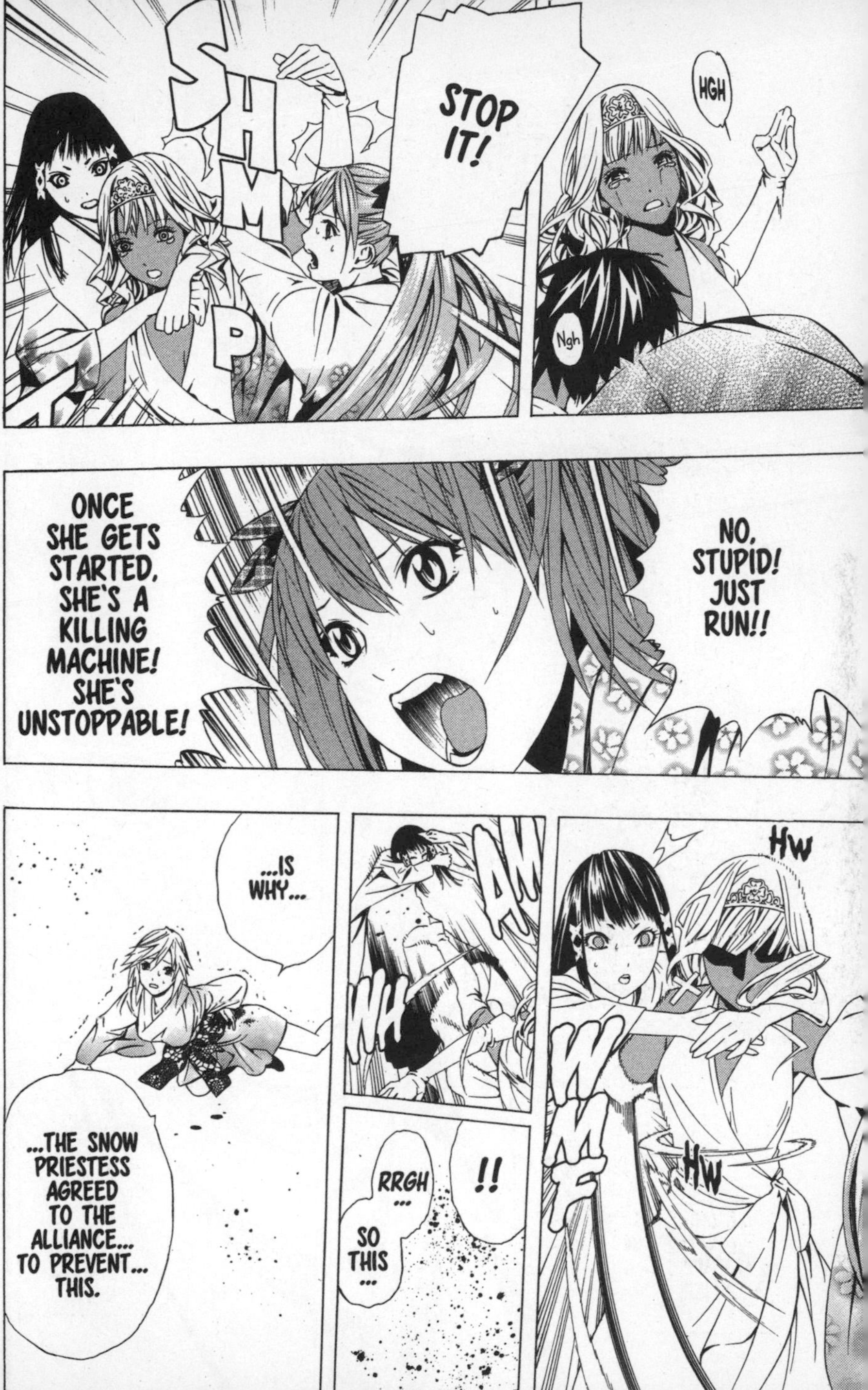
HGH
Ngh
STOP IT!
SHMP
NO, STUPID! JUST RUN!!
ONCE SHE GETS STARTED, SHE'S A KILLING MACHINE! SHE'S UNSTOPPABLE!
HW
HW
!!
RRGH...
SO THIS...
...IS WHY...
...THE SNOW PRIESTESS AGREED TO THE ALLIANCE... TO PREVENT... THIS.

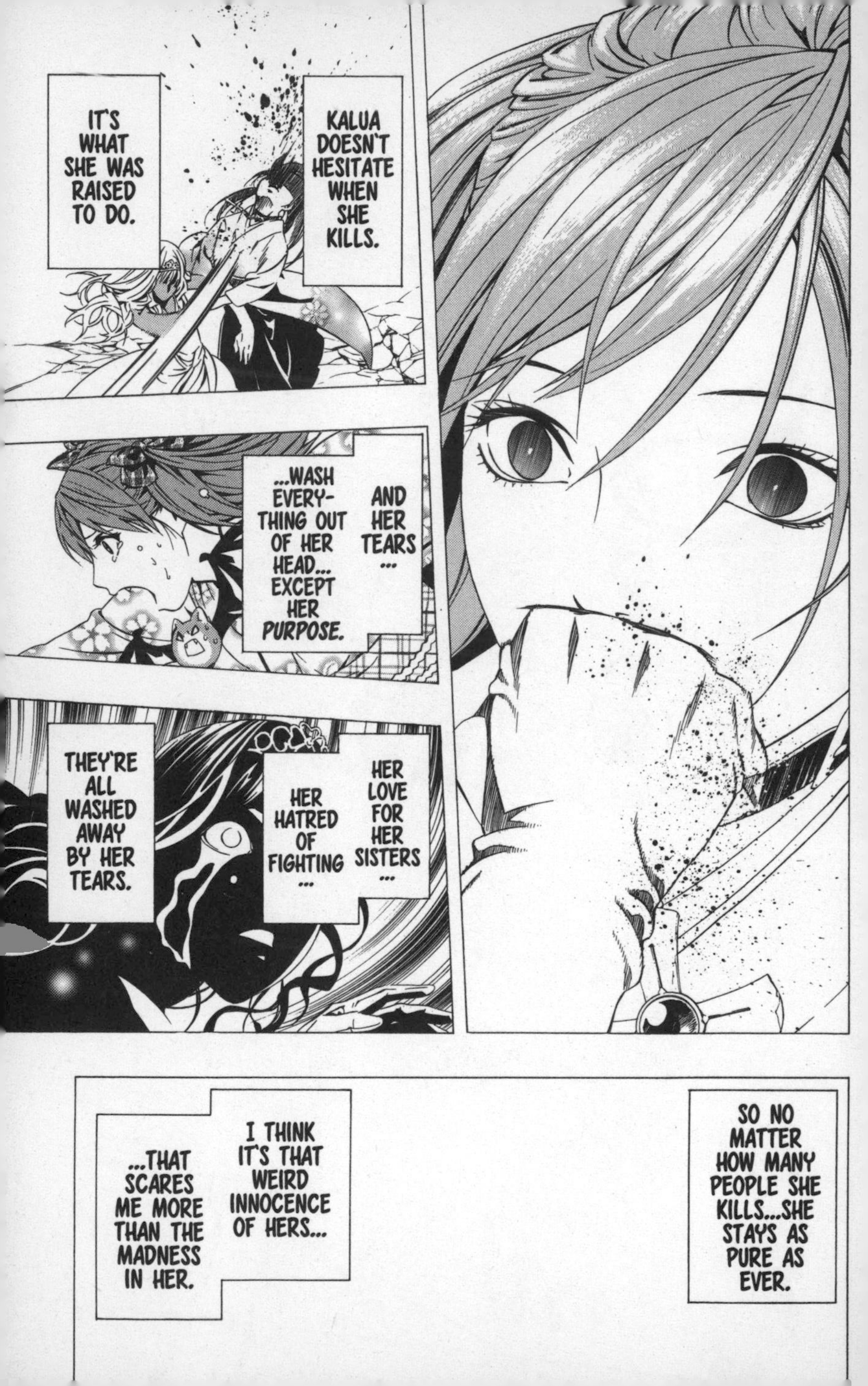
KALUA DOESN'T HESITATE WHEN SHE KILLS.
IT'S WHAT SHE WAS RAISED TO DO.
AND HER TEARS...
...WASH EVERY-THING OUT OF HER HEAD... EXCEPT HER PURPOSE.
HER LOVE FOR HER SISTERS...
HER HATRED OF FIGHTING...
THEY'RE ALL WASHED AWAY BY HER TEARS.
SO NO MATTER HOW MANY PEOPLE SHE KILLS...SHE STAYS AS PURE AS EVER.
I THINK IT'S THAT WEIRD INNOCENCE OF HERS...
...THAT SCARES ME MORE THAN THE MADNESS IN HER.

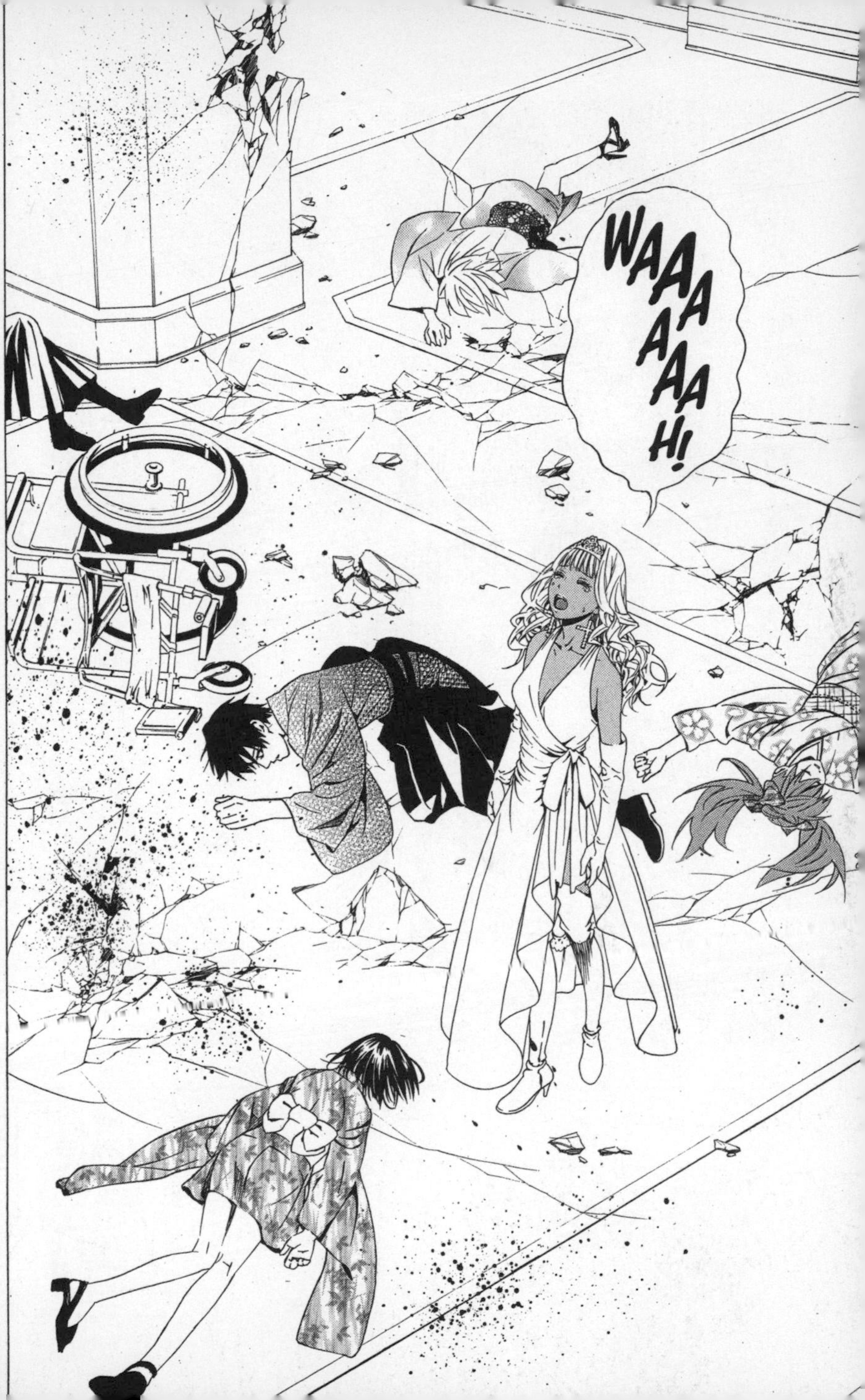
WAAAAAAAH!

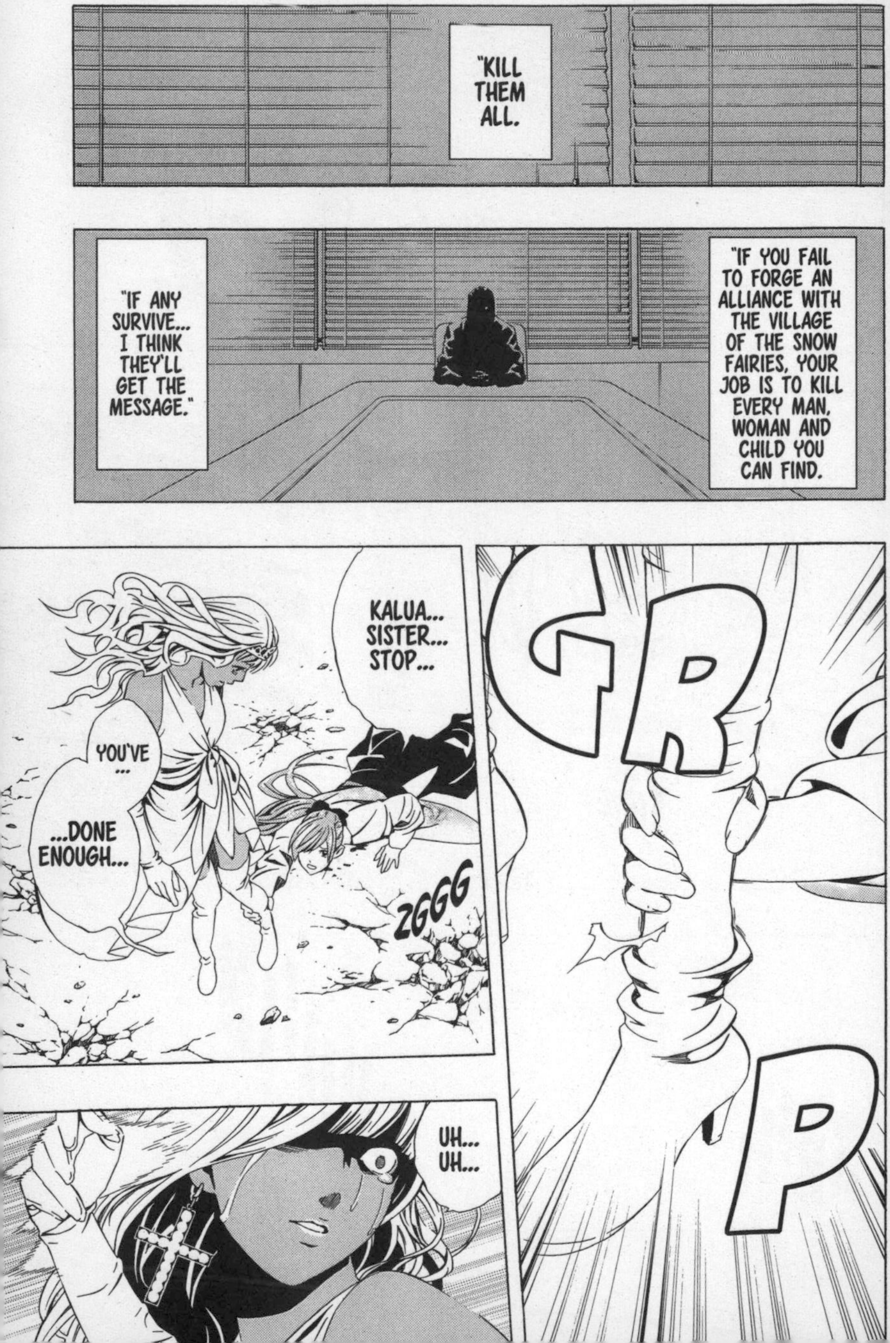
"KILL THEM ALL.
"IF YOU FAIL TO FORGE AN ALLIANCE WITH THE VILLAGE OF THE SNOW FAIRIES, YOUR JOB IS TO KILL EVERY MAN, WOMAN AND CHILD YOU CAN FIND.
"IF ANY SURVIVE... I THINK THEY'LL GET THE MESSAGE."
GR
P
KALUA... SISTER... STOP...
YOU'VE ...
...DONE ENOUGH...
ZGGG
UH... UH...

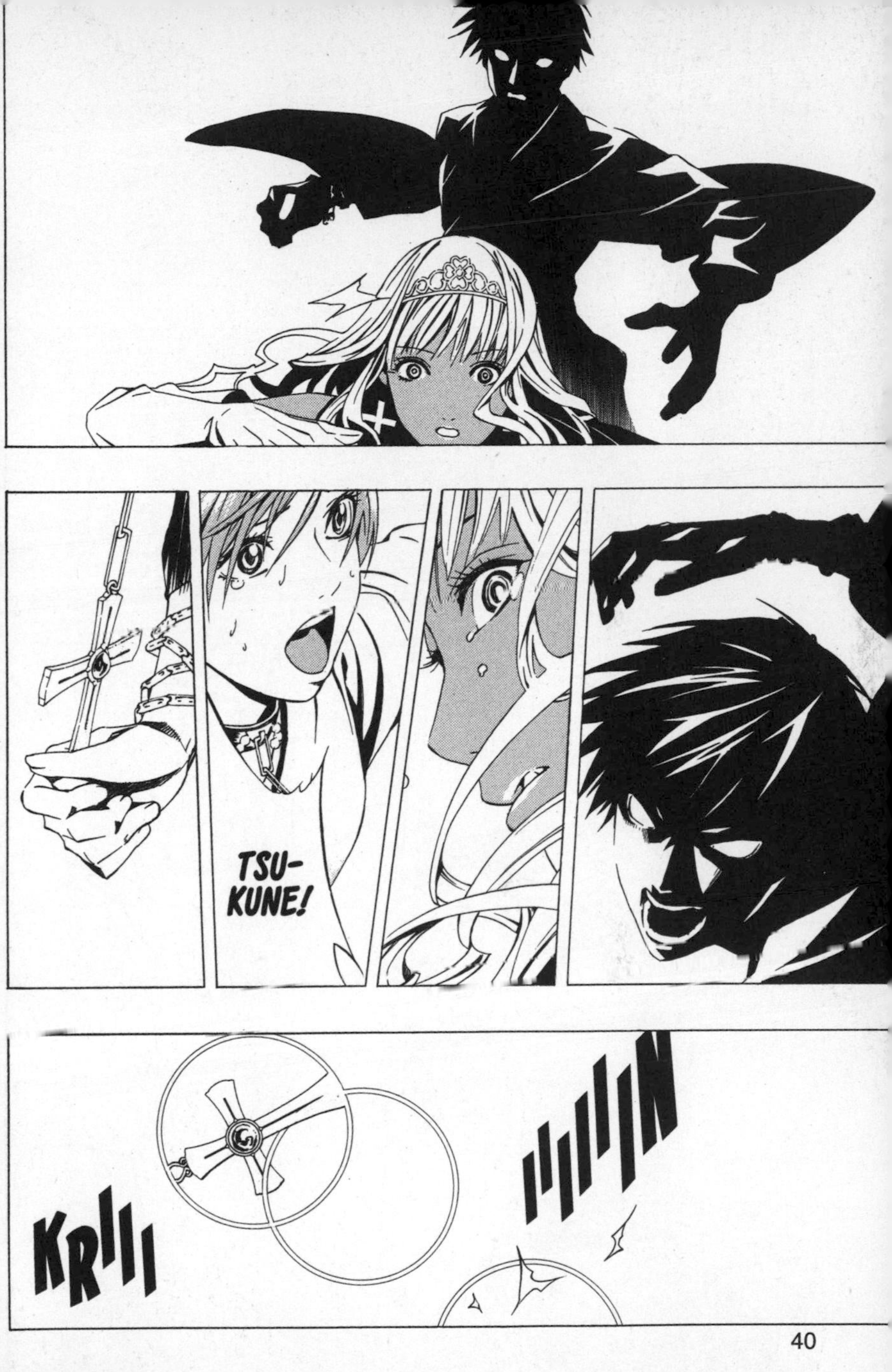
TSU-
KUNE!
KRIII
IIIIIN

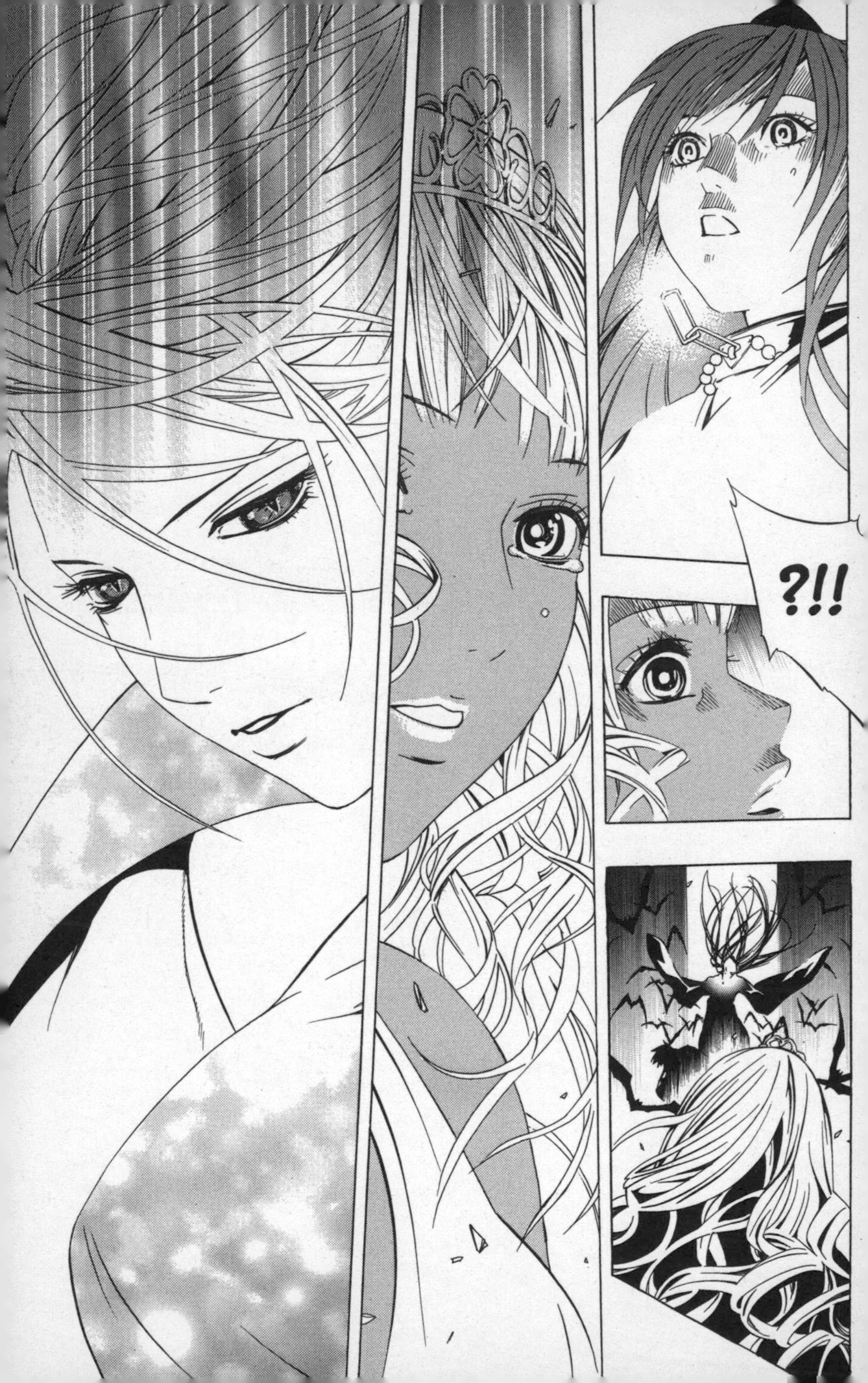
?!!

14: Something Important

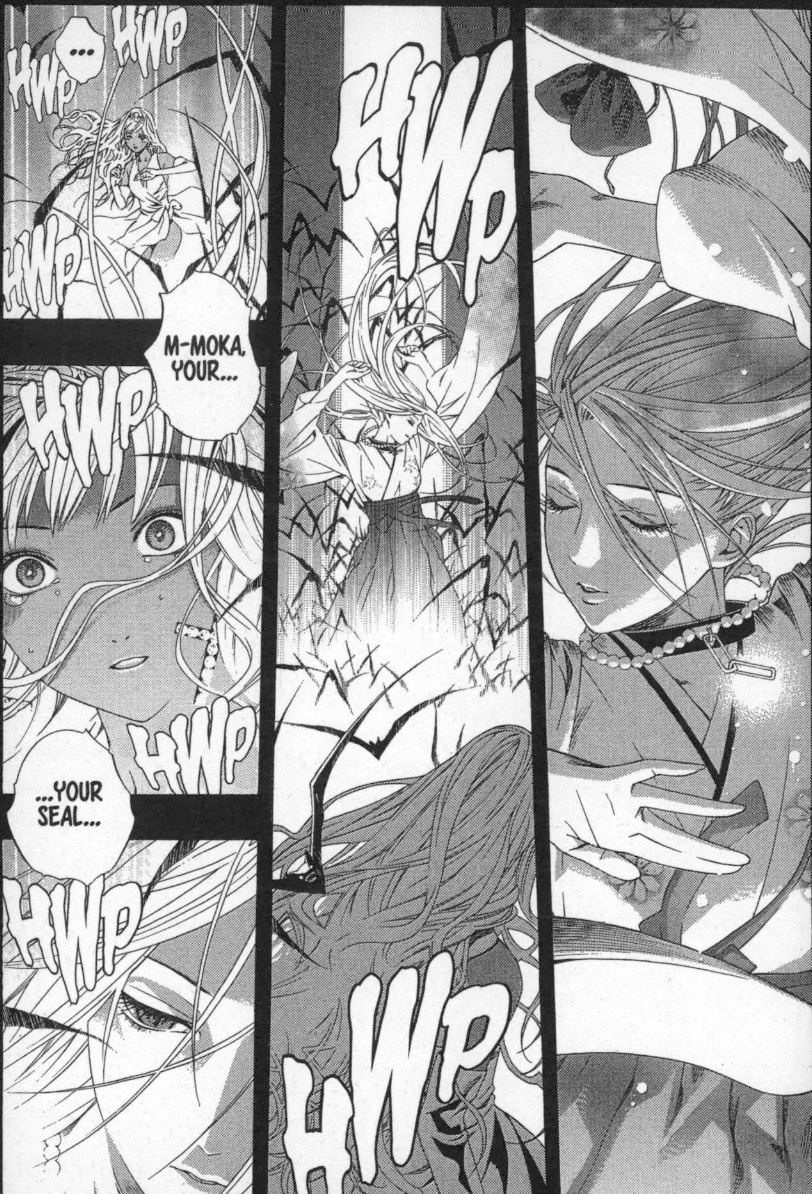
HWP
HWP
HWP
...
HWP
HWP
M-MOKA, YOUR...
HWP
HWP
...YOUR SEAL...
HWP

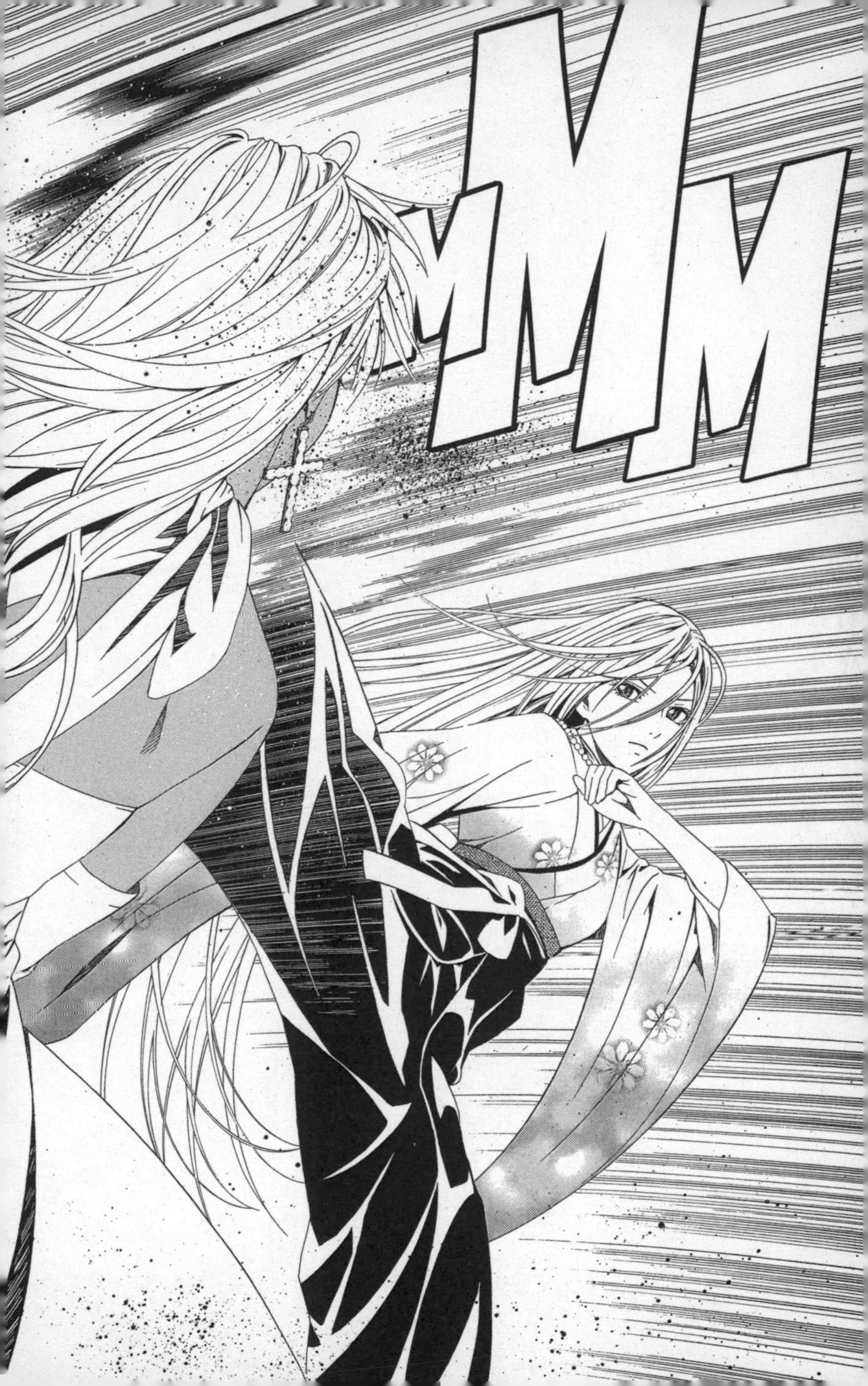
MMMM

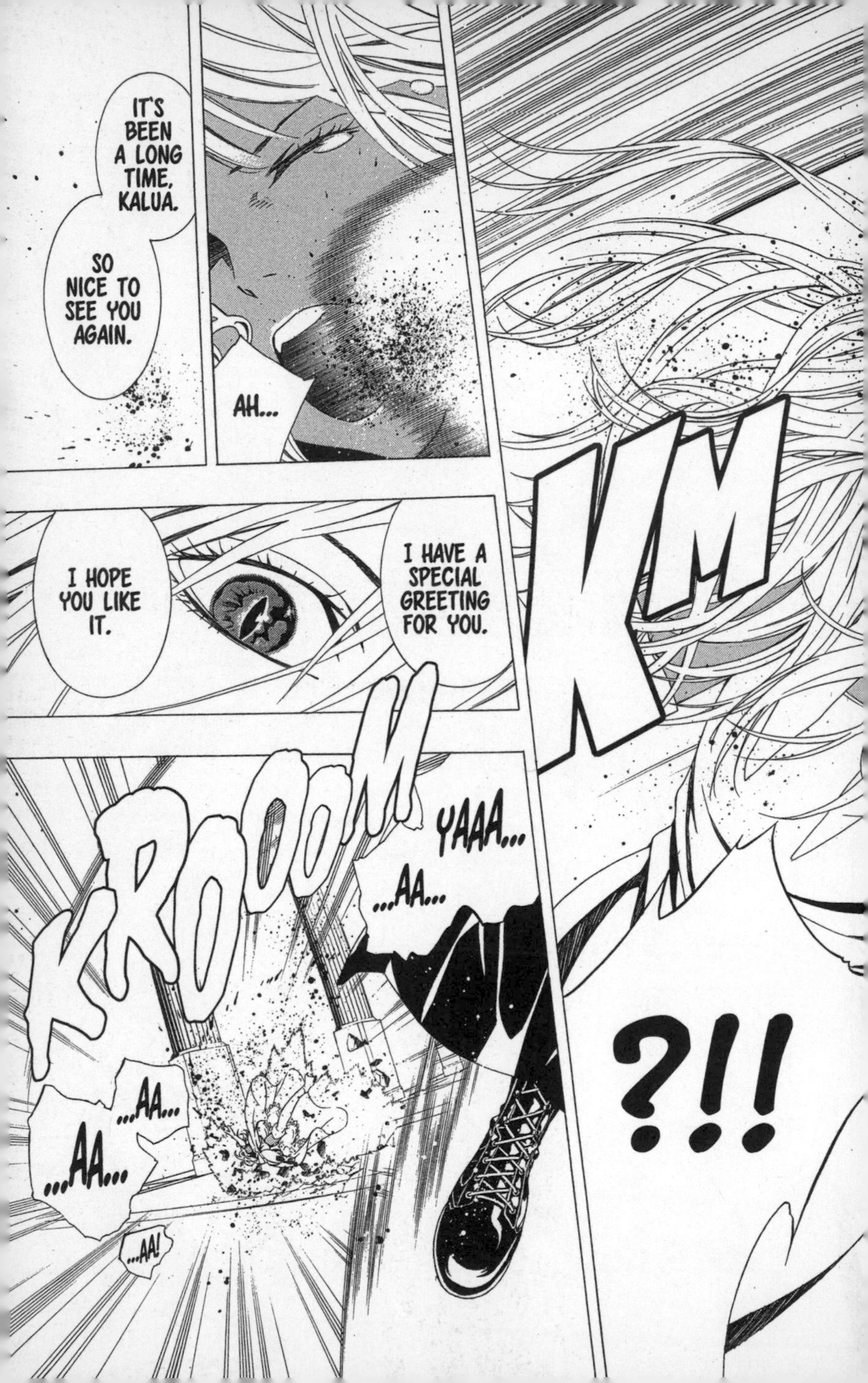
KM
?!!
AH...
IT'S BEEN A LONG TIME, KALUA.
SO NICE TO SEE YOU AGAIN.
I HAVE A SPECIAL GREETING FOR YOU.
I HOPE YOU LIKE IT.
YAAA...
...AA...
KROOOM
...AA...
...AA...
...AA!

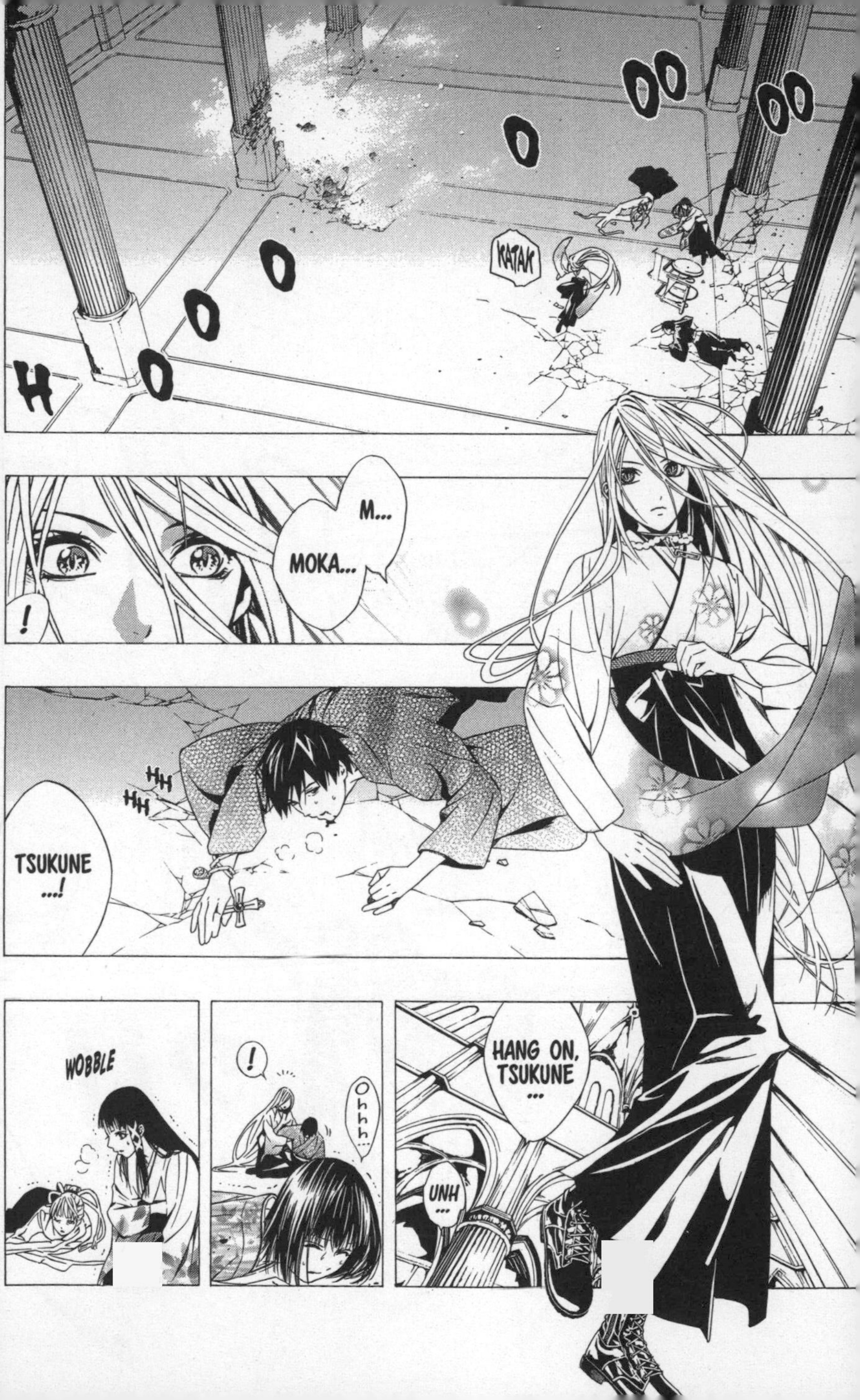
HOOOOOOOO
KATAK
M...
MOKA...
!
HH
HH
TSUKUNE ...!
HANG ON, TSUKUNE ...
UNH ...
!
Ohhh...
WOBBLE

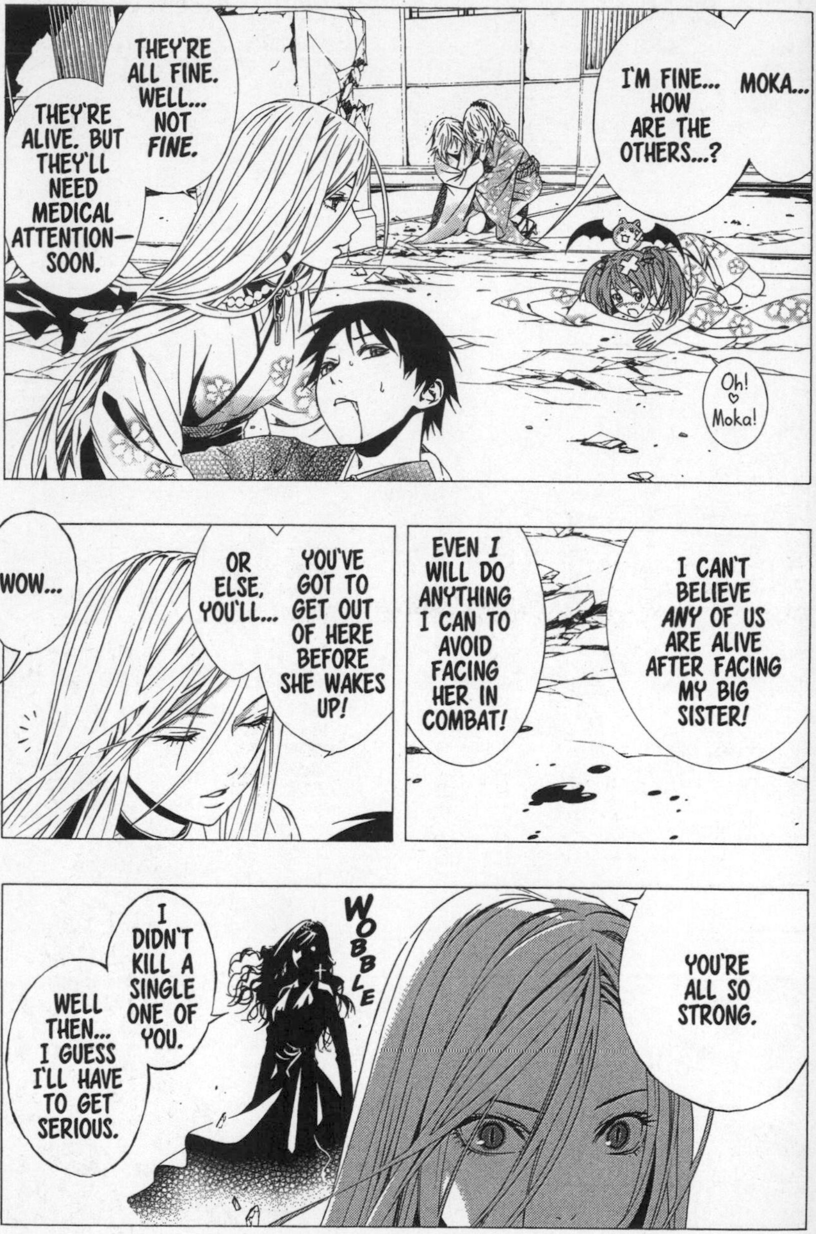
MOKA...
I'M FINE... HOW ARE THE OTHERS...?
THEY'RE ALL FINE. WELL... NOT *FINE.*
THEY'RE ALIVE. BUT THEY'LL NEED MEDICAL ATTENTION—SOON.
Oh! ♡ Moka!
I CAN'T BELIEVE *ANY* OF US ARE ALIVE AFTER FACING MY BIG SISTER!
EVEN *I* WILL DO ANYTHING I CAN TO AVOID FACING HER IN COMBAT!
YOU'VE GOT TO GET OUT OF HERE BEFORE SHE WAKES UP!
OR ELSE, YOU'LL...
WOW...
YOU'RE ALL SO STRONG.
WOBBLE
I DIDN'T KILL A SINGLE ONE OF YOU.
WELL THEN... I GUESS I'LL HAVE TO GET SERIOUS.

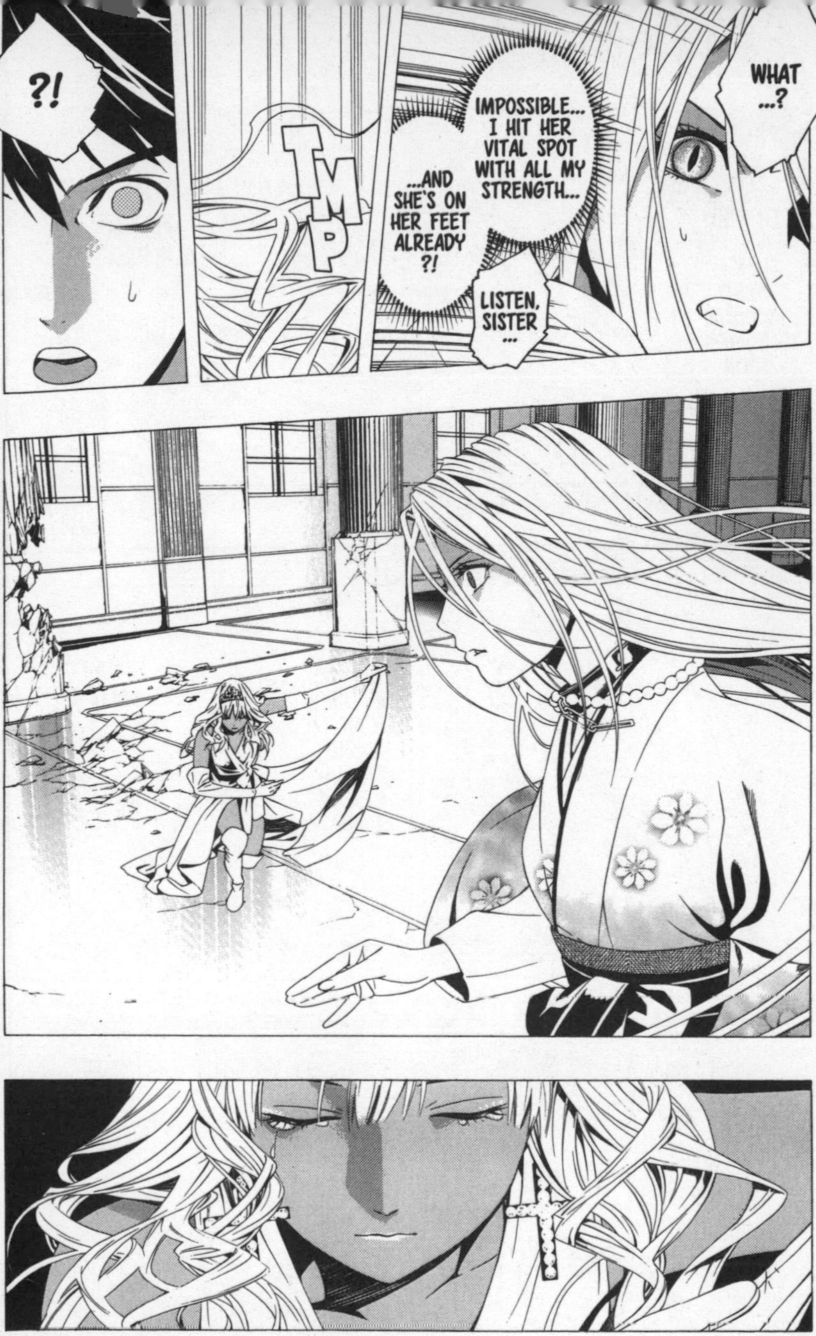
WHAT ...?
IMPOSSIBLE... I HIT HER VITAL SPOT WITH ALL MY STRENGTH...
...AND SHE'S ON HER FEET ALREADY ?!
LISTEN, SISTER ...
TMP
?!

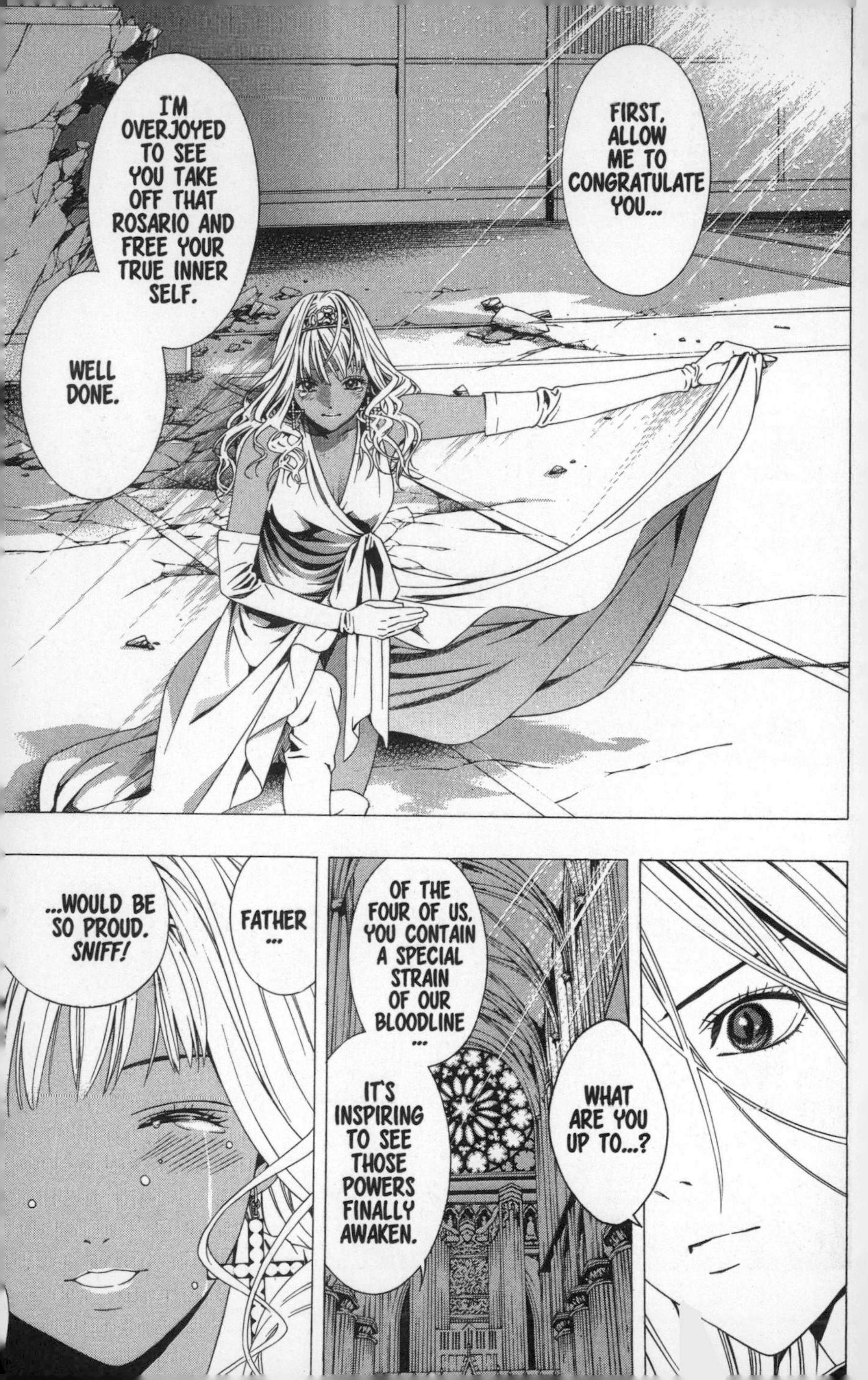
FIRST, ALLOW ME TO CONGRATULATE YOU...
I'M OVERJOYED TO SEE YOU TAKE OFF THAT ROSARIO AND FREE YOUR TRUE INNER SELF.
WELL DONE.
WHAT ARE YOU UP TO...?
OF THE FOUR OF US, YOU CONTAIN A SPECIAL STRAIN OF OUR BLOODLINE...
IT'S INSPIRING TO SEE THOSE POWERS FINALLY AWAKEN.
FATHER...
...WOULD BE SO PROUD. SNIFF!

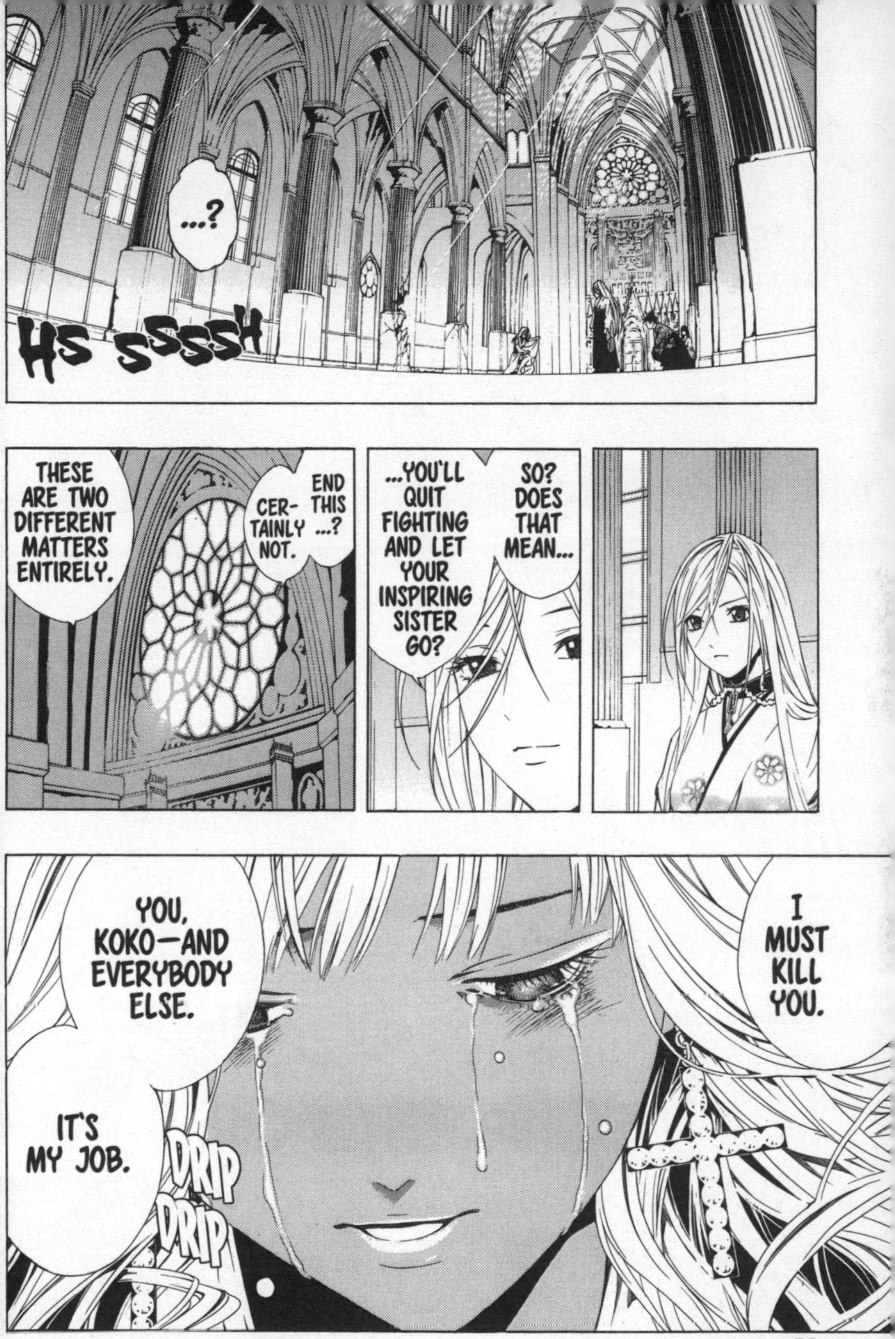
...?
HS SSSSH
SO? DOES THAT MEAN...
...YOU'LL QUIT FIGHTING AND LET YOUR INSPIRING SISTER GO?
END THIS ...?
CER-TAINLY NOT.
THESE ARE TWO DIFFERENT MATTERS ENTIRELY.
I MUST KILL YOU.
YOU, KOKO—AND EVERYBODY ELSE.
IT'S MY JOB.
DRIP
DRIP

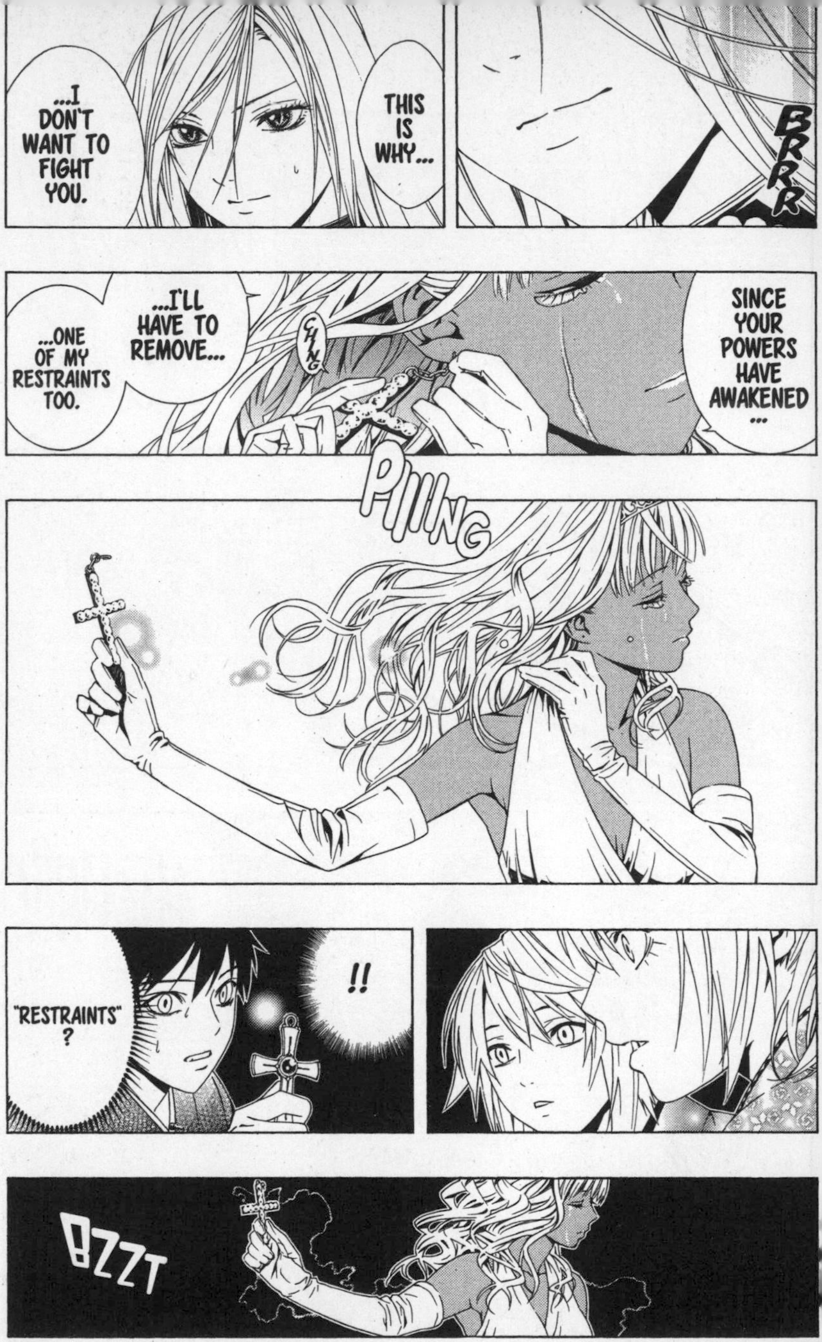
BRRR
THIS IS WHY...
...I DON'T WANT TO FIGHT YOU.
SINCE YOUR POWERS HAVE AWAKENED...
CHING
...I'LL HAVE TO REMOVE...
...ONE OF MY RESTRAINTS TOO.
PIIING
!!
"RESTRAINTS"?
BZZT

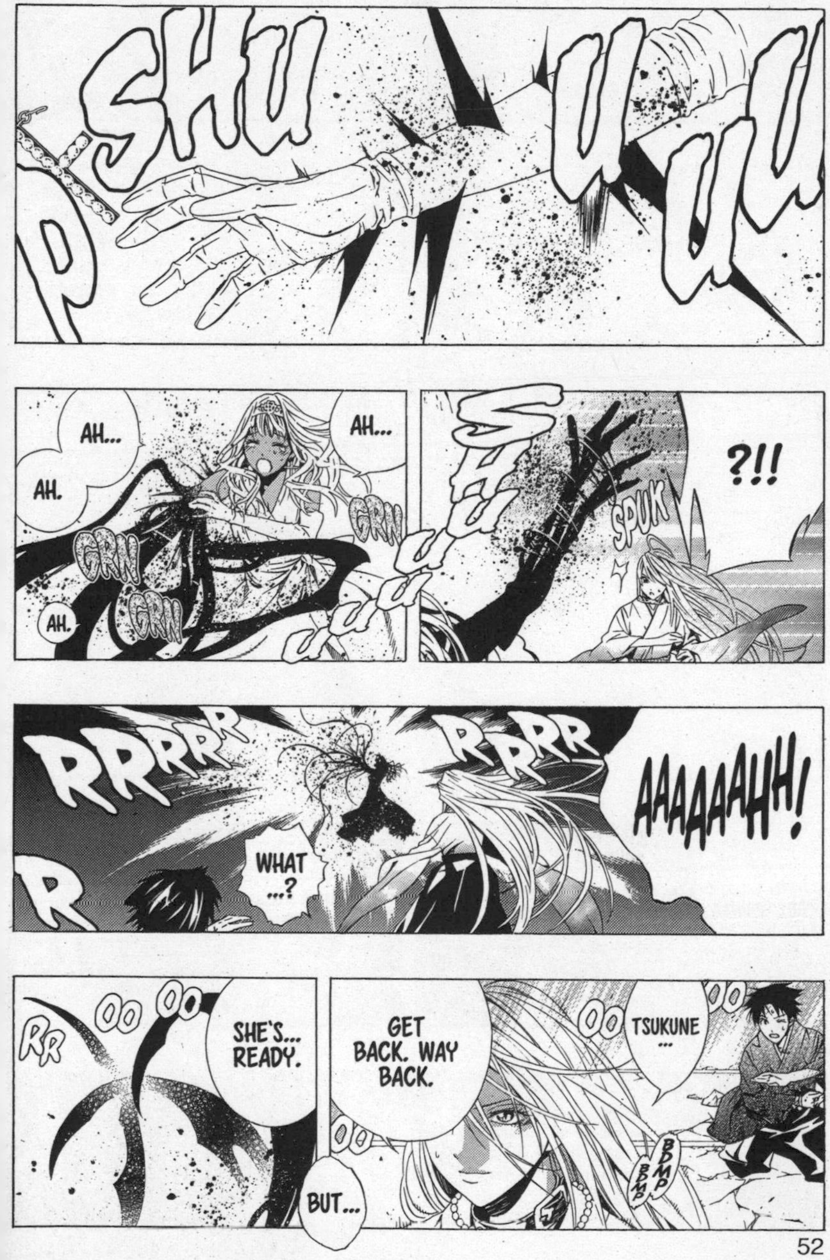
PSHUUUU
?!!
SHUUUU
SPUK
AH...
AH...
AH.
GRN
GRN
GRN
AH.
AAAAAAHH!
RRRR
WHAT ...?
RRRR
R
OO
TSUKUNE ...
GET BACK. WAY BACK.
OO
BDMP BDMP
BUT...
SHE'S... READY.
OO OO
RR

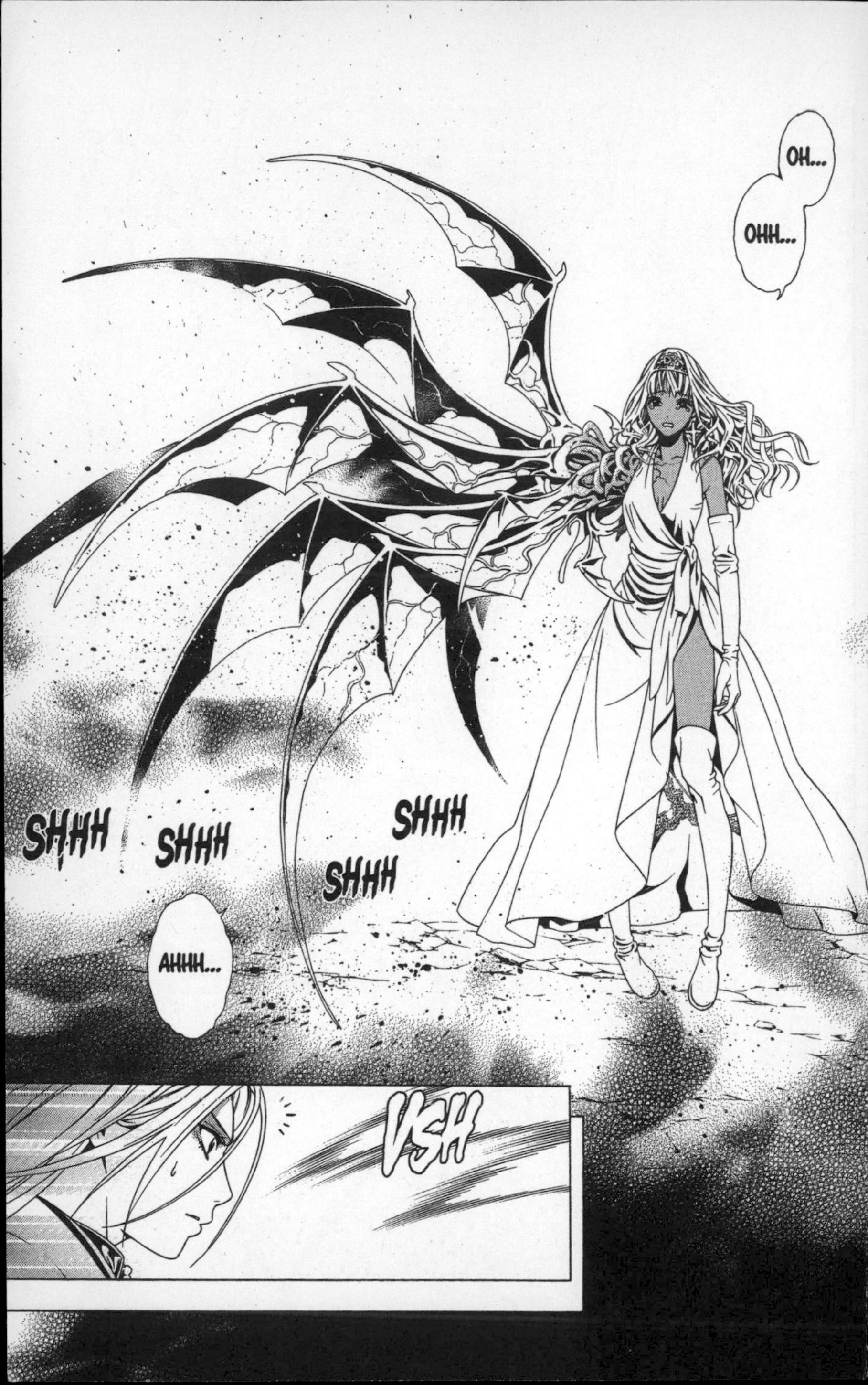
OH...
OHH...
SHHH
SHHH
SHHH
SHHH
AHHH...
VSH

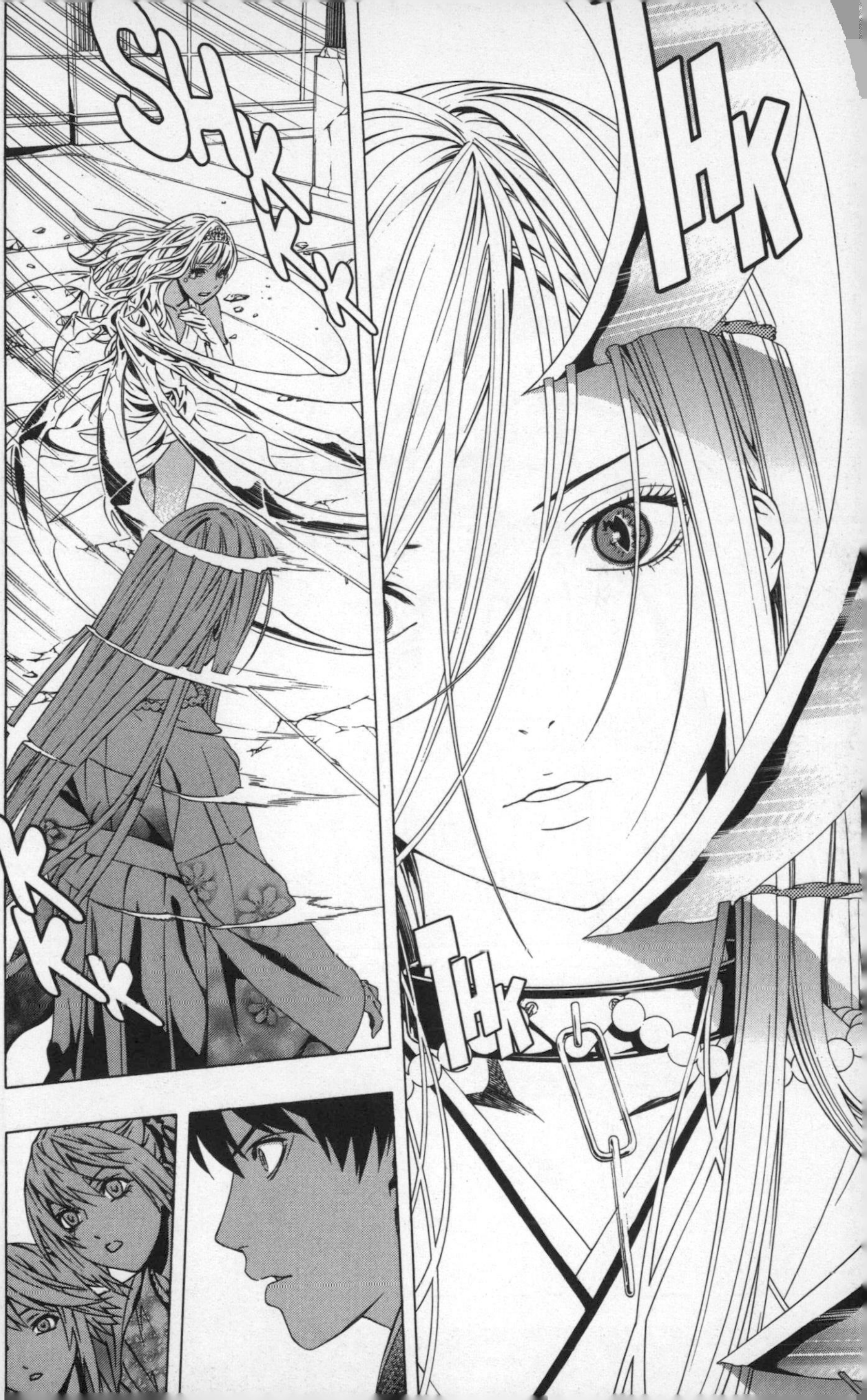
IHK
THK
SHKKK
KKKK

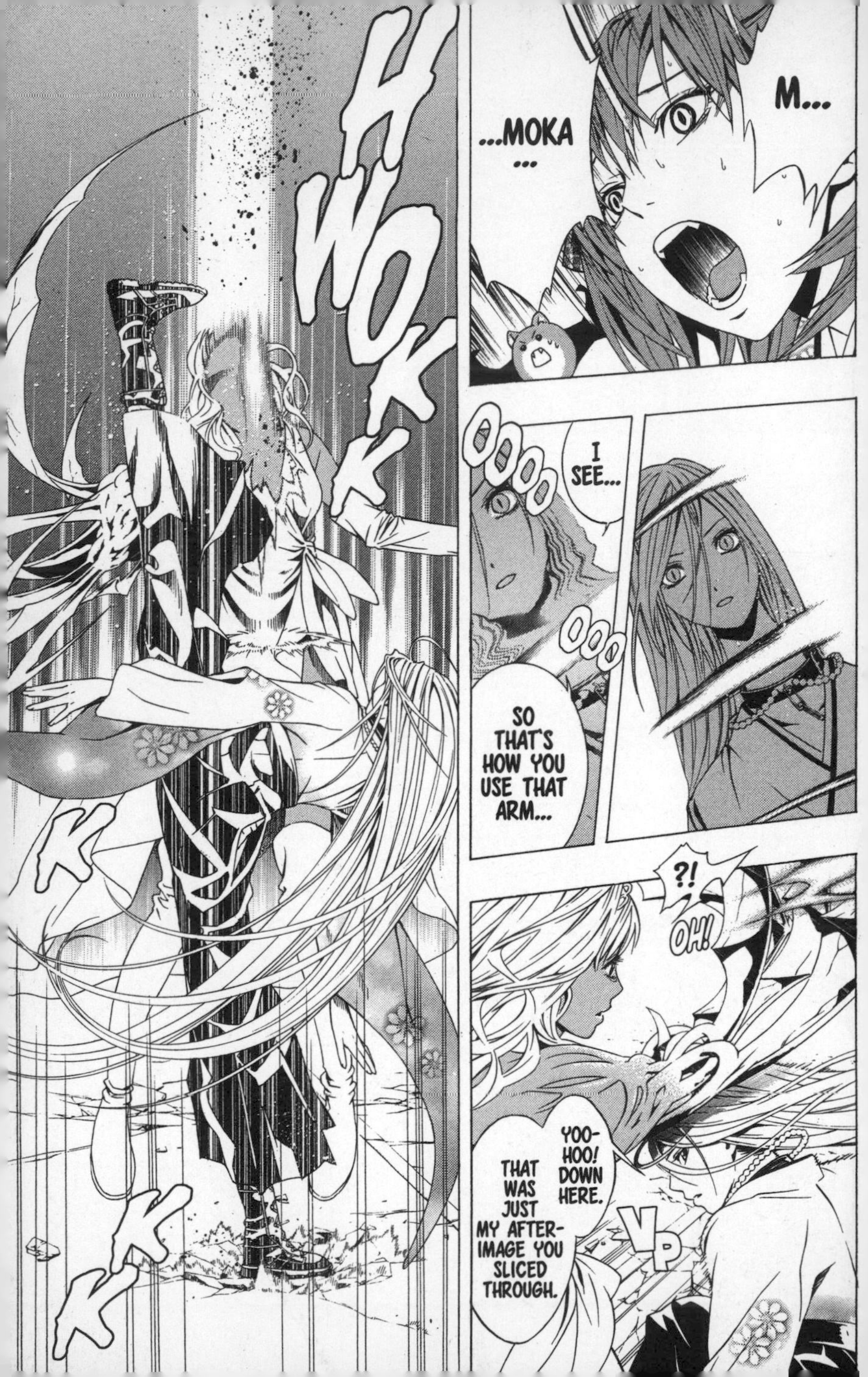
M...
...MOKA ...
OOOO
I SEE...
OOO
SO THAT'S HOW YOU USE THAT ARM...
?!
OH!
YOO-HOO! DOWN HERE.
THAT WAS JUST MY AFTER-IMAGE YOU SLICED THROUGH.
VP
HWOK
K
KKK

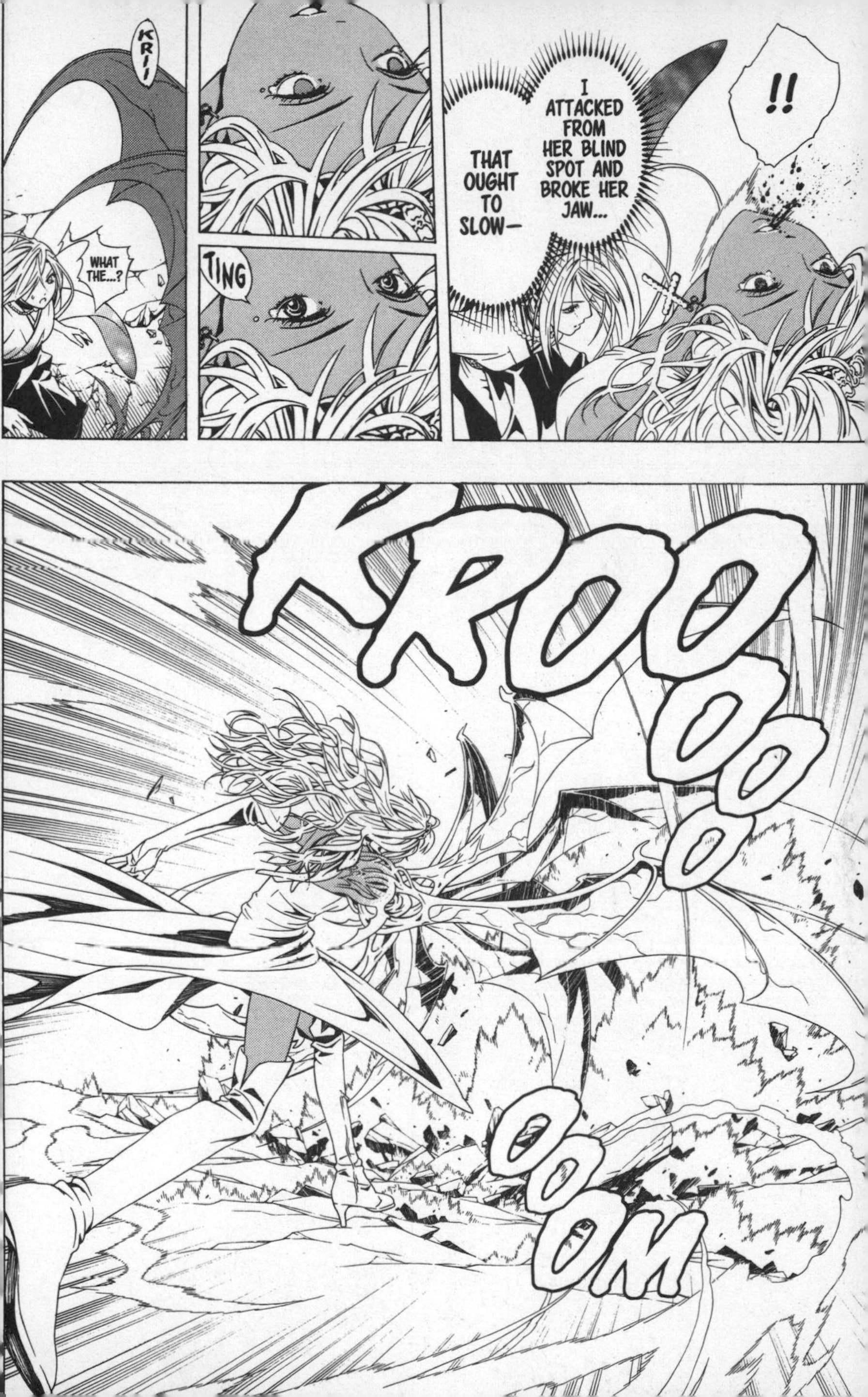
!!
I ATTACKED FROM HER BLIND SPOT AND BROKE HER JAW...
THAT OUGHT TO SLOW—
TING
KRII
WHAT THE...?
KROOOOO
OOOOM

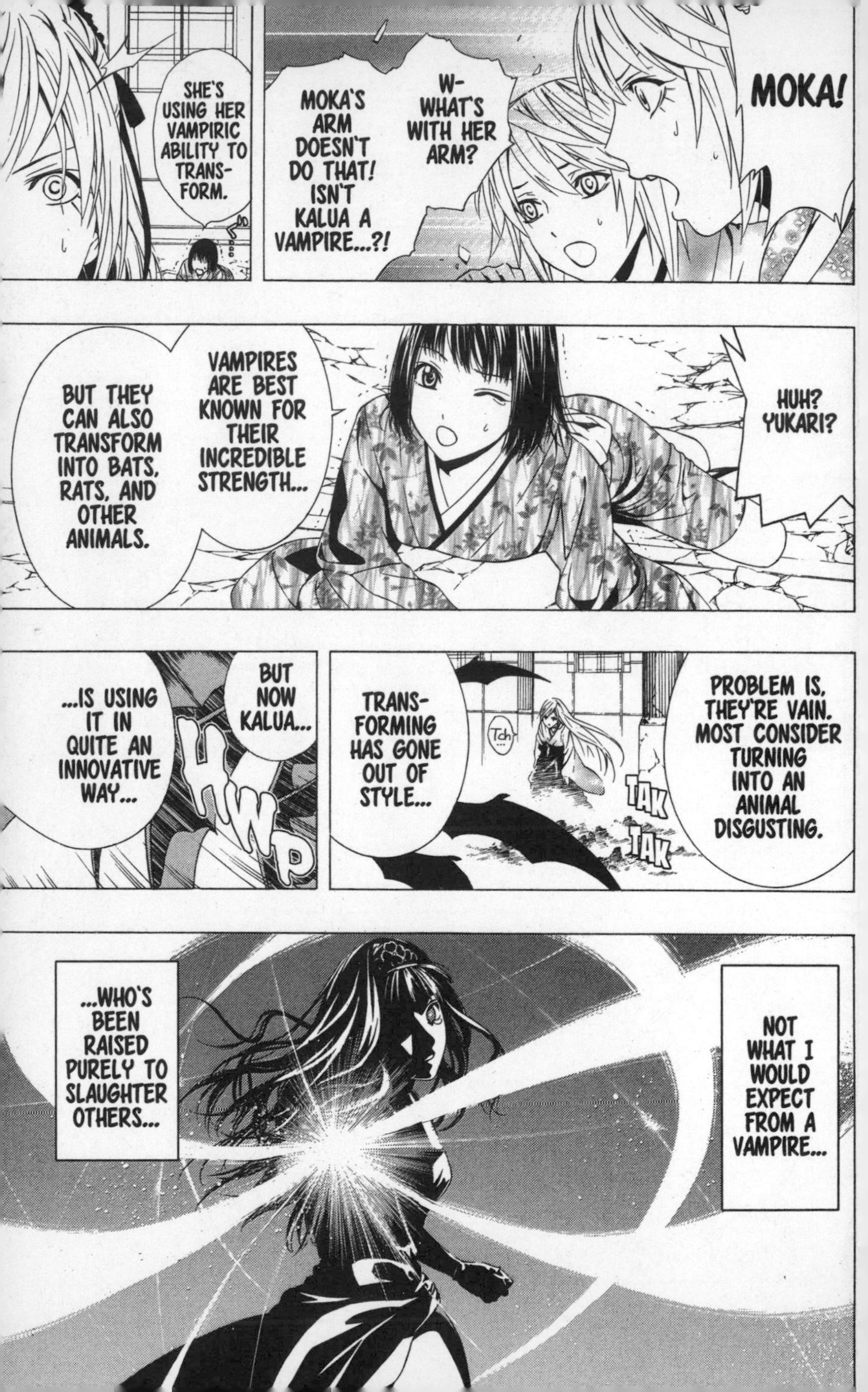
MOKA!
W- WHAT'S WITH HER ARM?
MOKA'S ARM DOESN'T DO THAT! ISN'T KALUA A VAMPIRE...?!
SHE'S USING HER VAMPIRIC ABILITY TO TRANS-FORM.
HUH? YUKARI?
VAMPIRES ARE BEST KNOWN FOR THEIR INCREDIBLE STRENGTH...
BUT THEY CAN ALSO TRANSFORM INTO BATS, RATS, AND OTHER ANIMALS.
PROBLEM IS, THEY'RE VAIN. MOST CONSIDER TURNING INTO AN ANIMAL DISGUSTING.
TAK
TAK
Tch...
TRANS-FORMING HAS GONE OUT OF STYLE...
BUT NOW KALUA...
...IS USING IT IN QUITE AN INNOVATIVE WAY...
NOT WHAT I WOULD EXPECT FROM A VAMPIRE...
...WHO'S BEEN RAISED PURELY TO SLAUGHTER OTHERS...

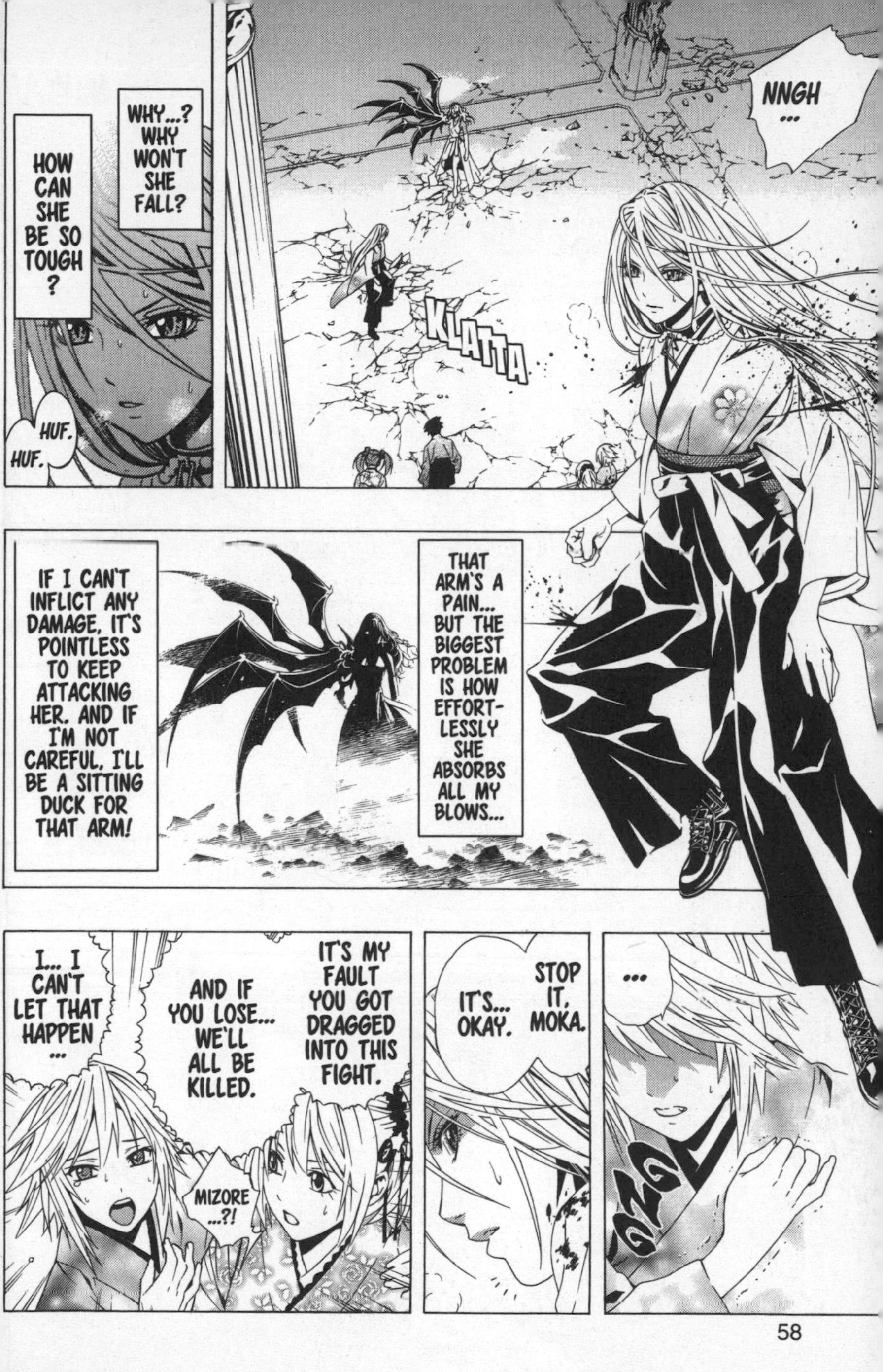
NNGH...
KLATTA
WHY...? WHY WON'T SHE FALL?
HOW CAN SHE BE SO TOUGH?
HUF. HUF.
THAT ARM'S A PAIN... BUT THE BIGGEST PROBLEM IS HOW EFFORTLESSLY SHE ABSORBS ALL MY BLOWS...
IF I CAN'T INFLICT ANY DAMAGE, IT'S POINTLESS TO KEEP ATTACKING HER. AND IF I'M NOT CAREFUL, I'LL BE A SITTING DUCK FOR THAT ARM!
...
STOP IT, MOKA.
IT'S... OKAY.
IT'S MY FAULT YOU GOT DRAGGED INTO THIS FIGHT.
AND IF YOU LOSE... WE'LL ALL BE KILLED.
I... I CAN'T LET THAT HAPPEN...
MIZORE...?!

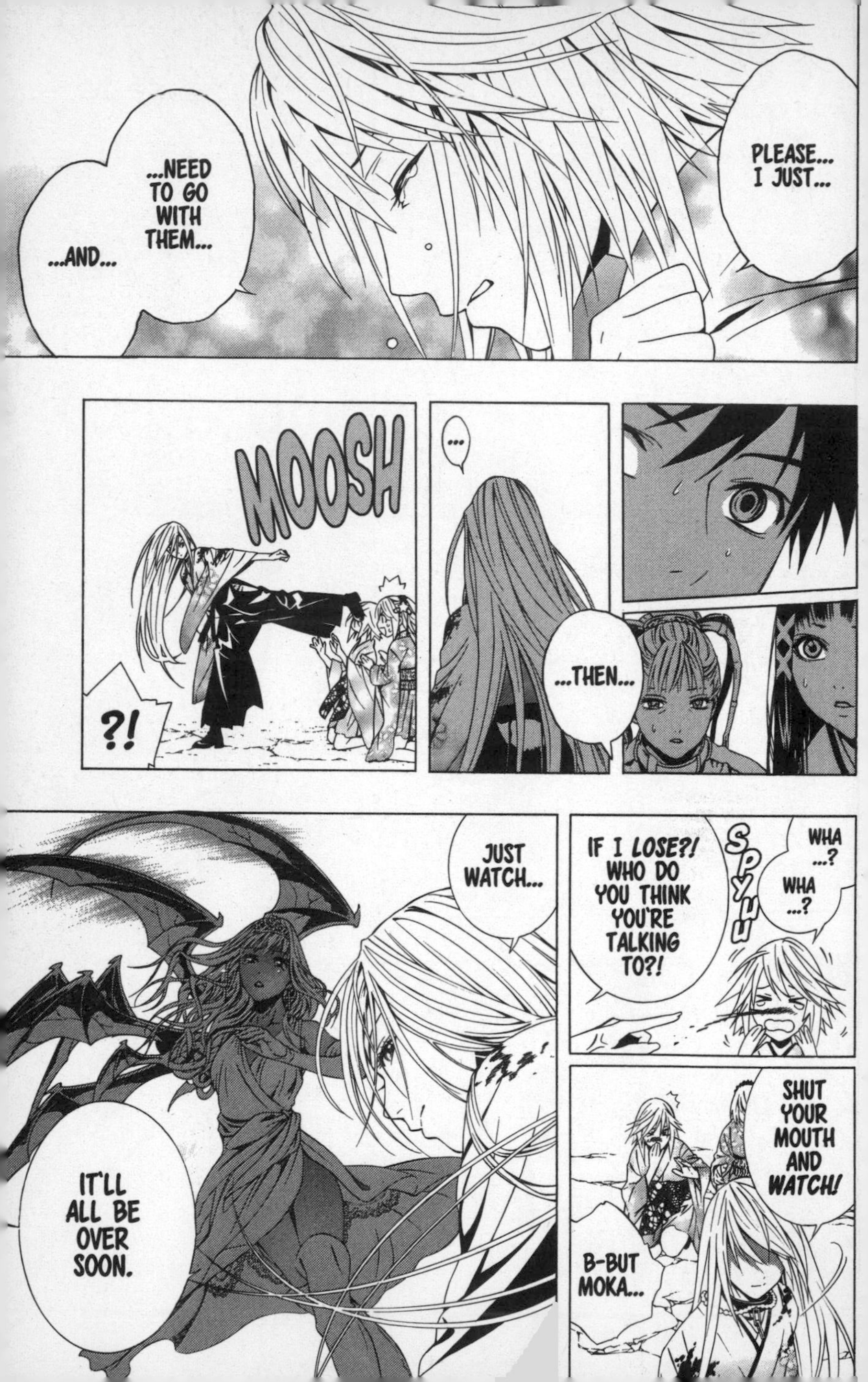
PLEASE... I JUST...
...NEED TO GO WITH THEM...
...AND...
...THEN...
...
MOOSH
?!
WHA ...?
WHA ...?
SPYUU
IF I *LOSE*?! WHO DO YOU THINK YOU'RE TALKING TO?!
SHUT YOUR MOUTH AND *WATCH!*
B-BUT MOKA...
JUST WATCH...
IT'LL ALL BE OVER SOON.

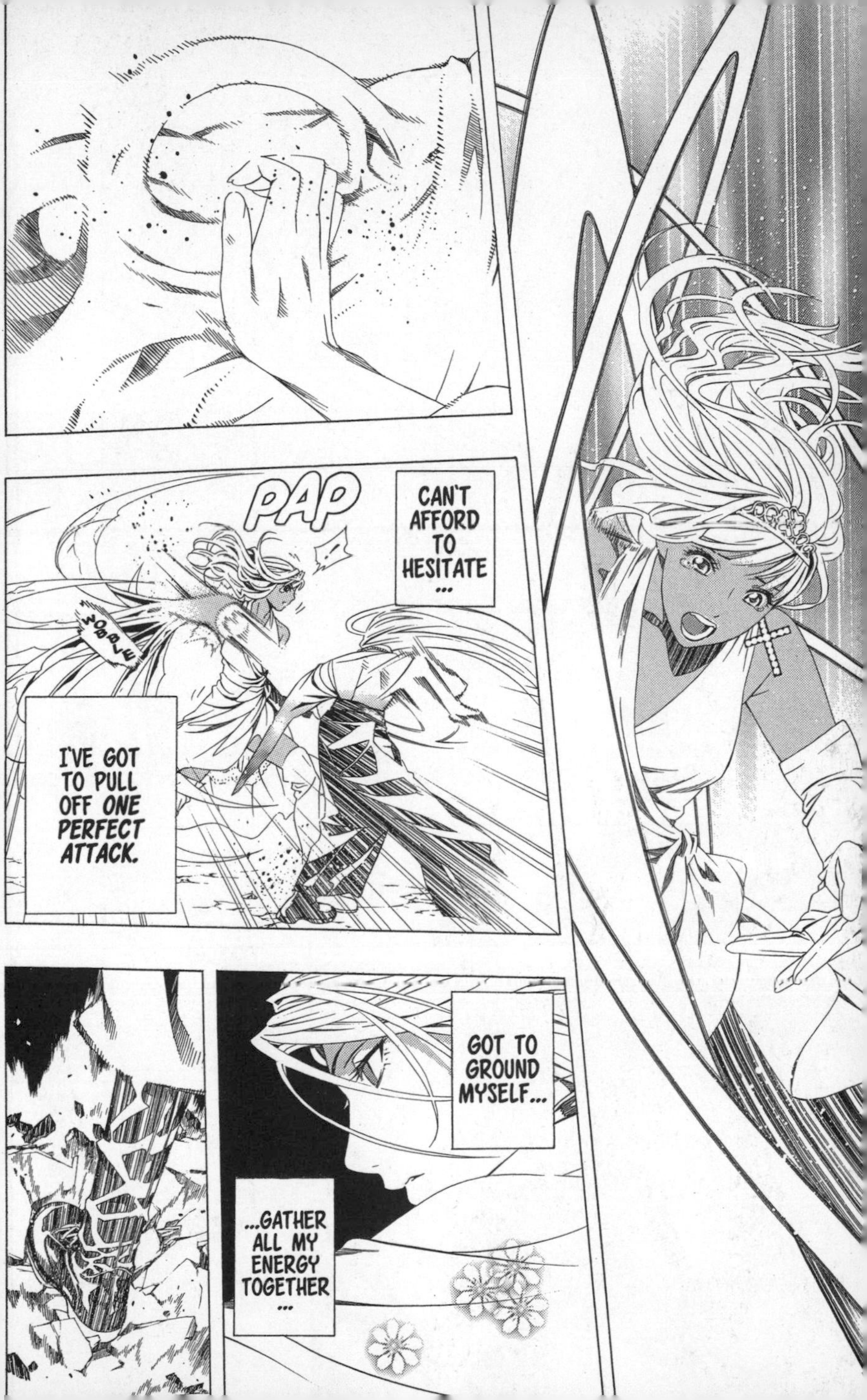
CAN'T AFFORD TO HESITATE ...
PAP
!
WOBBLE
I'VE GOT TO PULL OFF ONE PERFECT ATTACK.
GOT TO GROUND MYSELF...
...GATHER ALL MY ENERGY TOGETHER ...

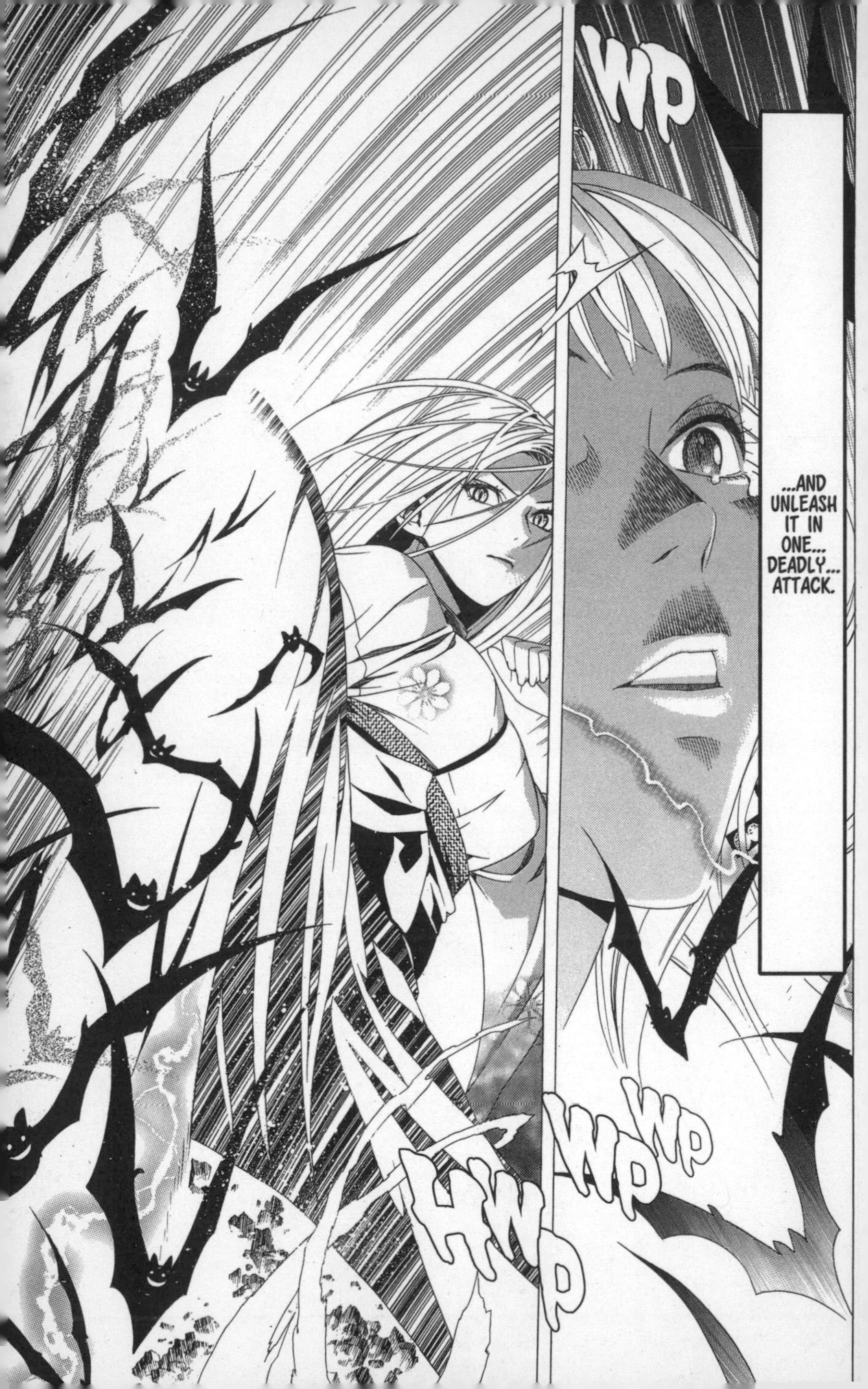
WP
...AND UNLEASH IT IN ONE... DEADLY... ATTACK.
WP
WP
WP
HWP

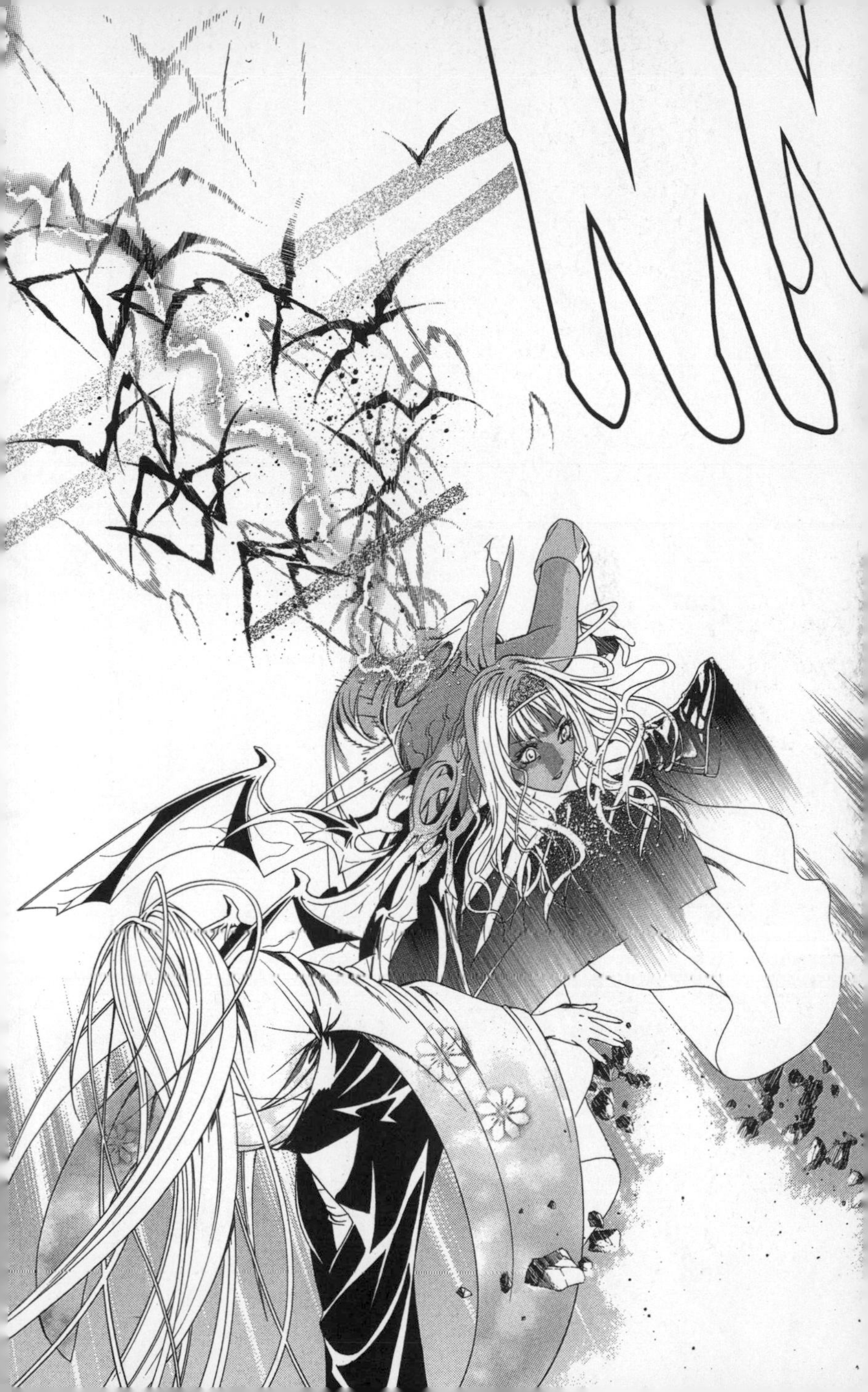

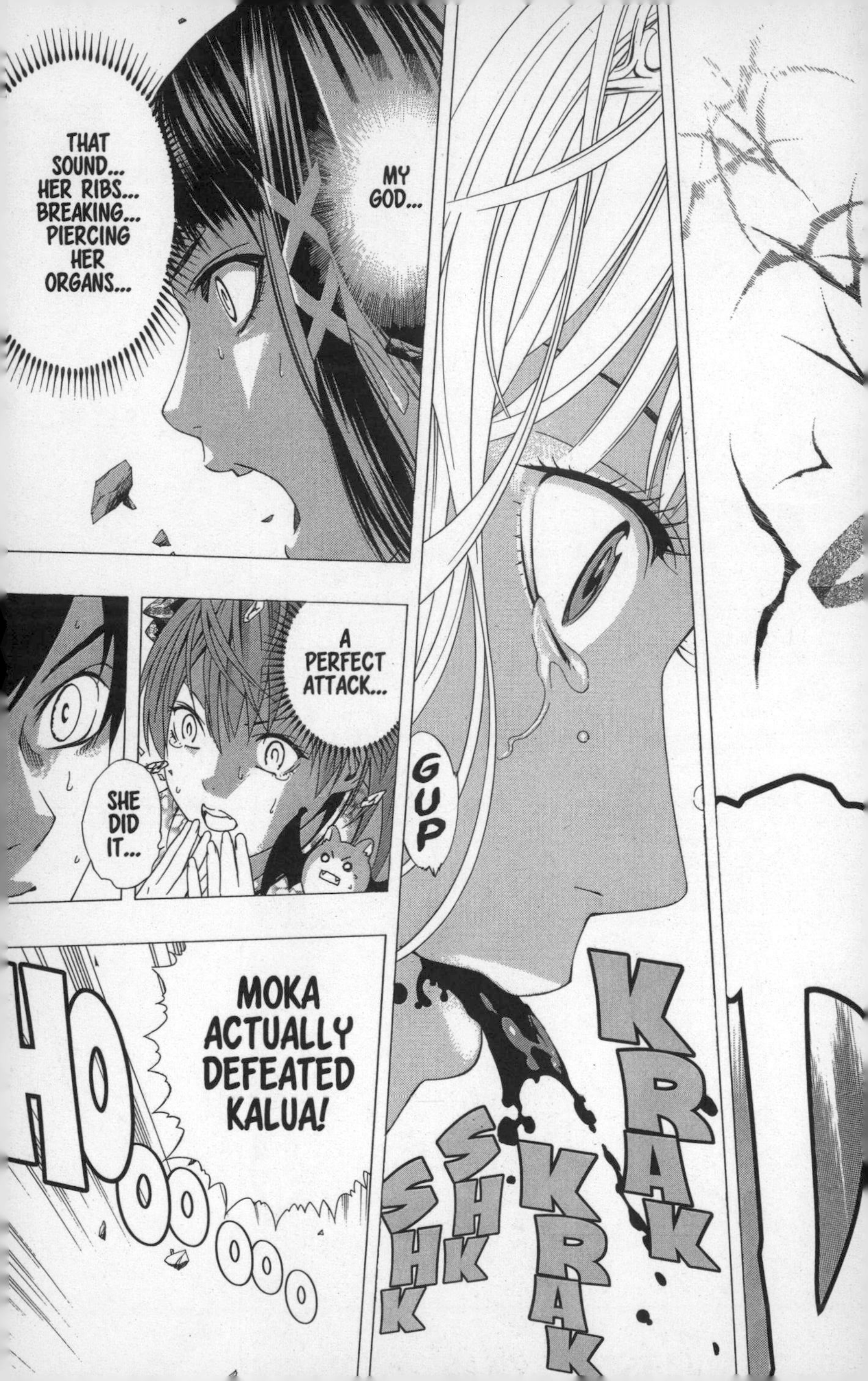
GUP
KRAK
KRAK
SHK
SHK
MY GOD...
THAT SOUND... HER RIBS... BREAKING... PIERCING HER ORGANS...
A PERFECT ATTACK...
SHE DID IT...
MOKA ACTUALLY DEFEATED KALUA!
HOOOOOOO

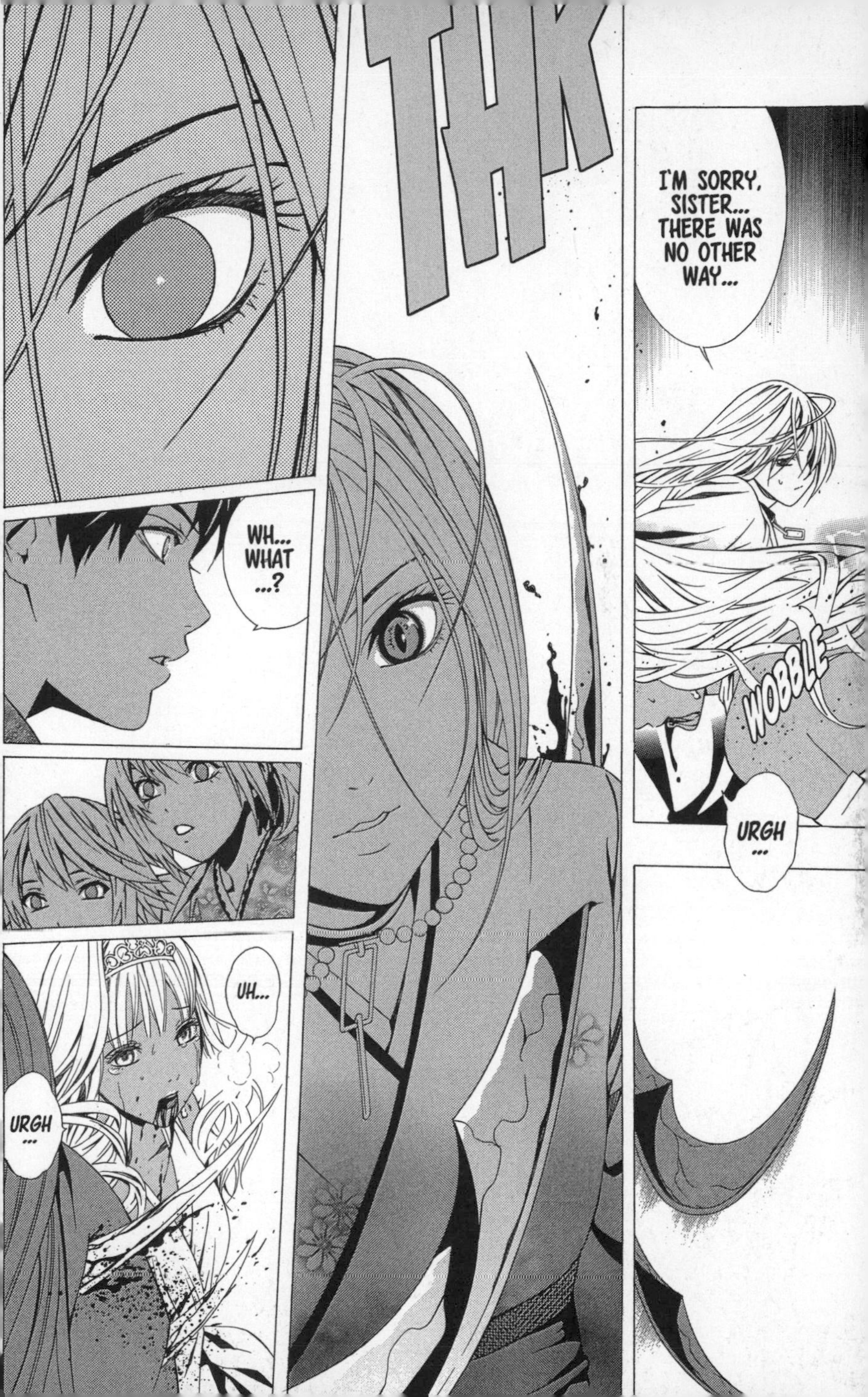
I'M SORRY, SISTER... THERE WAS NO OTHER WAY...
WOBBLE
URGH ...
THK
WH... WHAT ...?
UH...
URGH ...

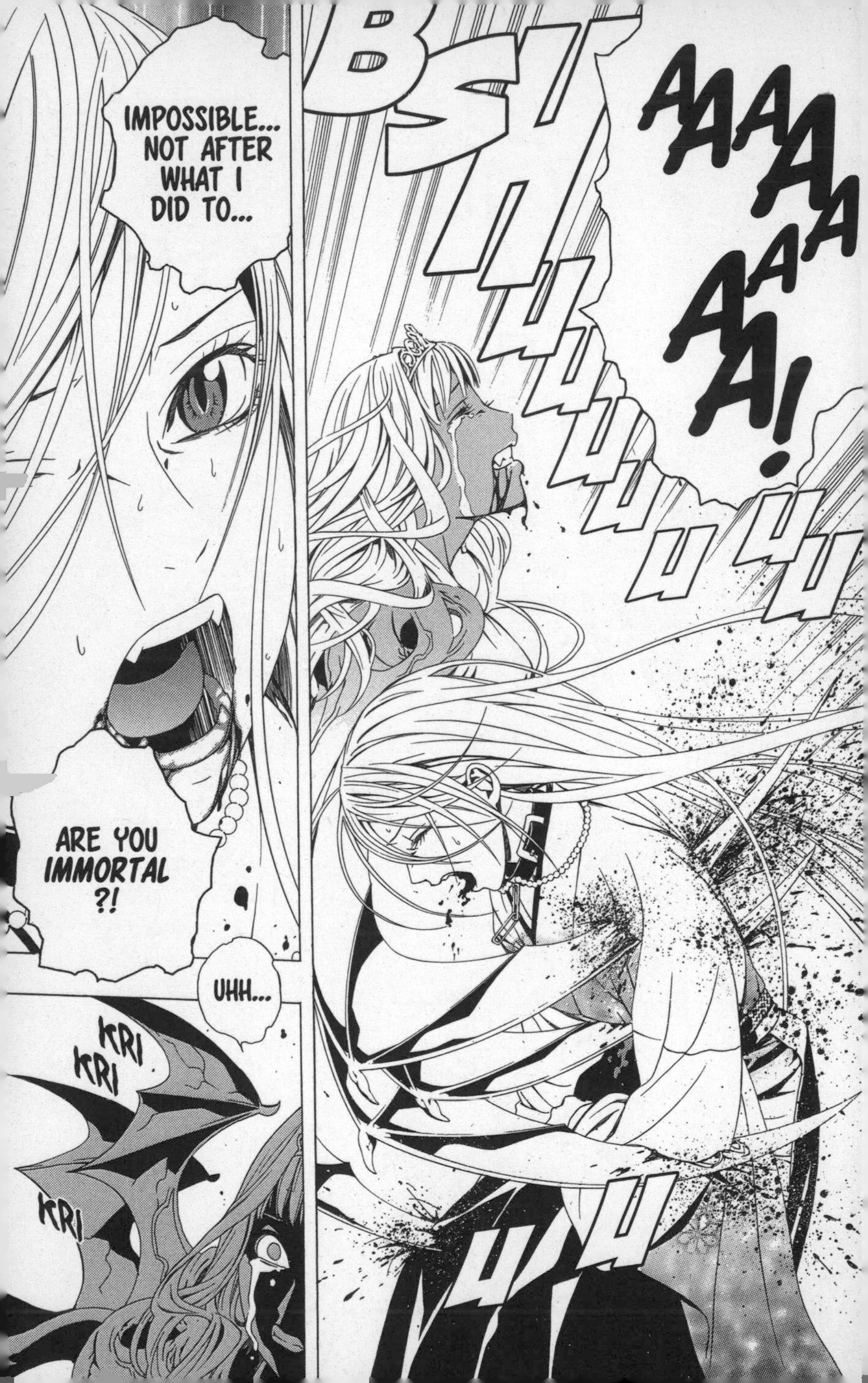
AAAAAAAAA!
IMPOSSIBLE... NOT AFTER WHAT I DID TO...
ARE YOU IMMORTAL ?!
UHH...
KRI KRI
KRI

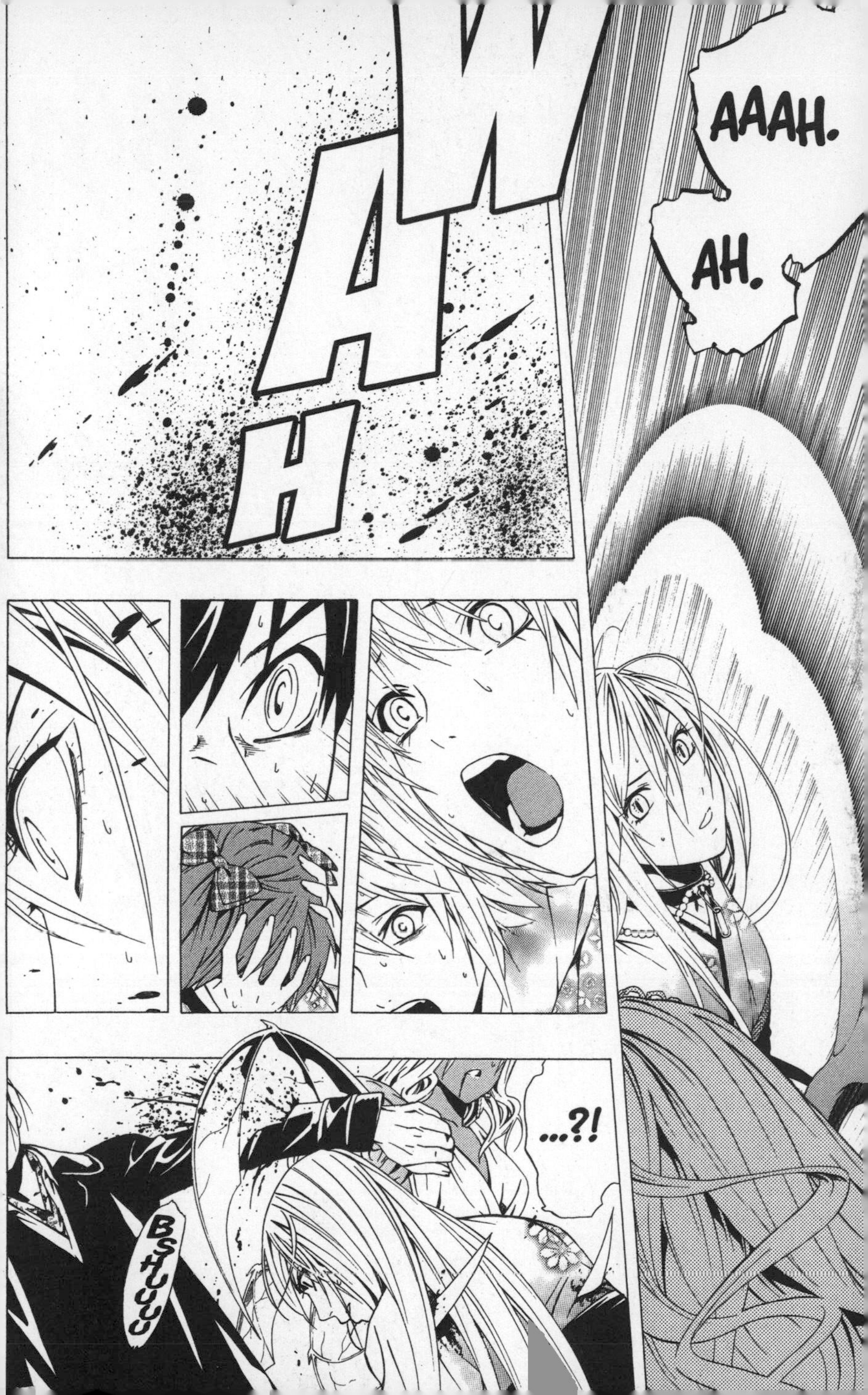
AAAH.
AH.
WAH
...?!
BSHUUUU

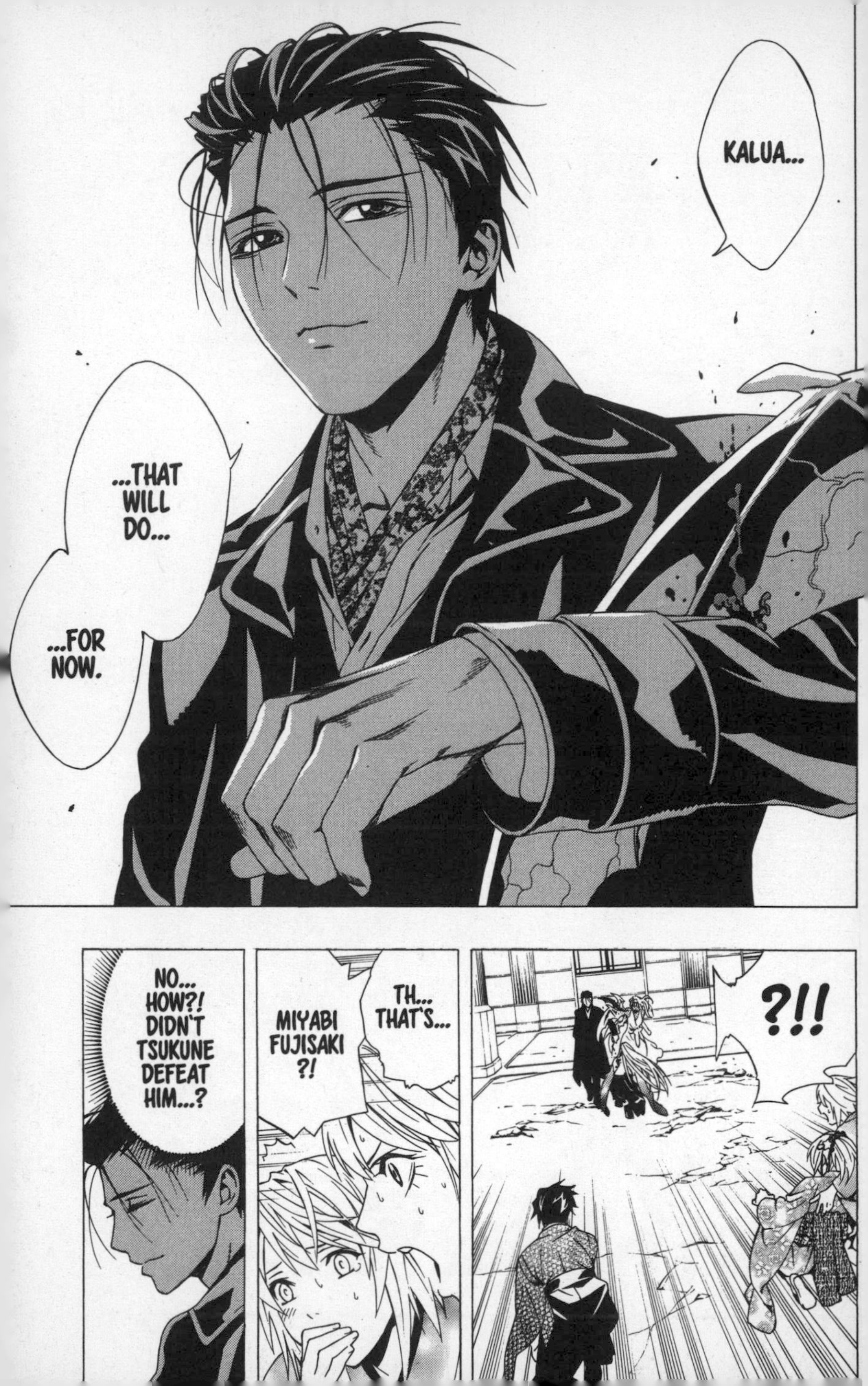
KALUA...
...THAT WILL DO...
...FOR NOW.
?!!
TH... THAT'S...
MIYABI FUJISAKI ?!
NO... HOW?! DIDN'T TSUKUNE DEFEAT HIM...?

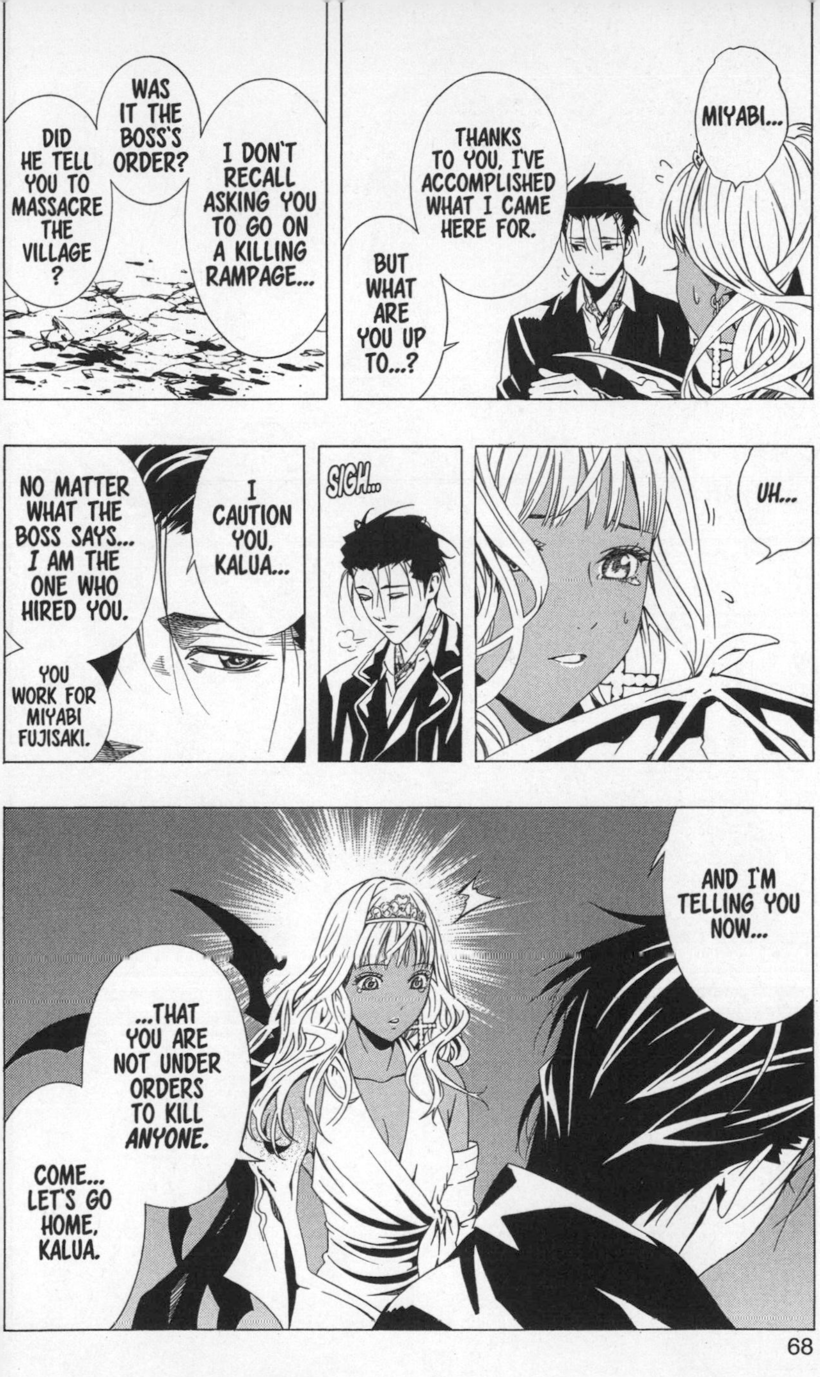
MIYABI...
THANKS TO YOU, I'VE ACCOMPLISHED WHAT I CAME HERE FOR.
BUT WHAT ARE YOU UP TO...?
I DON'T RECALL ASKING YOU TO GO ON A KILLING RAMPAGE...
WAS IT THE BOSS'S ORDER?
DID HE TELL YOU TO MASSACRE THE VILLAGE?
UH...
SIGH...
I CAUTION YOU, KALUA...
NO MATTER WHAT THE BOSS SAYS... I AM THE ONE WHO HIRED YOU.
YOU WORK FOR MIYABI FUJISAKI.
AND I'M TELLING YOU NOW...
...THAT YOU ARE NOT UNDER ORDERS TO KILL *ANYONE.*
COME... LET'S GO HOME, KALUA.

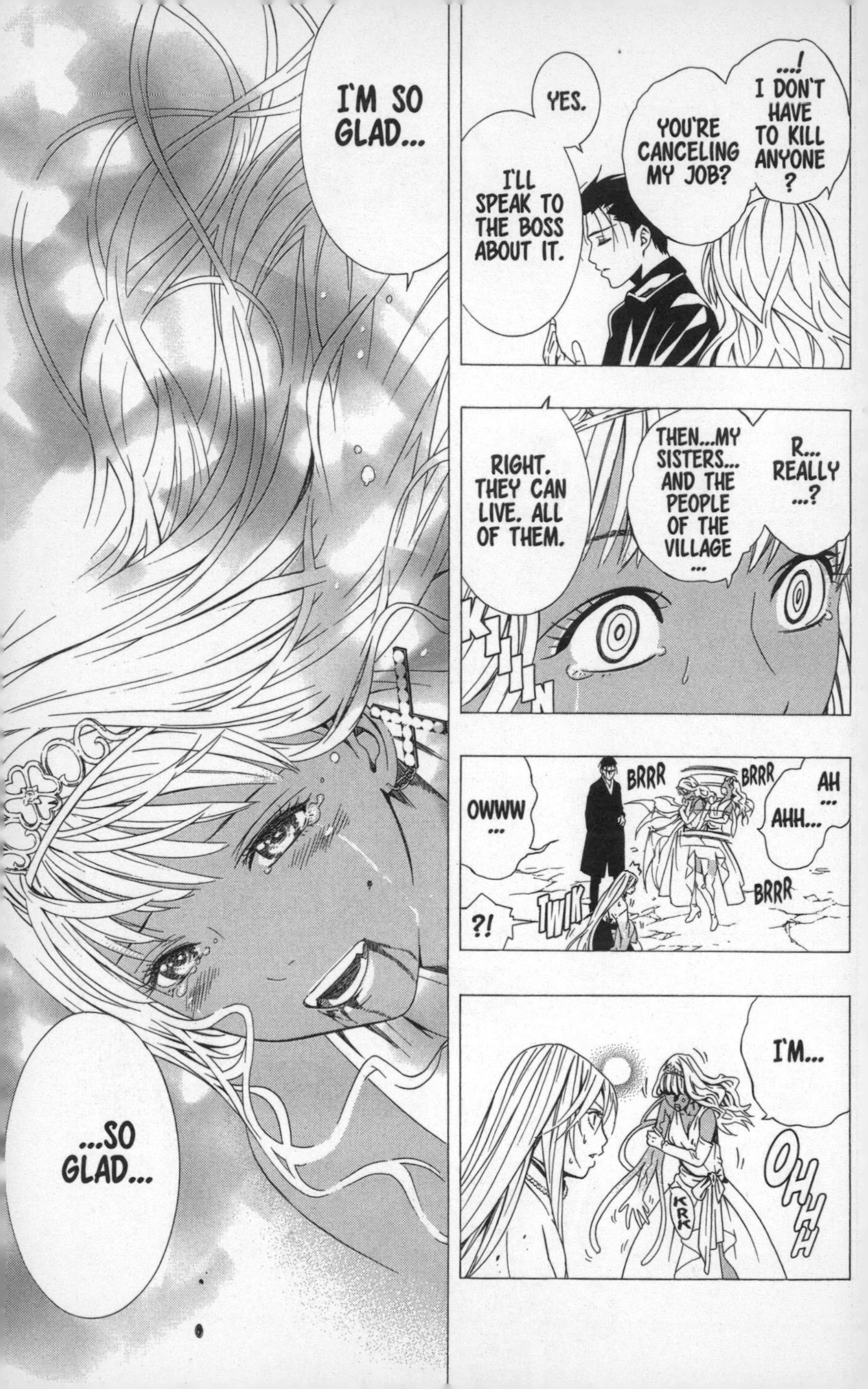
...! I DON'T HAVE TO KILL ANYONE ?
YOU'RE CANCELING MY JOB?
YES.
I'LL SPEAK TO THE BOSS ABOUT IT.
R... REALLY ...?
THEN...MY SISTERS... AND THE PEOPLE OF THE VILLAGE ...
RIGHT. THEY CAN LIVE. ALL OF THEM.
AH ... AHH...
BRRR
BRRR
BRRR
BRRR
OWWW ...
TWIK
?!
I'M...
OHHH
KRK
I'M SO GLAD...
...SO GLAD...

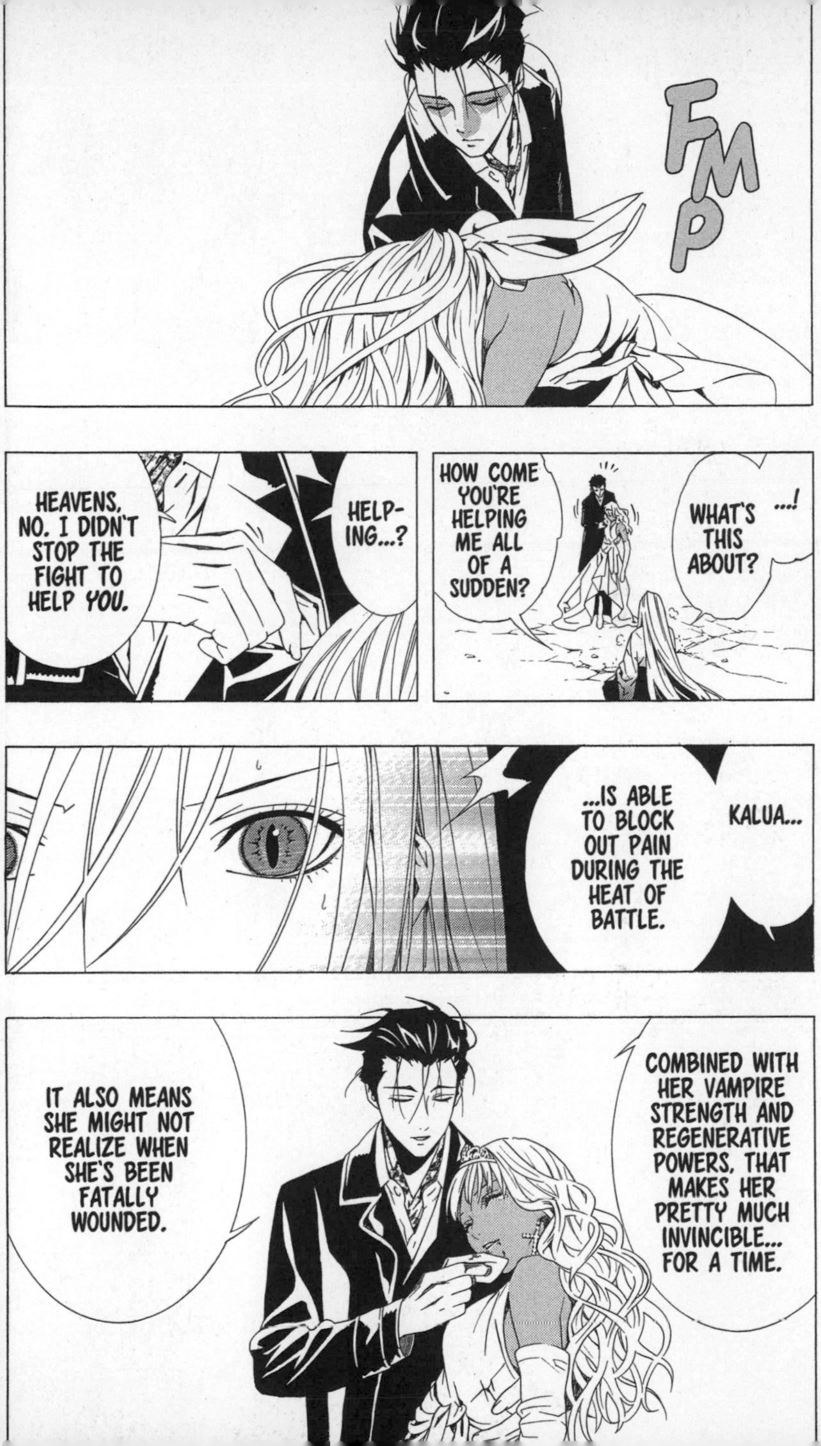
FMP
...!
WHAT'S THIS ABOUT?
HOW COME YOU'RE HELPING ME ALL OF A SUDDEN?
HELPING...?
HEAVENS, NO. I DIDN'T STOP THE FIGHT TO HELP YOU.
KALUA...
...IS ABLE TO BLOCK OUT PAIN DURING THE HEAT OF BATTLE.
COMBINED WITH HER VAMPIRE STRENGTH AND REGENERATIVE POWERS, THAT MAKES HER PRETTY MUCH INVINCIBLE... FOR A TIME.
IT ALSO MEANS SHE MIGHT NOT REALIZE WHEN SHE'S BEEN FATALLY WOUNDED.

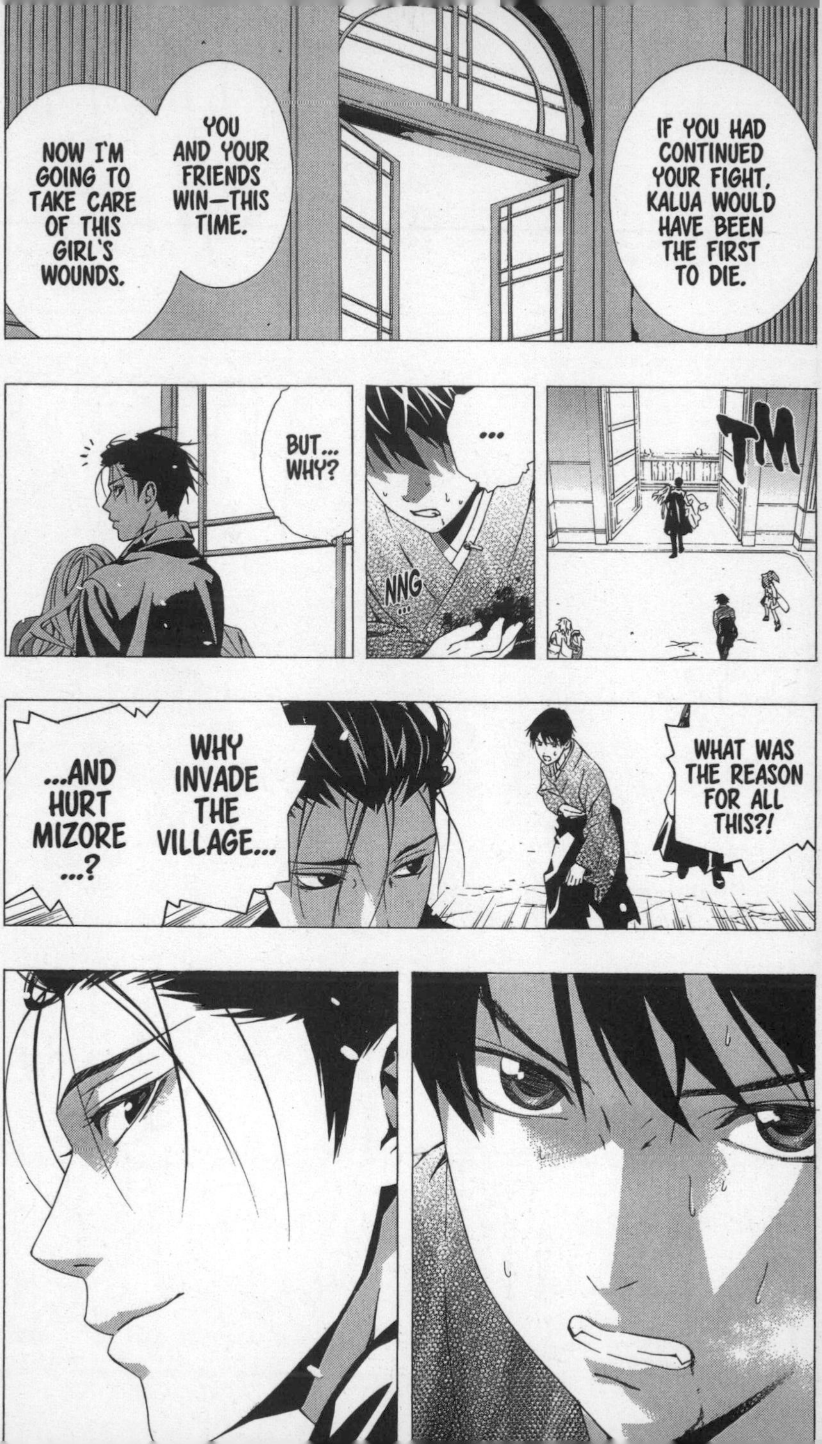
IF YOU HAD CONTINUED YOUR FIGHT, KALUA WOULD HAVE BEEN THE FIRST TO DIE.
YOU AND YOUR FRIENDS WIN—THIS TIME.
NOW I'M GOING TO TAKE CARE OF THIS GIRL'S WOUNDS.
TM
...
NNG...
BUT... WHY?
WHAT WAS THE REASON FOR ALL THIS?!
WHY INVADE THE VILLAGE...
...AND HURT MIZORE ...?

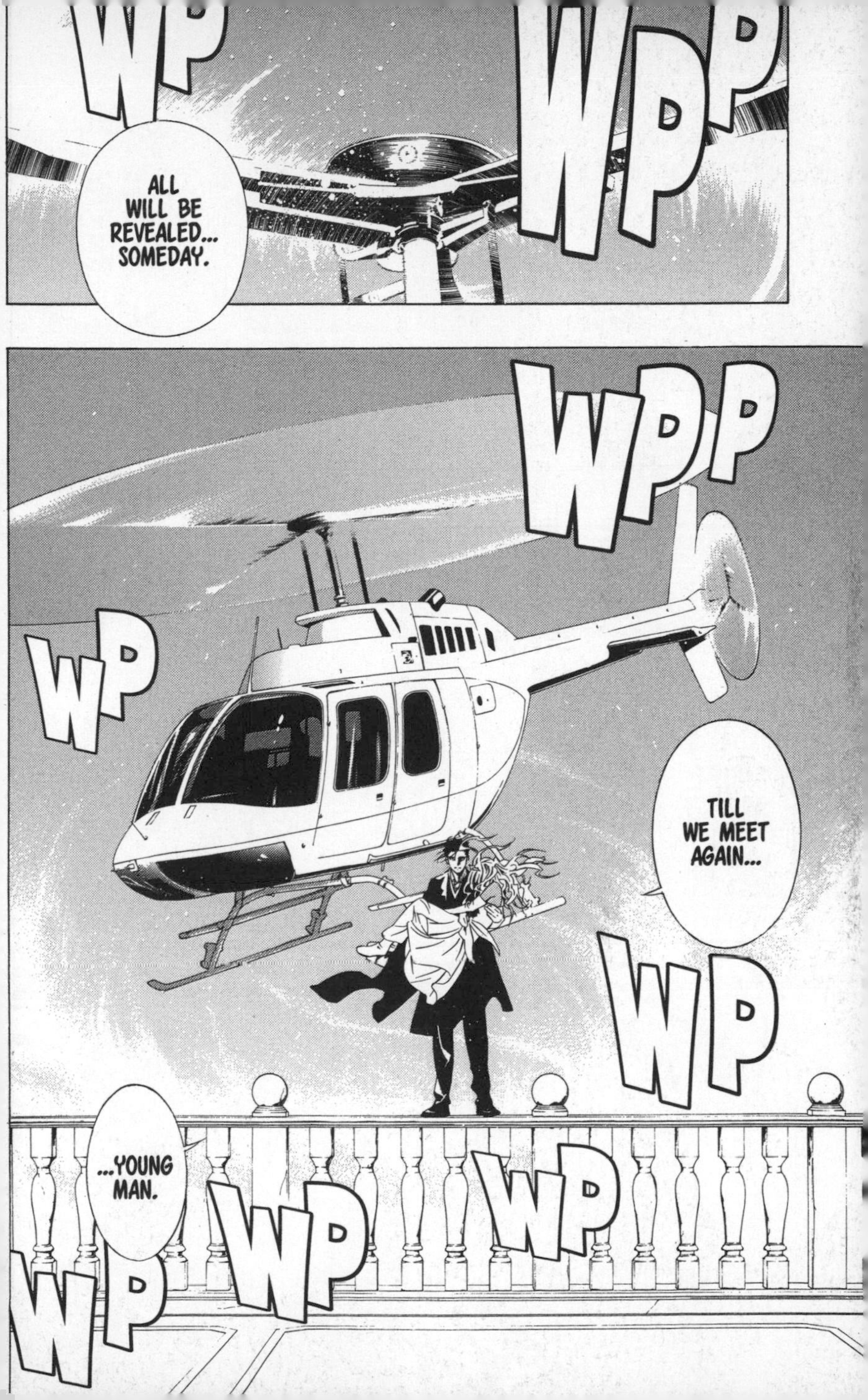
WPP
WP
ALL WILL BE REVEALED... SOMEDAY.
WPP
WP
TILL WE MEET AGAIN...
WP
WP
WP
...YOUNG MAN.
WP

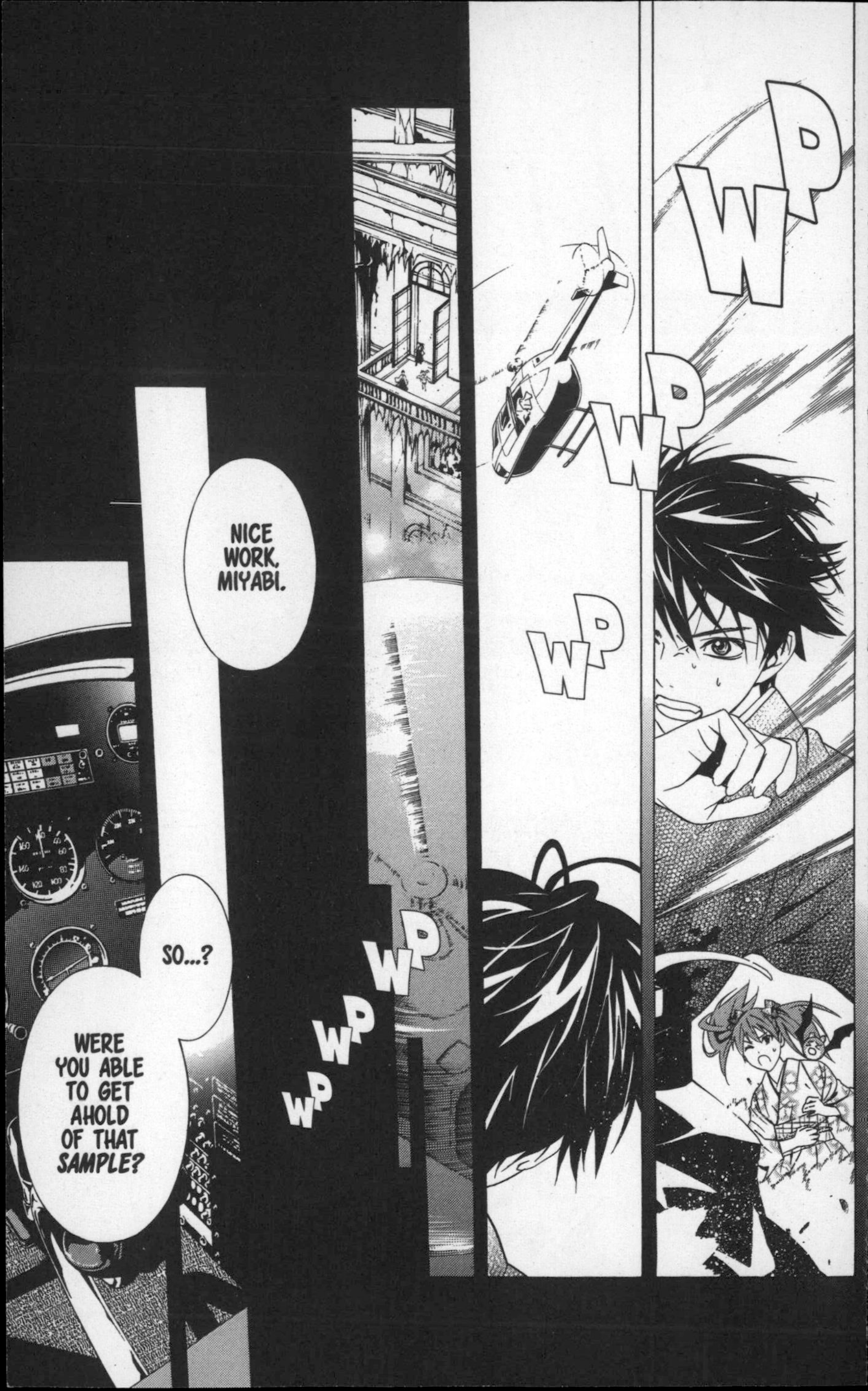
WP
WP
WP
WP
WP
WP
NICE WORK, MIYABI.
SO...?
WERE YOU ABLE TO GET AHOLD OF THAT SAMPLE?

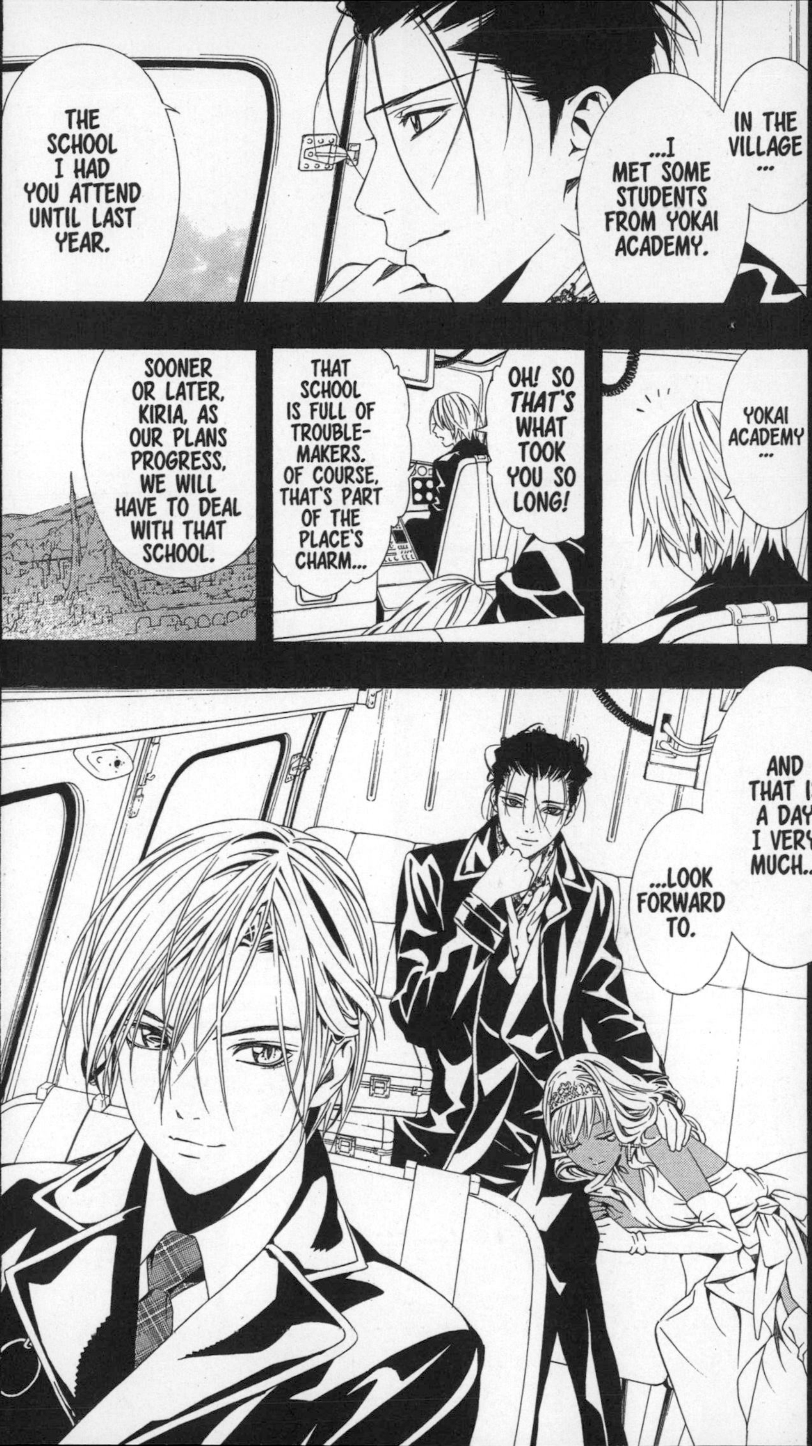
IN THE VILLAGE...
...I MET SOME STUDENTS FROM YOKAI ACADEMY.
THE SCHOOL I HAD YOU ATTEND UNTIL LAST YEAR.
YOKAI ACADEMY...
OH! SO THAT'S WHAT TOOK YOU SO LONG!
THAT SCHOOL IS FULL OF TROUBLE-MAKERS. OF COURSE, THAT'S PART OF THE PLACE'S CHARM...
SOONER OR LATER, KIRIA, AS OUR PLANS PROGRESS, WE WILL HAVE TO DEAL WITH THAT SCHOOL.
AND THAT IS A DAY I VERY MUCH...
...LOOK FORWARD TO.

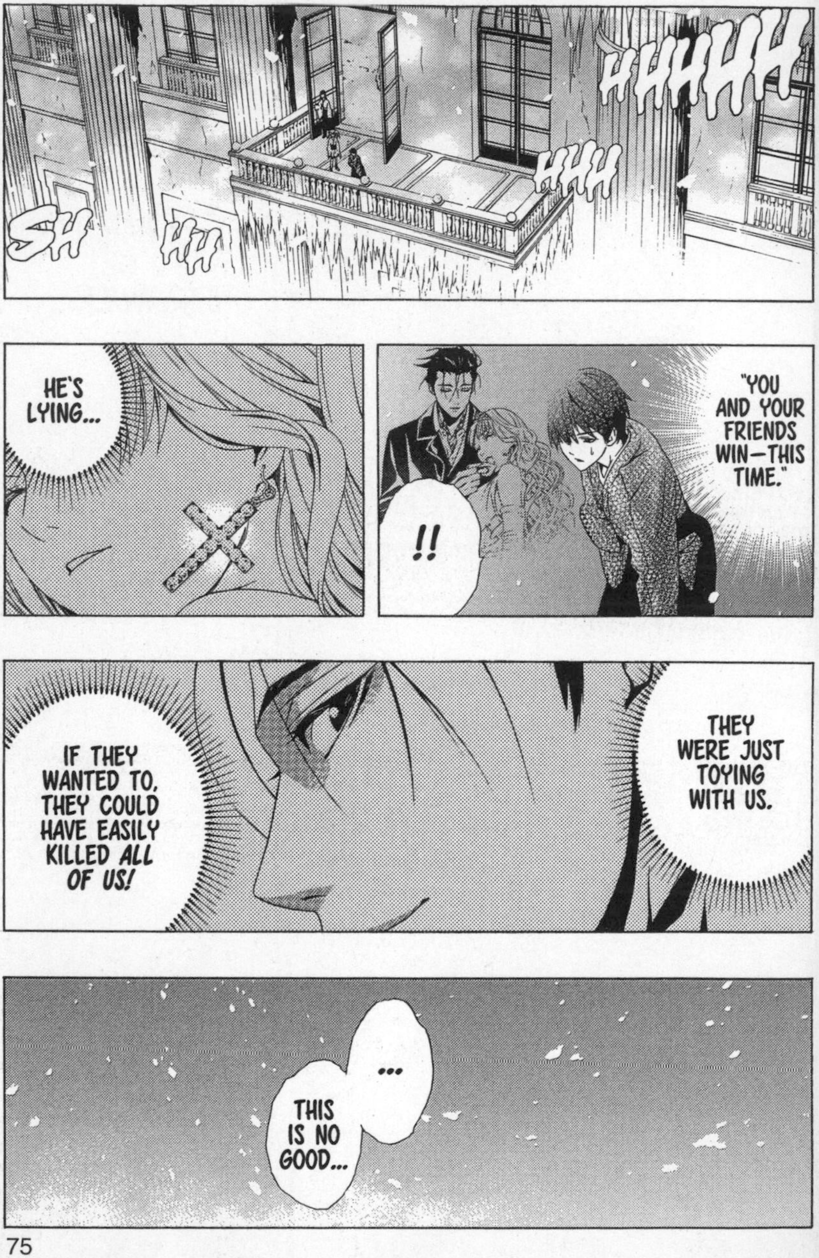
SH
HH
HHH
HHHHH
"YOU AND YOUR FRIENDS WIN—THIS TIME."
!!
HE'S LYING...
THEY WERE JUST TOYING WITH US.
IF THEY WANTED TO, THEY COULD HAVE EASILY KILLED ALL OF US!
...
THIS IS NO GOOD...

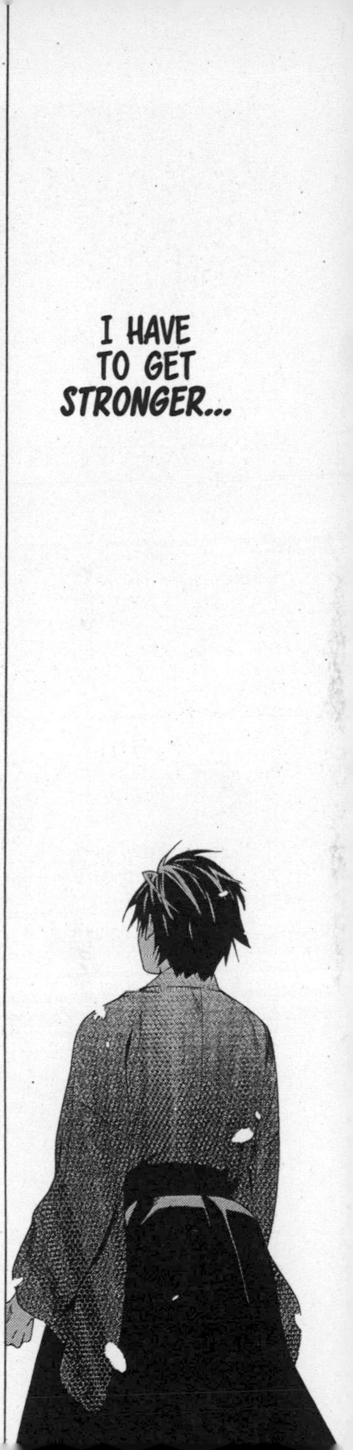
I HAVE TO GET STRONGER...

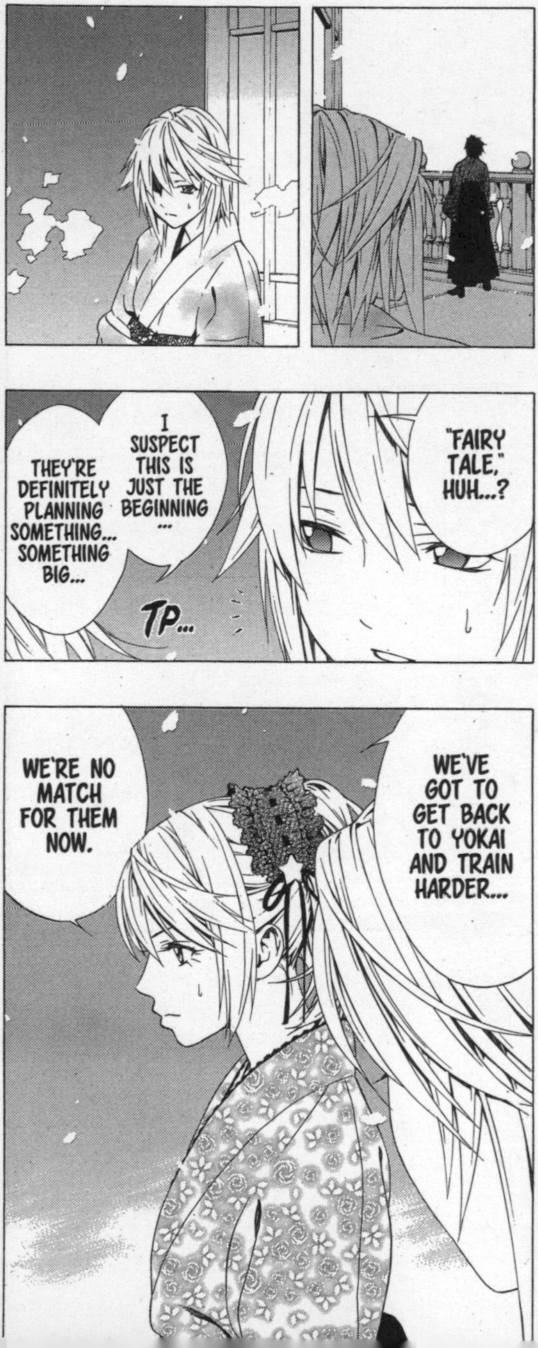
"FAIRY TALE," HUH...?
I SUSPECT THIS IS JUST THE BEGINNING...
THEY'RE DEFINITELY PLANNING SOMETHING... SOMETHING BIG...
TP...
WE'VE GOT TO GET BACK TO YOKAI AND TRAIN HARDER...
WE'RE NO MATCH FOR THEM NOW.

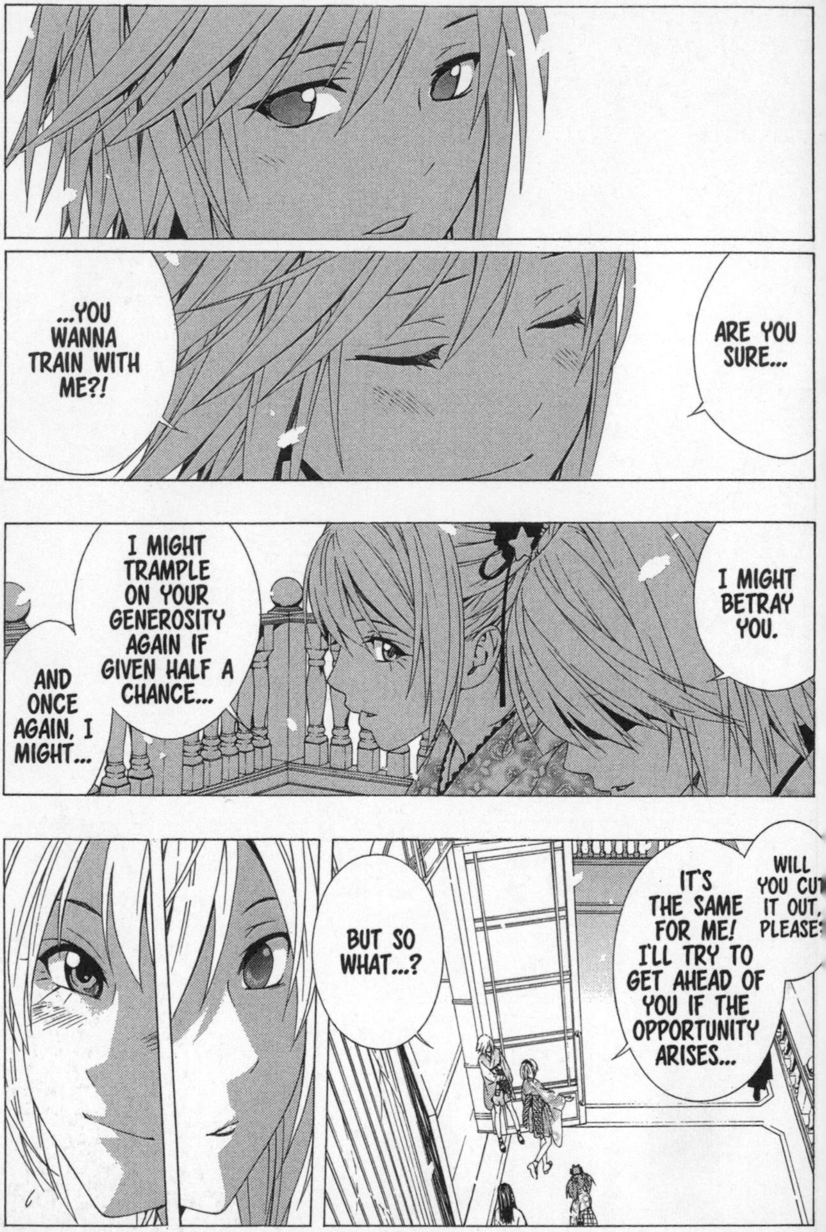
ARE YOU SURE...
...YOU WANNA TRAIN WITH ME?!
I MIGHT BETRAY YOU.
I MIGHT TRAMPLE ON YOUR GENEROSITY AGAIN IF GIVEN HALF A CHANCE...
AND ONCE AGAIN, I MIGHT...
WILL YOU CUT IT OUT, PLEASE?
IT'S THE SAME FOR ME! I'LL TRY TO GET AHEAD OF YOU IF THE OPPORTUNITY ARISES...
BUT SO WHAT...?

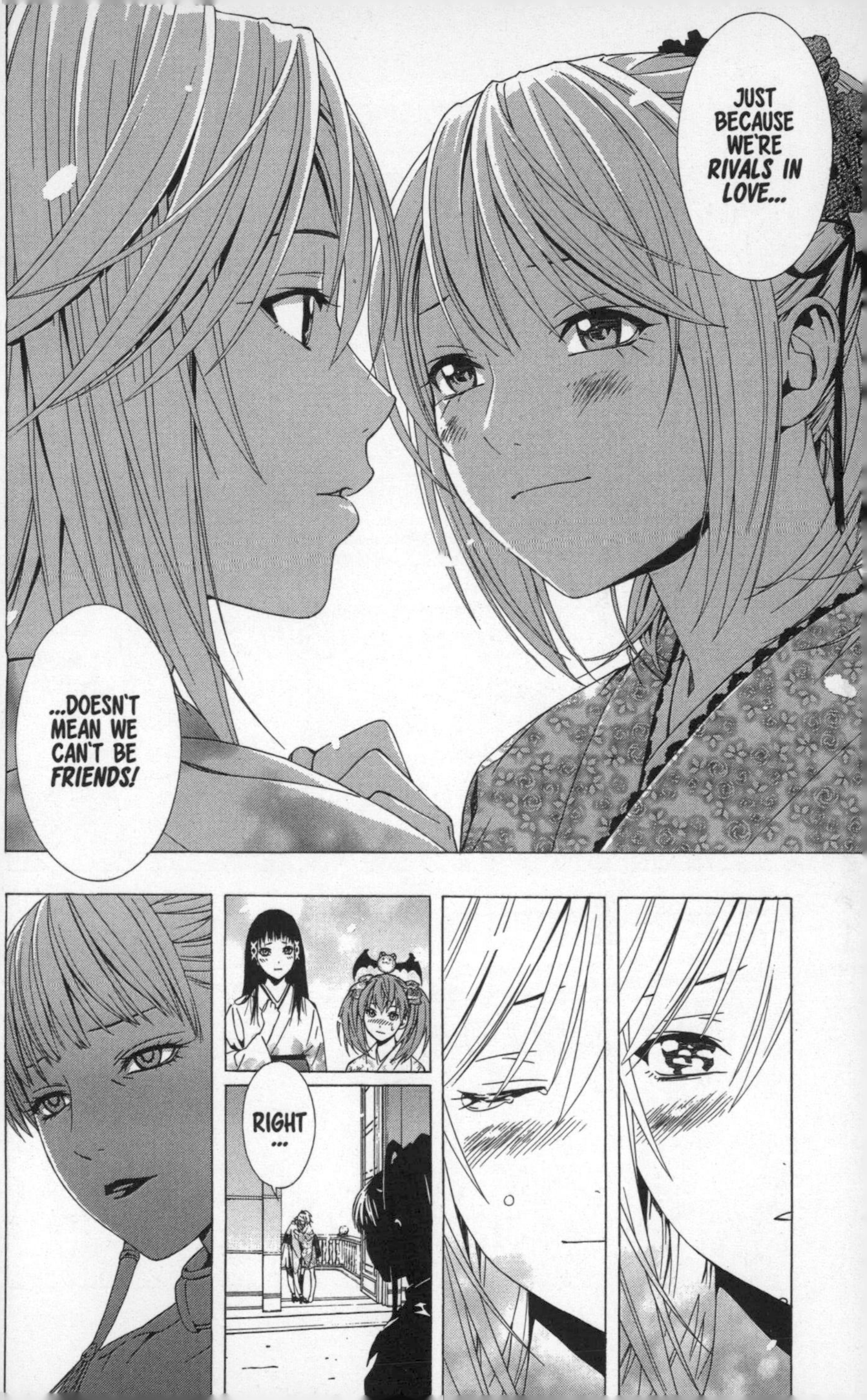
JUST BECAUSE WE'RE RIVALS IN LOVE...
...DOESN'T MEAN WE CAN'T BE FRIENDS!
RIGHT...

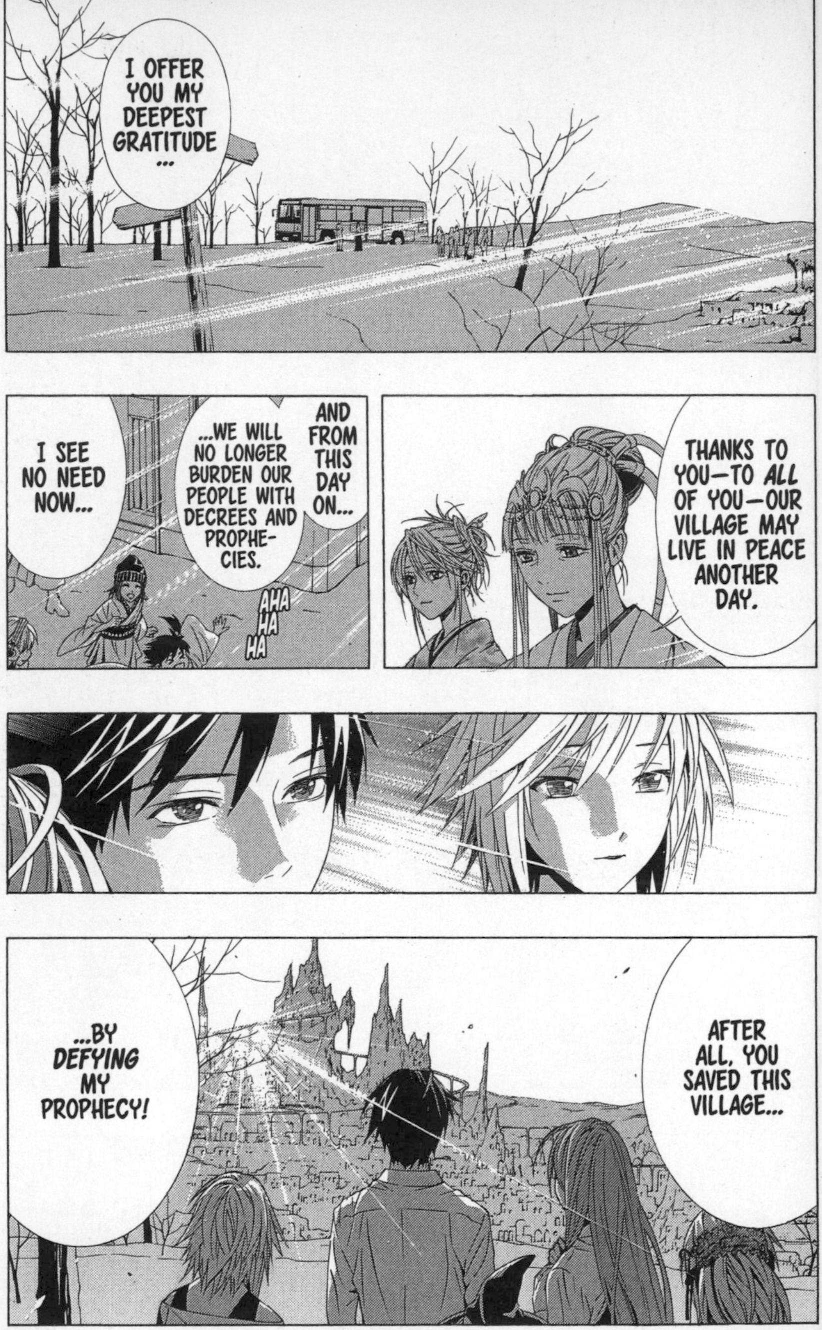
I OFFER YOU MY DEEPEST GRATITUDE...
THANKS TO YOU—TO ALL OF YOU—OUR VILLAGE MAY LIVE IN PEACE ANOTHER DAY.
AND FROM THIS DAY ON...
...WE WILL NO LONGER BURDEN OUR PEOPLE WITH DECREES AND PROPHE-CIES.
I SEE NO NEED NOW...
AHA HA HA
AFTER ALL, YOU SAVED THIS VILLAGE...
...BY DEFYING MY PROPHECY!

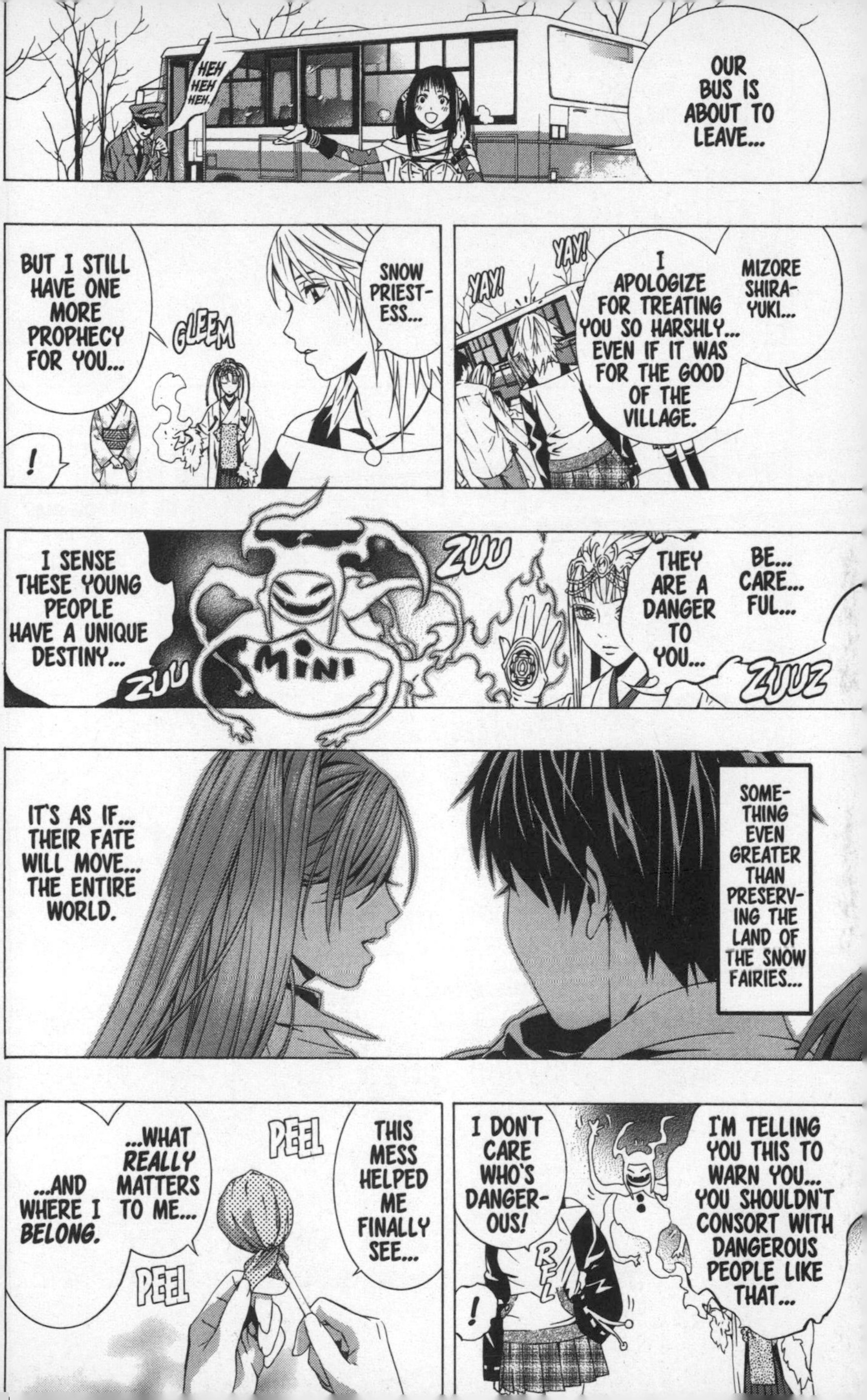

OUR BUS IS ABOUT TO LEAVE...
HEH HEH HEH.
MIZORE SHIRA-YUKI...
I APOLOGIZE FOR TREATING YOU SO HARSHLY... EVEN IF IT WAS FOR THE GOOD OF THE VILLAGE.
YAY!
YAY!
SNOW PRIEST-ESS...
GLEEM
BUT I STILL HAVE ONE MORE PROPHECY FOR YOU...
!
BE... CARE... FUL...
THEY ARE A DANGER TO YOU...
ZUUZ
ZUU
I SENSE THESE YOUNG PEOPLE HAVE A UNIQUE DESTINY...
MINI
ZUU
SOME-THING EVEN GREATER THAN PRESERV-ING THE LAND OF THE SNOW FAIRIES...
IT'S AS IF... THEIR FATE WILL MOVE... THE ENTIRE WORLD.
I'M TELLING YOU THIS TO WARN YOU... YOU SHOULDN'T CONSORT WITH DANGEROUS PEOPLE LIKE THAT...
I DON'T CARE WHO'S DANGER-OUS!
!
THIS MESS HELPED ME FINALLY SEE...
PEEL
...WHAT *REALLY* MATTERS TO ME...
...AND WHERE I *BELONG.*
PEEL

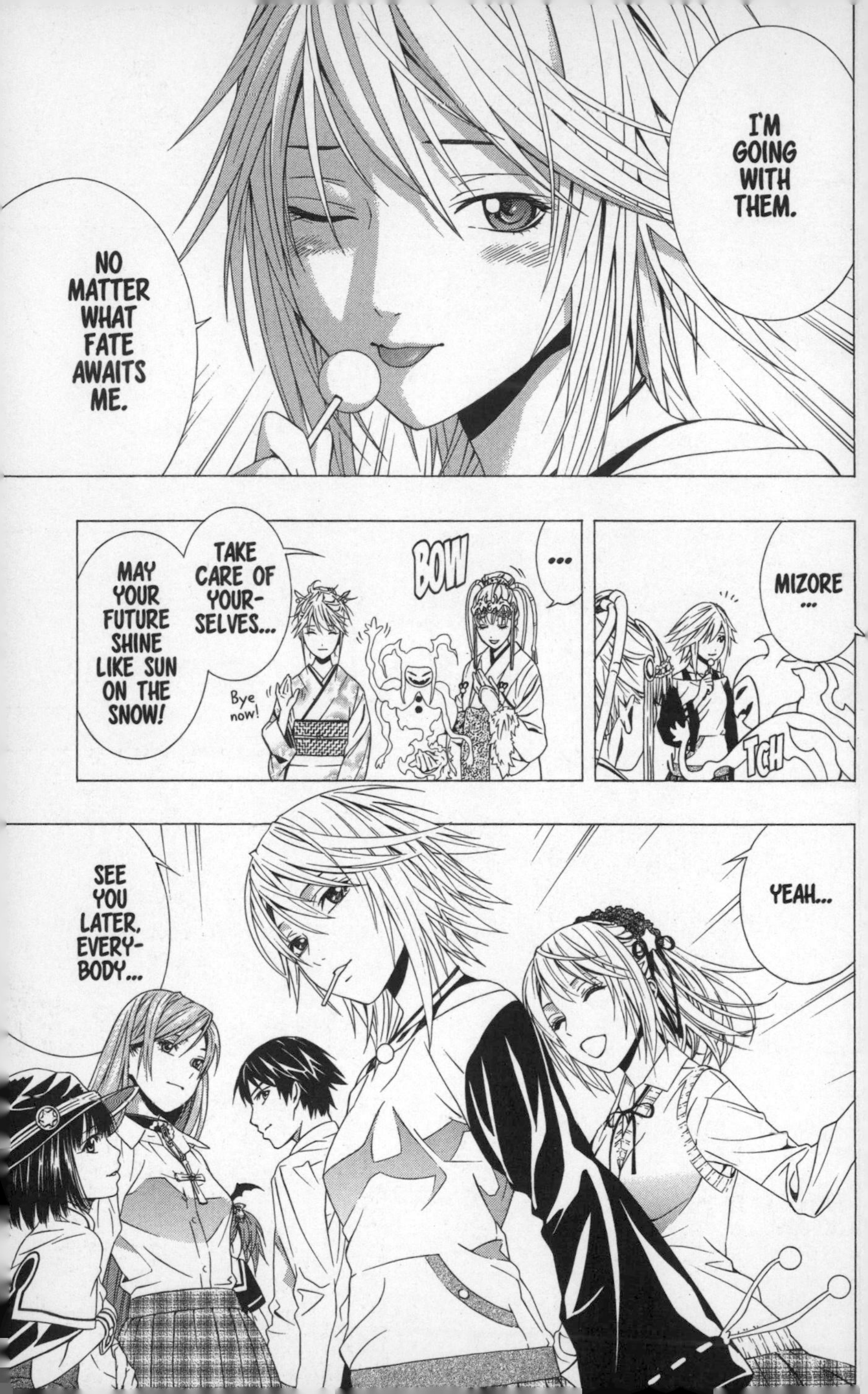
I'M GOING WITH THEM.
NO MATTER WHAT FATE AWAITS ME.
MIZORE ...
TCH
...
BOW
TAKE CARE OF YOURSELVES...
MAY YOUR FUTURE SHINE LIKE SUN ON THE SNOW!
Bye now!
YEAH...
SEE YOU LATER, EVERYBODY...

15: Paradise

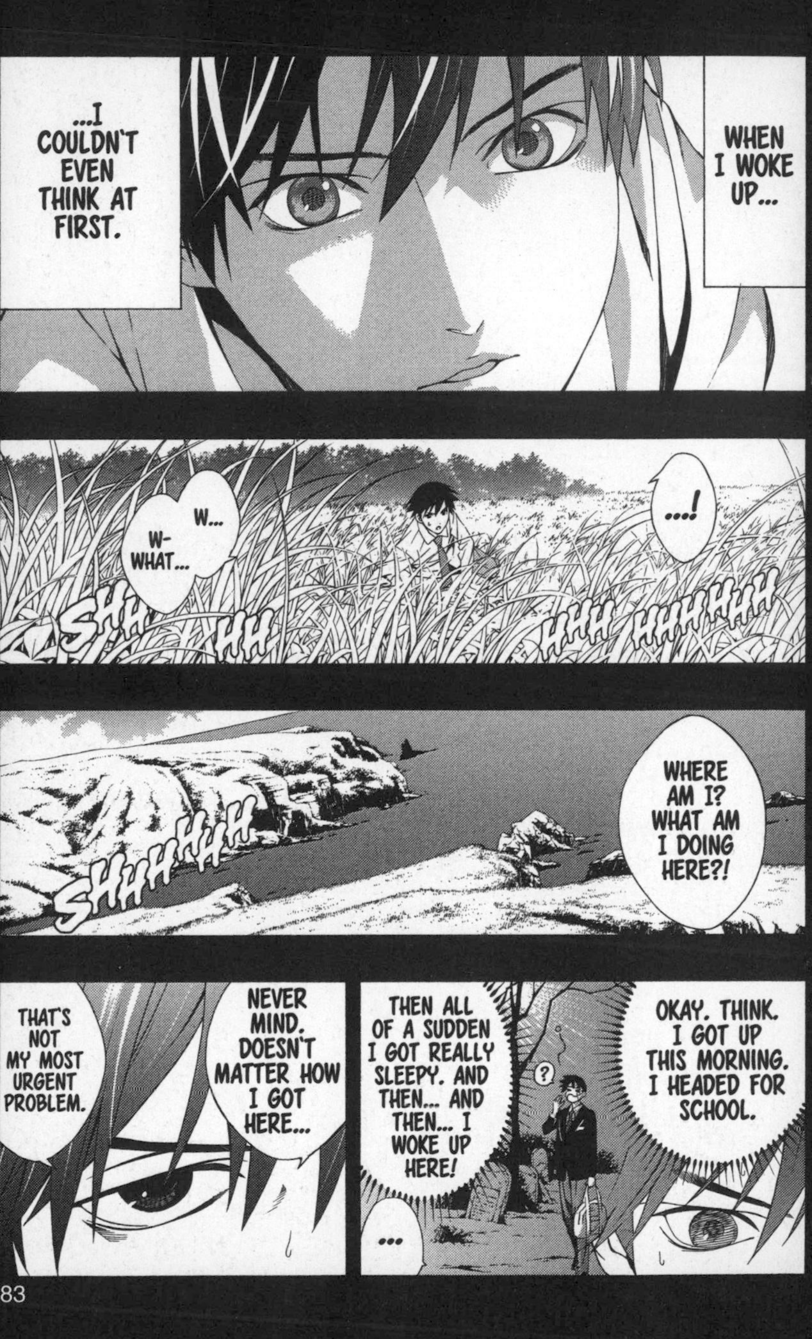
WHEN I WOKE UP...
...I COULDN'T EVEN THINK AT FIRST.
...!
W... W-WHAT...
SHHHHHHHHHHHH
WHERE AM I? WHAT AM I DOING HERE?!
SHHHHHH
OKAY. THINK. I GOT UP THIS MORNING. I HEADED FOR SCHOOL.
?
THEN ALL OF A SUDDEN I GOT REALLY SLEEPY. AND THEN... AND THEN... I WOKE UP HERE!
...
NEVER MIND. DOESN'T MATTER HOW I GOT HERE...
THAT'S NOT MY MOST URGENT PROBLEM.

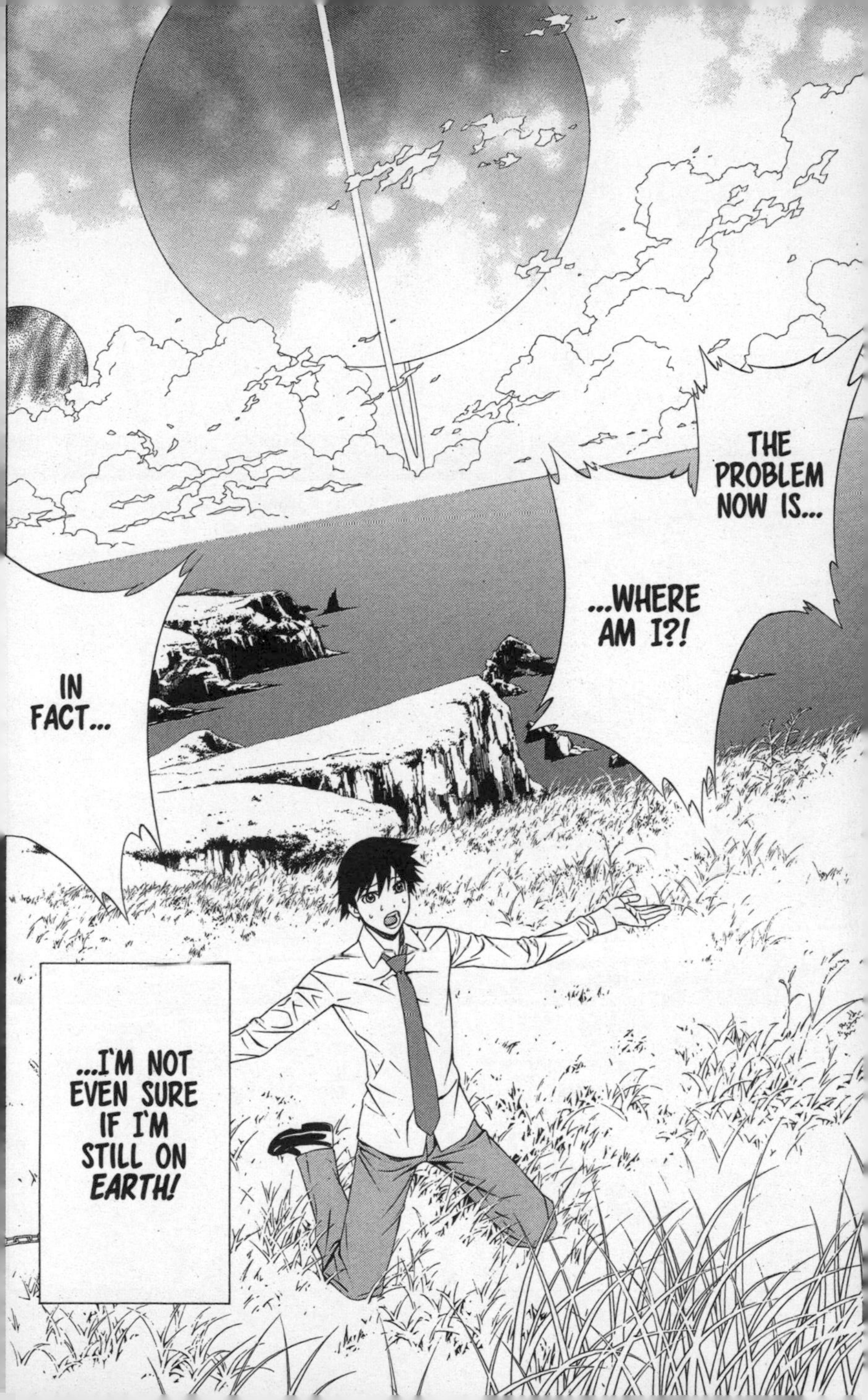
THE PROBLEM NOW IS...
...WHERE AM I?!
IN FACT...
...I'M NOT EVEN SURE IF I'M STILL ON EARTH!

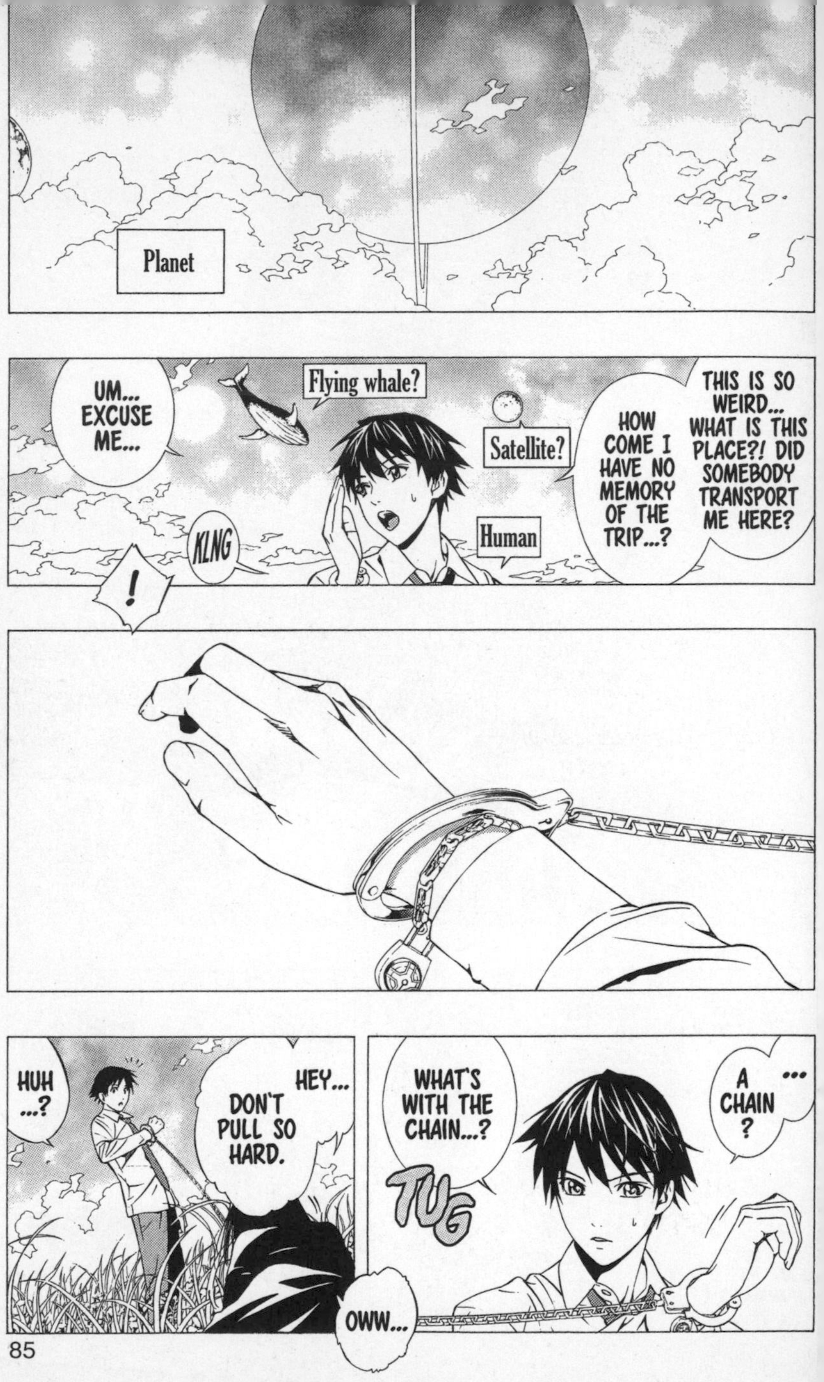
Planet
THIS IS SO WEIRD... WHAT IS THIS PLACE?! DID SOMEBODY TRANSPORT ME HERE?
HOW COME I HAVE NO MEMORY OF THE TRIP...?
Satellite?
Human
Flying whale?
UM... EXCUSE ME...
KLNG
!
...
A CHAIN ?
WHAT'S WITH THE CHAIN...?
TUG
OWW...
HEY... DON'T PULL SO HARD.
HUH ...?

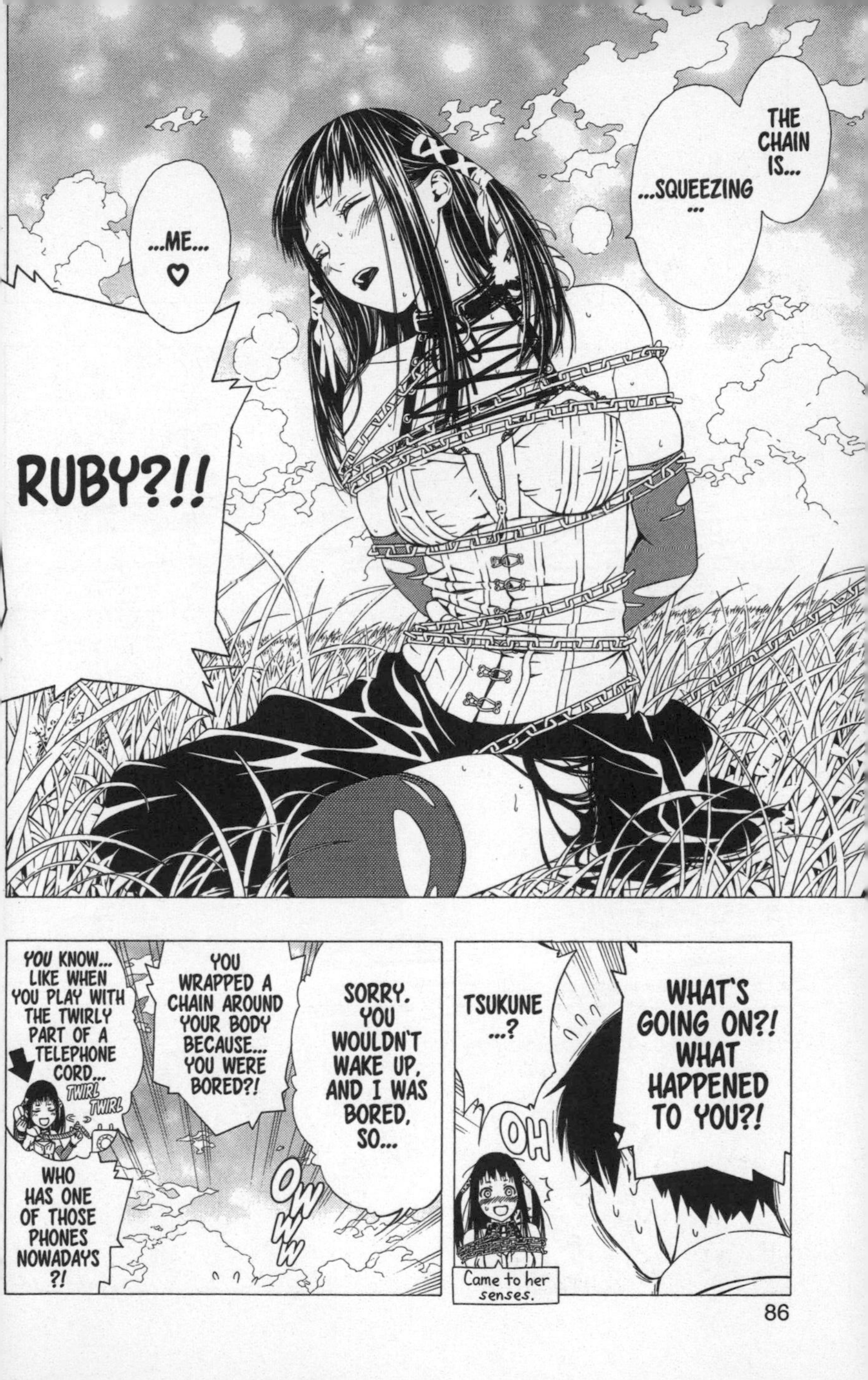
THE CHAIN IS... ...SQUEEZING...
...ME... ♡
RUBY?!!
WHAT'S GOING ON?! WHAT HAPPENED TO YOU?!
TSUKUNE ...?
OH
Came to her senses.
SORRY. YOU WOULDN'T WAKE UP, AND I WAS BORED, SO...
OWWW
YOU WRAPPED A CHAIN AROUND YOUR BODY BECAUSE... YOU WERE BORED?!
YOU KNOW... LIKE WHEN YOU PLAY WITH THE TWIRLY PART OF A TELEPHONE CORD...
TWIRL TWIRL
WHO HAS ONE OF THOSE PHONES NOWADAYS ?!

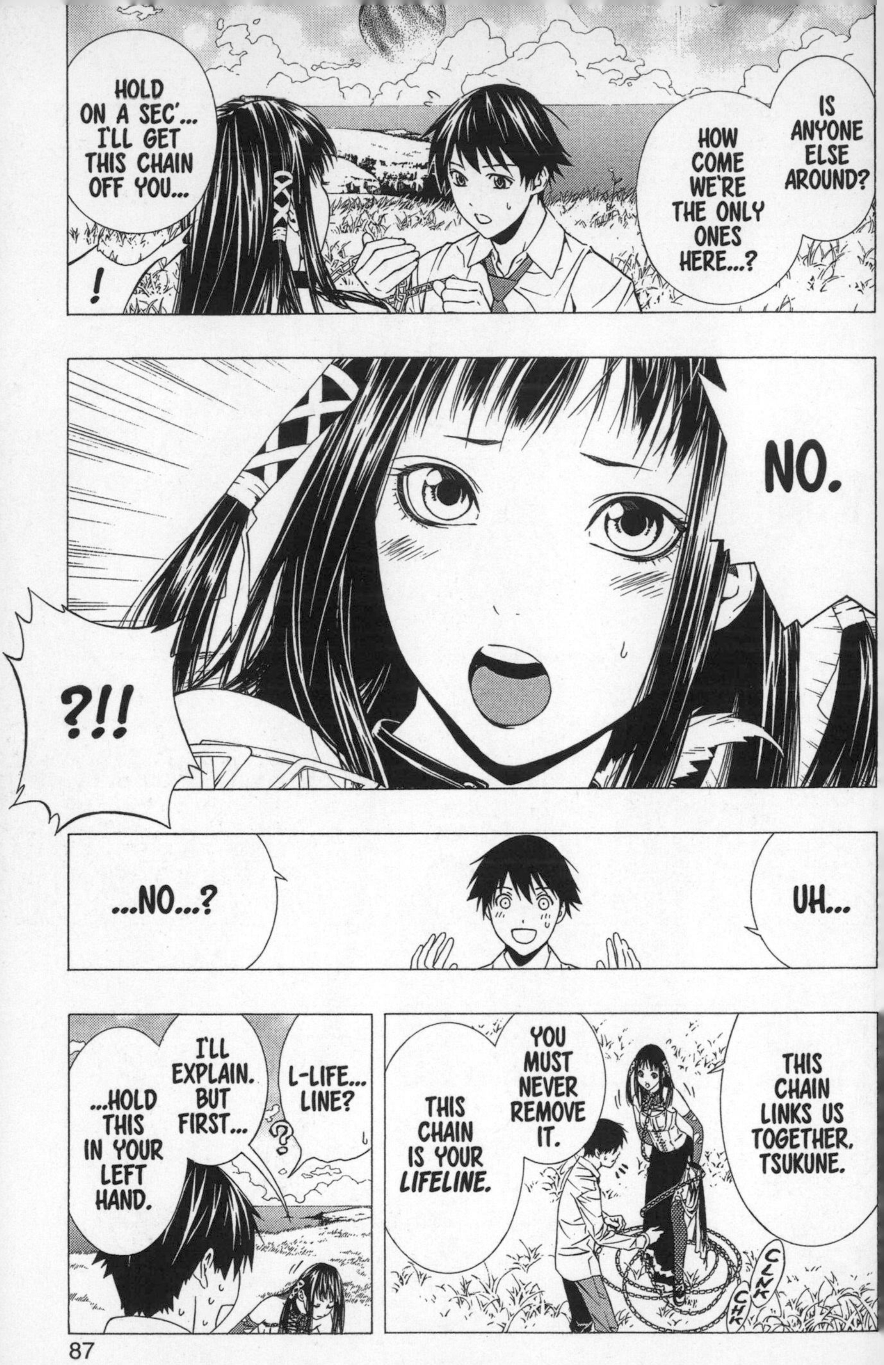
IS ANYONE ELSE AROUND?
HOW COME WE'RE THE ONLY ONES HERE...?
HOLD ON A SEC'... I'LL GET THIS CHAIN OFF YOU...
!
NO.
?!!
UH...
...NO...?
THIS CHAIN LINKS US TOGETHER, TSUKUNE.
YOU MUST NEVER REMOVE IT.
THIS CHAIN IS YOUR *LIFELINE.*
CLNK
CHK
L-LIFE... LINE?
?
I'LL EXPLAIN. BUT FIRST...
...HOLD THIS IN YOUR LEFT HAND.

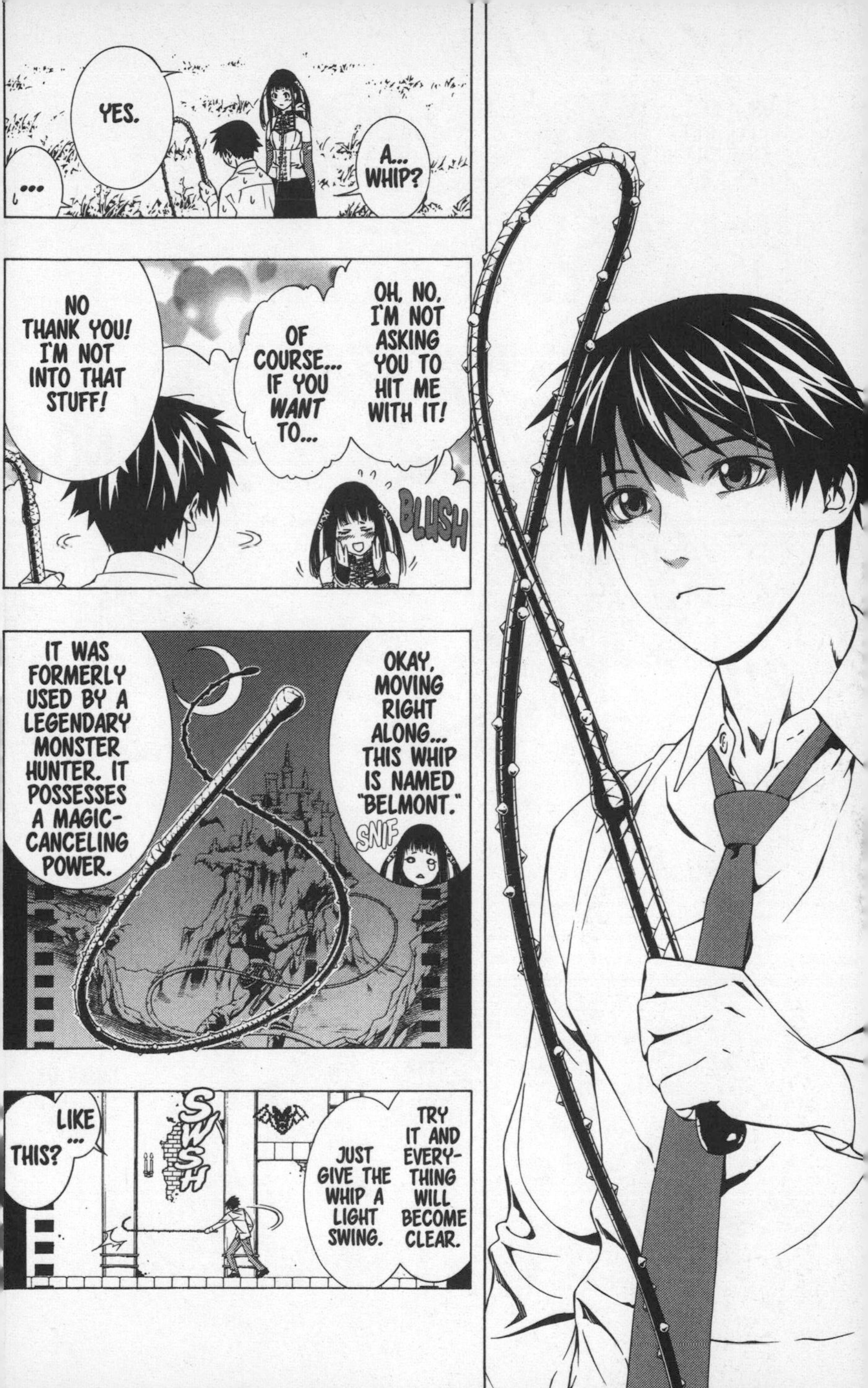
A... WHIP?
YES.
...
OH, NO, I'M NOT ASKING YOU TO HIT ME WITH IT!
OF COURSE... IF YOU WANT TO...
BLUSH
NO THANK YOU! I'M NOT INTO THAT STUFF!
OKAY, MOVING RIGHT ALONG... THIS WHIP IS NAMED "BELMONT."
SNIF
IT WAS FORMERLY USED BY A LEGENDARY MONSTER HUNTER. IT POSSESSES A MAGIC-CANCELING POWER.
TRY IT AND EVERYTHING WILL BECOME CLEAR.
JUST GIVE THE WHIP A LIGHT SWING.
SWSH
LIKE... THIS?

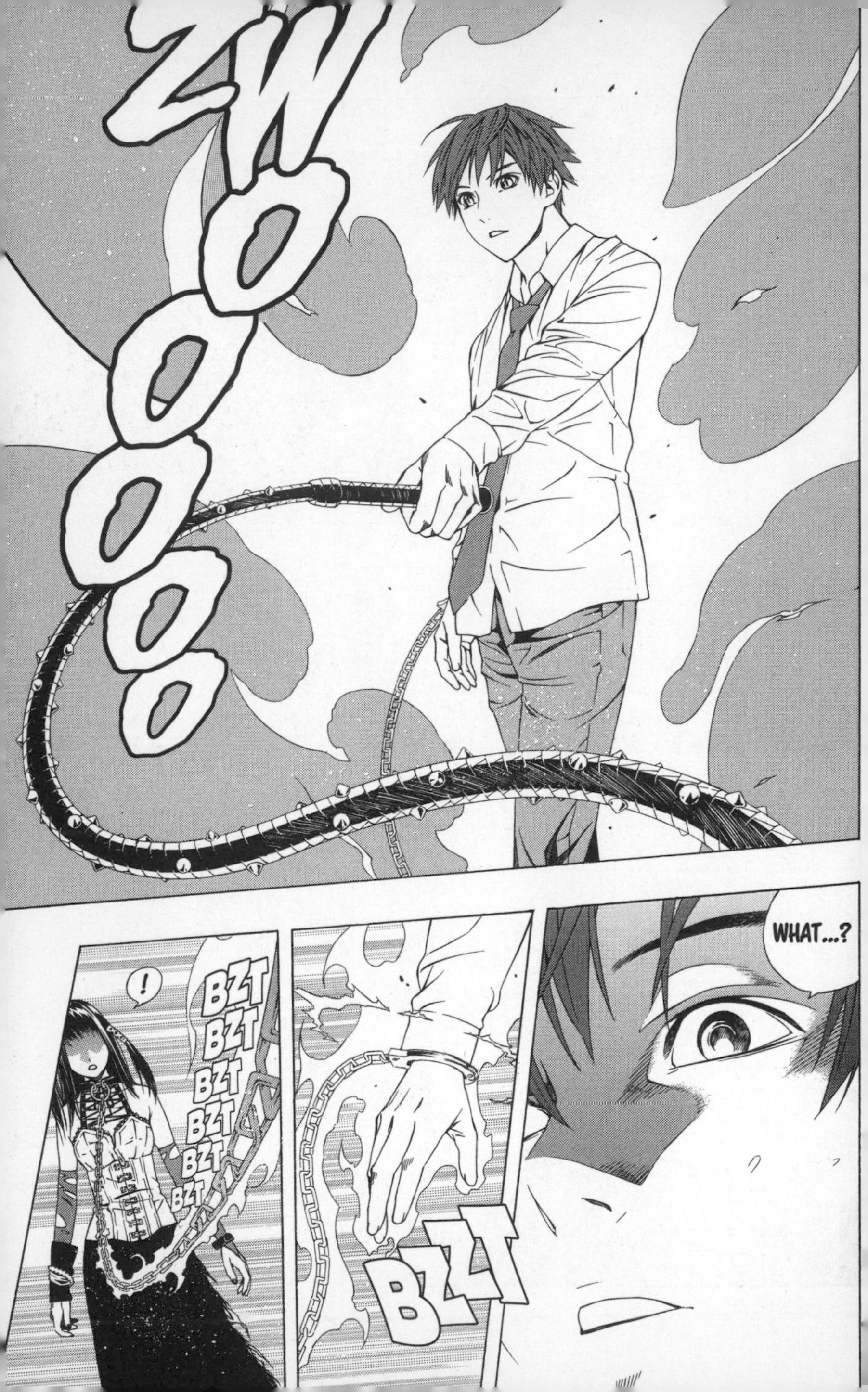
ZWOOOOOO
WHAT...?
BZZT
!
BZT
BZT
BZT
BZT
BZT
BZT

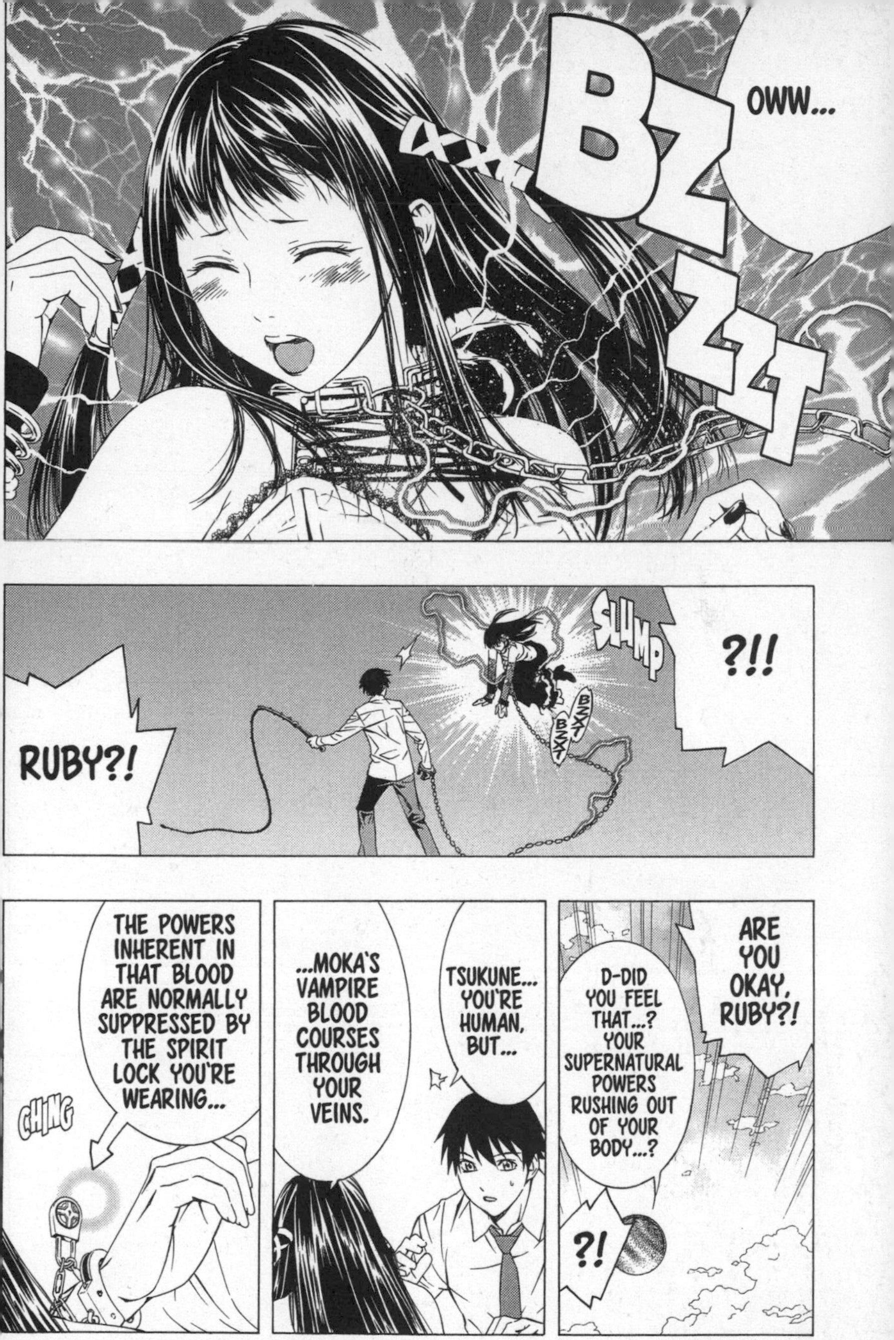
OWW...
BZZZT
?!!
SLUMP
BZZT BZZT
RUBY?!
ARE YOU OKAY, RUBY?!
D-DID YOU FEEL THAT...? YOUR SUPERNATURAL POWERS RUSHING OUT OF YOUR BODY...?
?!
TSUKUNE... YOU'RE HUMAN, BUT...
...MOKA'S VAMPIRE BLOOD COURSES THROUGH YOUR VEINS.
THE POWERS INHERENT IN THAT BLOOD ARE NORMALLY SUPPRESSED BY THE SPIRIT LOCK YOU'RE WEARING...
CHING

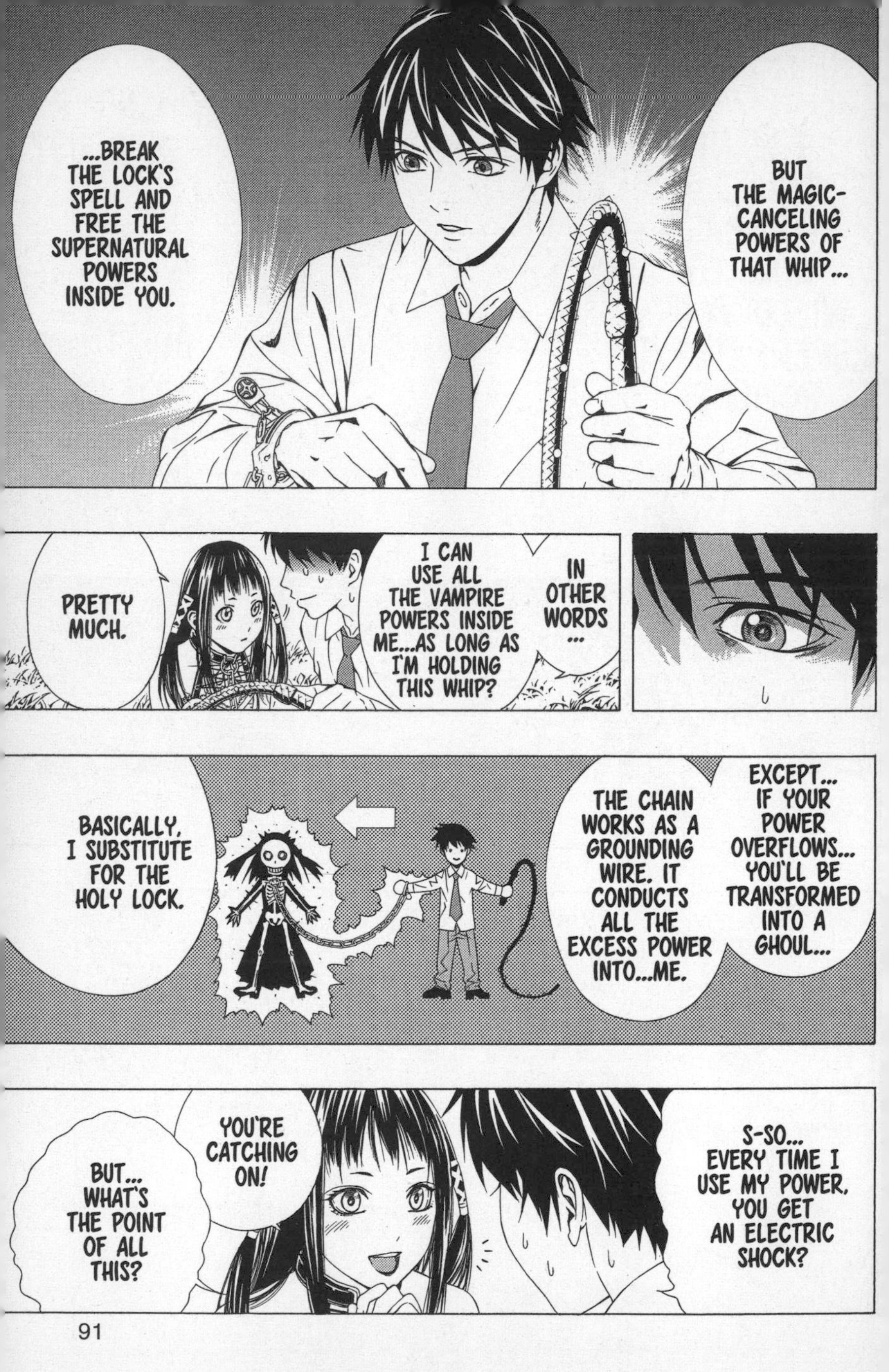
BUT THE MAGIC-CANCELING POWERS OF THAT WHIP...
...BREAK THE LOCK'S SPELL AND FREE THE SUPERNATURAL POWERS INSIDE YOU.
IN OTHER WORDS...
I CAN USE ALL THE VAMPIRE POWERS INSIDE ME...AS LONG AS I'M HOLDING THIS WHIP?
PRETTY MUCH.
EXCEPT... IF YOUR POWER OVERFLOWS... YOU'LL BE TRANSFORMED INTO A GHOUL...
THE CHAIN WORKS AS A GROUNDING WIRE. IT CONDUCTS ALL THE EXCESS POWER INTO...ME.
BASICALLY, I SUBSTITUTE FOR THE HOLY LOCK.
S-SO... EVERY TIME I USE MY POWER, YOU GET AN ELECTRIC SHOCK?
YOU'RE CATCHING ON!
BUT... WHAT'S THE POINT OF ALL THIS?

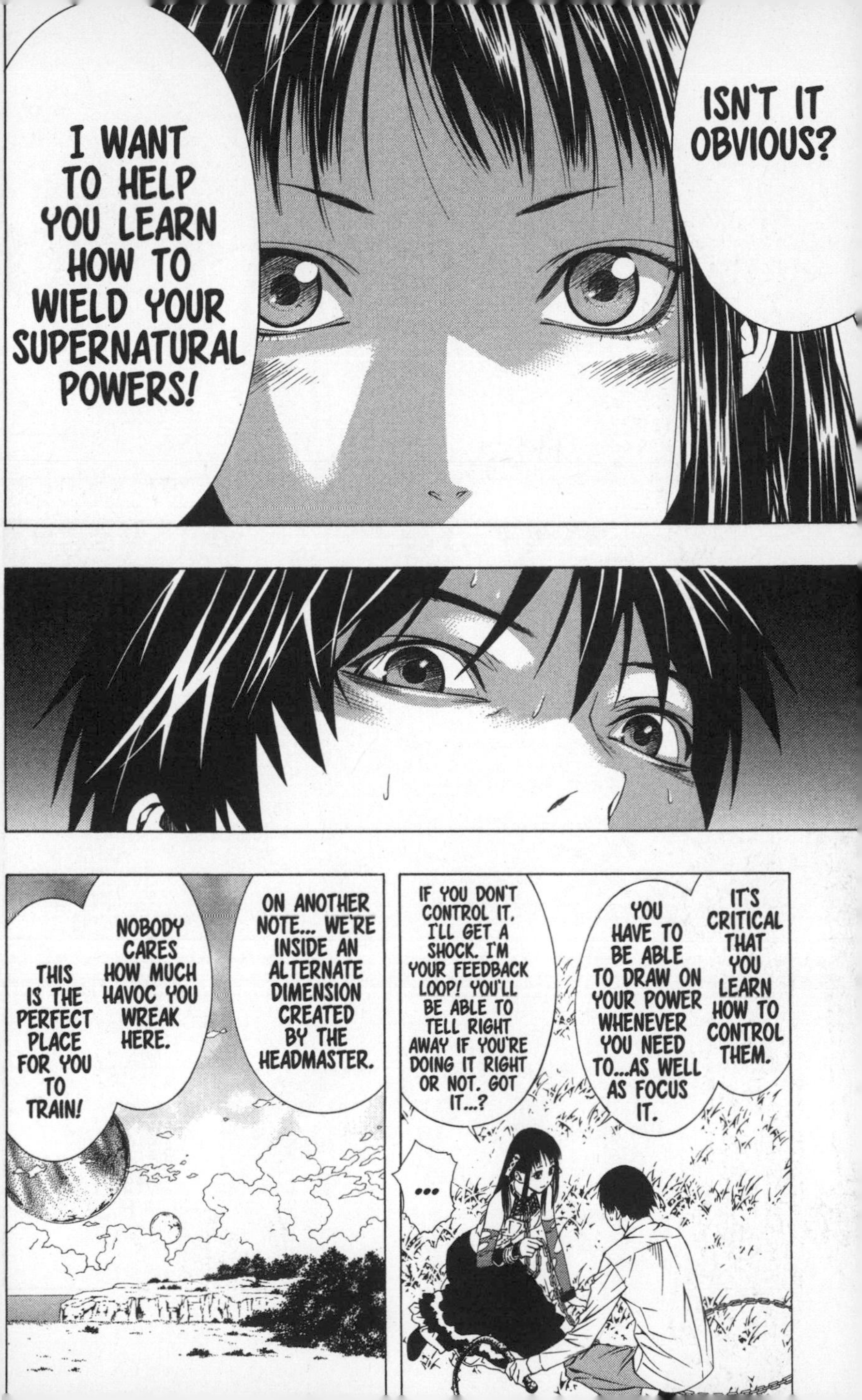
ISN'T IT OBVIOUS?
I WANT TO HELP YOU LEARN HOW TO WIELD YOUR SUPERNATURAL POWERS!
IT'S CRITICAL THAT YOU LEARN HOW TO CONTROL THEM.
YOU HAVE TO BE ABLE TO DRAW ON YOUR POWER WHENEVER YOU NEED TO...AS WELL AS FOCUS IT.
IF YOU DON'T CONTROL IT, I'LL GET A SHOCK. I'M YOUR FEEDBACK LOOP! YOU'LL BE ABLE TO TELL RIGHT AWAY IF YOU'RE DOING IT RIGHT OR NOT. GOT IT...?
...
ON ANOTHER NOTE... WE'RE INSIDE AN ALTERNATE DIMENSION CREATED BY THE HEADMASTER.
NOBODY CARES HOW MUCH HAVOC YOU WREAK HERE.
THIS IS THE PERFECT PLACE FOR YOU TO TRAIN!

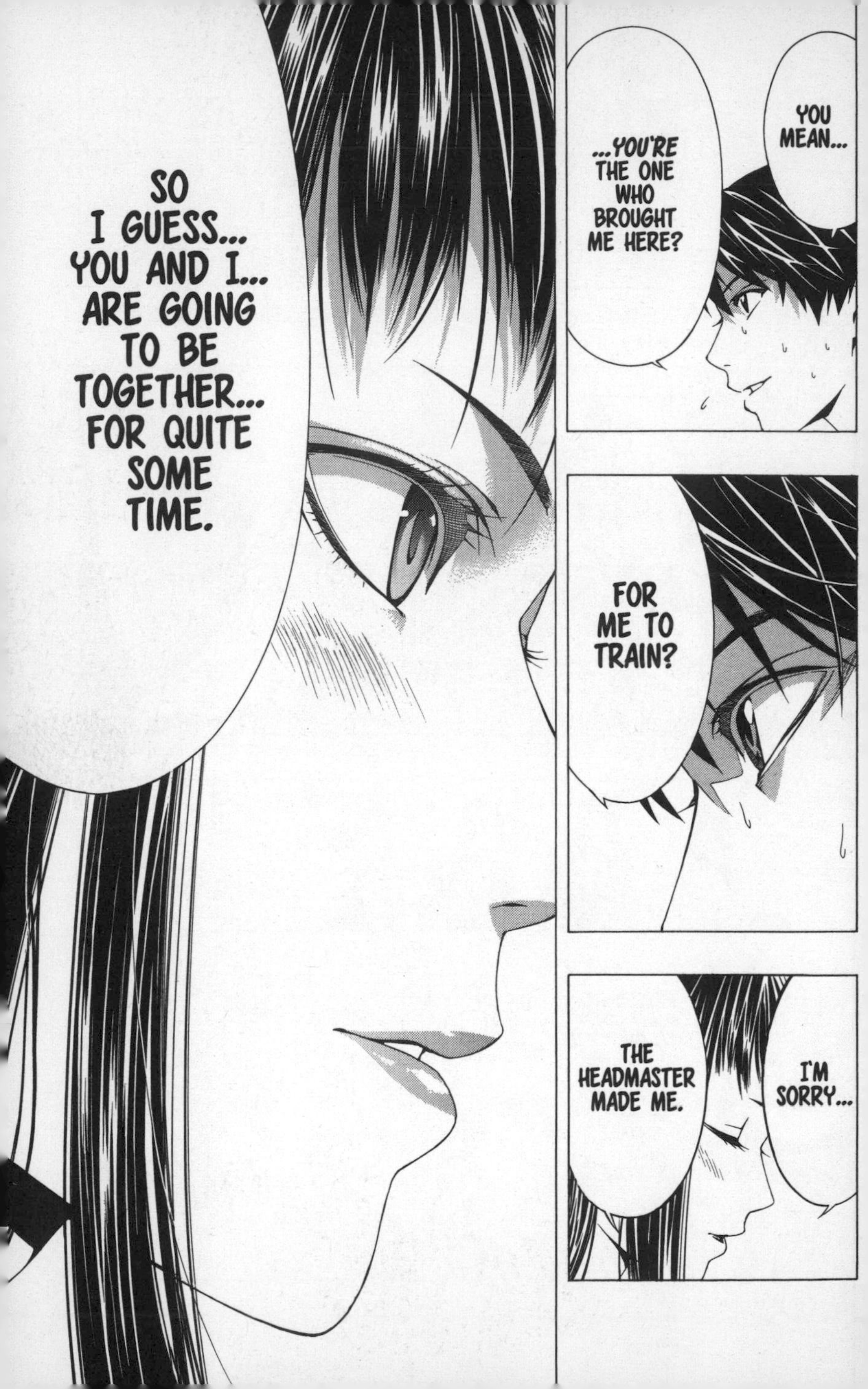
YOU MEAN...
...YOU'RE THE ONE WHO BROUGHT ME HERE?
FOR ME TO TRAIN?
I'M SORRY...
THE HEADMASTER MADE ME.
SO I GUESS... YOU AND I... ARE GOING TO BE TOGETHER... FOR QUITE SOME TIME.

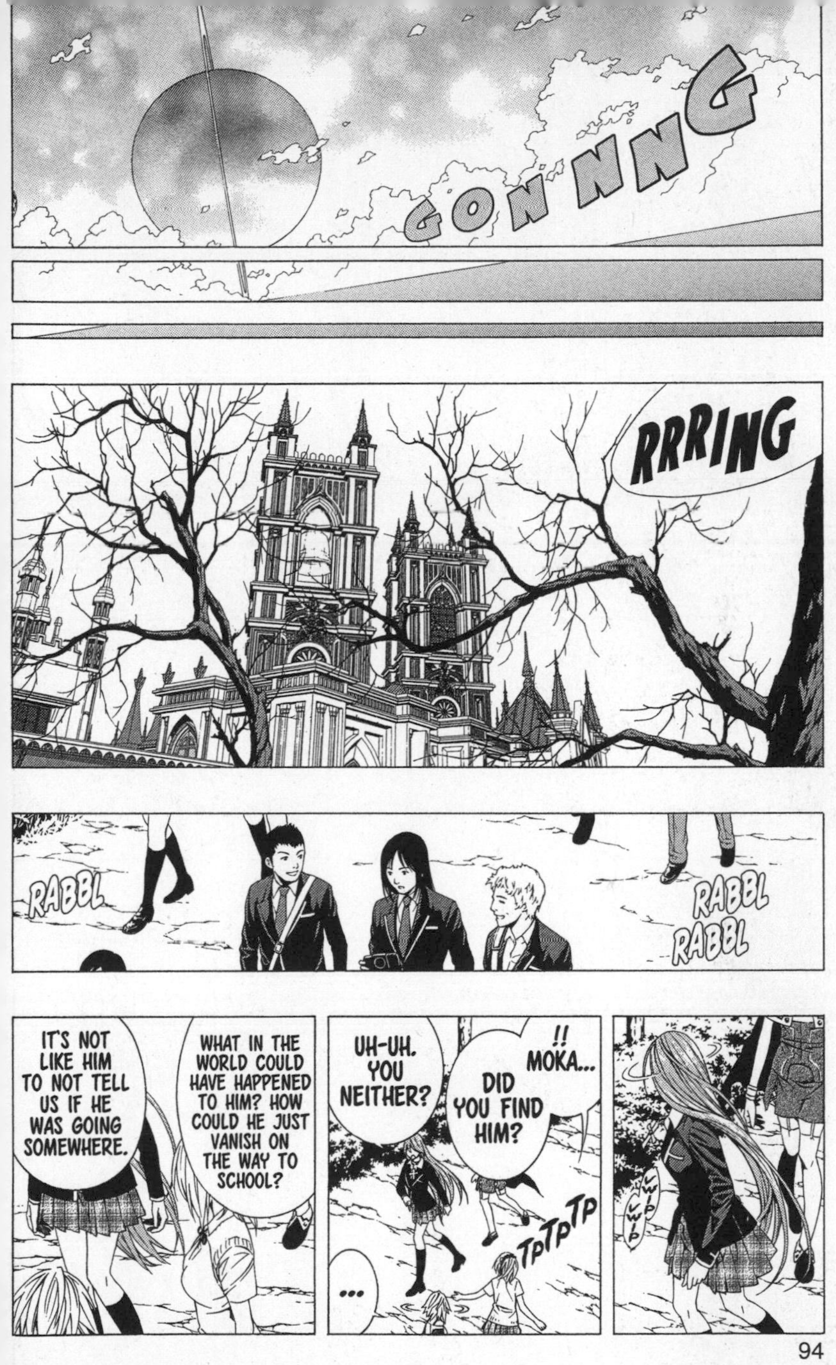
GONNNG
RRRING
RABBL RABBL
RABBL
!! MOKA...
DID YOU FIND HIM?
UH-UH. YOU NEITHER?
TPTPTP
...
WHAT IN THE WORLD COULD HAVE HAPPENED TO HIM? HOW COULD HE JUST VANISH ON THE WAY TO SCHOOL?
IT'S NOT LIKE HIM TO NOT TELL US IF HE WAS GOING SOMEWHERE.

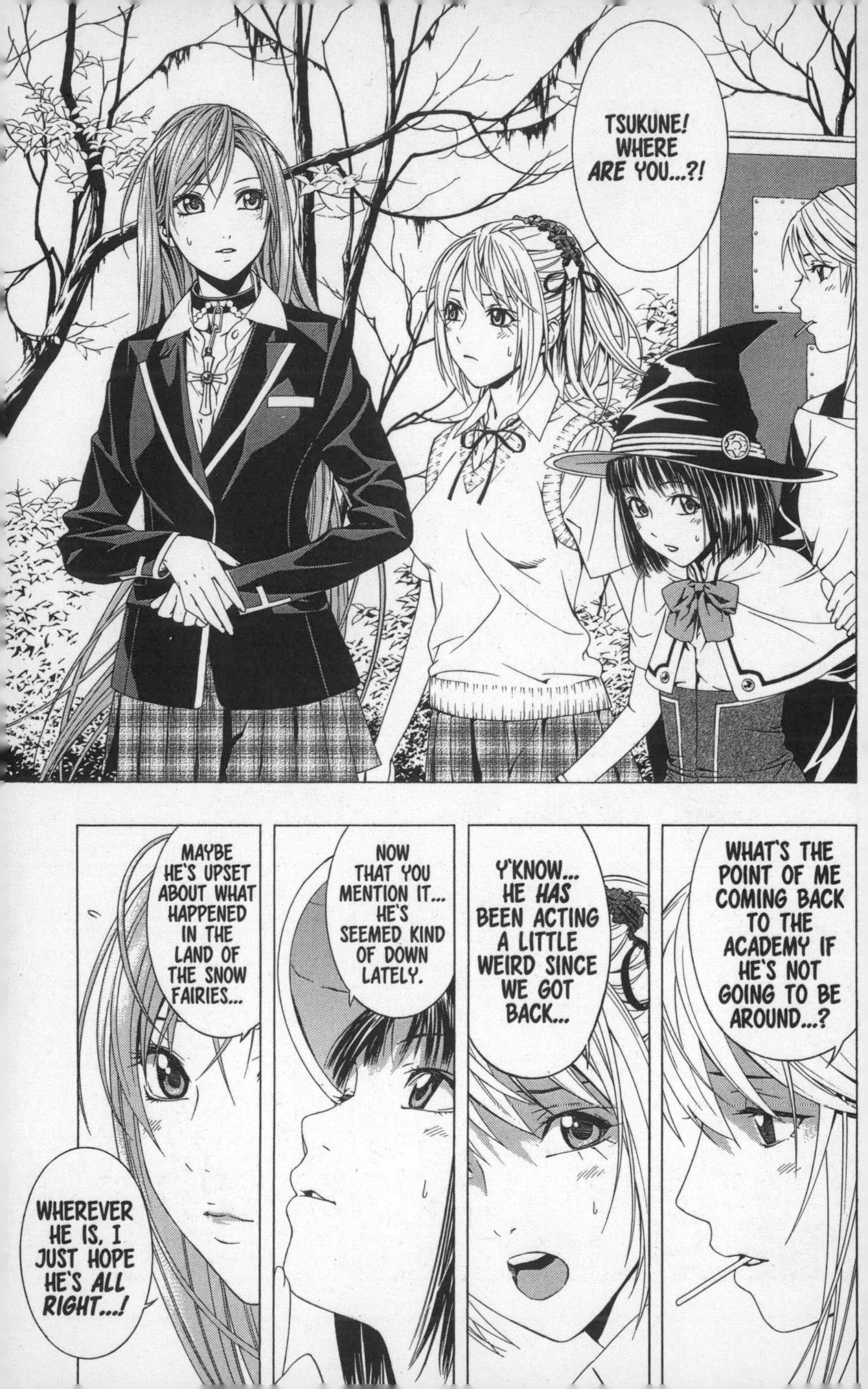
TSUKUNE! WHERE ARE YOU...?!
WHAT'S THE POINT OF ME COMING BACK TO THE ACADEMY IF HE'S NOT GOING TO BE AROUND...?
Y'KNOW... HE *HAS* BEEN ACTING A LITTLE WEIRD SINCE WE GOT BACK...
NOW THAT YOU MENTION IT... HE'S SEEMED KIND OF DOWN LATELY.
MAYBE HE'S UPSET ABOUT WHAT HAPPENED IN THE LAND OF THE SNOW FAIRIES...
WHEREVER HE IS, I JUST HOPE HE'S *ALL RIGHT*...!

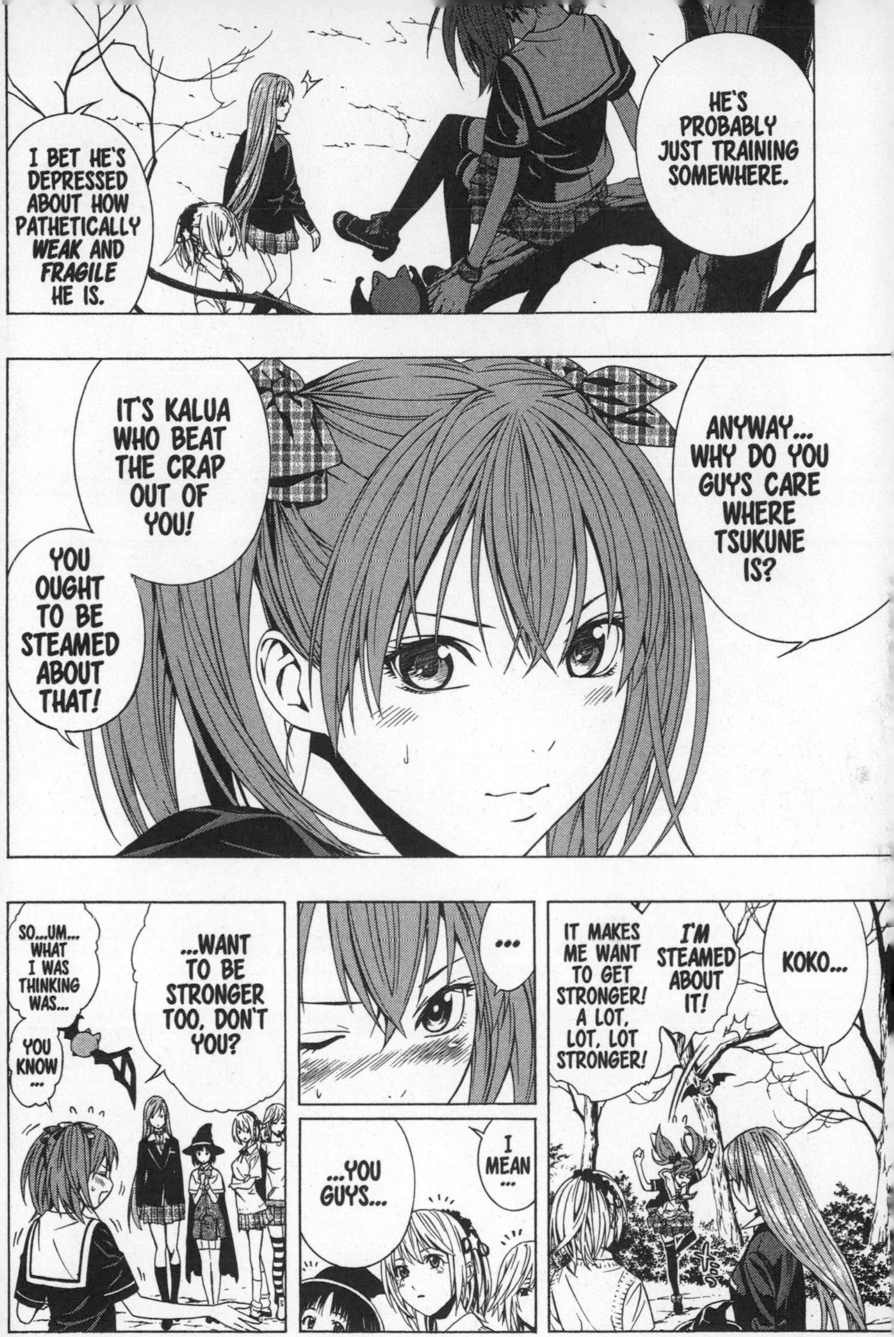
HE'S PROBABLY JUST TRAINING SOMEWHERE.
I BET HE'S DEPRESSED ABOUT HOW PATHETICALLY WEAK AND FRAGILE HE IS.
ANYWAY... WHY DO YOU GUYS CARE WHERE TSUKUNE IS?
IT'S KALUA WHO BEAT THE CRAP OUT OF YOU!
YOU OUGHT TO BE STEAMED ABOUT THAT!
KOKO...
I'M STEAMED ABOUT IT!
IT MAKES ME WANT TO GET STRONGER! A LOT, LOT, LOT STRONGER!
...
I MEAN...
...YOU GUYS...
...WANT TO BE STRONGER TOO, DON'T YOU?
SO...UM... WHAT I WAS THINKING WAS...
YOU KNOW...

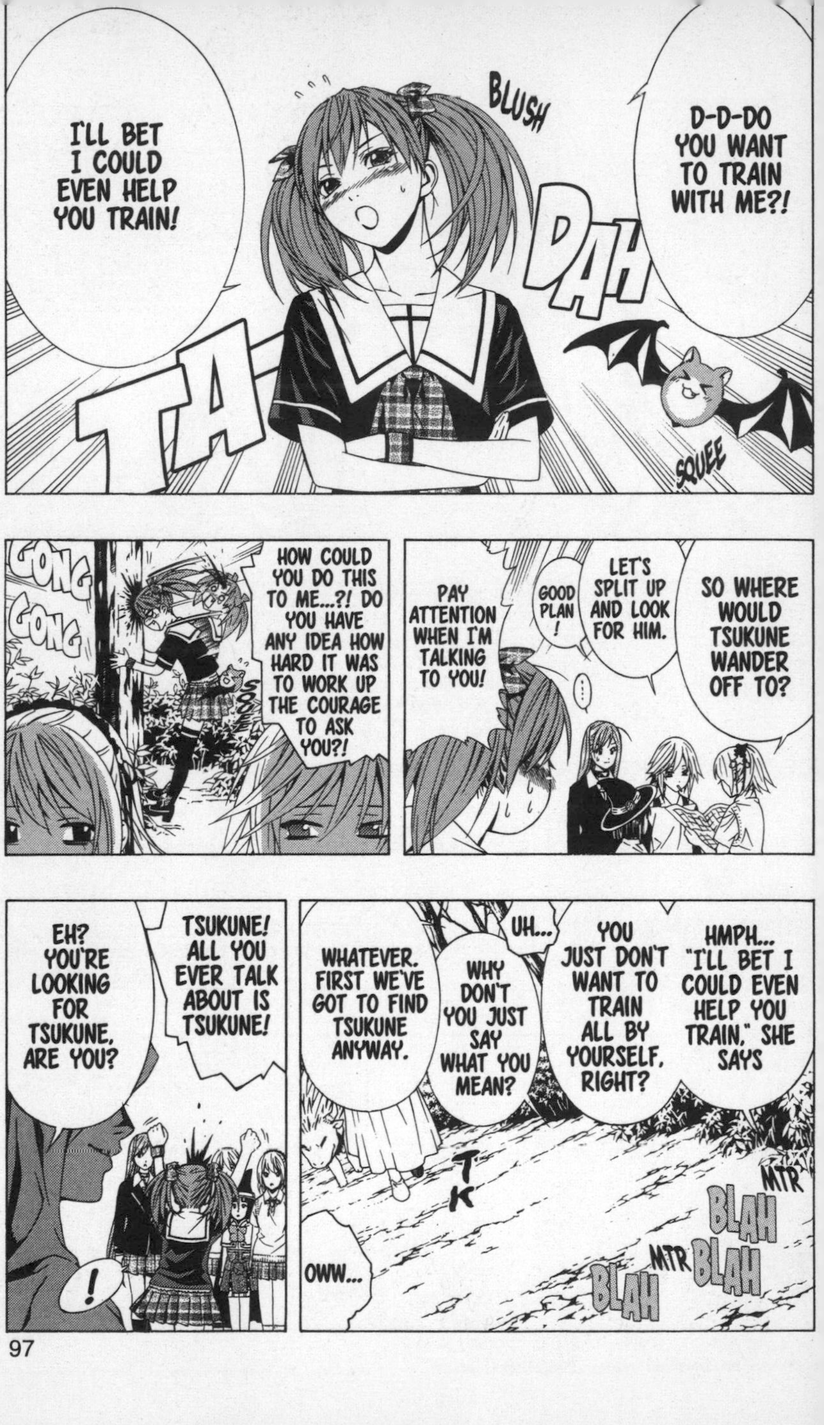
D-D-DO YOU WANT TO TRAIN WITH ME?!
BLUSH
I'LL BET I COULD EVEN HELP YOU TRAIN!
TA-
DAH
SQUEE
SO WHERE WOULD TSUKUNE WANDER OFF TO?
LET'S SPLIT UP AND LOOK FOR HIM.
GOOD PLAN!
...
PAY ATTENTION WHEN I'M TALKING TO YOU!
HOW COULD YOU DO THIS TO ME...?! DO YOU HAVE ANY IDEA HOW HARD IT WAS TO WORK UP THE COURAGE TO ASK YOU?!
GONG
GONG
HMPH... "I'LL BET I COULD EVEN HELP YOU TRAIN," SHE SAYS
YOU JUST DON'T WANT TO TRAIN ALL BY YOURSELF, RIGHT?
UH...
WHY DON'T YOU JUST SAY WHAT YOU MEAN?
WHATEVER. FIRST WE'VE GOT TO FIND TSUKUNE ANYWAY.
TK
MTR
BLAH
MTR
BLAH
BLAH
OWW...
TSUKUNE! ALL YOU EVER TALK ABOUT IS TSUKUNE!
EH? YOU'RE LOOKING FOR TSUKUNE, ARE YOU?
!

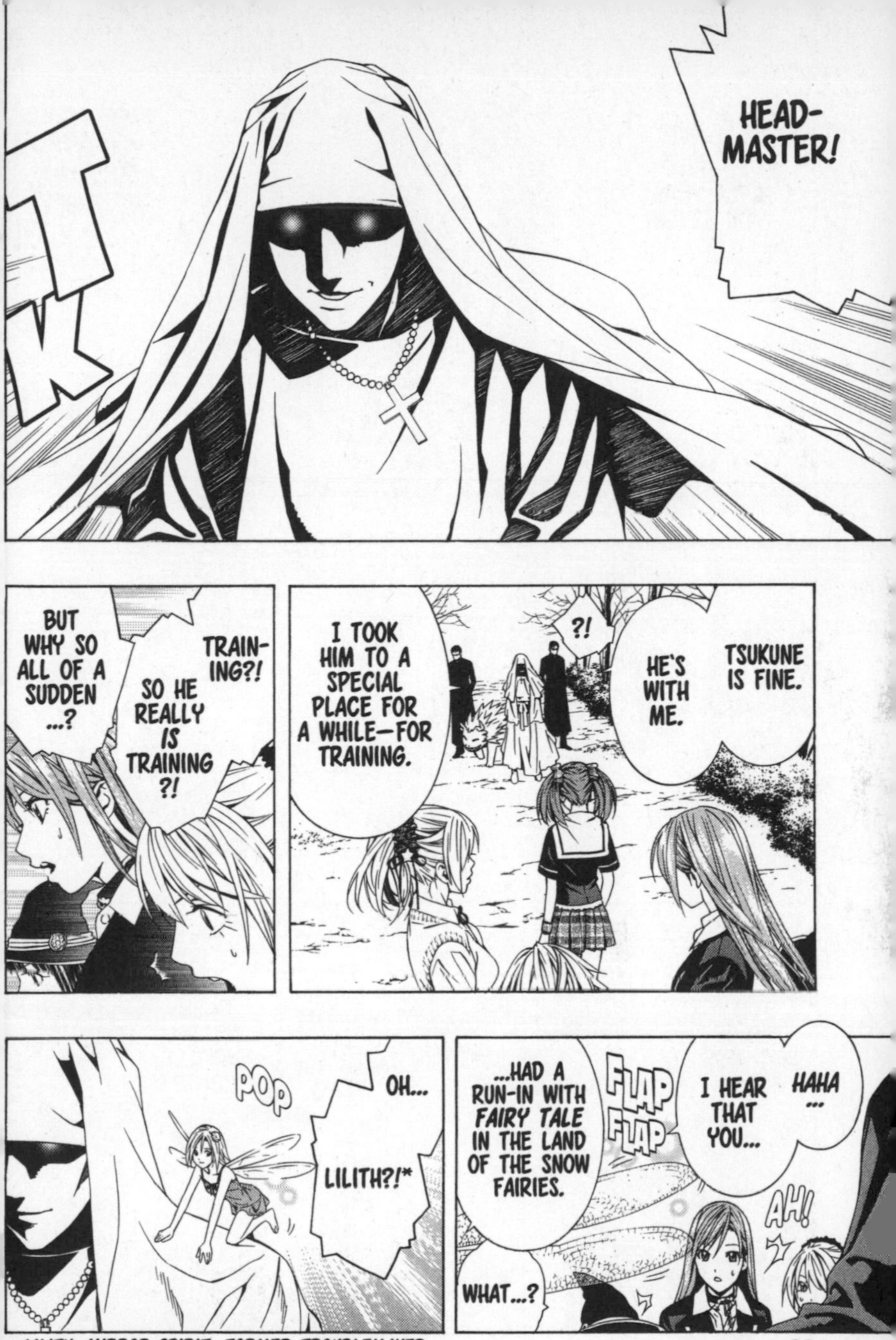
HEAD-MASTER!
TSUKUNE IS FINE.
HE'S WITH ME.
?!
I TOOK HIM TO A SPECIAL PLACE FOR A WHILE—FOR TRAINING.
TRAINING?!
SO HE REALLY IS TRAINING?!
BUT WHY SO ALL OF A SUDDEN...?
HAHA...
I HEAR THAT YOU...
FLAP FLAP
...HAD A RUN-IN WITH FAIRY TALE IN THE LAND OF THE SNOW FAIRIES.
AH!
WHAT...?
OH...
LILITH?!*
POP

*LILITH: MIRROR SPIRIT. FORMER TROUBLEMAKER NOW WORKING FOR THE HEADMASTER.

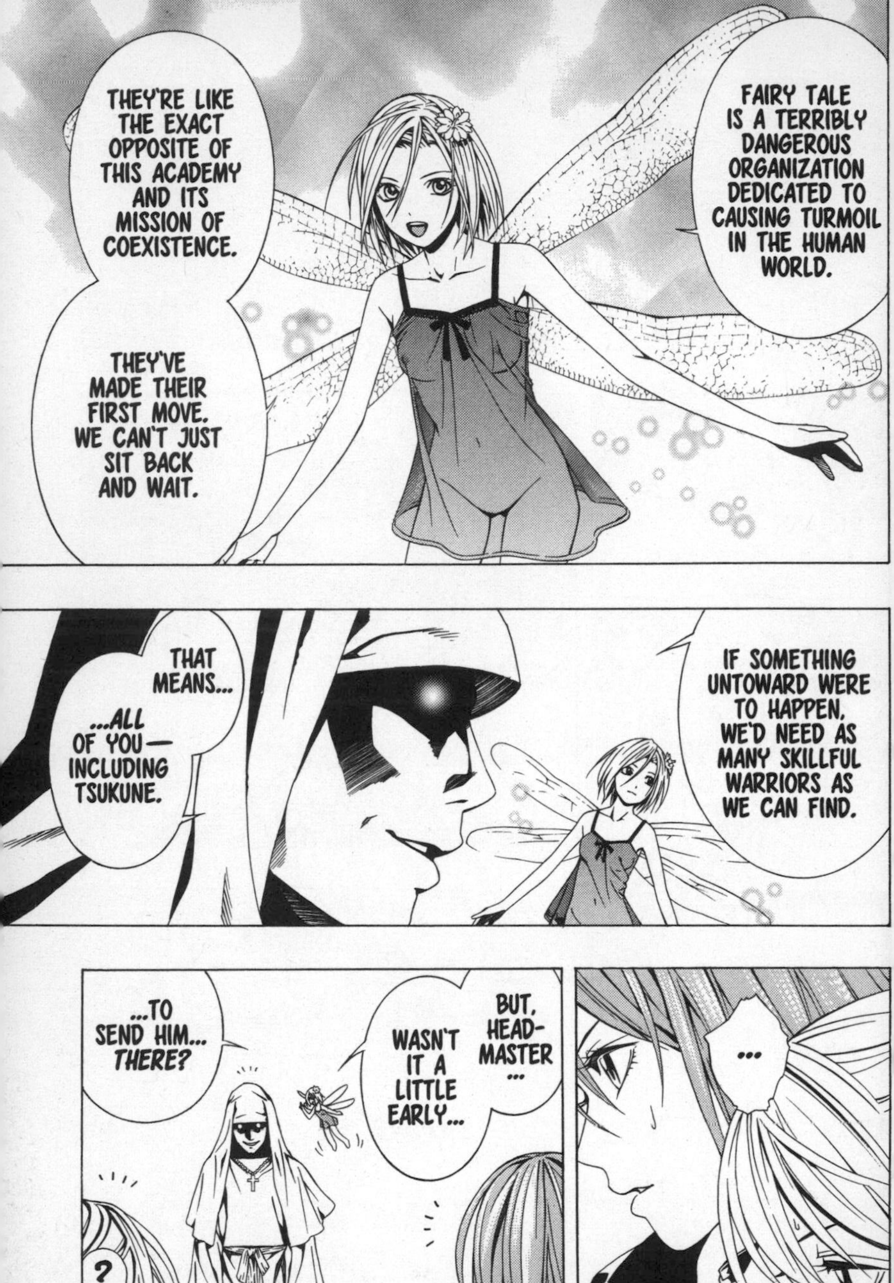
FAIRY TALE IS A TERRIBLY DANGEROUS ORGANIZATION DEDICATED TO CAUSING TURMOIL IN THE HUMAN WORLD.
THEY'RE LIKE THE EXACT OPPOSITE OF THIS ACADEMY AND ITS MISSION OF COEXISTENCE.
THEY'VE MADE THEIR FIRST MOVE. WE CAN'T JUST SIT BACK AND WAIT.
IF SOMETHING UNTOWARD WERE TO HAPPEN, WE'D NEED AS MANY SKILLFUL WARRIORS AS WE CAN FIND.
THAT MEANS...
...ALL OF YOU— INCLUDING TSUKUNE.
...
BUT, HEAD-MASTER...
WASN'T IT A LITTLE EARLY...
...TO SEND HIM... *THERE?*
?

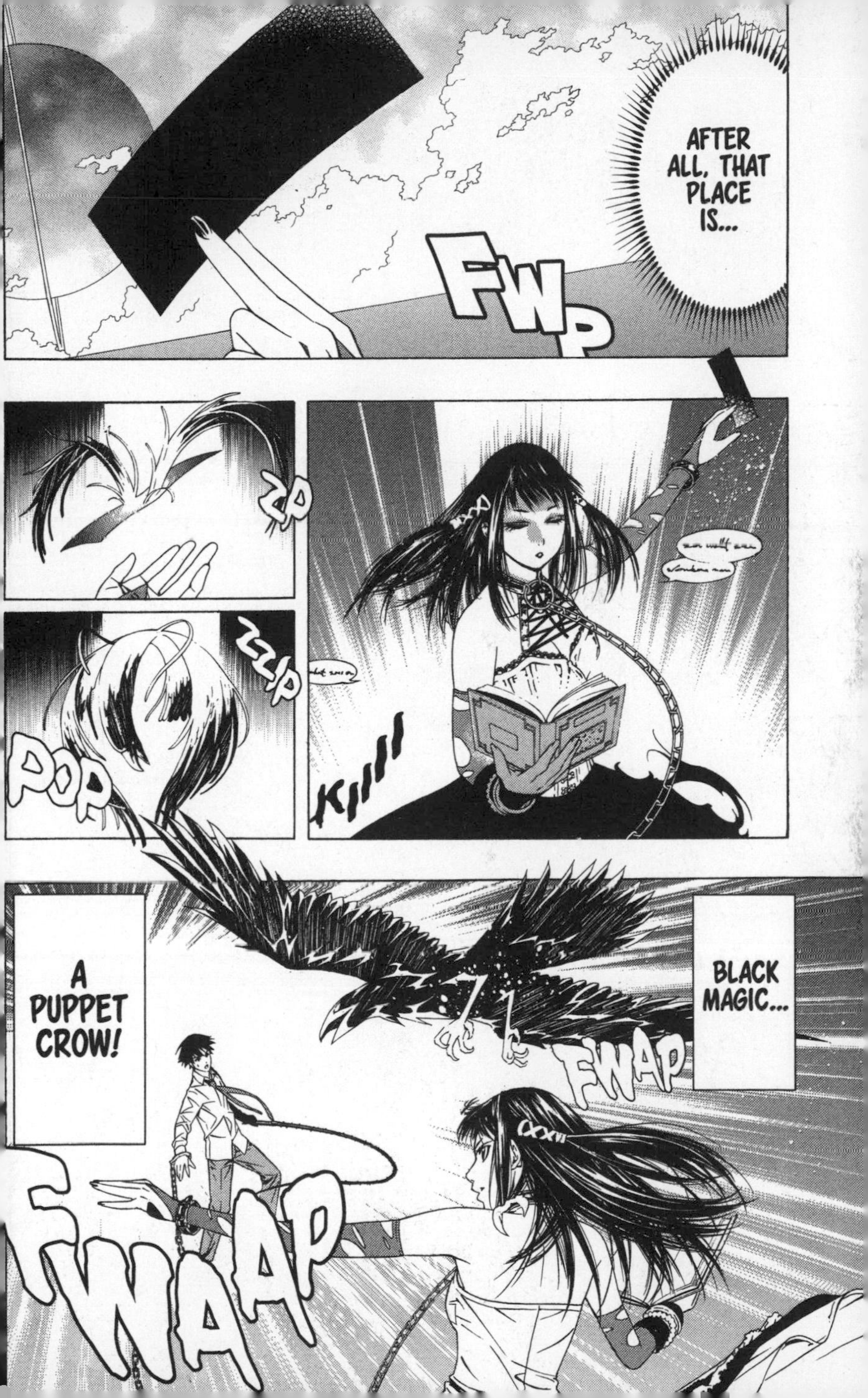
AFTER ALL, THAT PLACE IS...
FWP
KIIII
ZIP
ZZIP
POP
BLACK MAGIC...
FWAP
A PUPPET CROW!
FWAAP

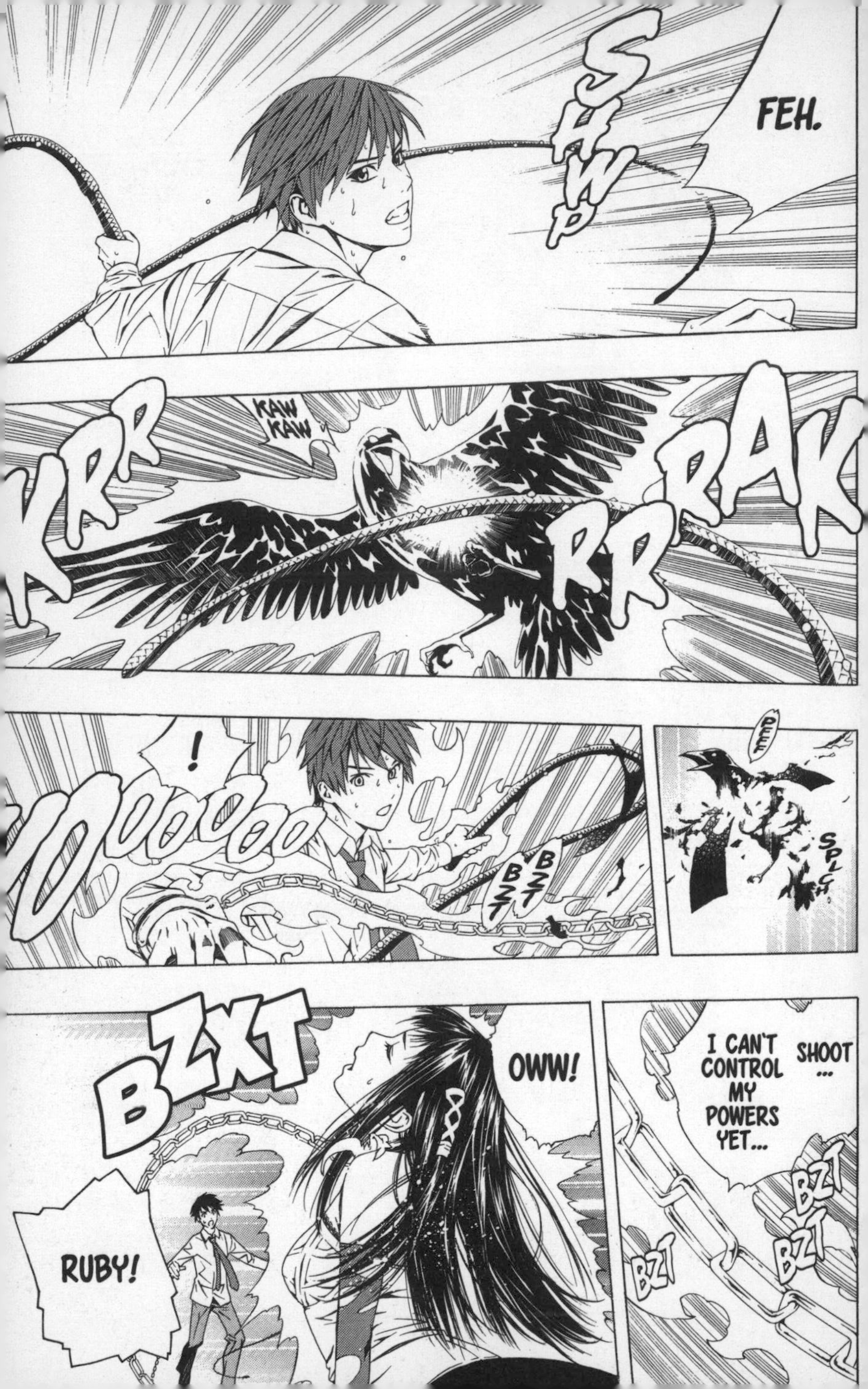
FEH.
SHWP
KAW KAW
RAK
RR
KRR
PEEF
SPLCH
!
BZT BZT
BZT
OOOOOOO
SHOOT...
I CAN'T CONTROL MY POWERS YET...
BZT
BZT
BZT
BZT
OWW!
BZXT
RUBY!

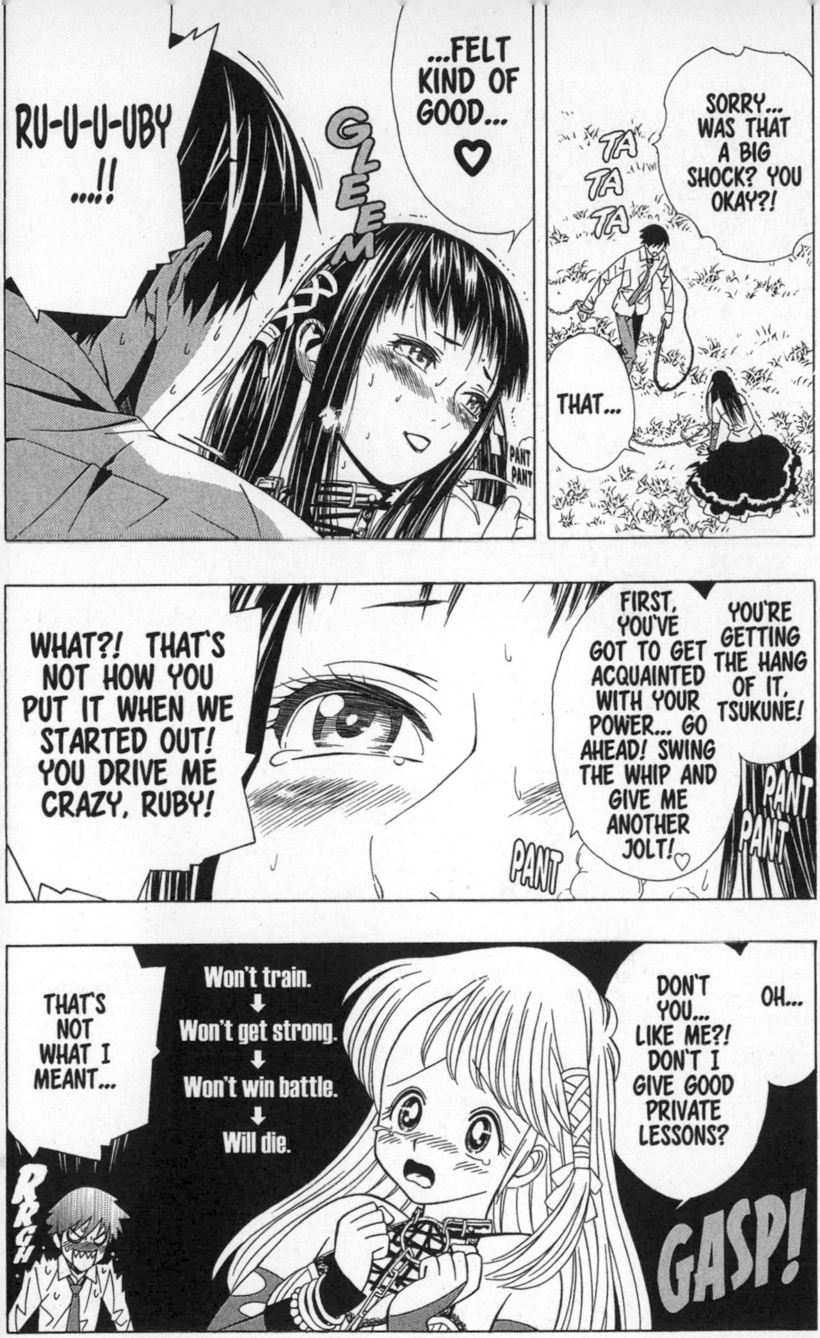
SORRY... WAS THAT A BIG SHOCK? YOU OKAY?!
TA TA TA
THAT...
...FELT KIND OF GOOD... ♡
GLEEM
PANT PANT
RU-U-U-UBY ...!!
YOU'RE GETTING THE HANG OF IT, TSUKUNE!
FIRST, YOU'VE GOT TO GET ACQUAINTED WITH YOUR POWER... GO AHEAD! SWING THE WHIP AND GIVE ME ANOTHER JOLT! ♡
PANT PANT
PANT
WHAT?! THAT'S NOT HOW YOU PUT IT WHEN WE STARTED OUT! YOU DRIVE ME CRAZY, RUBY!
OH...
DON'T YOU... LIKE ME?! DON'T I GIVE GOOD PRIVATE LESSONS?
GASP!
Won't train. ↓ Won't get strong. ↓ Won't win battle. ↓ Will die.
THAT'S NOT WHAT I MEANT...
RRGH

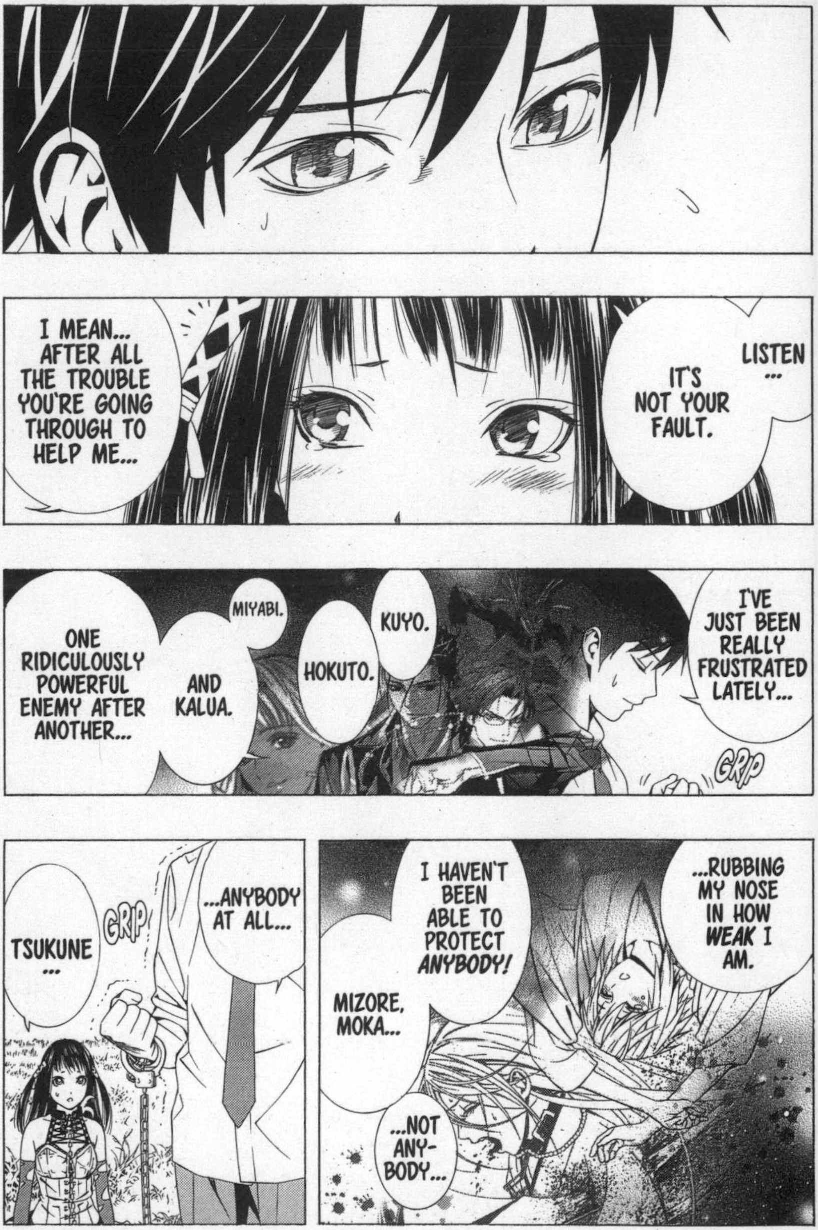
LISTEN...
IT'S NOT YOUR FAULT.
I MEAN... AFTER ALL THE TROUBLE YOU'RE GOING THROUGH TO HELP ME...
I'VE JUST BEEN REALLY FRUSTRATED LATELY...
GRIP
KUYO.
HOKUTO.
MIYABI.
AND KALUA.
ONE RIDICULOUSLY POWERFUL ENEMY AFTER ANOTHER...
...RUBBING MY NOSE IN HOW *WEAK* I AM.
I HAVEN'T BEEN ABLE TO PROTECT *ANYBODY!*
MIZORE, MOKA...
...NOT ANY-BODY...
...ANYBODY AT ALL...
GRIP
TSUKUNE...

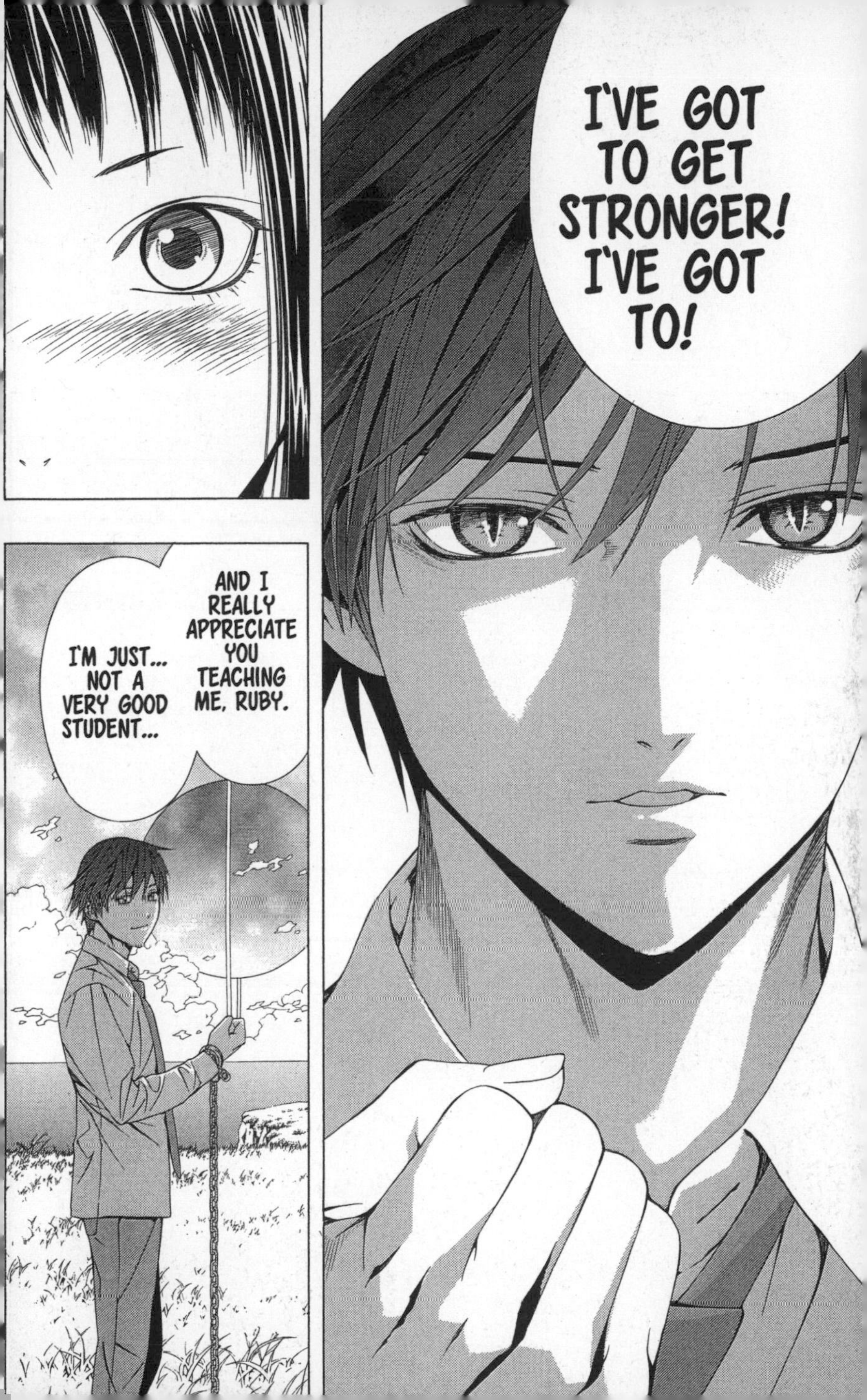
I'VE GOT TO GET STRONGER! I'VE GOT TO!
AND I REALLY APPRECIATE YOU TEACHING ME, RUBY.
I'M JUST... NOT A VERY GOOD STUDENT...

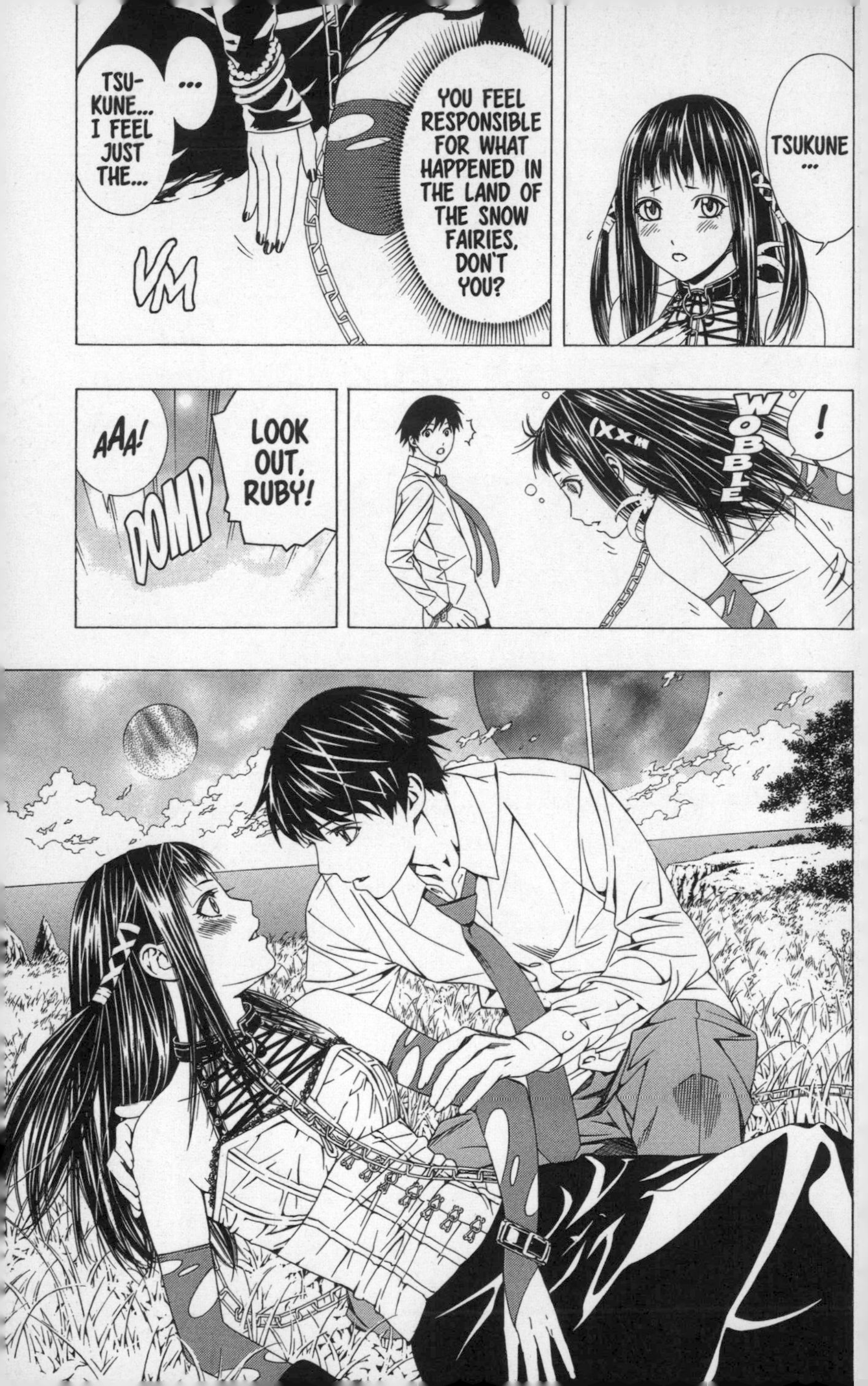
TSUKUNE...
YOU FEEL RESPONSIBLE FOR WHAT HAPPENED IN THE LAND OF THE SNOW FAIRIES, DON'T YOU?
...
TSU-KUNE... I FEEL JUST THE...
VM
!
WOBBLE
LOOK OUT, RUBY!
AAA!
DOMP

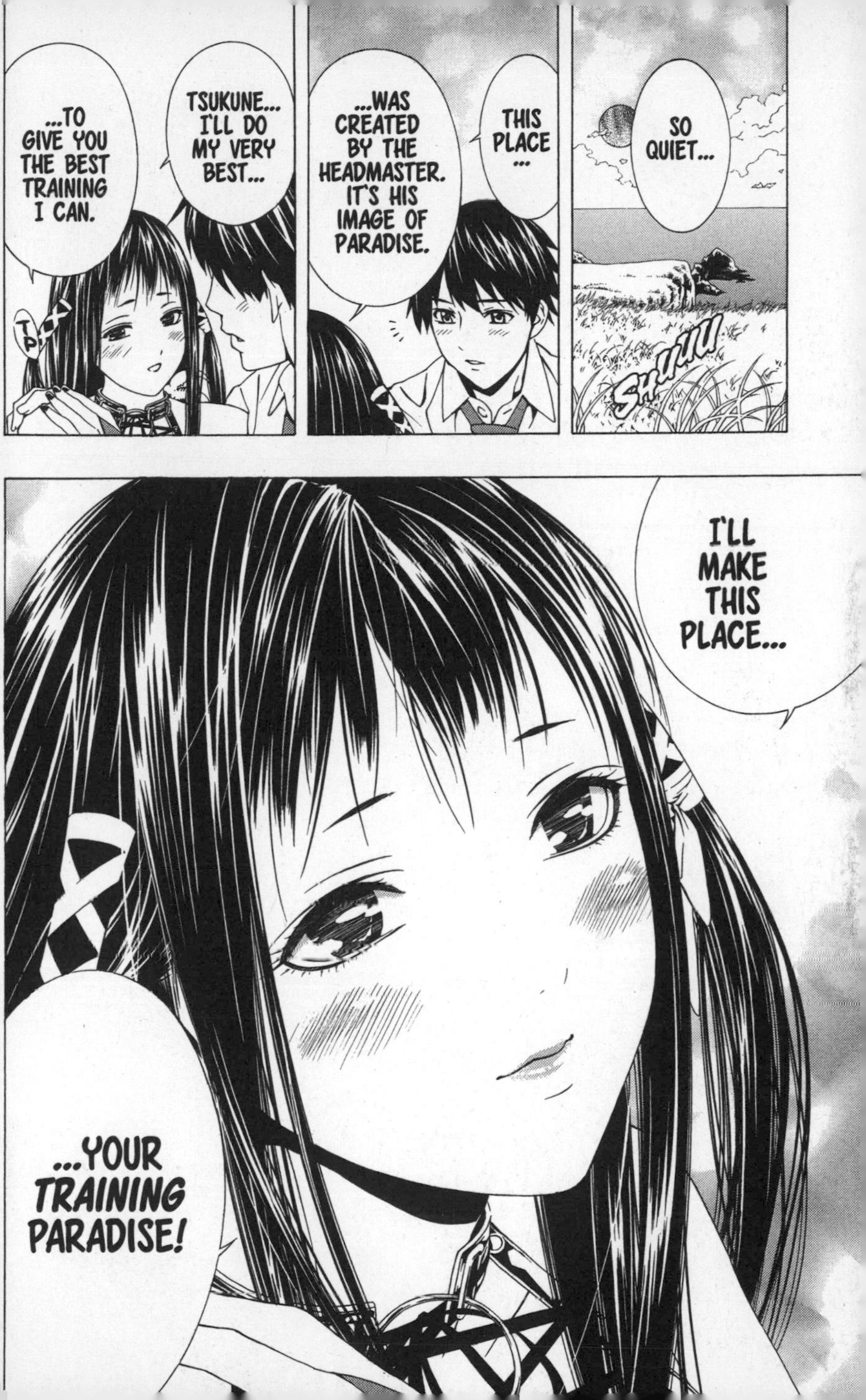
SO QUIET...
SHUUU
THIS PLACE...
...WAS CREATED BY THE HEADMASTER. IT'S HIS IMAGE OF PARADISE.
TSUKUNE... I'LL DO MY VERY BEST...
...TO GIVE YOU THE BEST TRAINING I CAN.
TP
I'LL MAKE THIS PLACE...
...YOUR TRAINING PARADISE!

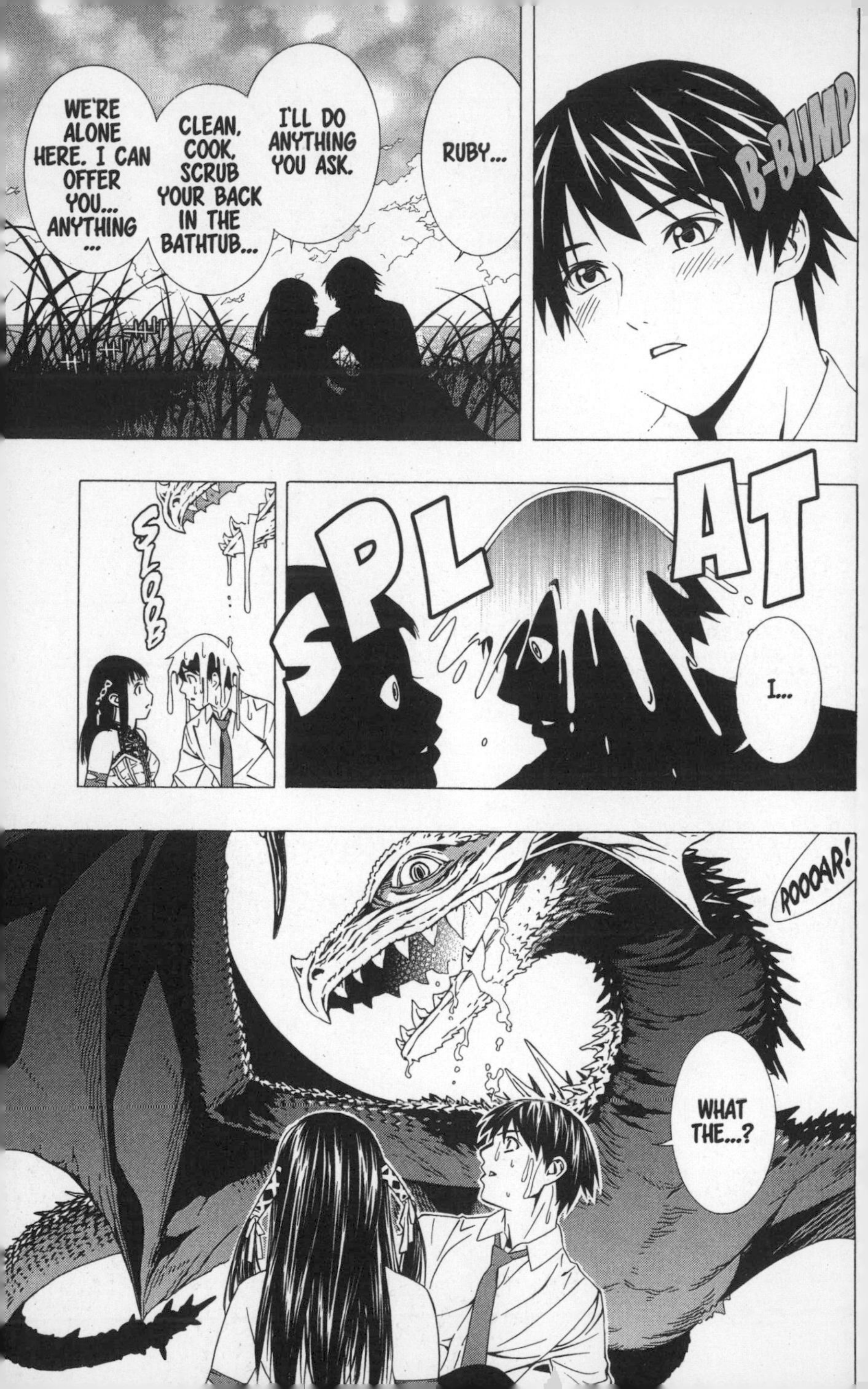
B-BUMP
RUBY...
I'LL DO ANYTHING YOU ASK.
CLEAN, COOK, SCRUB YOUR BACK IN THE BATHTUB...
WE'RE ALONE HERE. I CAN OFFER YOU... ANYTHING ...
SPLAT
I...
SLOBB
...
ROOOAR!
WHAT THE...?

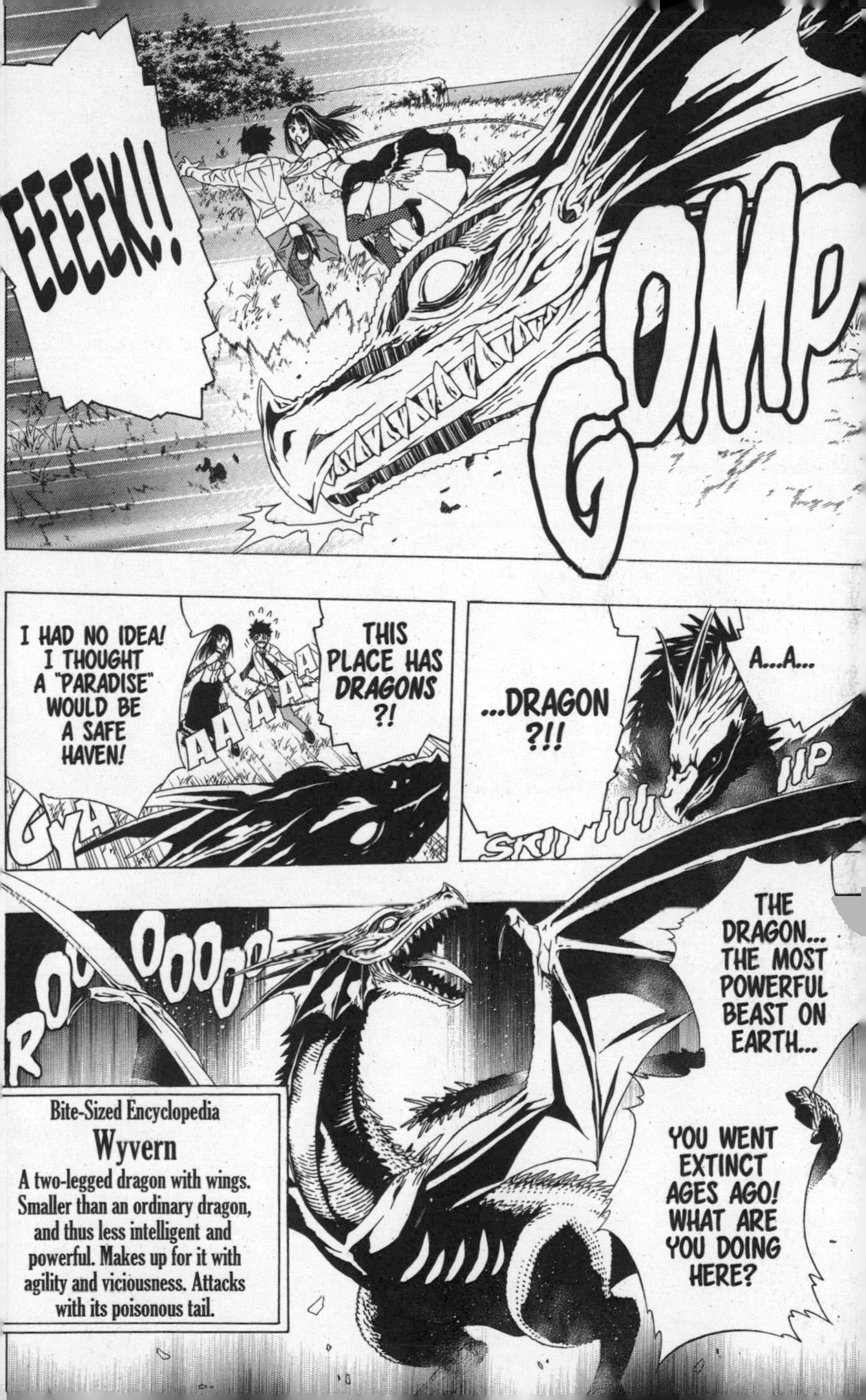
GOMP
EEEEK!!
A...A...
...DRAGON ?!!
SKI
IIP
THIS PLACE HAS DRAGONS ?!
I HAD NO IDEA! I THOUGHT A "PARADISE" WOULD BE A SAFE HAVEN!
AAAAA
GYA
THE DRAGON... THE MOST POWERFUL BEAST ON EARTH...
YOU WENT EXTINCT AGES AGO! WHAT ARE YOU DOING HERE?
ROOOOOOO
Bite-Sized Encyclopedia
Wyvern
A two-legged dragon with wings. Smaller than an ordinary dragon, and thus less intelligent and powerful. Makes up for it with agility and viciousness. Attacks with its poisonous tail.

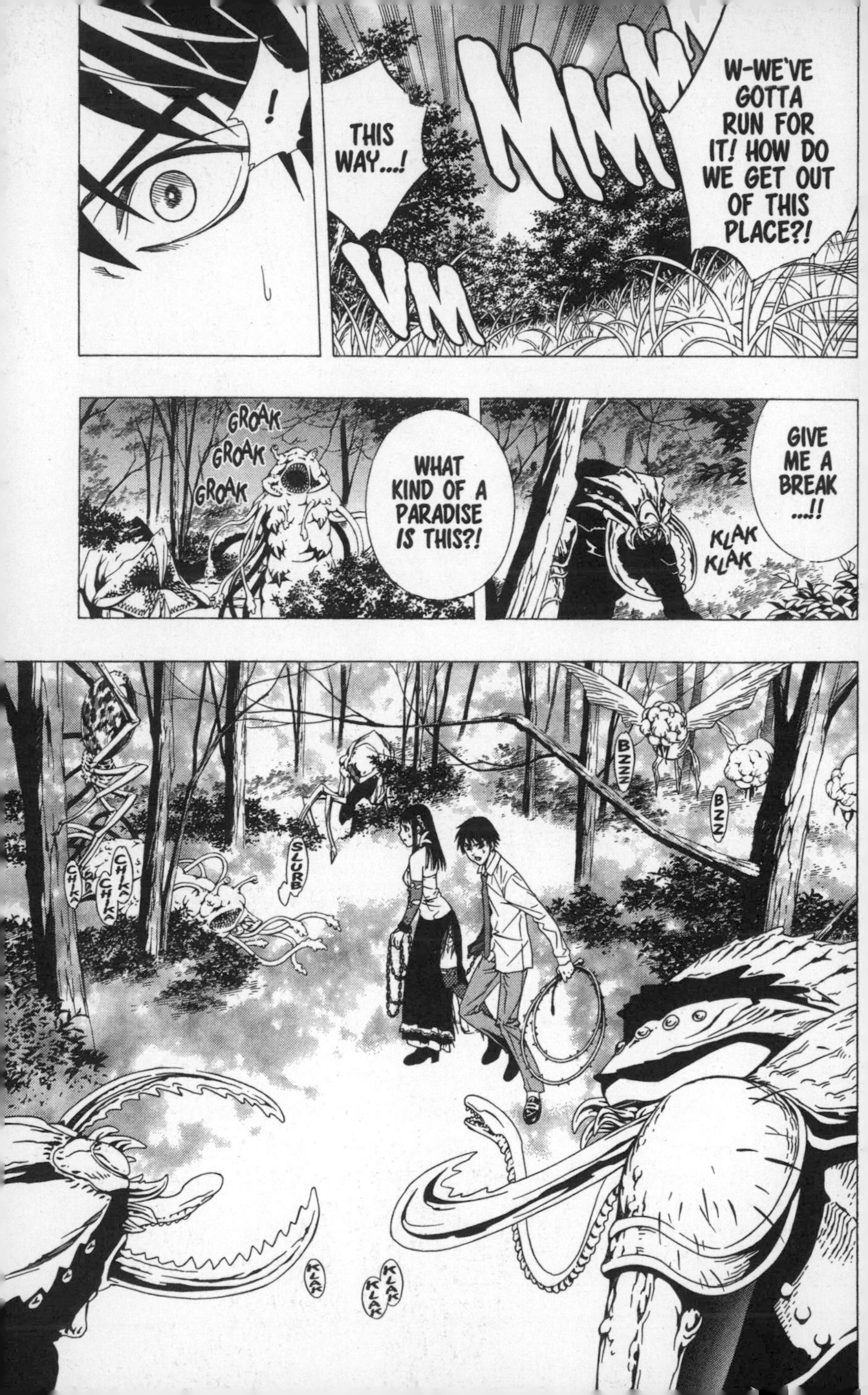
W-WE'VE GOTTA RUN FOR IT! HOW DO WE GET OUT OF THIS PLACE?!
MMM
THIS WAY...!
VM
!
GIVE ME A BREAK ...!!
KLAK KLAK
WHAT KIND OF A PARADISE IS THIS?!
GROAK
GROAK
GROAK
BZZZ
BZZ
SLURB
CHIKA
CHIKA
KLAK
KLAK
KLAK

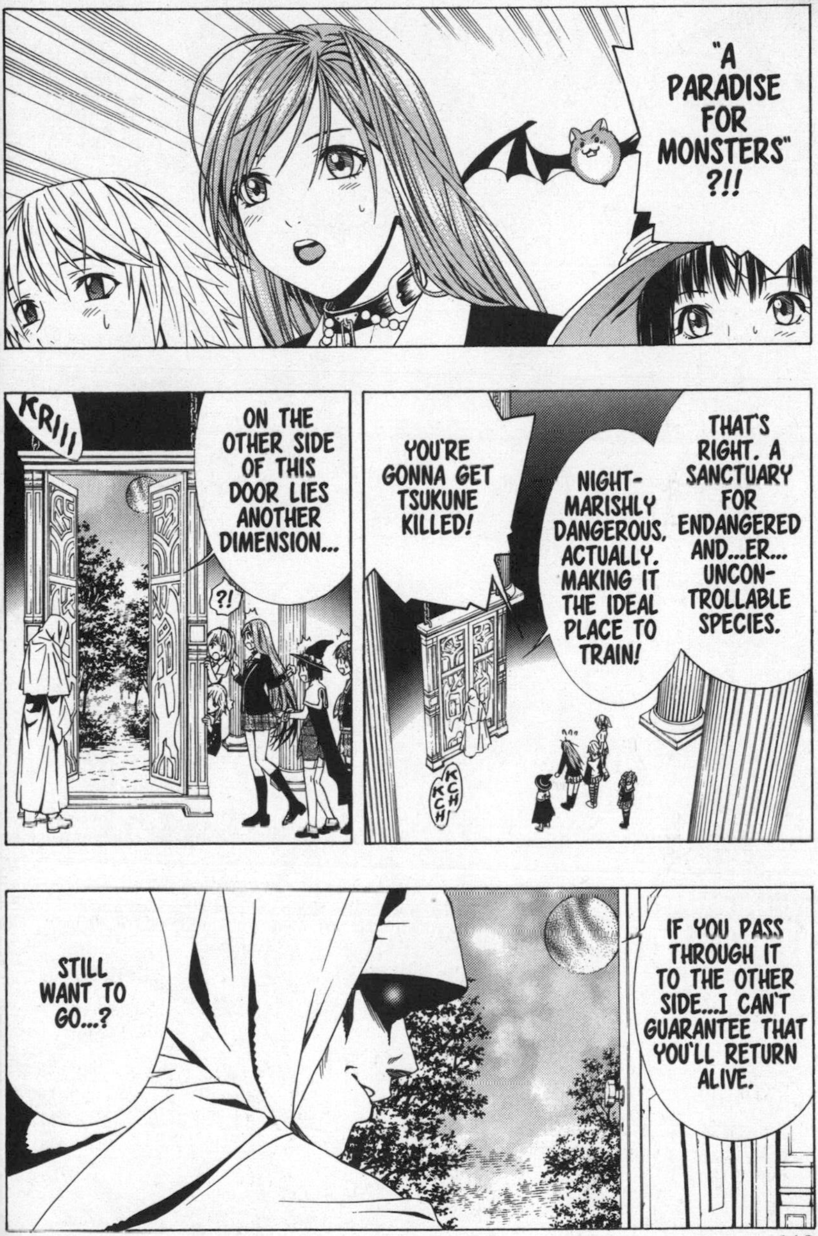
"A PARADISE FOR MONSTERS" ?!!
THAT'S RIGHT. A SANCTUARY FOR ENDANGERED AND...ER... UNCONTROLLABLE SPECIES.
NIGHTMARISHLY DANGEROUS, ACTUALLY. MAKING IT THE IDEAL PLACE TO TRAIN!
YOU'RE GONNA GET TSUKUNE KILLED!
KCH KCH
ON THE OTHER SIDE OF THIS DOOR LIES ANOTHER DIMENSION...
KRIII
?!
IF YOU PASS THROUGH IT TO THE OTHER SIDE...I CAN'T GUARANTEE THAT YOU'LL RETURN ALIVE.
STILL WANT TO GO...?

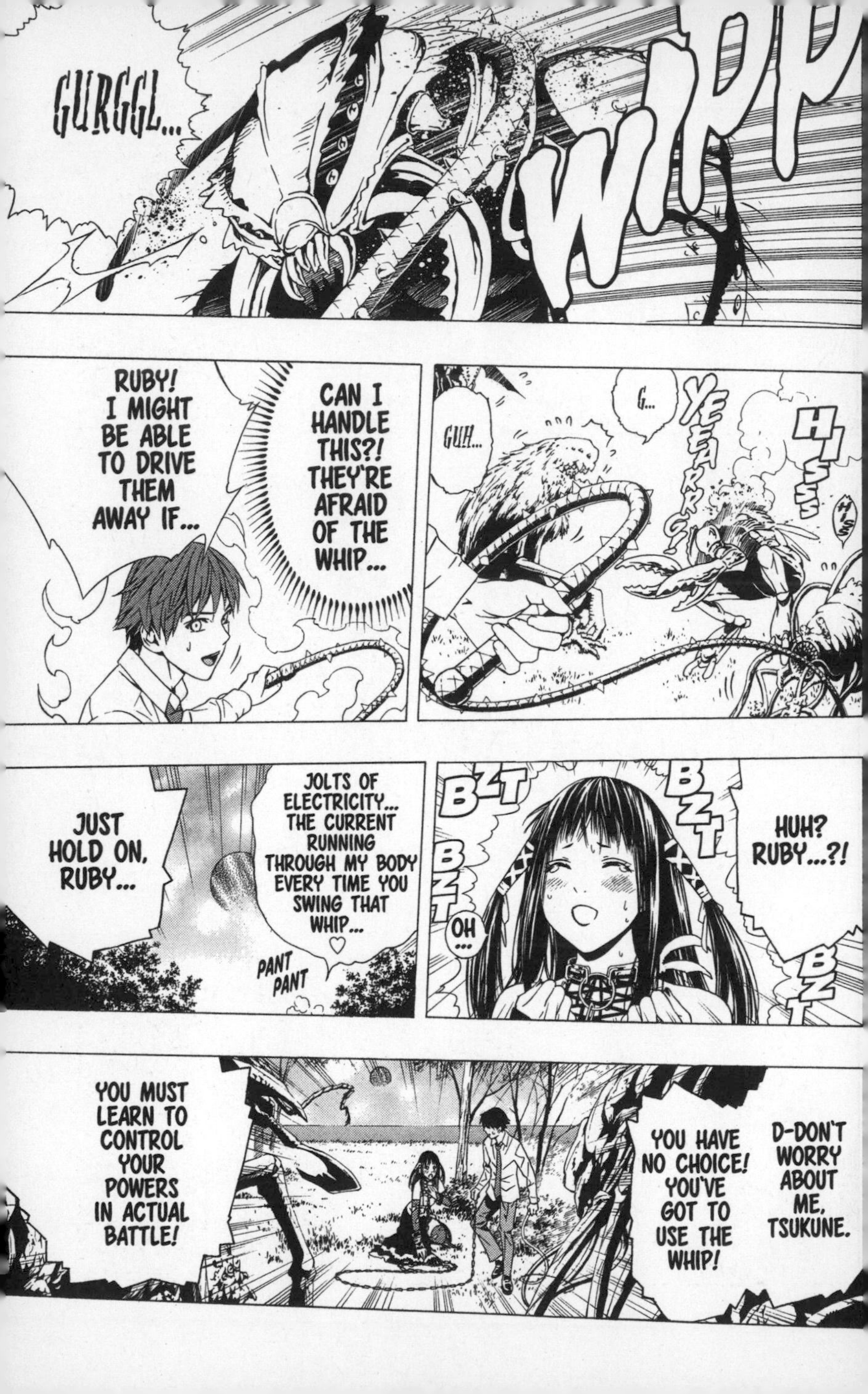
WHIPP
GURGGL...
HISSS
HISS
YEEARRG!
G...
GUH...
CAN I HANDLE THIS?! THEY'RE AFRAID OF THE WHIP...
RUBY! I MIGHT BE ABLE TO DRIVE THEM AWAY IF...
HUH? RUBY...?!
BZT
BZT
BZT
BZT
OH...
JOLTS OF ELECTRICITY... THE CURRENT RUNNING THROUGH MY BODY EVERY TIME YOU SWING THAT WHIP... ♡
PANT PANT
JUST HOLD ON, RUBY...
D-DON'T WORRY ABOUT ME, TSUKUNE.
YOU HAVE NO CHOICE! YOU'VE GOT TO USE THE WHIP!
YOU MUST LEARN TO CONTROL YOUR POWERS IN ACTUAL BATTLE!

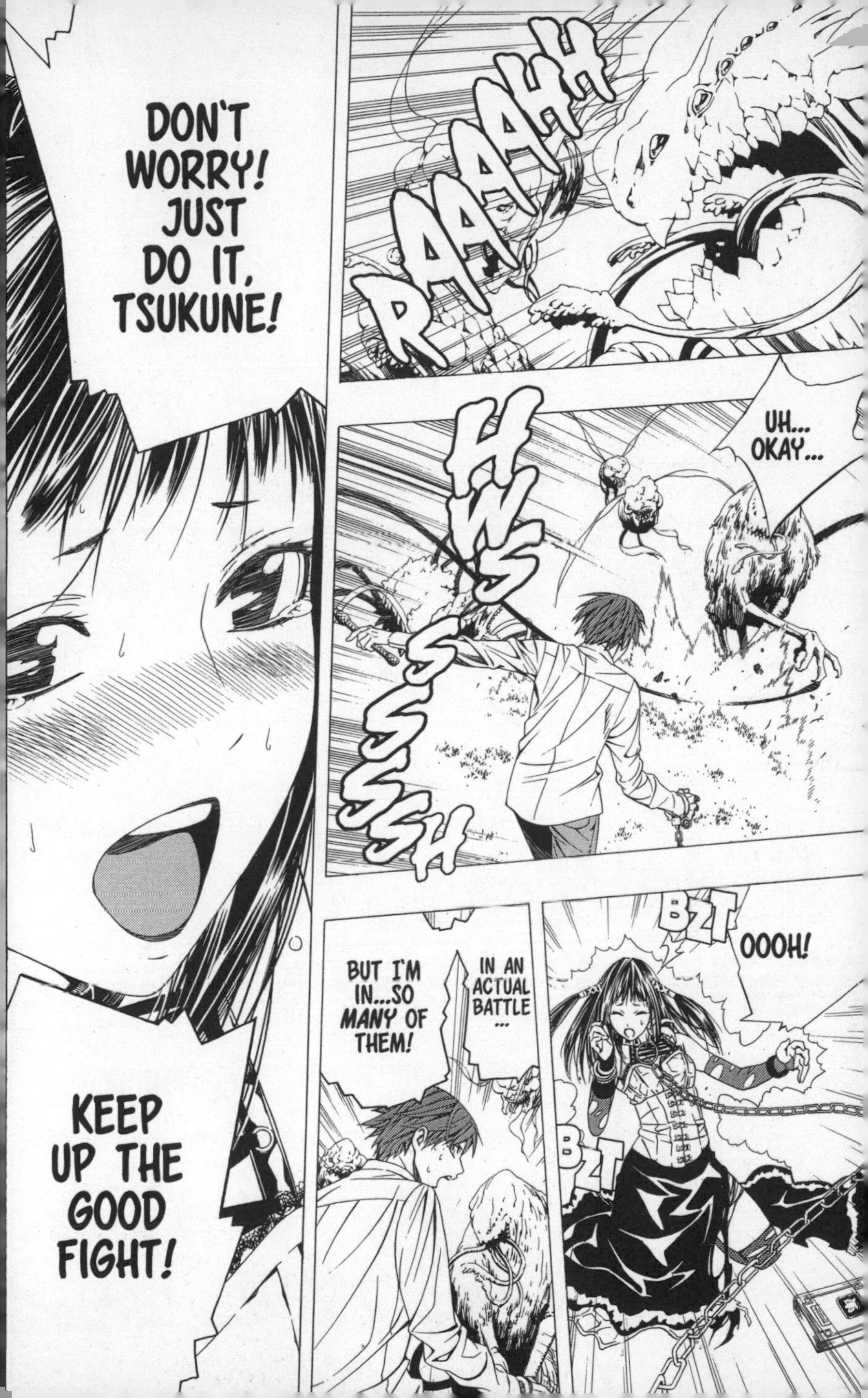
RAAAAHH
HWSSSSSH
UH... OKAY...
BZT
OOOH!
BZT
IN AN ACTUAL BATTLE ...
BUT I'M IN...SO MANY OF THEM!
DON'T WORRY! JUST DO IT, TSUKUNE!
KEEP UP THE GOOD FIGHT!

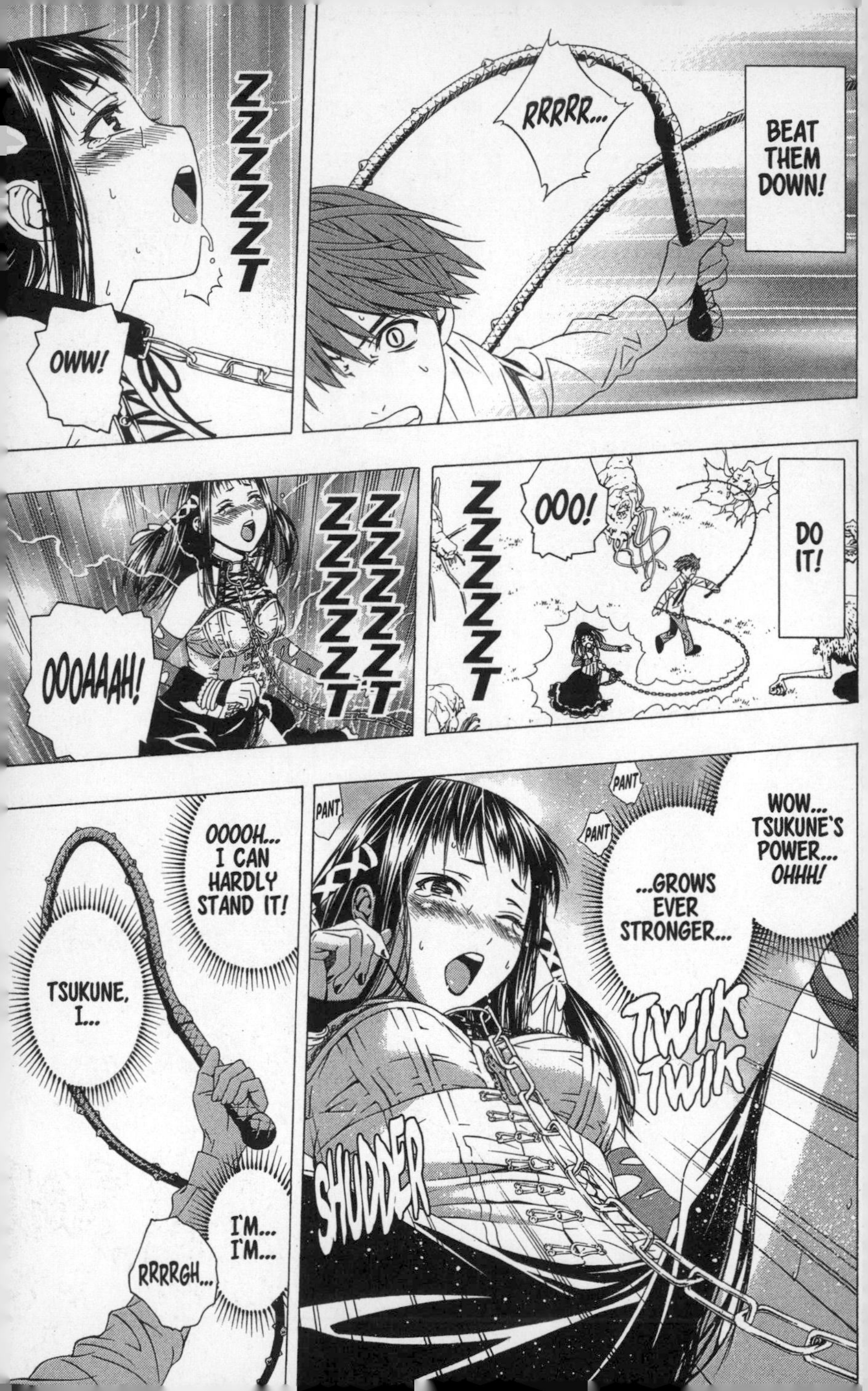

BEAT THEM DOWN!
RRRRR...
ZZZZZT
OWW!
DO IT!
OOO!
ZZZZZT
ZZZZZZT
ZZZZZZT
OOOAAAH!
PANT
PANT
WOW... TSUKUNE'S POWER... OHHH!
...GROWS EVER STRONGER...
PANT
TWIK TWIK
SHUDDER
OOOOH... I CAN HARDLY STAND IT!
TSUKUNE, I...
I'M... I'M...
RRRRGH...

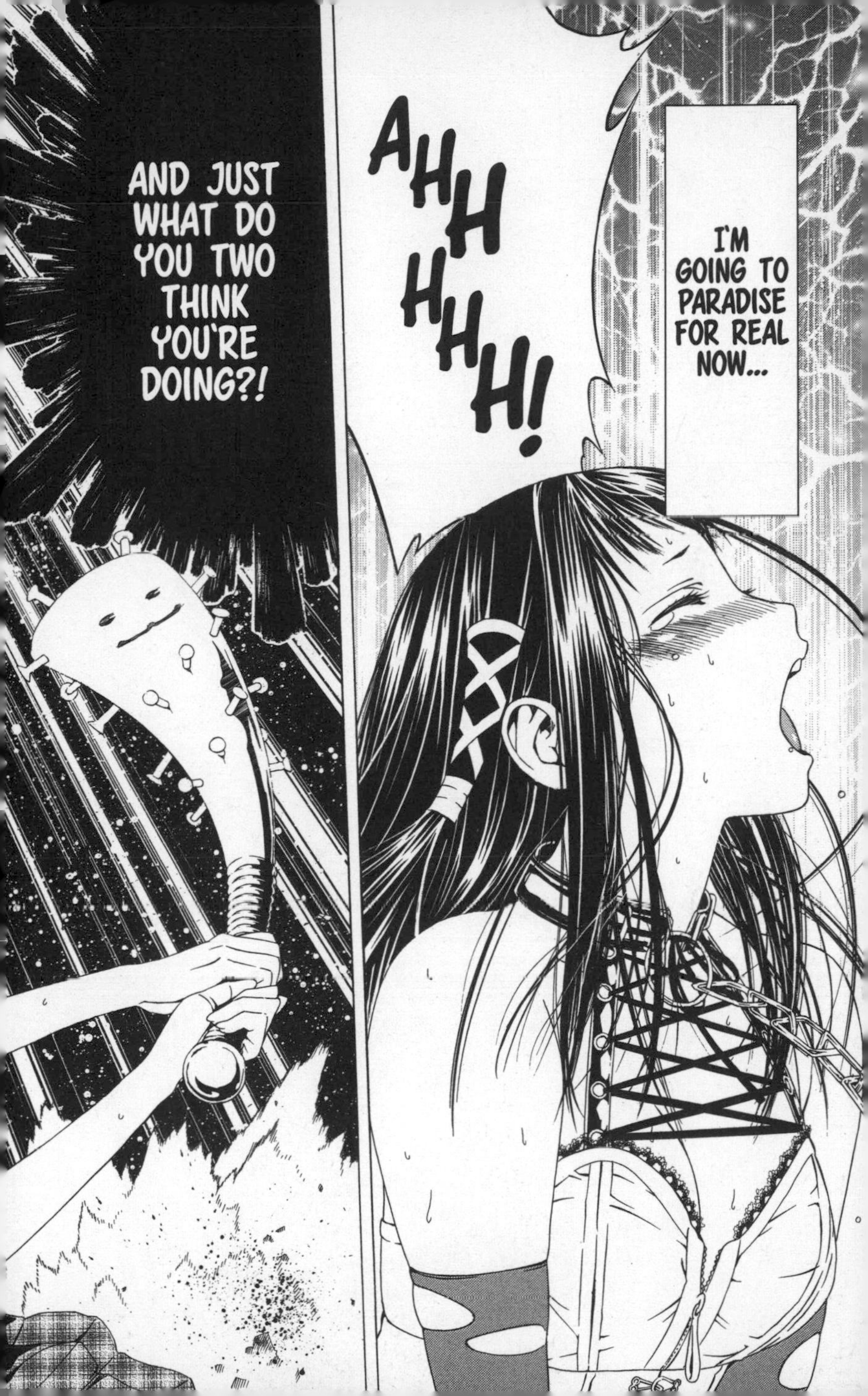

I'M GOING TO PARADISE FOR REAL NOW...
AHHHHHH!
AND JUST WHAT DO YOU TWO THINK YOU'RE DOING?!

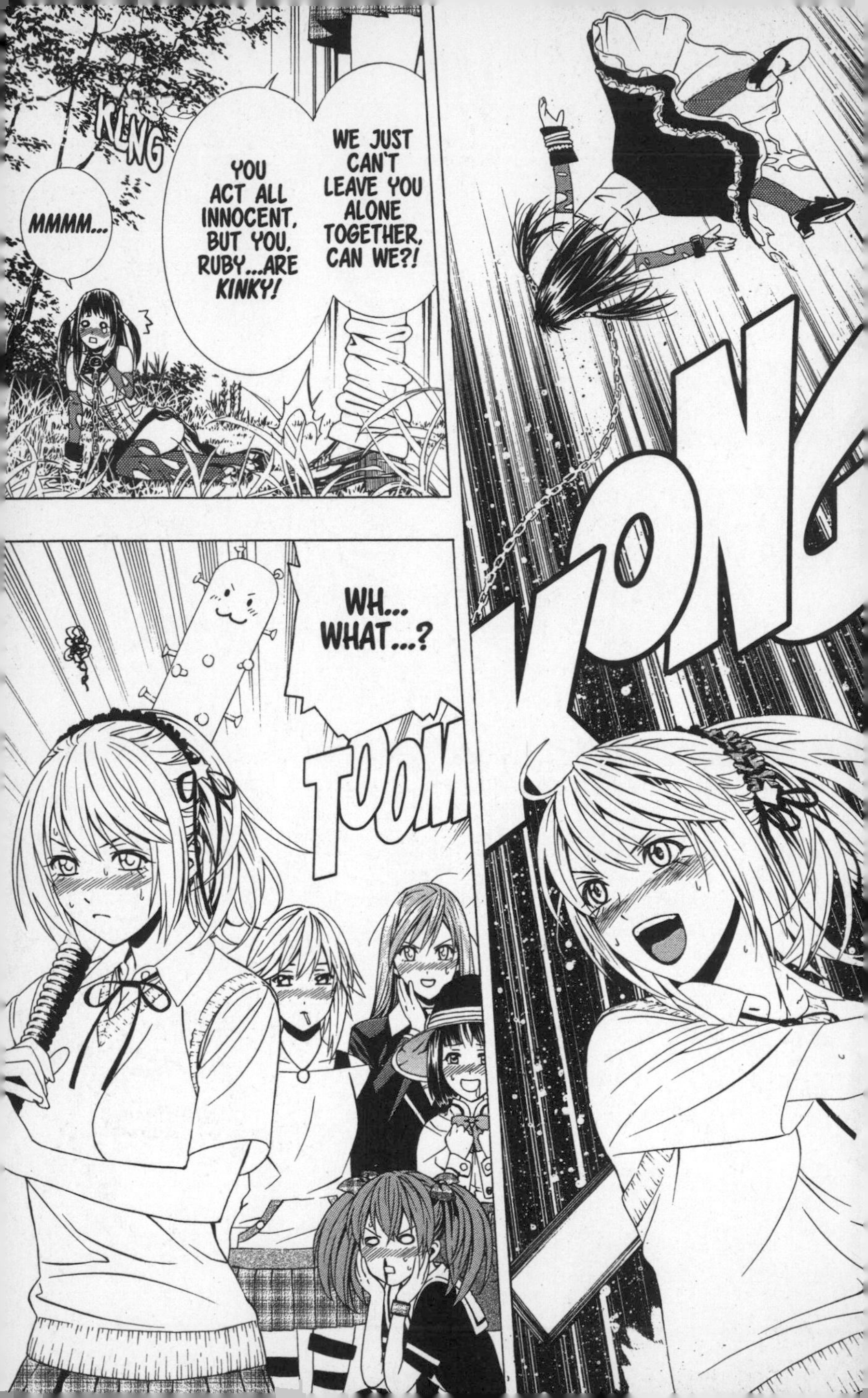
KONG
WE JUST CAN'T LEAVE YOU ALONE TOGETHER, CAN WE?!
YOU ACT ALL INNOCENT, BUT YOU, RUBY...ARE KINKY!
KLNG
MMMM...
WH... WHAT...?
TOOM

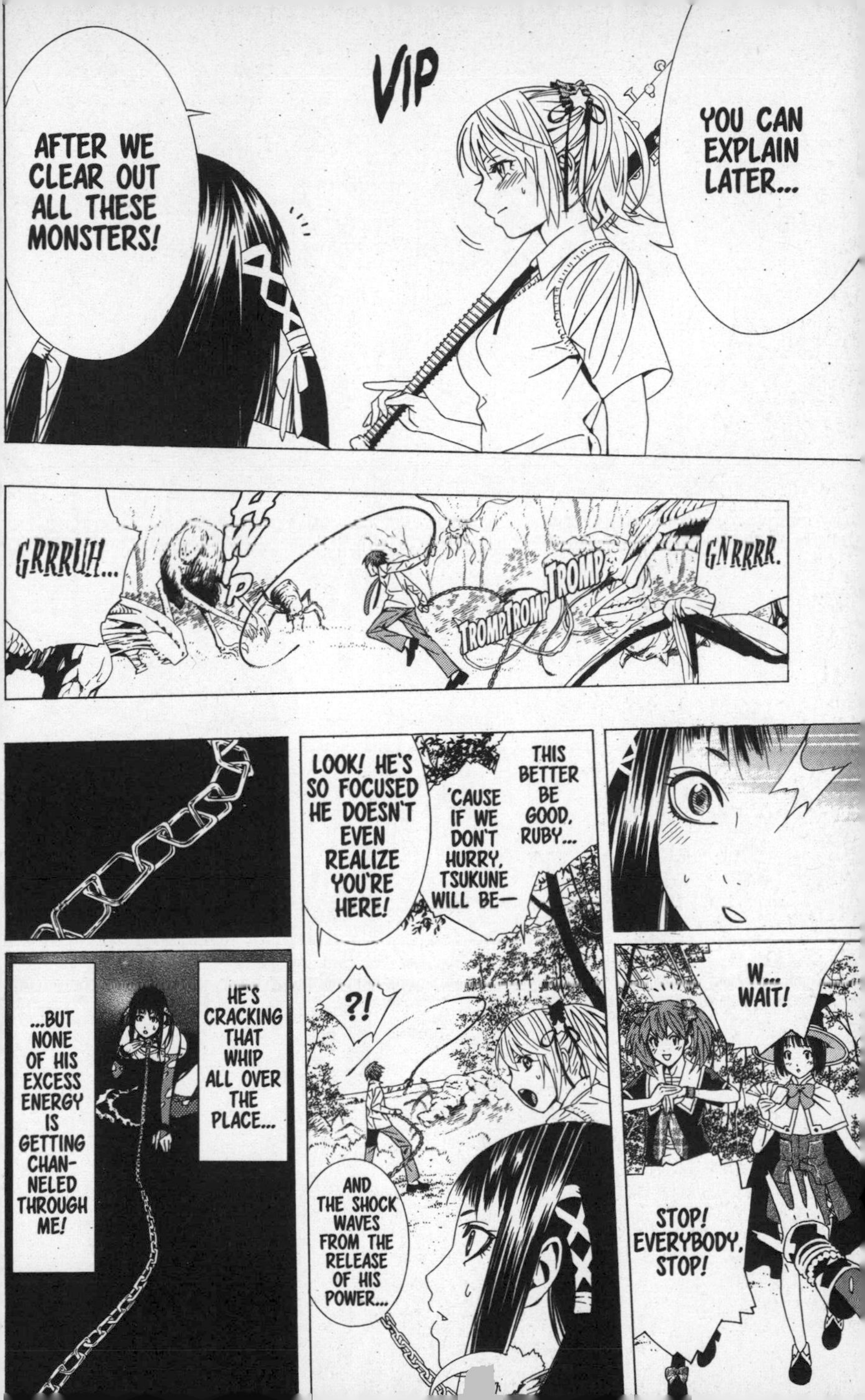
YOU CAN EXPLAIN LATER...
VIP
AFTER WE CLEAR OUT ALL THESE MONSTERS!
GNRRRR.
TROMP TROMP TROMP
GRRRUH...
W... WAIT!
STOP! EVERYBODY, STOP!
THIS BETTER BE GOOD, RUBY...
'CAUSE IF WE DON'T HURRY, TSUKUNE WILL BE—
LOOK! HE'S SO FOCUSED HE DOESN'T EVEN REALIZE YOU'RE HERE!
?!
AND THE SHOCK WAVES FROM THE RELEASE OF HIS POWER...
HE'S CRACKING THAT WHIP ALL OVER THE PLACE...
...BUT NONE OF HIS EXCESS ENERGY IS GETTING CHAN-NELED THROUGH ME!

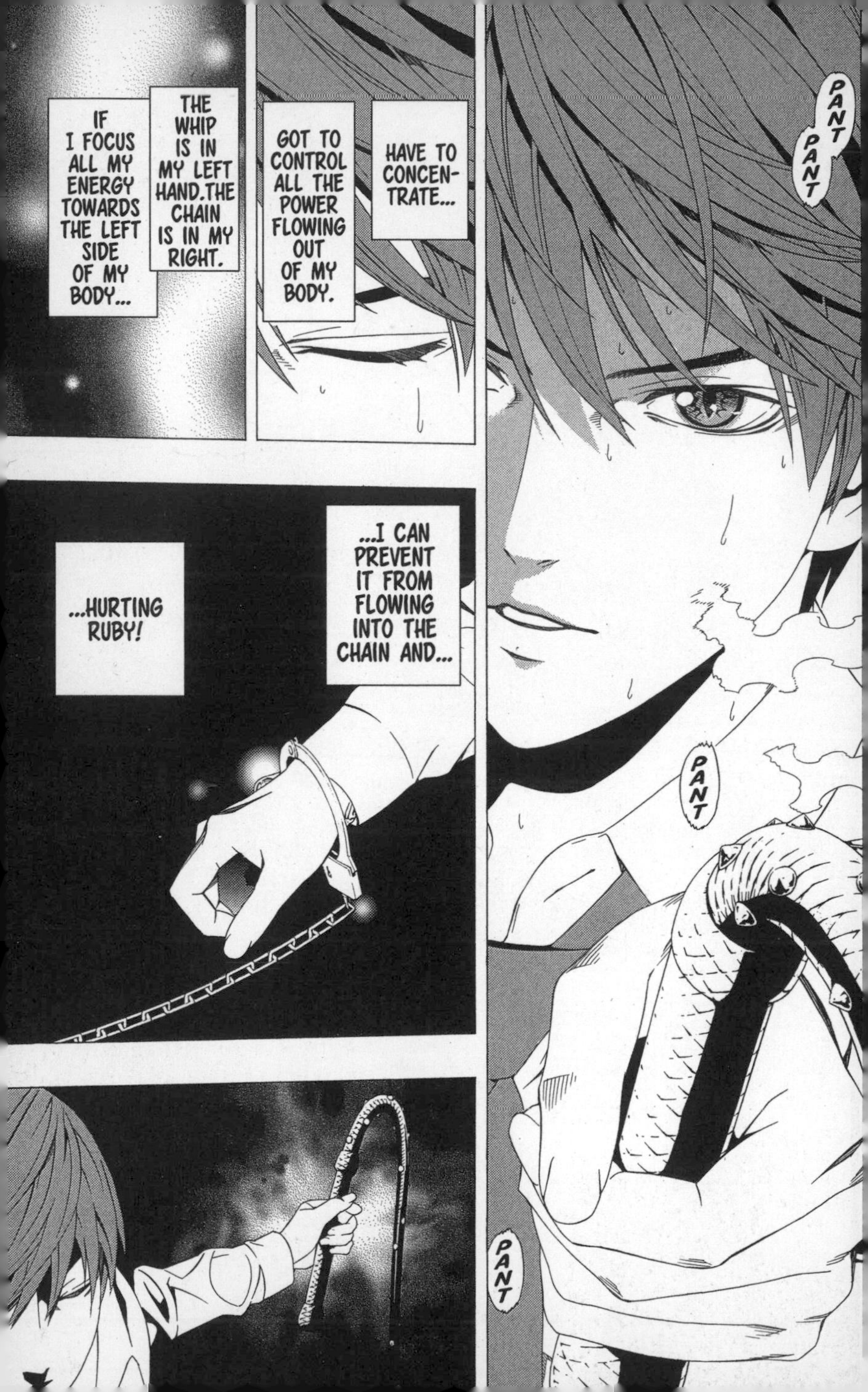
PANT PANT
PANT
PANT
HAVE TO CONCENTRATE...
GOT TO CONTROL ALL THE POWER FLOWING OUT OF MY BODY.
THE WHIP IS IN MY LEFT HAND. THE CHAIN IS IN MY RIGHT.
IF I FOCUS ALL MY ENERGY TOWARDS THE LEFT SIDE OF MY BODY...
...I CAN PREVENT IT FROM FLOWING INTO THE CHAIN AND...
...HURTING RUBY!

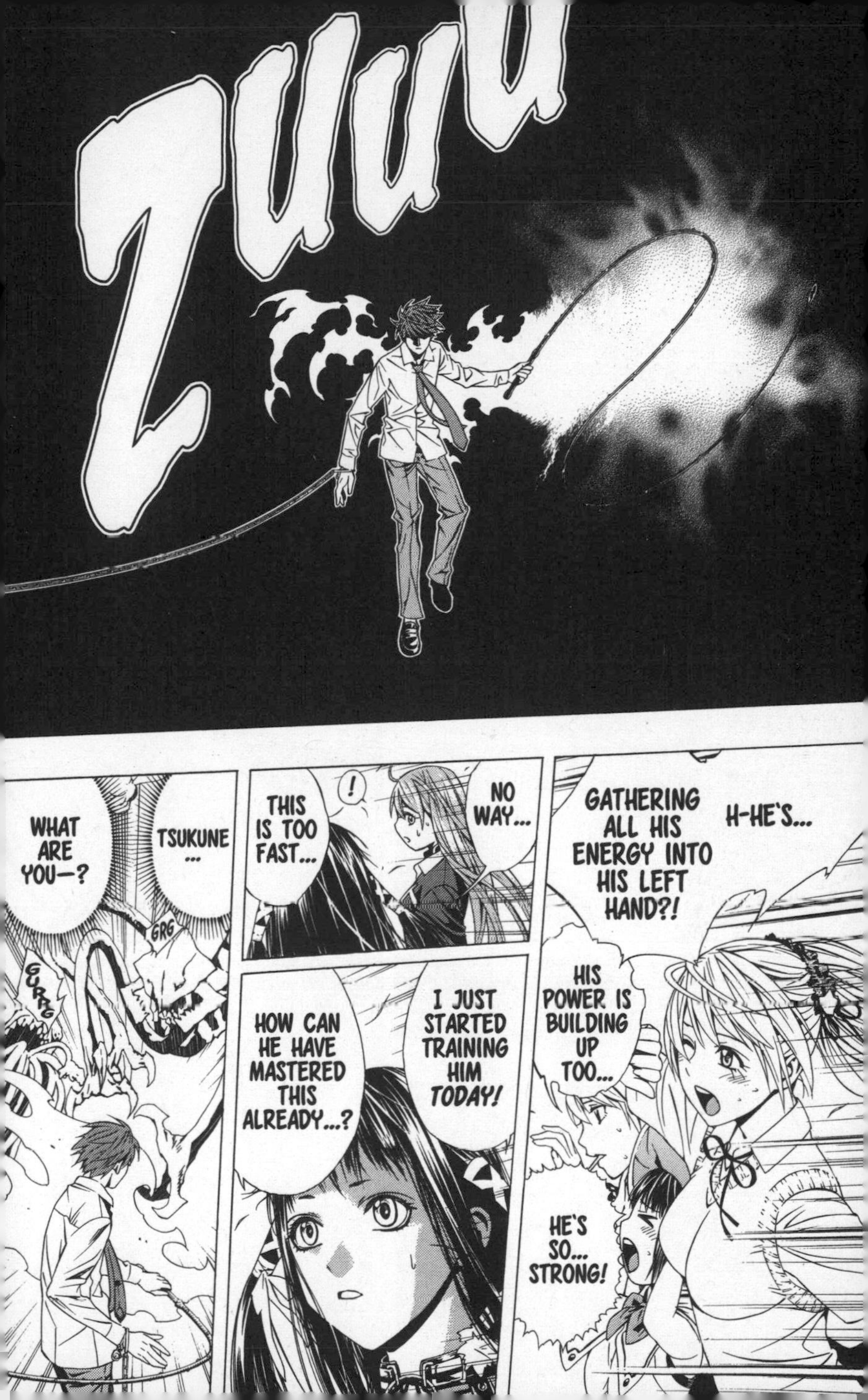
ZUUU
H-HE'S...
GATHERING ALL HIS ENERGY INTO HIS LEFT HAND?!
HIS POWER IS BUILDING UP TOO...
HE'S SO... STRONG!
NO WAY...
!
THIS IS TOO FAST...
I JUST STARTED TRAINING HIM *TODAY!*
HOW CAN HE HAVE MASTERED THIS ALREADY...?
TSUKUNE...
WHAT ARE YOU—?
GRG
GURRG

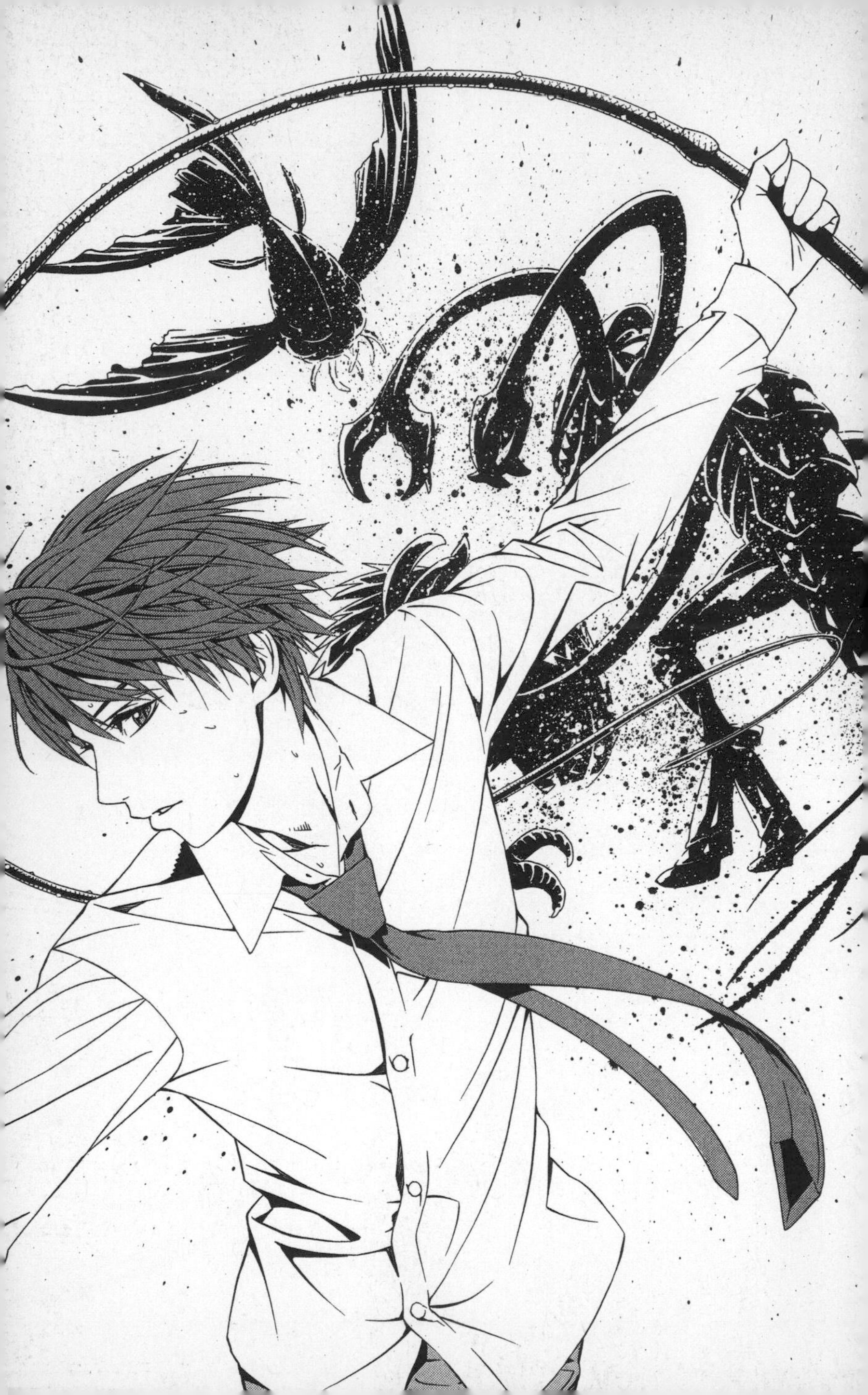

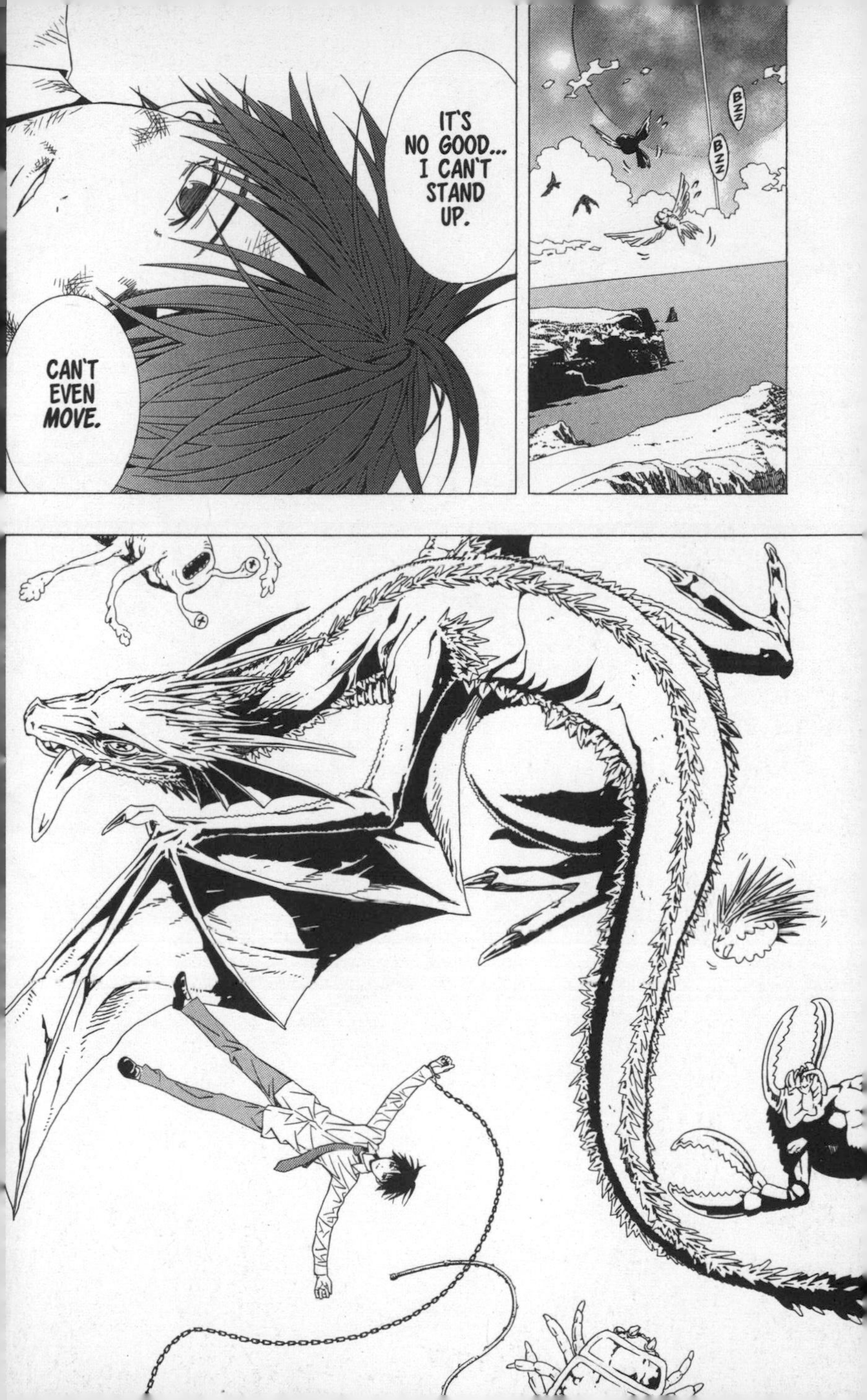
BZZ
BZZ
IT'S NO GOOD... I CAN'T STAND UP.
CAN'T EVEN MOVE.

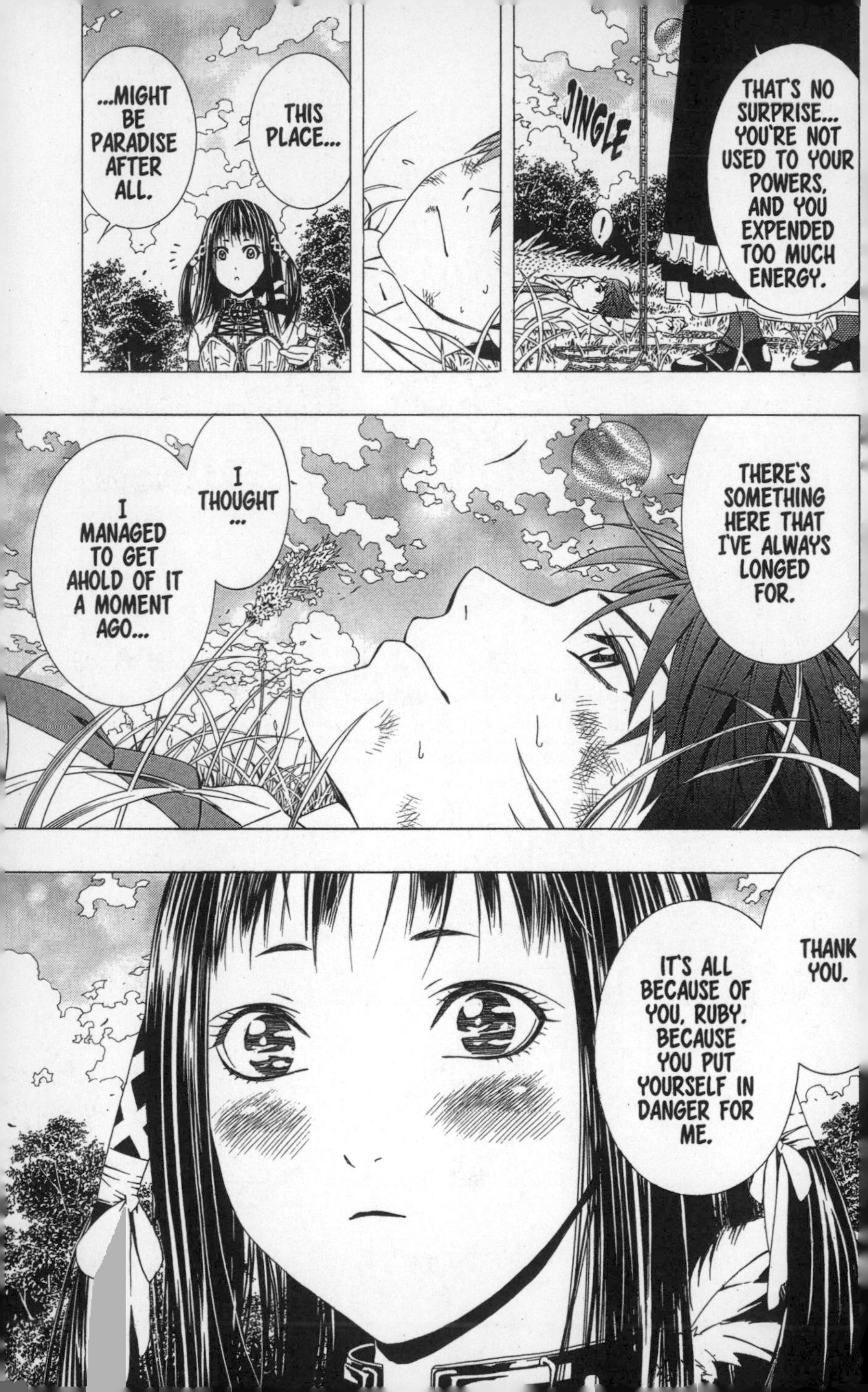
THAT'S NO SURPRISE... YOU'RE NOT USED TO YOUR POWERS, AND YOU EXPENDED TOO MUCH ENERGY.
JINGLE
!
THIS PLACE...
...MIGHT BE PARADISE AFTER ALL.
THERE'S SOMETHING HERE THAT I'VE ALWAYS LONGED FOR.
I THOUGHT...
I MANAGED TO GET AHOLD OF IT A MOMENT AGO...
THANK YOU.
IT'S ALL BECAUSE OF YOU, RUBY. BECAUSE YOU PUT YOURSELF IN DANGER FOR ME.

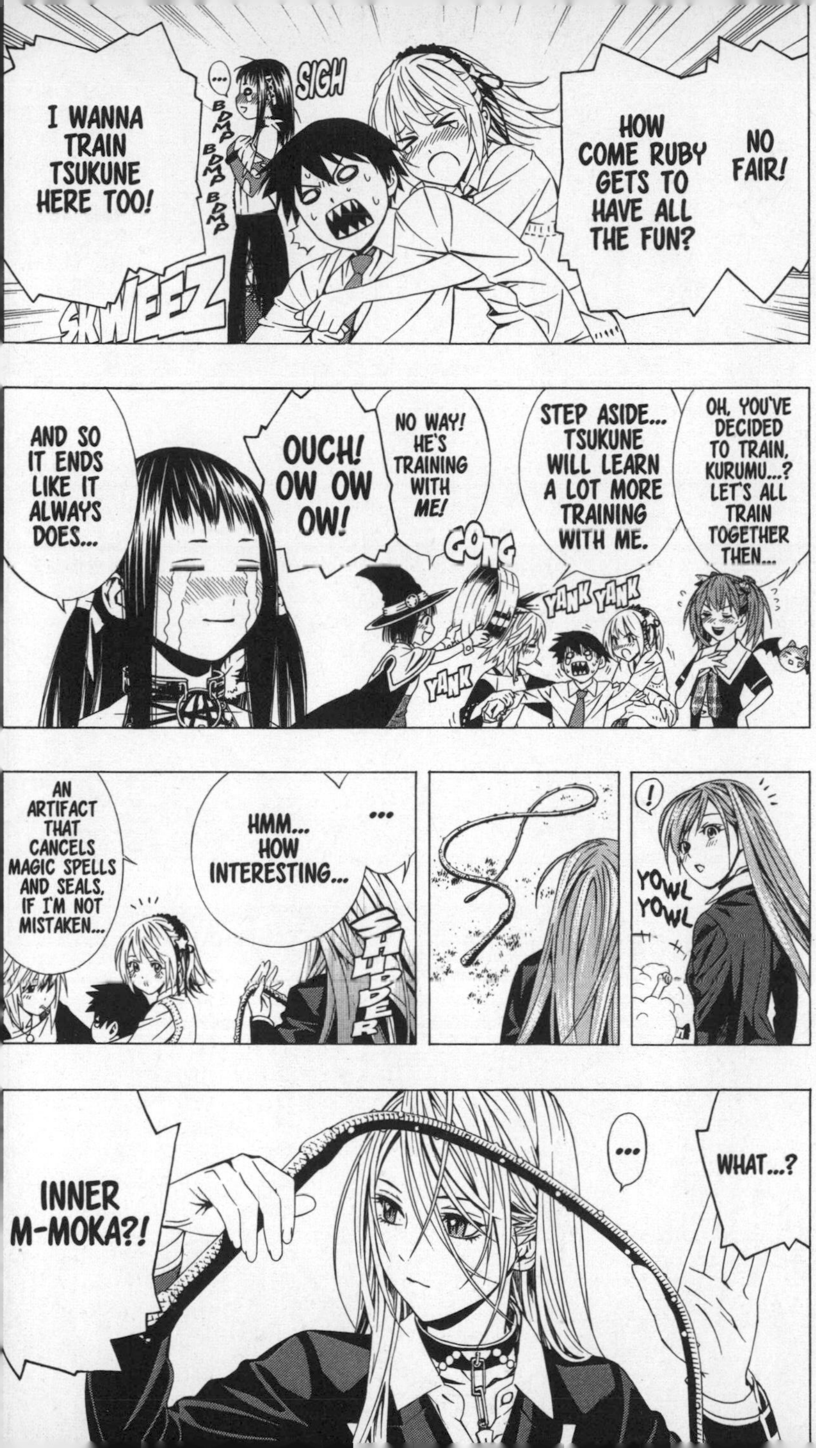
NO FAIR!
HOW COME RUBY GETS TO HAVE ALL THE FUN?
SIGH
...
BDMP BDMP BDMP
I WANNA TRAIN TSUKUNE HERE TOO!
SKWEEZ
OH, YOU'VE DECIDED TO TRAIN, KURUMU...? LET'S ALL TRAIN TOGETHER THEN...
STEP ASIDE... TSUKUNE WILL LEARN A LOT MORE TRAINING WITH ME.
NO WAY! HE'S TRAINING WITH ME!
YANK YANK
GONG
OUCH! OW OW OW!
YANK
AND SO IT ENDS LIKE IT ALWAYS DOES...
!
YOWL YOWL
...
HMM... HOW INTERESTING...
AN ARTIFACT THAT CANCELS MAGIC SPELLS AND SEALS, IF I'M NOT MISTAKEN...
SHUDDER
WHAT...?
...
INNER M-MOKA?!

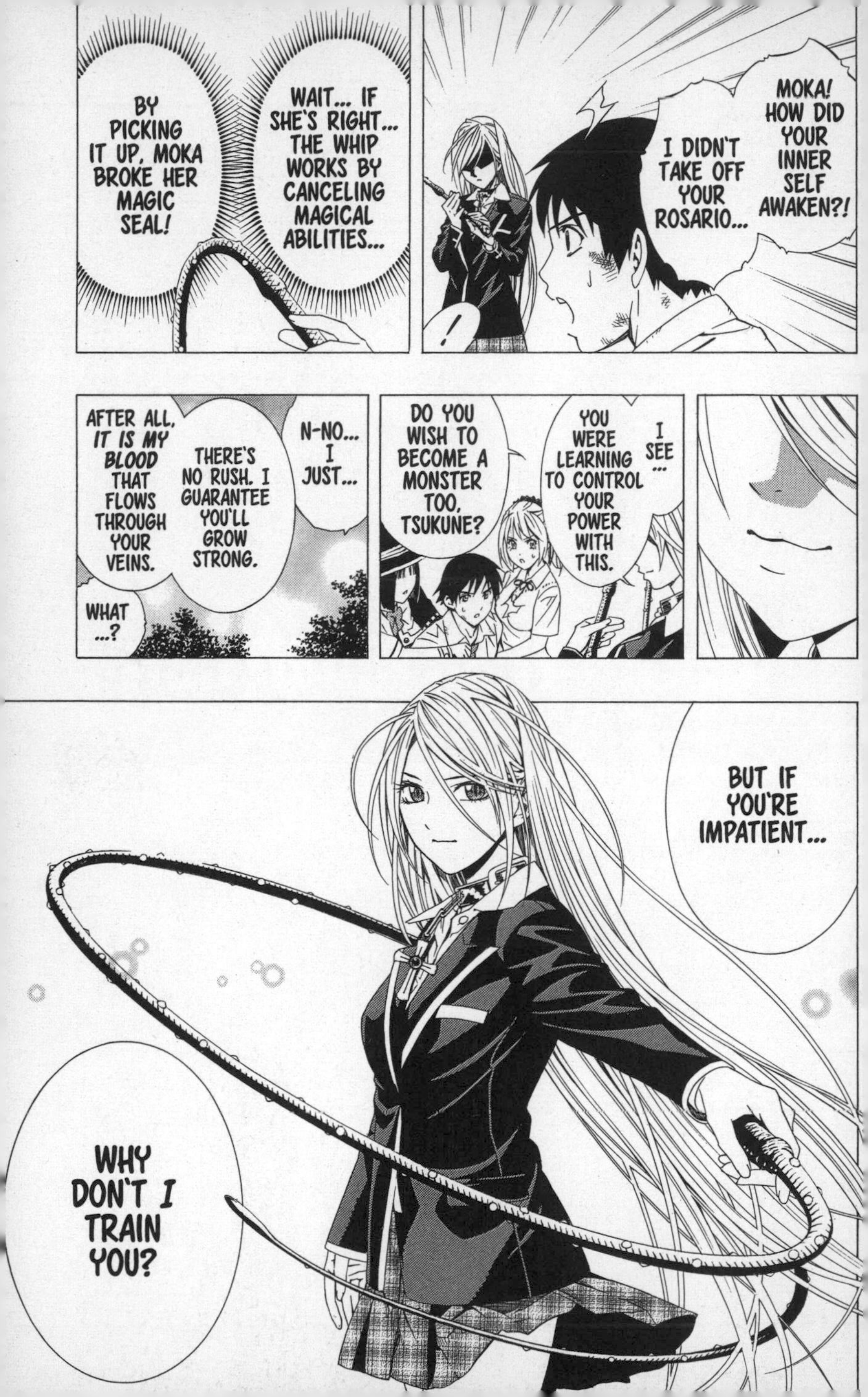
MOKA! HOW DID YOUR INNER SELF AWAKEN?!
I DIDN'T TAKE OFF YOUR ROSARIO...
!
WAIT... IF SHE'S RIGHT... THE WHIP WORKS BY CANCELING MAGICAL ABILITIES...
BY PICKING IT UP, MOKA BROKE HER MAGIC SEAL!
I SEE...
YOU WERE LEARNING TO CONTROL YOUR POWER WITH THIS.
DO YOU WISH TO BECOME A MONSTER TOO, TSUKUNE?
N-NO... I JUST...
THERE'S NO RUSH. I GUARANTEE YOU'LL GROW STRONG.
AFTER ALL, *IT IS MY BLOOD* THAT FLOWS THROUGH YOUR VEINS.
WHAT...?
BUT IF YOU'RE IMPATIENT...
WHY DON'T *I* TRAIN YOU?

16: The True Inner Self

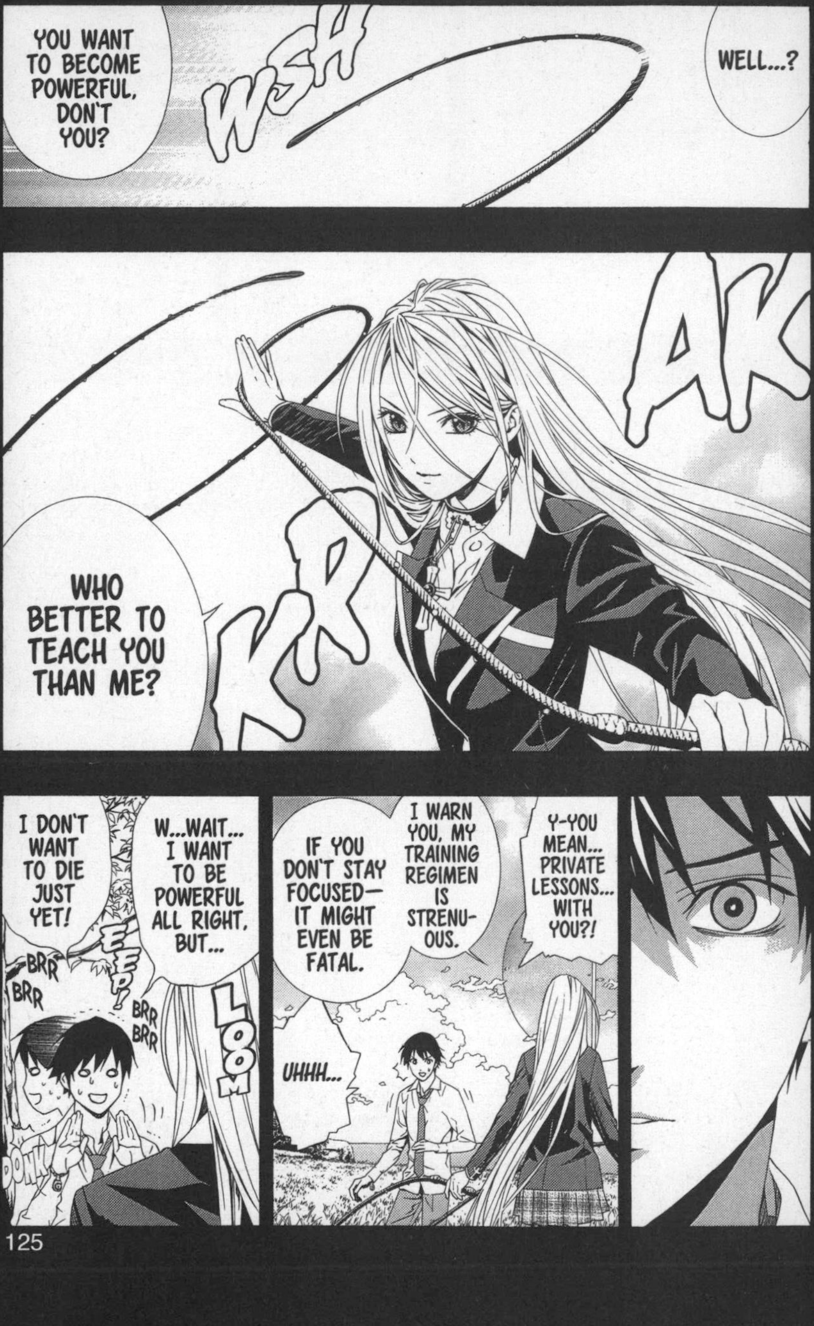

WELL...?
WSH
YOU WANT TO BECOME POWERFUL, DON'T YOU?
AK
KR
WHO BETTER TO TEACH YOU THAN ME?
Y-YOU MEAN... PRIVATE LESSONS... WITH YOU?!
I WARN YOU, MY TRAINING REGIMEN IS STRENU-OUS.
IF YOU DON'T STAY FOCUSED— IT MIGHT EVEN BE FATAL.
UHHH...
LOOM
W...WAIT... I WANT TO BE POWERFUL ALL RIGHT, BUT...
I DON'T WANT TO DIE JUST YET!
EEP!
BRR BRR
BRR BRR
DONK

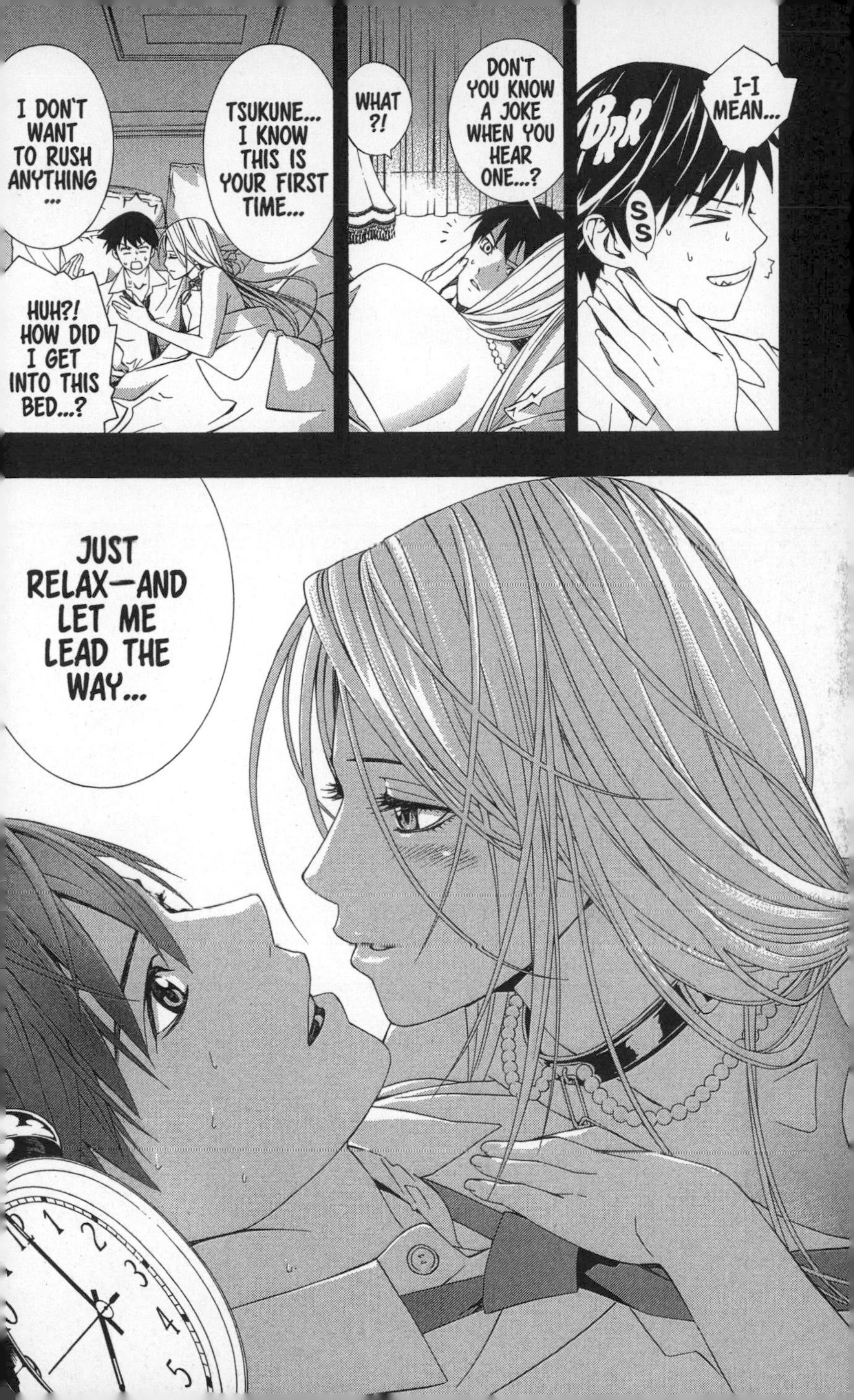
I-I MEAN...
BRR
SS
DON'T YOU KNOW A JOKE WHEN YOU HEAR ONE...?
WHAT ?!
TSUKUNE... I KNOW THIS IS YOUR FIRST TIME...
I DON'T WANT TO RUSH ANYTHING...
HUH?! HOW DID I GET INTO THIS BED...?
JUST RELAX—AND LET ME LEAD THE WAY...

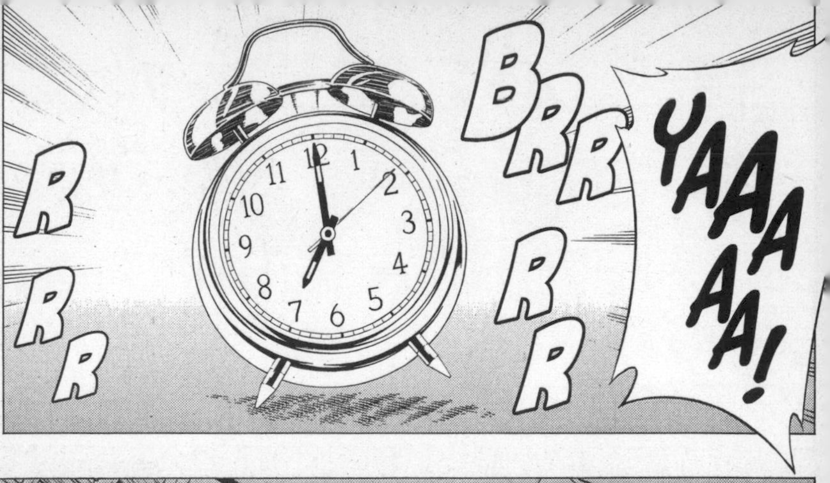
YAAAAA!
BRRRR
RRR
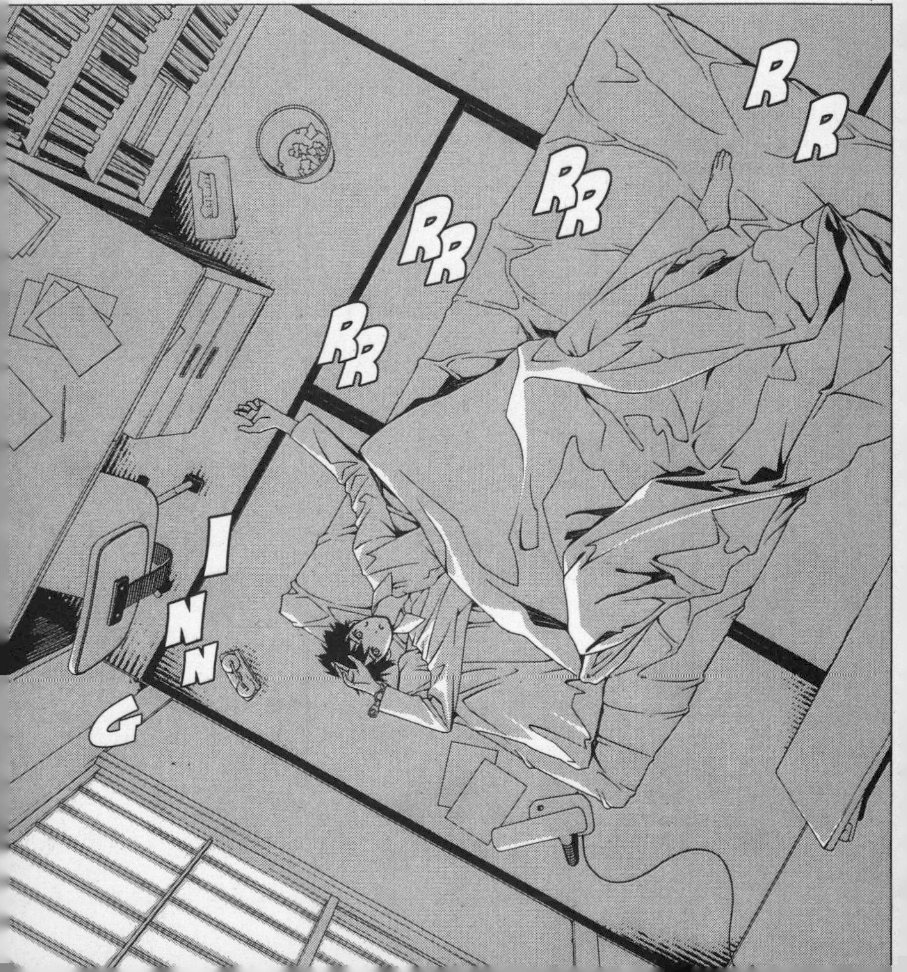
RR
RR
RR
RR
INNG

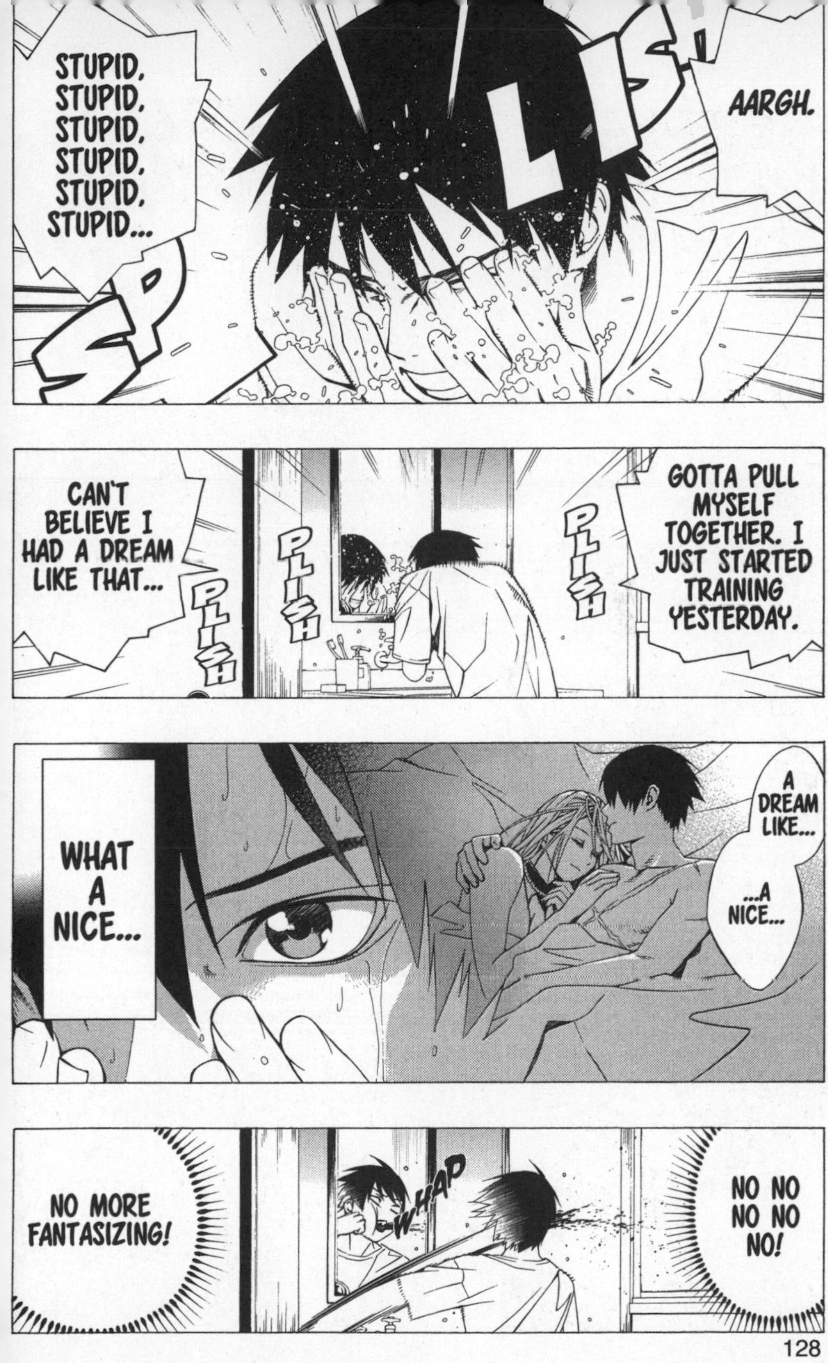
AARGH.
SPLISH
STUPID, STUPID, STUPID, STUPID, STUPID, STUPID...
GOTTA PULL MYSELF TOGETHER. I JUST STARTED TRAINING YESTERDAY.
PLISH
PLISH
PLISH
CAN'T BELIEVE I HAD A DREAM LIKE THAT...
A DREAM LIKE...
...A NICE...
WHAT A NICE...
NO NO NO NO NO!
WHAP
NO MORE FANTASIZING!

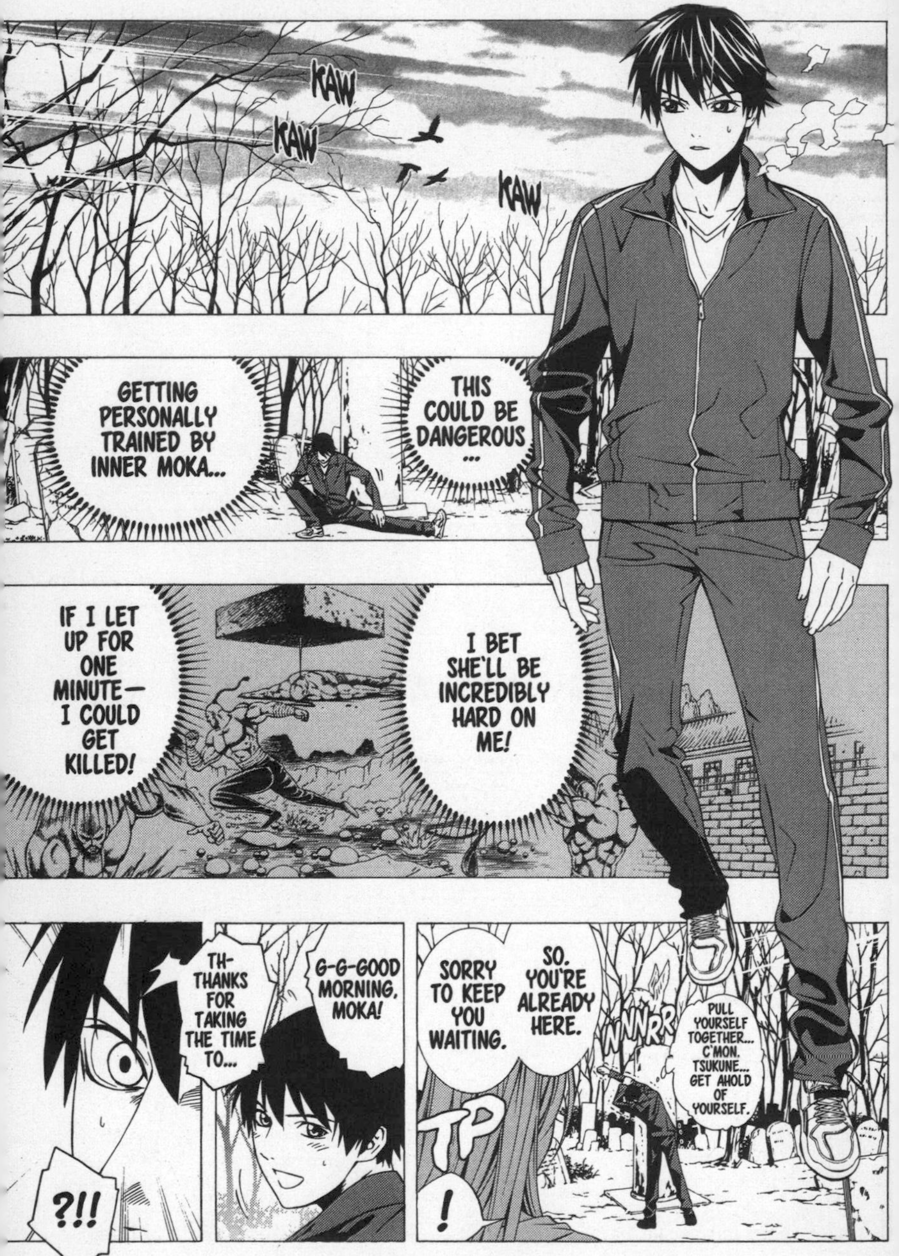
KAW
KAW
KAW
THIS COULD BE DANGEROUS...
GETTING PERSONALLY TRAINED BY INNER MOKA...
I BET SHE'LL BE INCREDIBLY HARD ON ME!
IF I LET UP FOR ONE MINUTE— I COULD GET KILLED!
PULL YOURSELF TOGETHER... C'MON, TSUKUNE... GET AHOLD OF YOURSELF.
NNNRR
SO. YOU'RE ALREADY HERE.
SORRY TO KEEP YOU WAITING.
TP
!
G-G-GOOD MORNING, MOKA!
TH-THANKS FOR TAKING THE TIME TO...
?!!

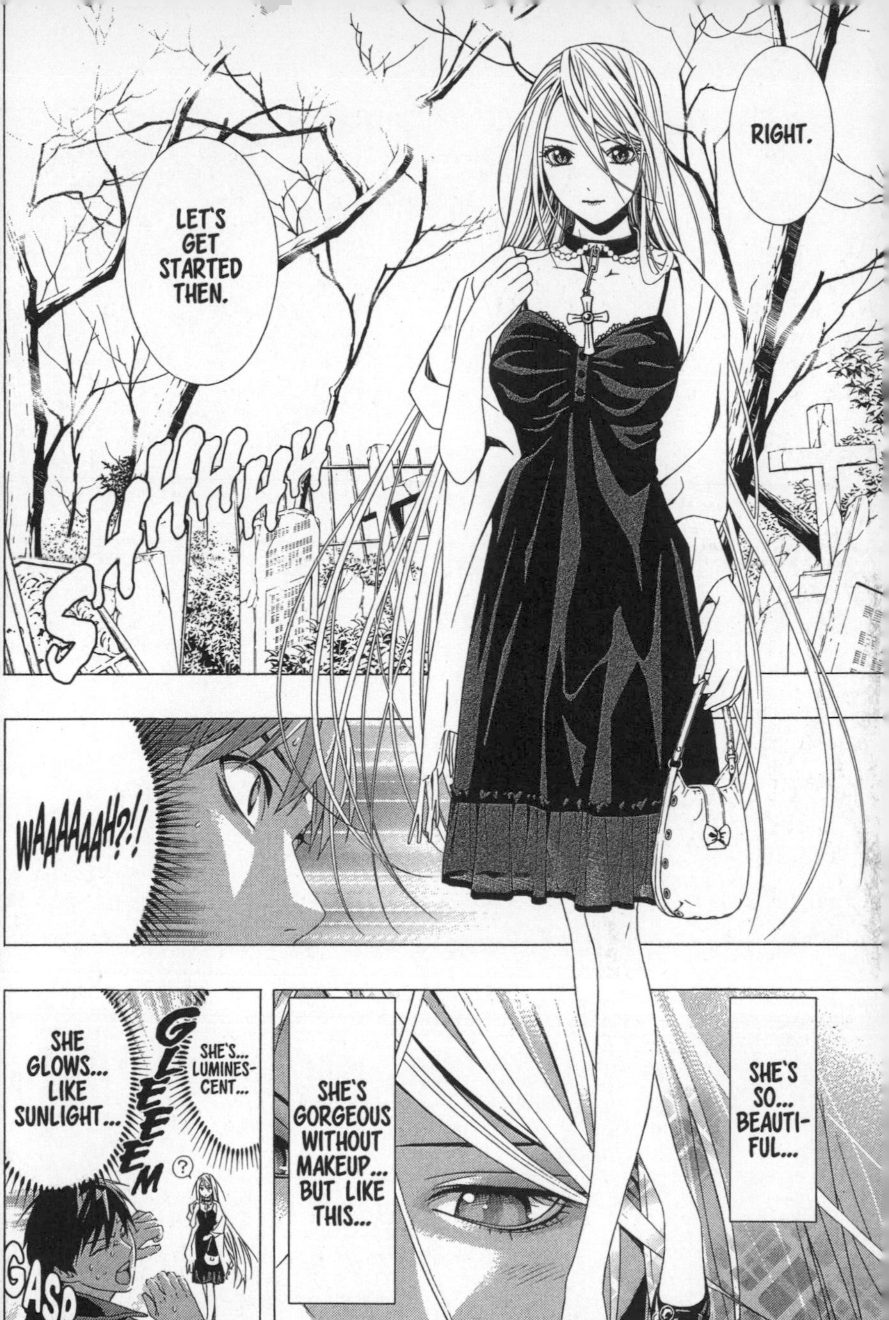
RIGHT.
LET'S GET STARTED THEN.
SHHHHH
WAAAAAAH?!!
SHE'S SO... BEAUTIFUL...
SHE'S GORGEOUS WITHOUT MAKEUP... BUT LIKE THIS...
SHE'S... LUMINESCENT...
GLEEEEM
SHE GLOWS... LIKE SUNLIGHT...
?
GASP

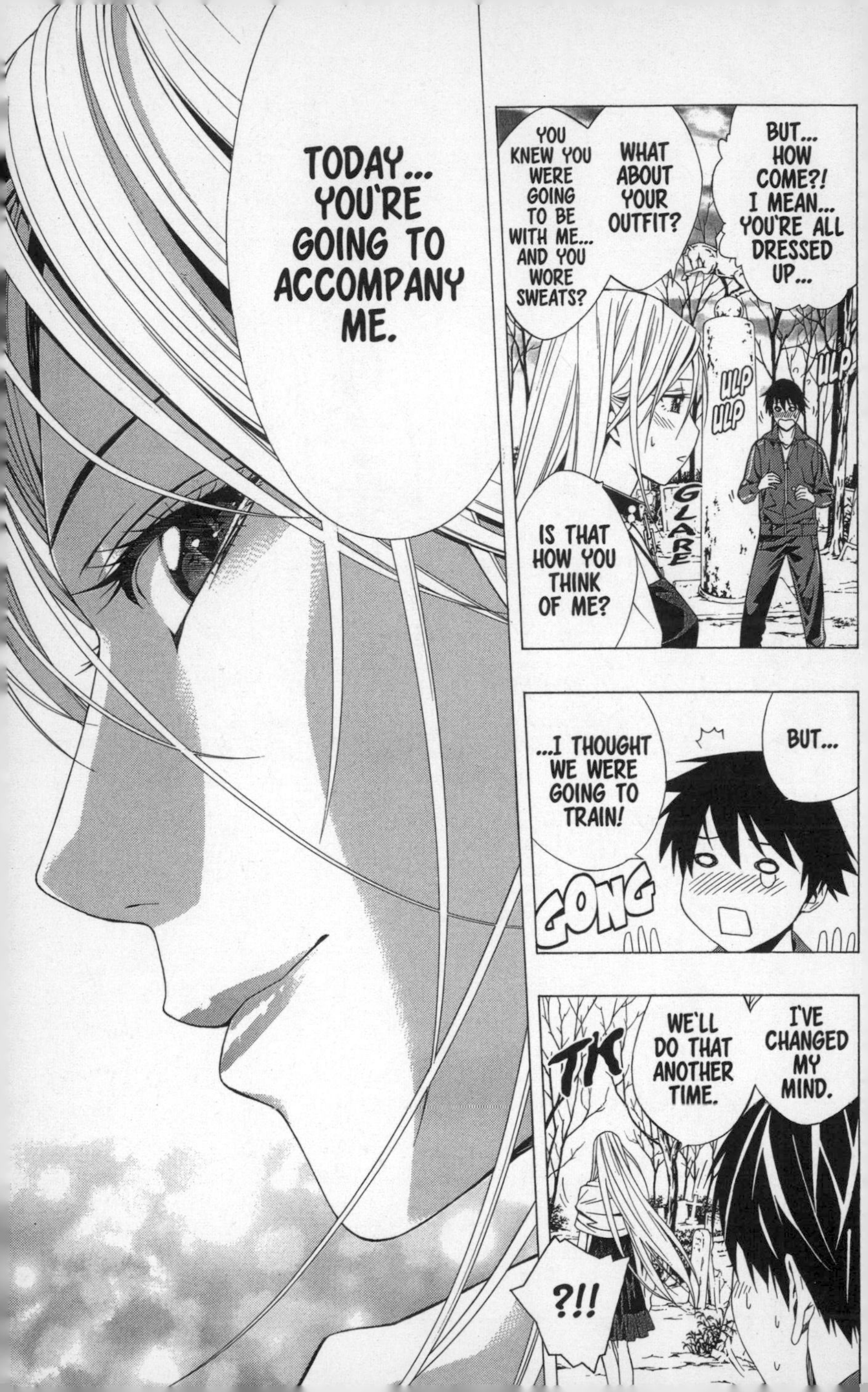
BUT... HOW COME?! I MEAN... YOU'RE ALL DRESSED UP...
ULP
ULP ULP
WHAT ABOUT YOUR OUTFIT?
YOU KNEW YOU WERE GOING TO BE WITH ME... AND YOU WORE SWEATS?
GLARE
IS THAT HOW YOU THINK OF ME?
BUT...
...I THOUGHT WE WERE GOING TO TRAIN!
GONG
I'VE CHANGED MY MIND.
WE'LL DO THAT ANOTHER TIME.
TK
?!!
TODAY... YOU'RE GOING TO ACCOMPANY ME.

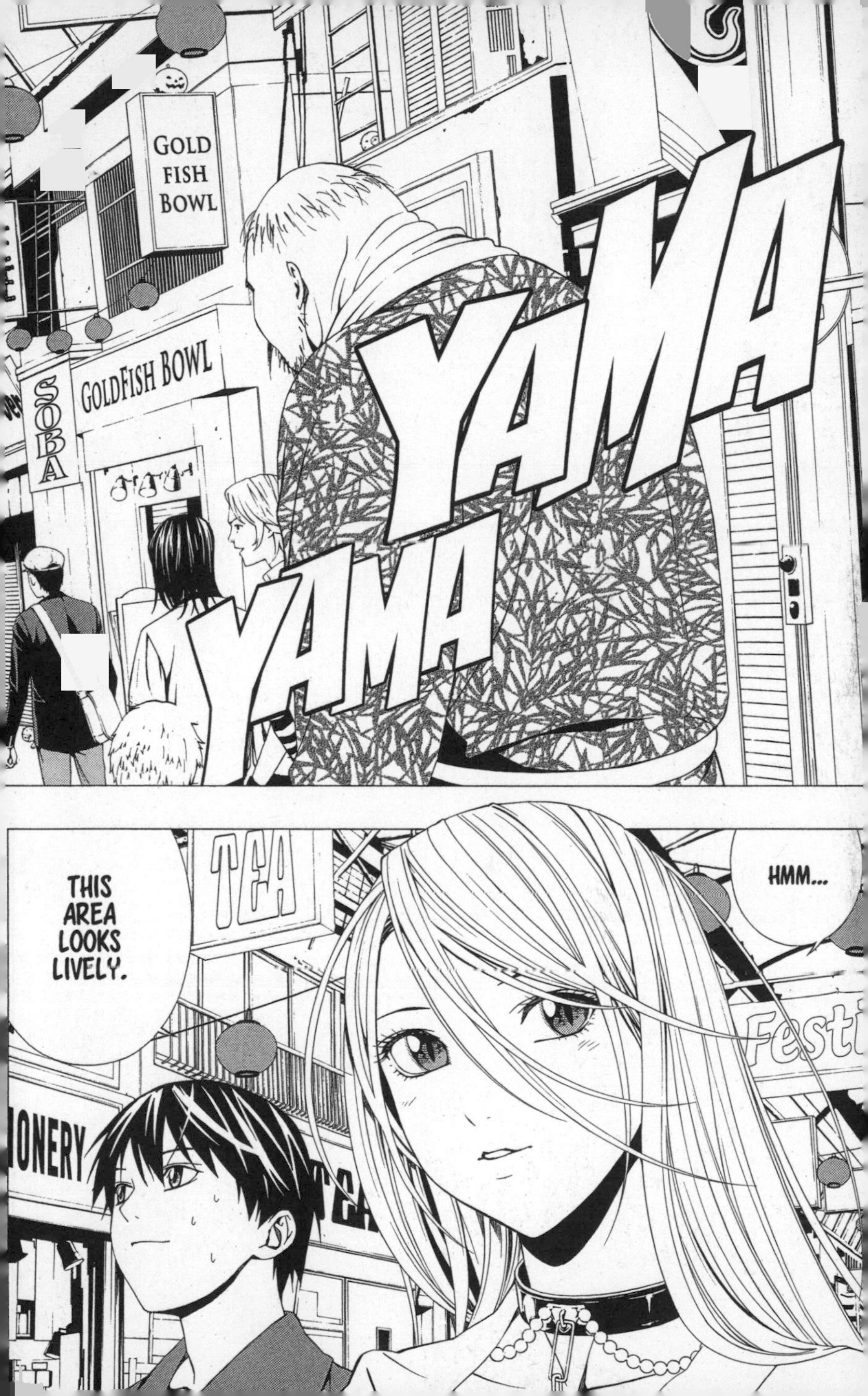
GOLD FISH BOWL
GOLDFISH BOWL
SOBA
YAMA
YAMA
TEA
HMM...
THIS AREA LOOKS LIVELY.

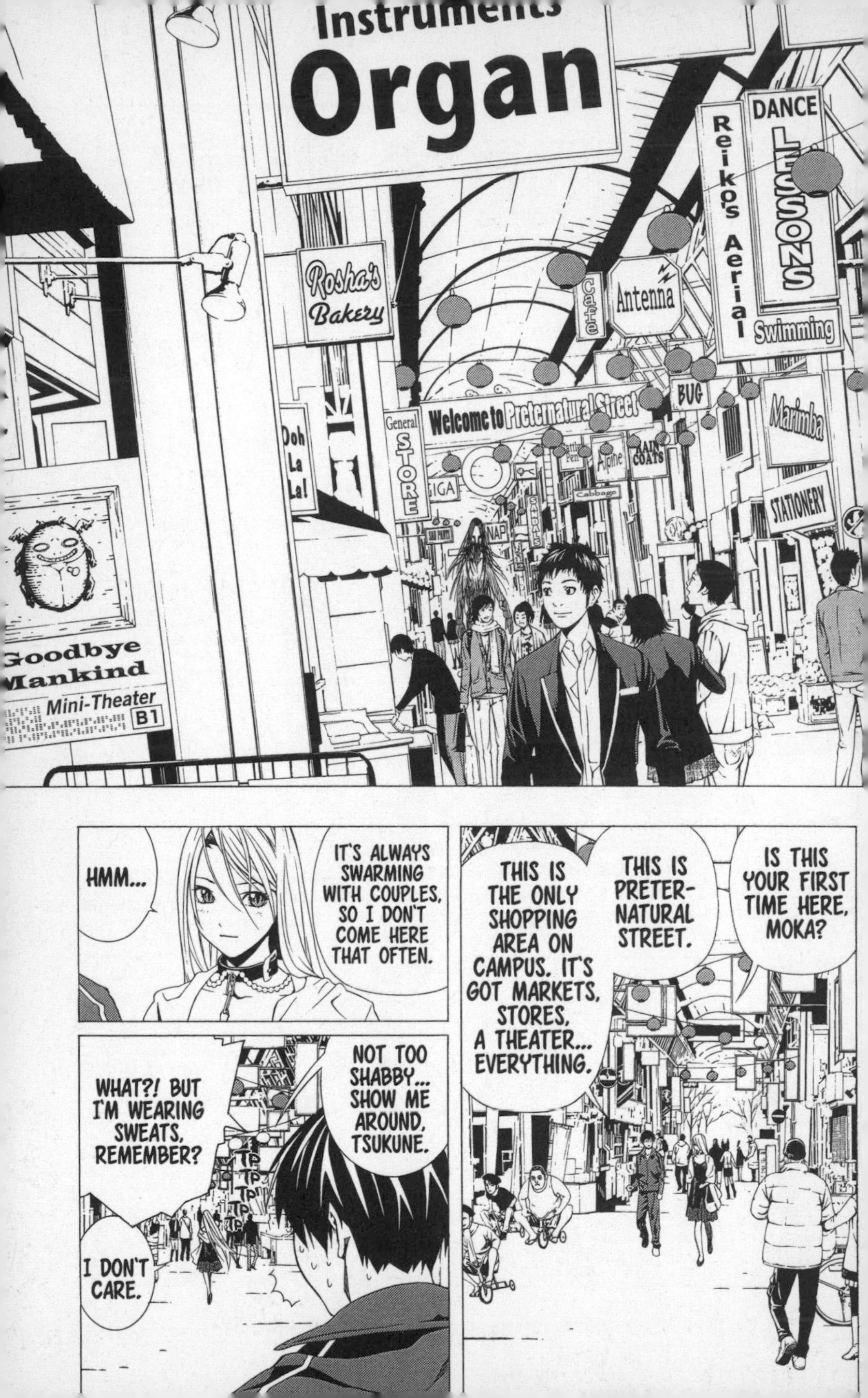
Instruments
Organ
DANCE
LESSONS
Reiko's Aerial
Swimming
Antenna
Cafe
Rosha's Bakery
BUG
Marimba
Welcome to Preternatural Street
General STORE
Doh La La!
GIGA
RAIN COATS
Alpine
Cabbage
SANDALS
NAP
STATIONERY
Goodbye Mankind
Mini-Theater
B1
IS THIS YOUR FIRST TIME HERE, MOKA?
THIS IS PRETER-NATURAL STREET.
THIS IS THE ONLY SHOPPING AREA ON CAMPUS. IT'S GOT MARKETS, STORES, A THEATER... EVERYTHING.
IT'S ALWAYS SWARMING WITH COUPLES, SO I DON'T COME HERE THAT OFTEN.
HMM...
NOT TOO SHABBY... SHOW ME AROUND, TSUKUNE.
WHAT?! BUT I'M WEARING SWEATS, REMEMBER?
TP TP TP TP
I DON'T CARE.

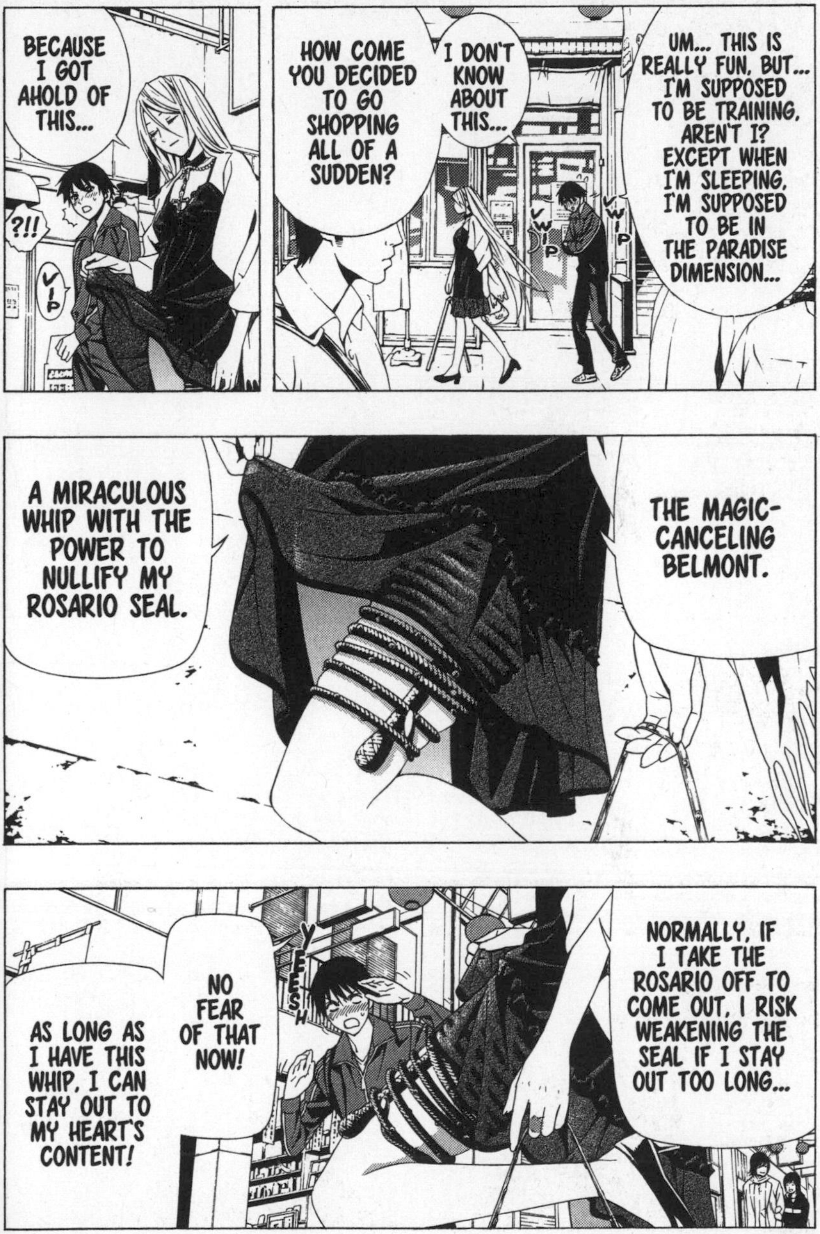
UM... THIS IS REALLY FUN, BUT... I'M SUPPOSED TO BE TRAINING, AREN'T I? EXCEPT WHEN I'M SLEEPING, I'M SUPPOSED TO BE IN THE PARADISE DIMENSION...
VWIP
VWIP
VWIP
I DON'T KNOW ABOUT THIS...
HOW COME YOU DECIDED TO GO SHOPPING ALL OF A SUDDEN?
BECAUSE I GOT AHOLD OF THIS...
?!!
VIP
THE MAGIC-CANCELING BELMONT.
A MIRACULOUS WHIP WITH THE POWER TO NULLIFY MY ROSARIO SEAL.
NORMALLY, IF I TAKE THE ROSARIO OFF TO COME OUT, I RISK WEAKENING THE SEAL IF I STAY OUT TOO LONG...
YEESH
NO FEAR OF THAT NOW!
AS LONG AS I HAVE THIS WHIP, I CAN STAY OUT TO MY HEART'S CONTENT!

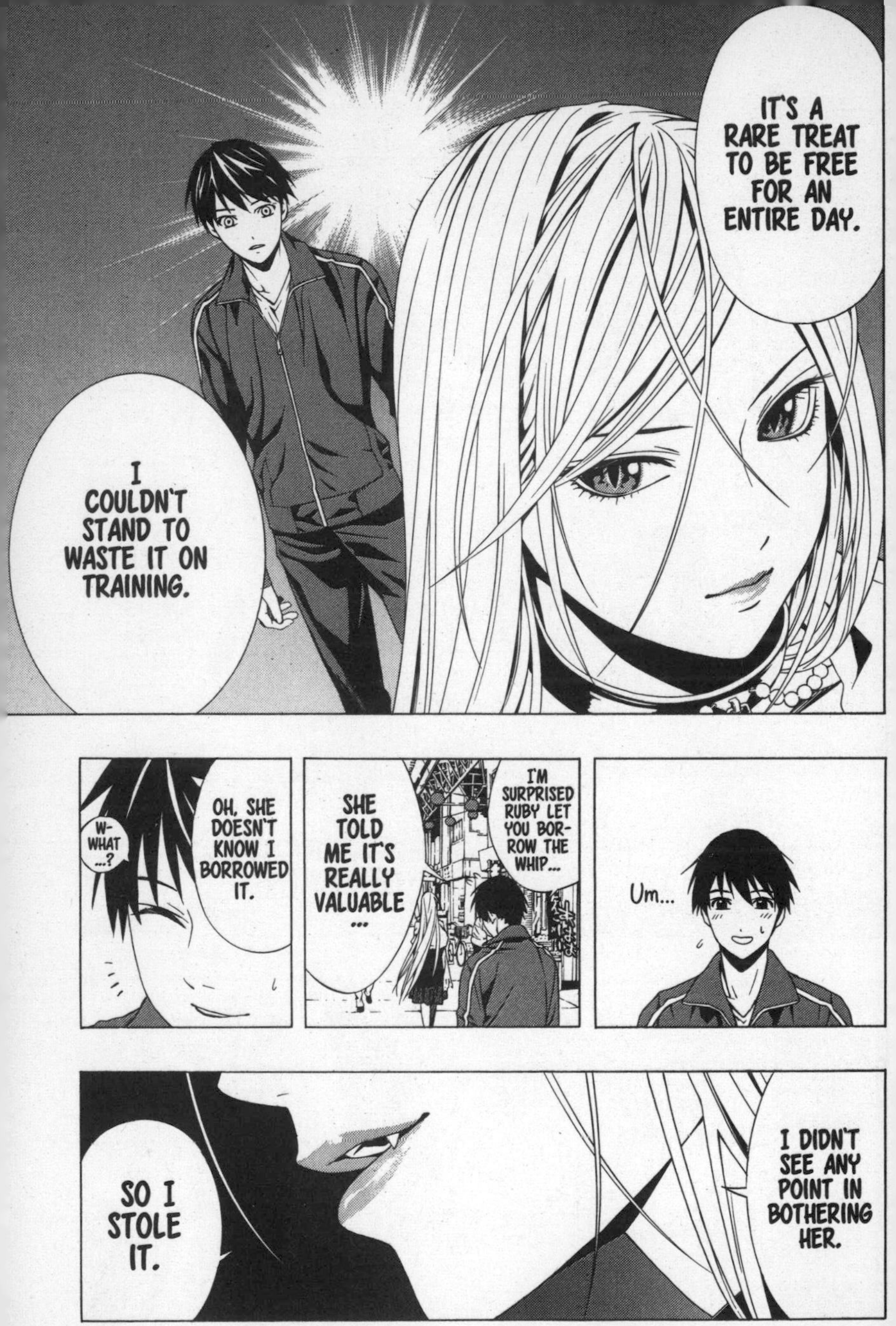
IT'S A RARE TREAT TO BE FREE FOR AN ENTIRE DAY.
I COULDN'T STAND TO WASTE IT ON TRAINING.
Um...
I'M SURPRISED RUBY LET YOU BOR-ROW THE WHIP...
SHE TOLD ME IT'S REALLY VALUABLE...
OH, SHE DOESN'T KNOW I BORROWED IT.
W-WHAT...?
I DIDN'T SEE ANY POINT IN BOTHERING HER.
SO I STOLE IT.

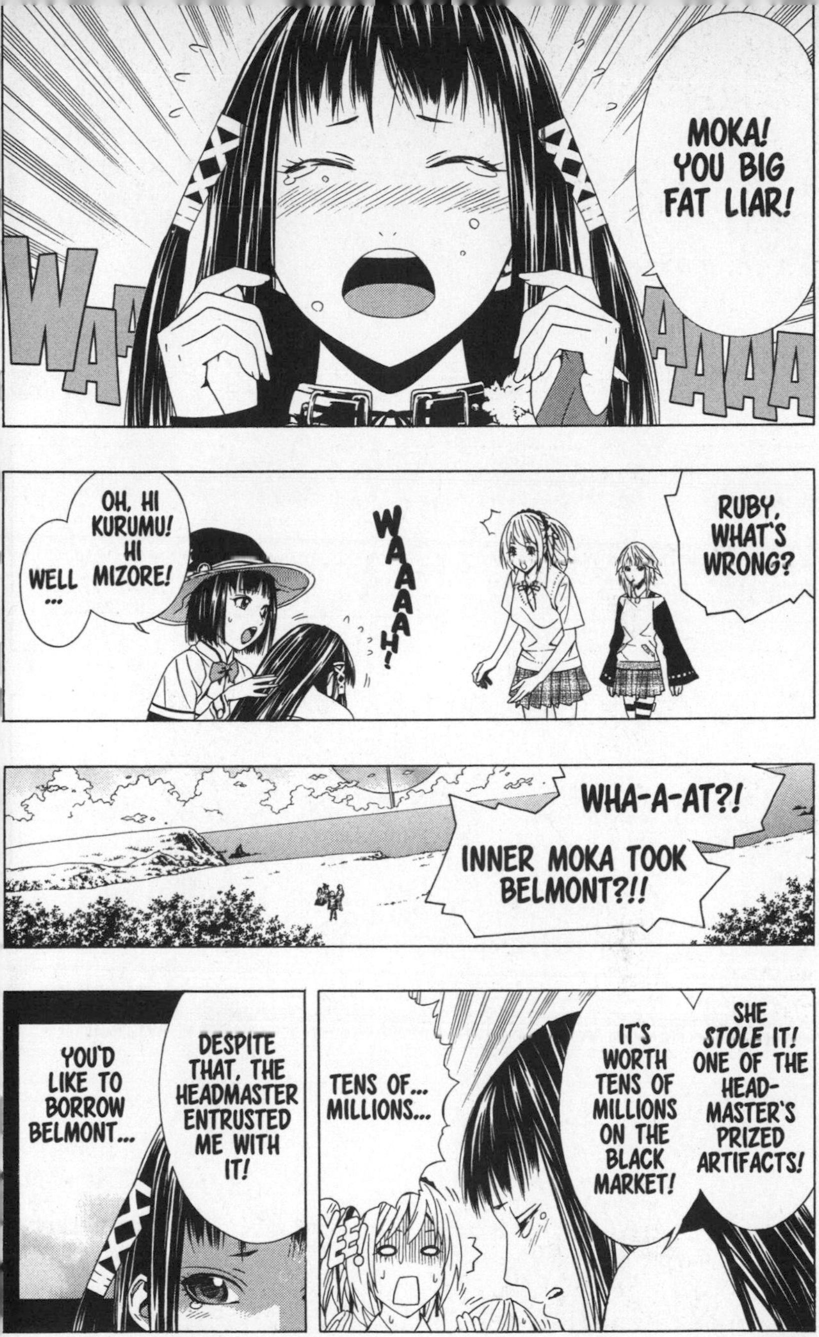
MOKA! YOU BIG FAT LIAR!
WAA
AAAA
RUBY, WHAT'S WRONG?
WAAAAAH!
OH, HI KURUMU! HI MIZORE!
WELL ...
WHA-A-AT?!
INNER MOKA TOOK BELMONT?!!
SHE *STOLE* IT! ONE OF THE HEAD-MASTER'S PRIZED ARTIFACTS!
IT'S WORTH TENS OF MILLIONS ON THE BLACK MARKET!
TENS OF... MILLIONS...
YEE!
DESPITE THAT, THE HEADMASTER ENTRUSTED ME WITH IT!
YOU'D LIKE TO BORROW BELMONT...

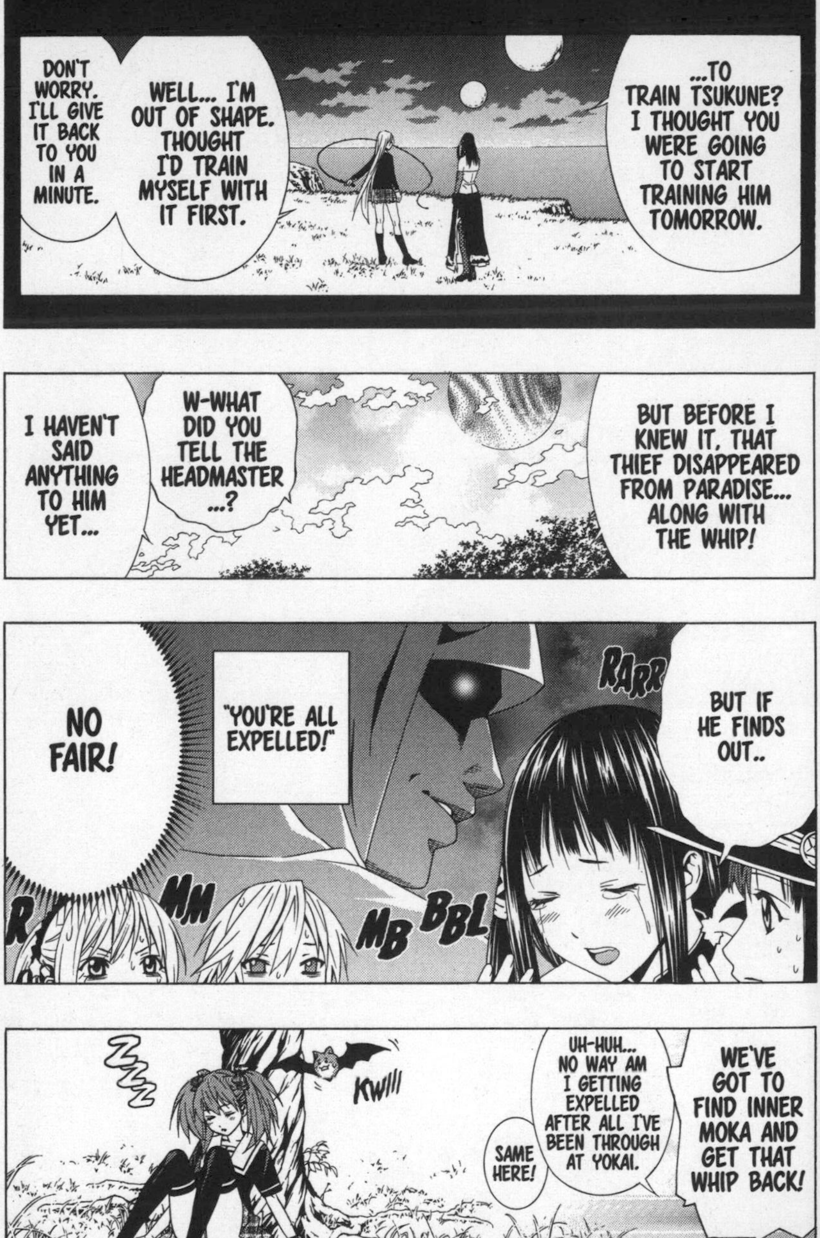
...TO TRAIN TSUKUNE? I THOUGHT YOU WERE GOING TO START TRAINING HIM TOMORROW.
WELL... I'M OUT OF SHAPE. THOUGHT I'D TRAIN MYSELF WITH IT FIRST.
DON'T WORRY. I'LL GIVE IT BACK TO YOU IN A MINUTE.
BUT BEFORE I KNEW IT, THAT THIEF DISAPPEARED FROM PARADISE... ALONG WITH THE WHIP!
W-WHAT DID YOU TELL THE HEADMASTER ...?
I HAVEN'T SAID ANYTHING TO HIM YET...
BUT IF HE FINDS OUT..
RARR
"YOU'RE ALL EXPELLED!"
NO FAIR!
R MM MB BBL
WE'VE GOT TO FIND INNER MOKA AND GET THAT WHIP BACK!
UH-HUH... NO WAY AM I GETTING EXPELLED AFTER ALL I'VE BEEN THROUGH AT YOKAI.
SAME HERE!
KWIII
ZZZ

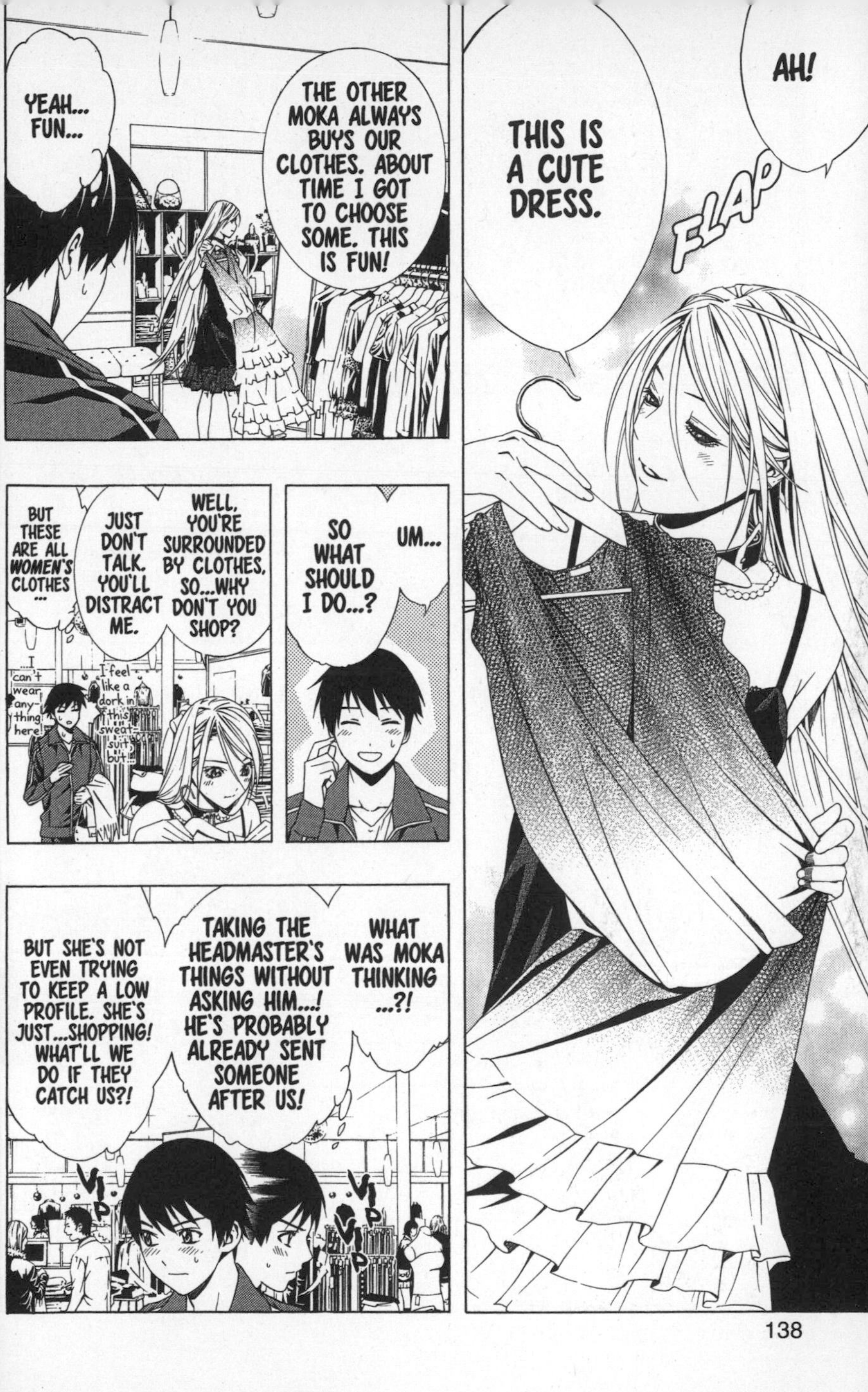
AH!
FLAP
THIS IS A CUTE DRESS.
THE OTHER MOKA ALWAYS BUYS OUR CLOTHES. ABOUT TIME I GOT TO CHOOSE SOME. THIS IS FUN!
YEAH... FUN...
UM...
SO WHAT SHOULD I DO...?
WELL, YOU'RE SURROUNDED BY CLOTHES, SO...WHY DON'T YOU SHOP?
JUST DON'T TALK. YOU'LL DISTRACT ME.
BUT THESE ARE ALL *WOMEN'S* CLOTHES...
I feel like a dork in this sweat-suit but...
...I can't wear anything here!
WHAT WAS MOKA THINKING...?!
TAKING THE HEADMASTER'S THINGS WITHOUT ASKING HIM...! HE'S PROBABLY ALREADY SENT SOMEONE AFTER US!
BUT SHE'S NOT EVEN TRYING TO KEEP A LOW PROFILE. SHE'S JUST...SHOPPING! WHAT'LL WE DO IF THEY CATCH US?!
VIP
VIP
VIP

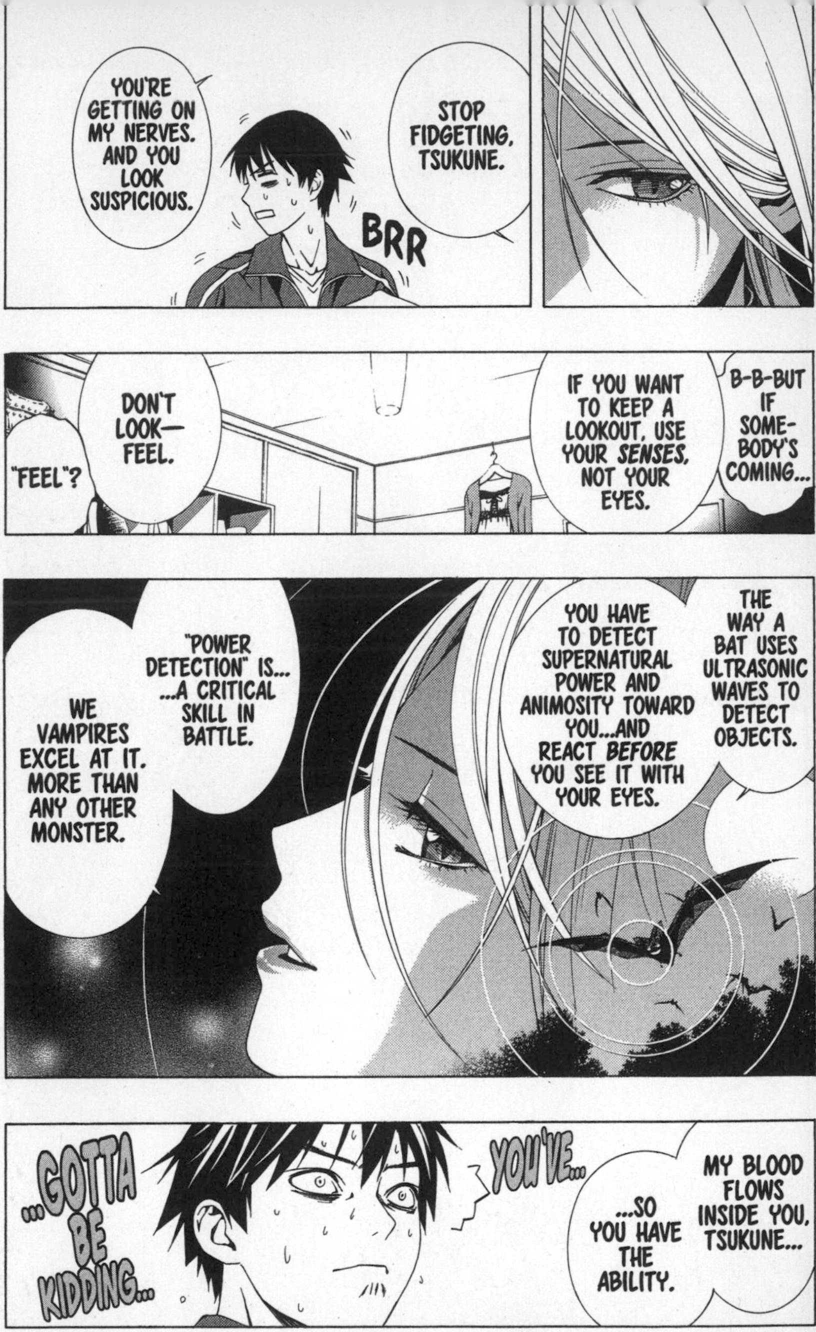
STOP FIDGETING, TSUKUNE.
YOU'RE GETTING ON MY NERVES. AND YOU LOOK SUSPICIOUS.
BRR
B-B-BUT IF SOMEBODY'S COMING...
IF YOU WANT TO KEEP A LOOKOUT, USE YOUR *SENSES*, NOT YOUR EYES.
DON'T LOOK—FEEL.
"FEEL"?
THE WAY A BAT USES ULTRASONIC WAVES TO DETECT OBJECTS.
YOU HAVE TO DETECT SUPERNATURAL POWER AND ANIMOSITY TOWARD YOU...AND REACT *BEFORE* YOU SEE IT WITH YOUR EYES.
"POWER DETECTION" IS... ...A CRITICAL SKILL IN BATTLE.
WE VAMPIRES EXCEL AT IT. MORE THAN ANY OTHER MONSTER.
MY BLOOD FLOWS INSIDE YOU, TSUKUNE...
...SO YOU HAVE THE ABILITY.
YOU'VE...
...GOTTA BE KIDDING...

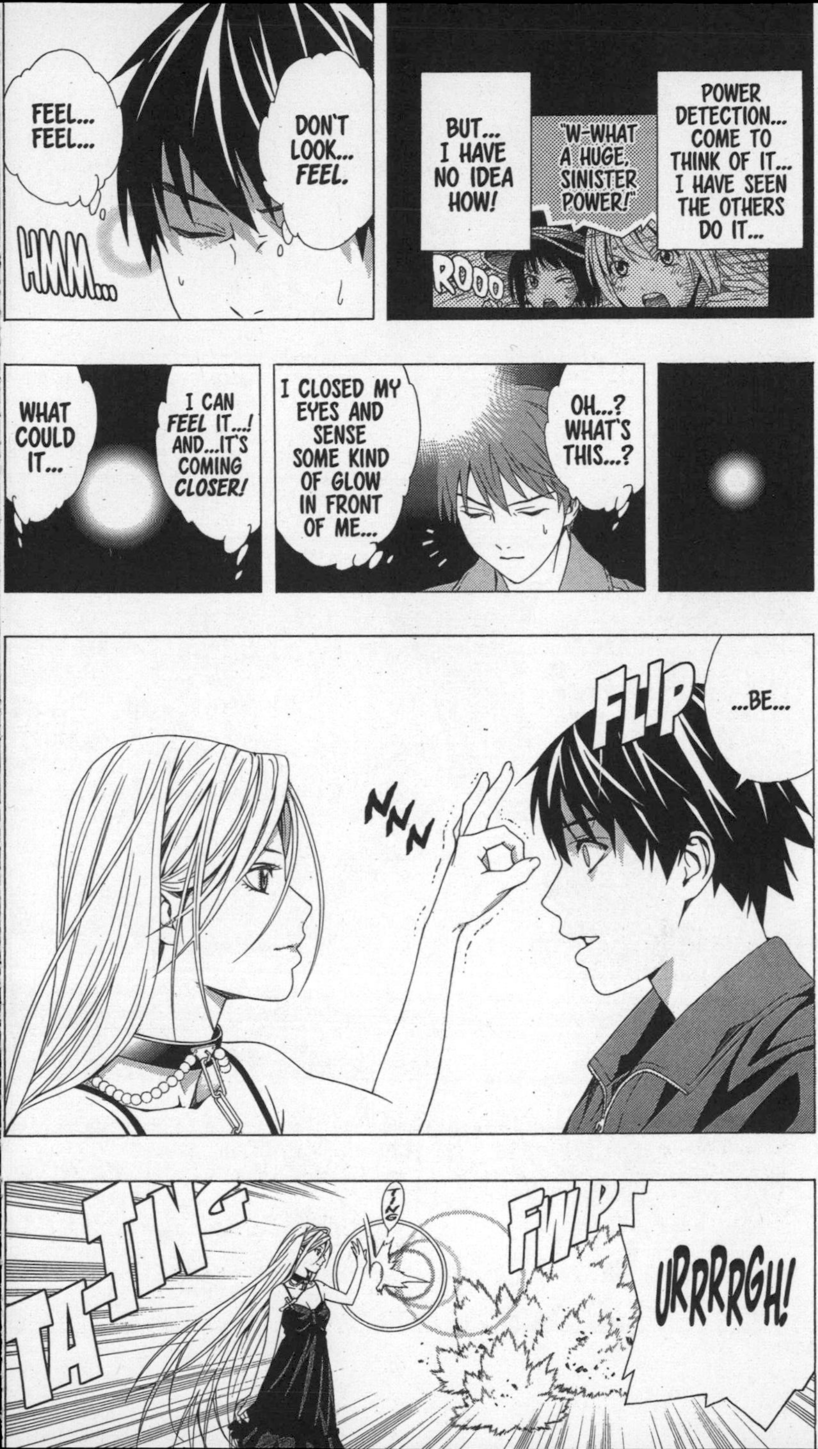
POWER DETECTION... COME TO THINK OF IT... I HAVE SEEN THE OTHERS DO IT...
"W-WHAT A HUGE, SINISTER POWER!"
ROOO
BUT... I HAVE NO IDEA HOW!
DON'T LOOK... FEEL.
FEEL... FEEL...
HMM...
OH...? WHAT'S THIS...?
I CLOSED MY EYES AND SENSE SOME KIND OF GLOW IN FRONT OF ME...
I CAN FEEL IT...! AND...IT'S COMING CLOSER!
WHAT COULD IT...
...BE...
FLIP
NNN
URRRRGH!
FWIP
TING
TA-TING

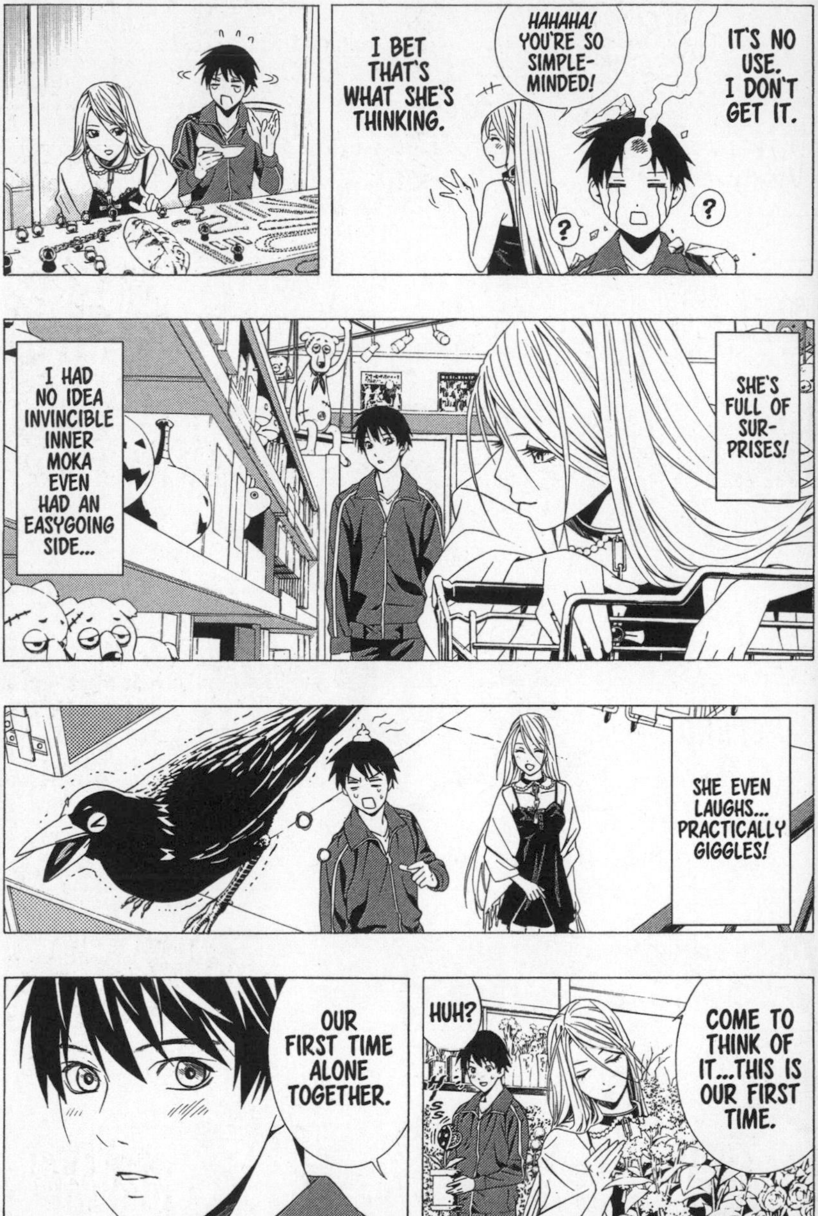
IT'S NO USE. I DON'T GET IT.
HAHAHA! YOU'RE SO SIMPLE-MINDED!
I BET THAT'S WHAT SHE'S THINKING.
SHE'S FULL OF SUR-PRISES!
I HAD NO IDEA INVINCIBLE INNER MOKA EVEN HAD AN EASYGOING SIDE...
SHE EVEN LAUGHS... PRACTICALLY GIGGLES!
COME TO THINK OF IT...THIS IS OUR FIRST TIME.
HUH?
OUR FIRST TIME ALONE TOGETHER.

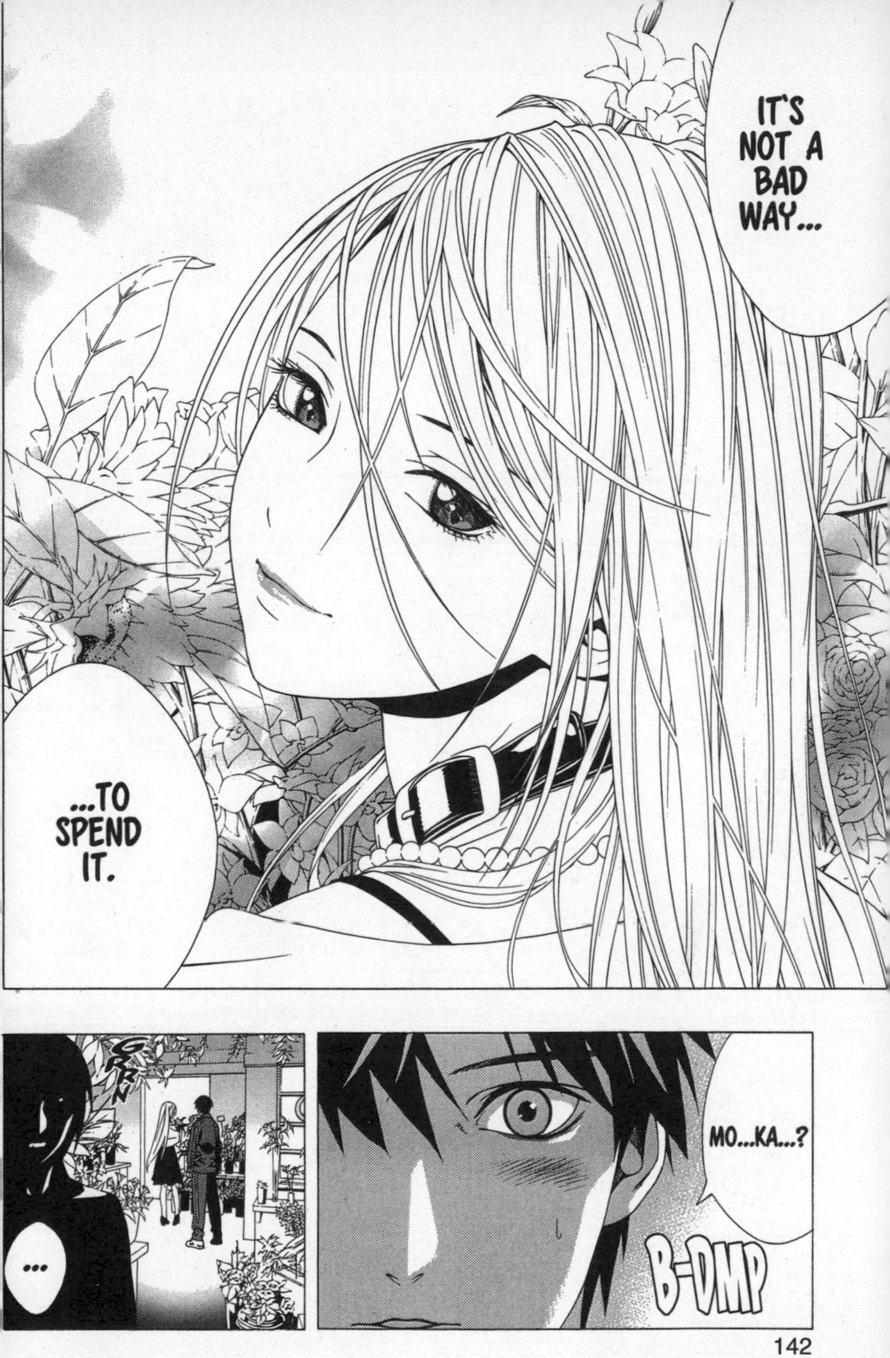
IT'S NOT A BAD WAY...
...TO SPEND IT.
MO...KA...?
B-DMP
GRRN
...

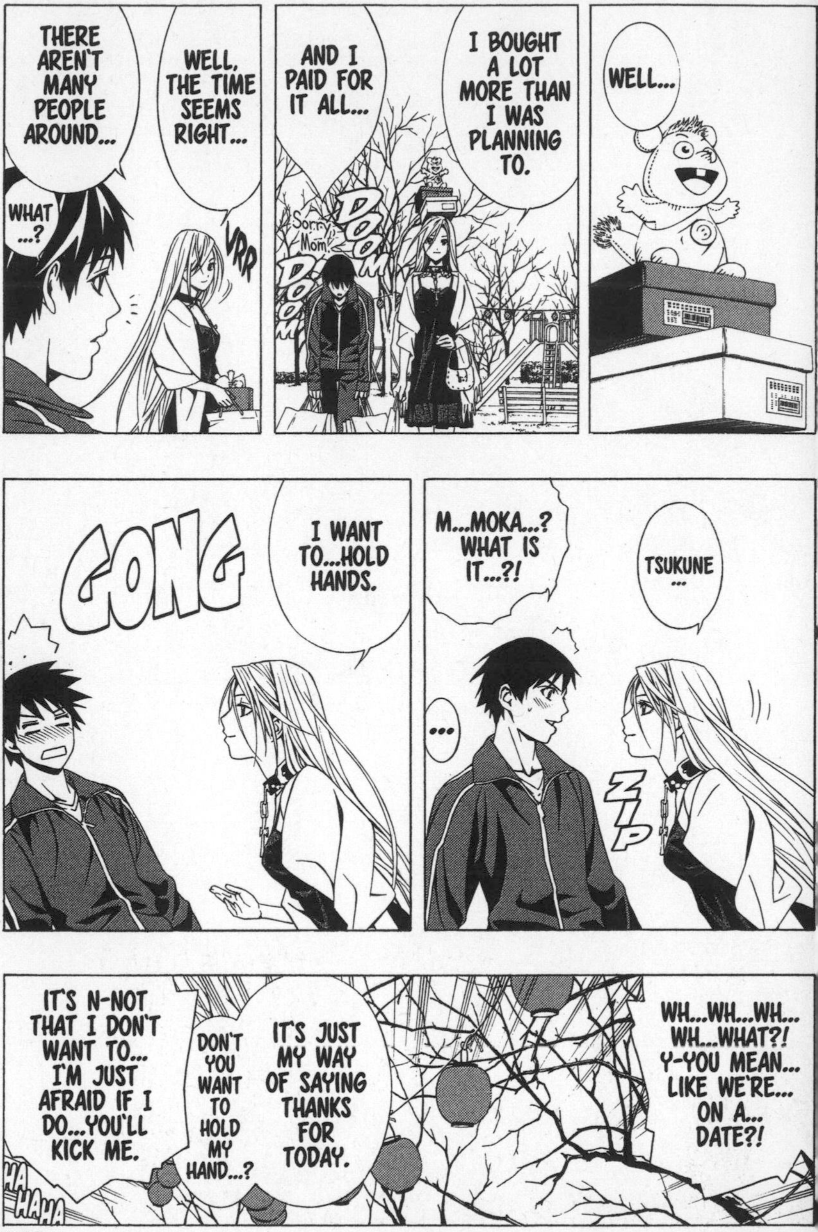
WELL...
I BOUGHT A LOT MORE THAN I WAS PLANNING TO.
AND I PAID FOR IT ALL...
DOOM
Sorry, Mom!
DOOM
WELL, THE TIME SEEMS RIGHT...
VRR
THERE AREN'T MANY PEOPLE AROUND...
WHAT ...?
TSUKUNE ...
M...MOKA...? WHAT IS IT...?!
...
ZIP
I WANT TO...HOLD HANDS.
GONG
WH...WH...WH... WH...WHAT?! Y-YOU MEAN... LIKE WE'RE... ON A... DATE?!
IT'S JUST MY WAY OF SAYING THANKS FOR TODAY.
DON'T YOU WANT TO HOLD MY HAND...?
IT'S N-NOT THAT I DON'T WANT TO... I'M JUST AFRAID IF I DO...YOU'LL KICK ME.
HA HA
HAHA

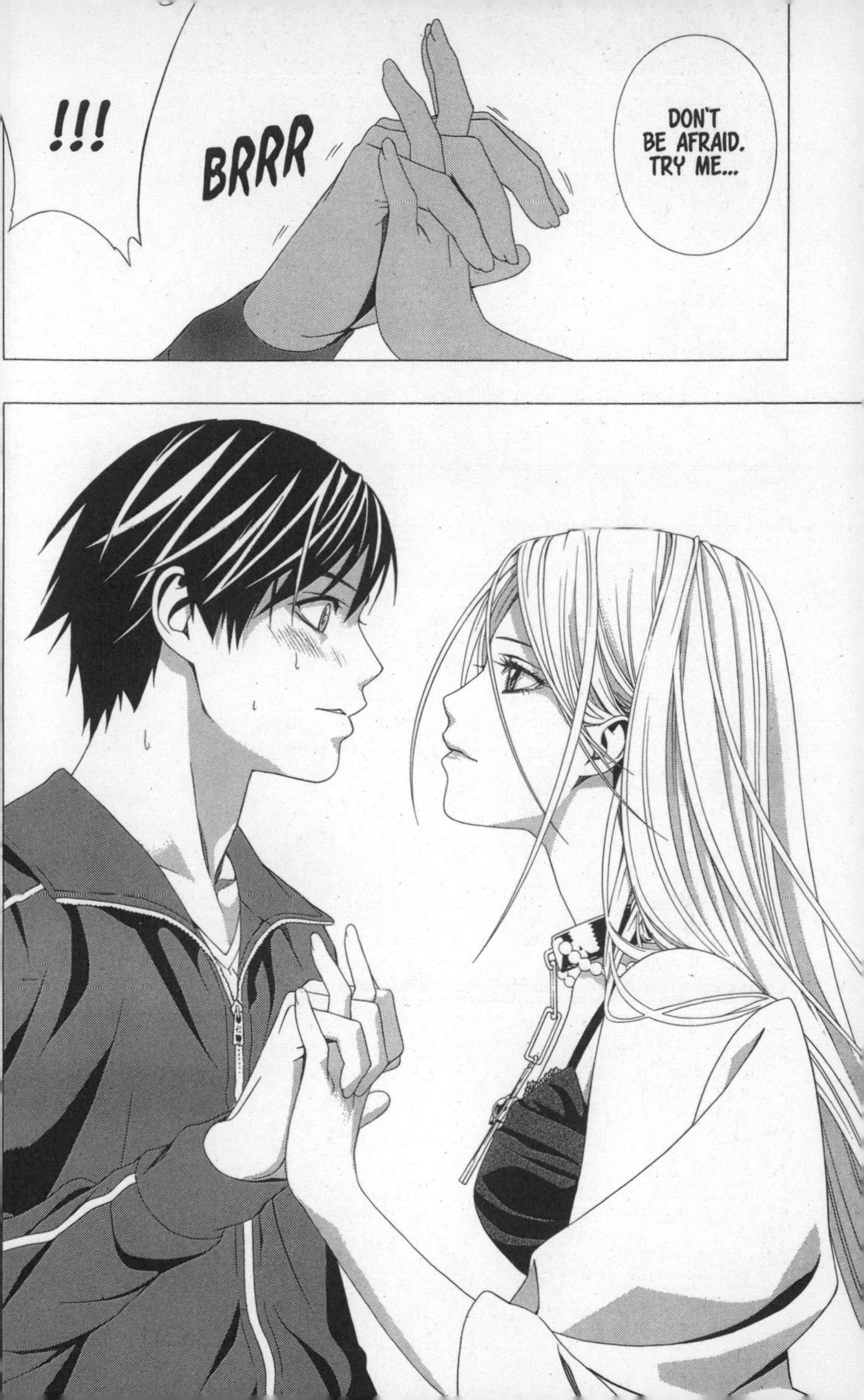
DON'T BE AFRAID. TRY ME...
BRRR
!!!

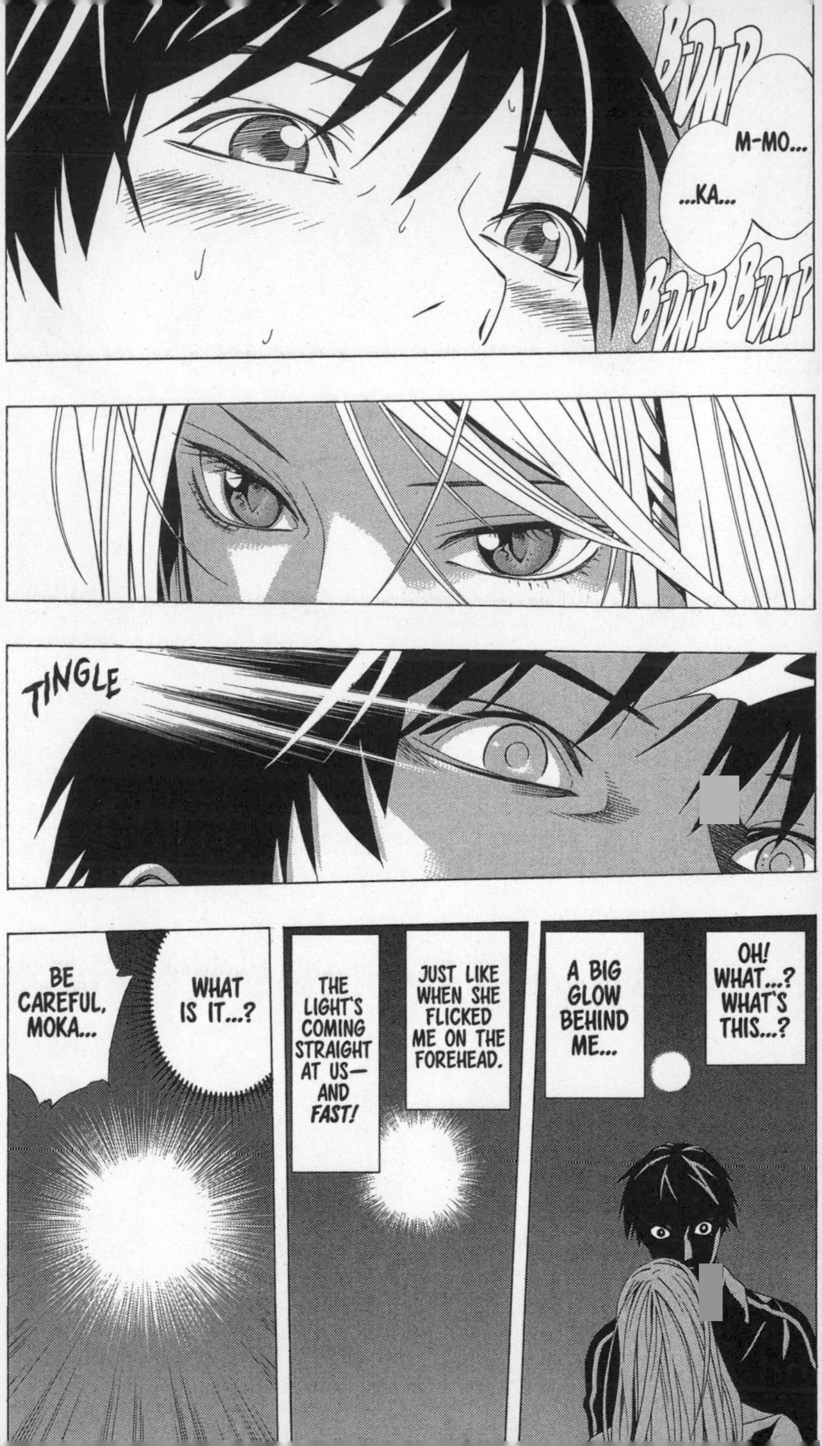
BUMP
M-MO...
...KA...
BUMP BUMP
TINGLE
OH! WHAT...? WHAT'S THIS...?
A BIG GLOW BEHIND ME...
JUST LIKE WHEN SHE FLICKED ME ON THE FOREHEAD.
THE LIGHT'S COMING STRAIGHT AT US— AND *FAST!*
WHAT IS IT...?
BE CAREFUL, MOKA...

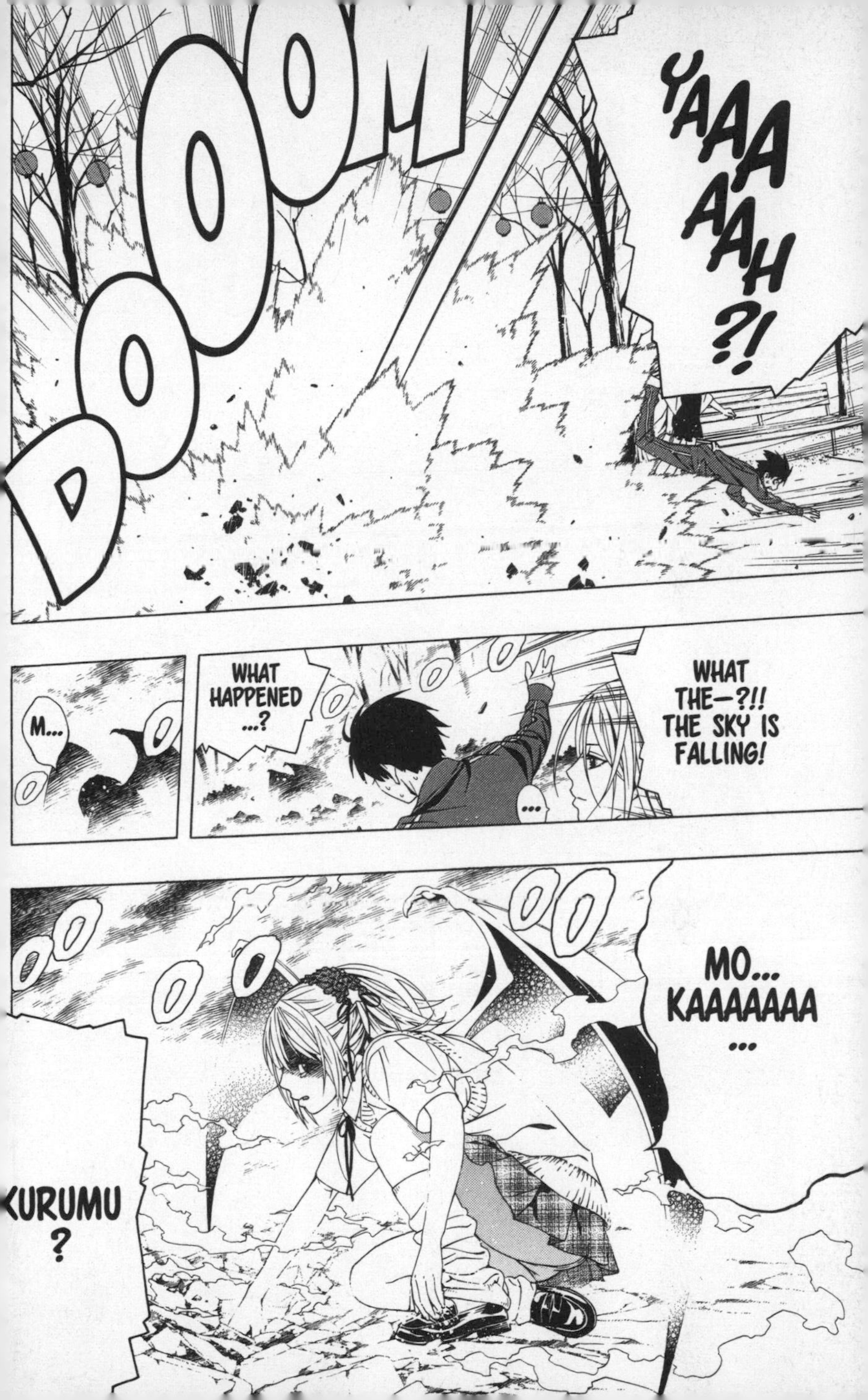
YAAAAAH?!
DOOOM
WHAT THE—?!! THE SKY IS FALLING!
WHAT HAPPENED ...?
...
M...
MO... KAAAAAAA ...
KURUMU ?

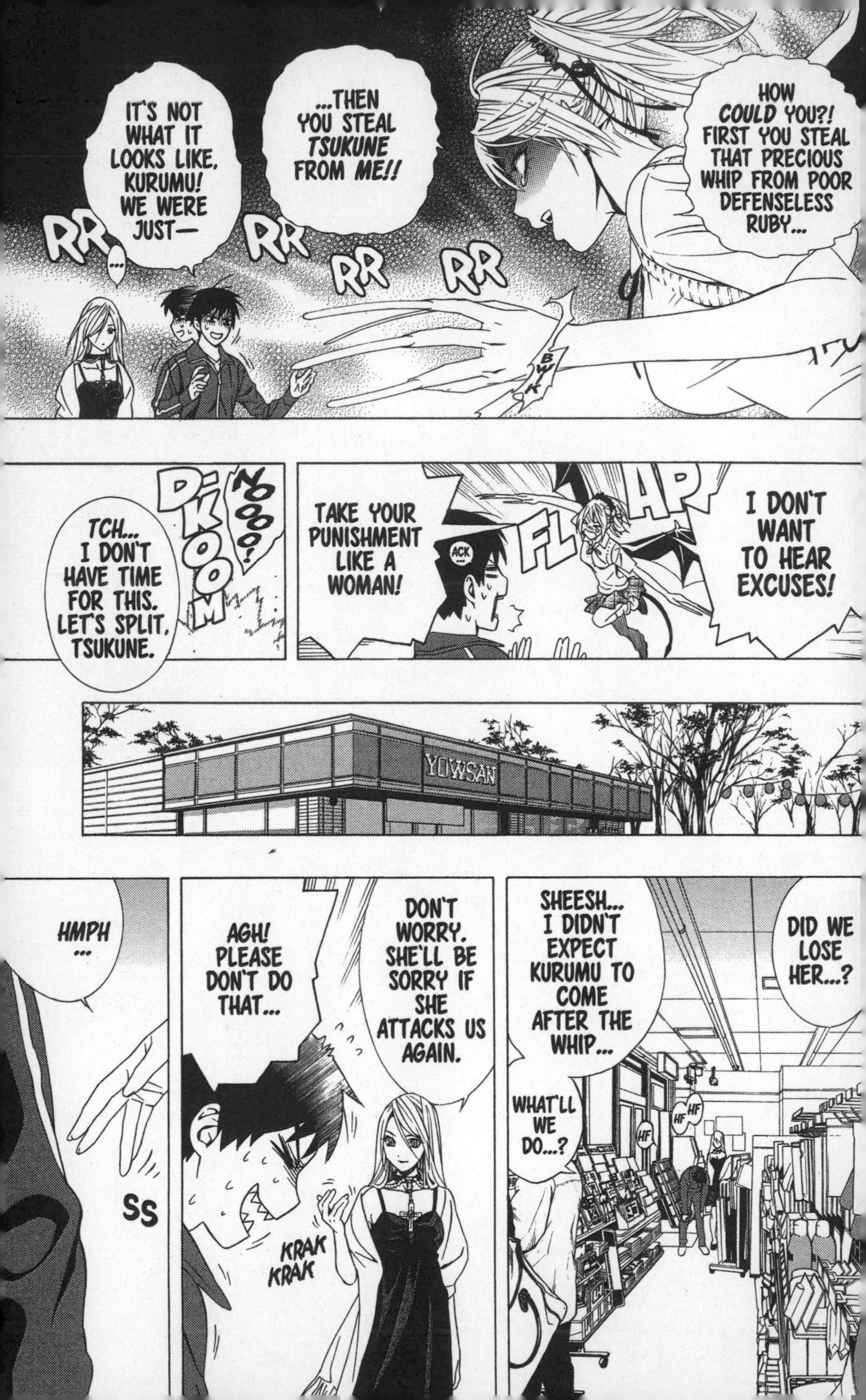
HOW COULD YOU?! FIRST YOU STEAL THAT PRECIOUS WHIP FROM POOR DEFENSELESS RUBY...
...THEN YOU STEAL TSUKUNE FROM ME!!
IT'S NOT WHAT IT LOOKS LIKE, KURUMU! WE WERE JUST—
RR RR RR RR
...
BWIK
I DON'T WANT TO HEAR EXCUSES!
FLAP
ACK...
TAKE YOUR PUNISHMENT LIKE A WOMAN!
NOOOOO!
D-KOOOM
TCH... I DON'T HAVE TIME FOR THIS. LET'S SPLIT, TSUKUNE.
YOWSAN
DID WE LOSE HER...?
SHEESH... I DIDN'T EXPECT KURUMU TO COME AFTER THE WHIP...
WHAT'LL WE DO...?
HF HF HF
DON'T WORRY. SHE'LL BE SORRY IF SHE ATTACKS US AGAIN.
AGH! PLEASE DON'T DO THAT...
KRAK KRAK
HMPH...
SS

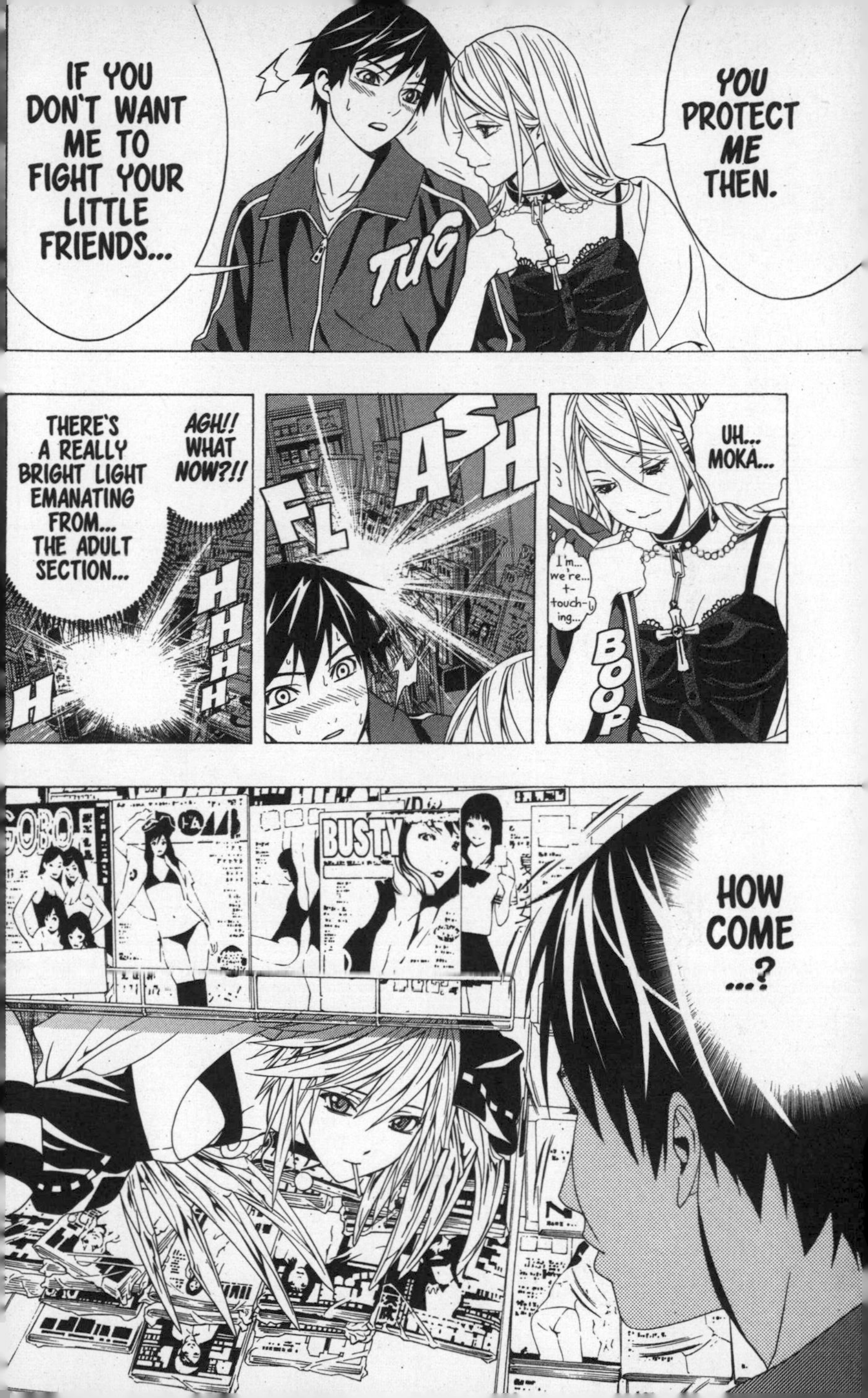
YOU PROTECT ME THEN.
IF YOU DON'T WANT ME TO FIGHT YOUR LITTLE FRIENDS...
TUG
UH... MOKA...
I'm... we're... t-touching...
BOOP
FLASH
AGH!! WHAT NOW?!!
THERE'S A REALLY BRIGHT LIGHT EMANATING FROM... THE ADULT SECTION...
HHHHH
HOW COME ...?
BUSTY

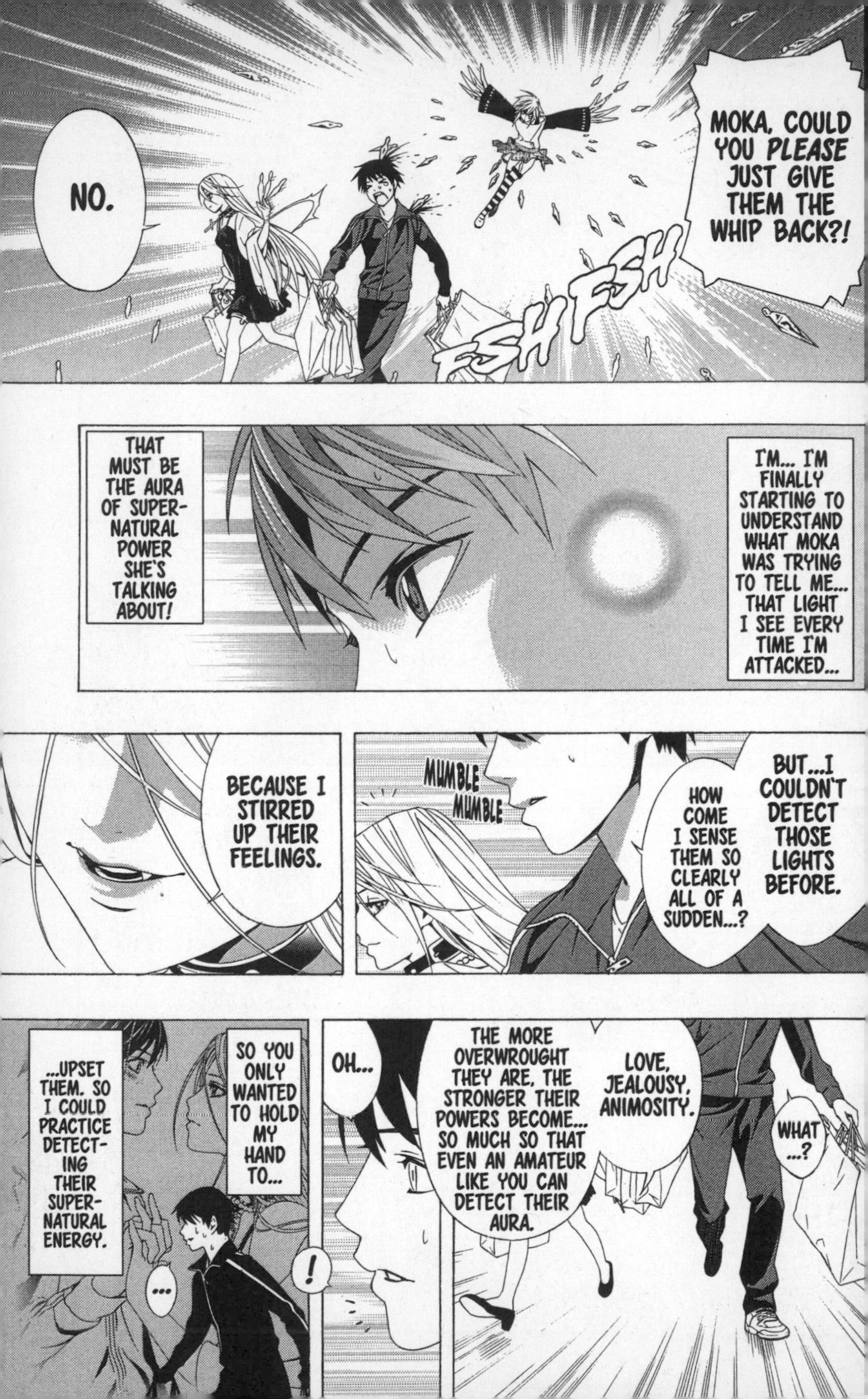
MOKA, COULD YOU *PLEASE* JUST GIVE THEM THE WHIP BACK?!
FSH FSH
NO.
I'M... I'M FINALLY STARTING TO UNDERSTAND WHAT MOKA WAS TRYING TO TELL ME... THAT LIGHT I SEE EVERY TIME I'M ATTACKED...
THAT MUST BE THE AURA OF SUPER-NATURAL POWER SHE'S TALKING ABOUT!
BUT...I COULDN'T DETECT THOSE LIGHTS BEFORE.
HOW COME I SENSE THEM SO CLEARLY ALL OF A SUDDEN...?
MUMBLE MUMBLE
BECAUSE I STIRRED UP THEIR FEELINGS.
WHAT ...?
LOVE, JEALOUSY, ANIMOSITY.
THE MORE OVERWROUGHT THEY ARE, THE STRONGER THEIR POWERS BECOME... SO MUCH SO THAT EVEN AN AMATEUR LIKE YOU CAN DETECT THEIR AURA.
OH...
!
SO YOU ONLY WANTED TO HOLD MY HAND TO...
...UPSET THEM. SO I COULD PRACTICE DETECT-ING THEIR SUPER-NATURAL ENERGY.
...

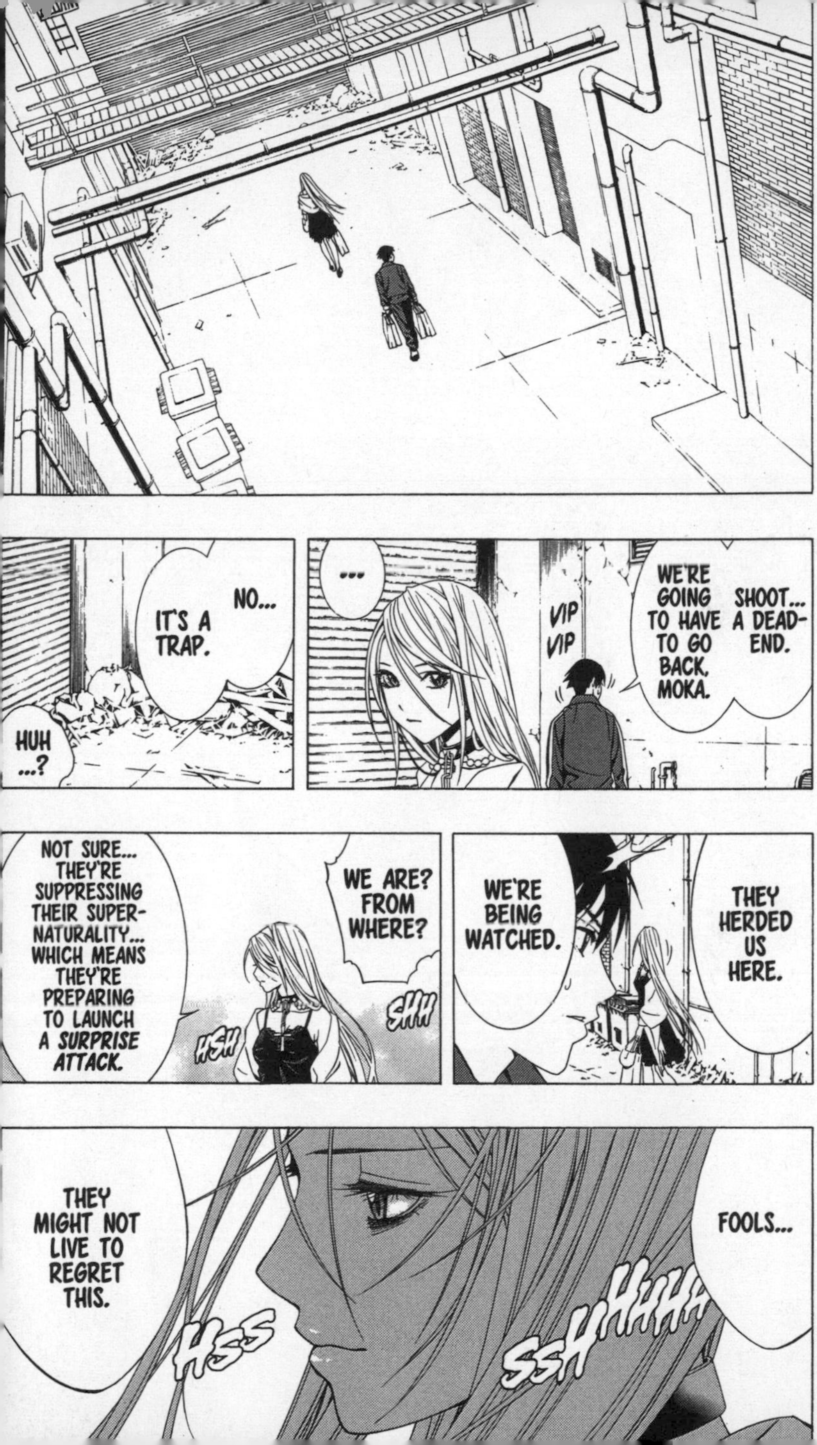
SHOOT... A DEAD-END.
WE'RE GOING TO HAVE TO GO BACK, MOKA.
VIP VIP
...
NO... IT'S A TRAP.
HUH...?
THEY HERDED US HERE.
WE'RE BEING WATCHED.
WE ARE? FROM WHERE?
SHH
NOT SURE... THEY'RE SUPPRESSING THEIR SUPER-NATURALITY... WHICH MEANS THEY'RE PREPARING TO LAUNCH A SURPRISE ATTACK.
HSH
FOOLS...
SSHHHHHH
THEY MIGHT NOT LIVE TO REGRET THIS.
HSS

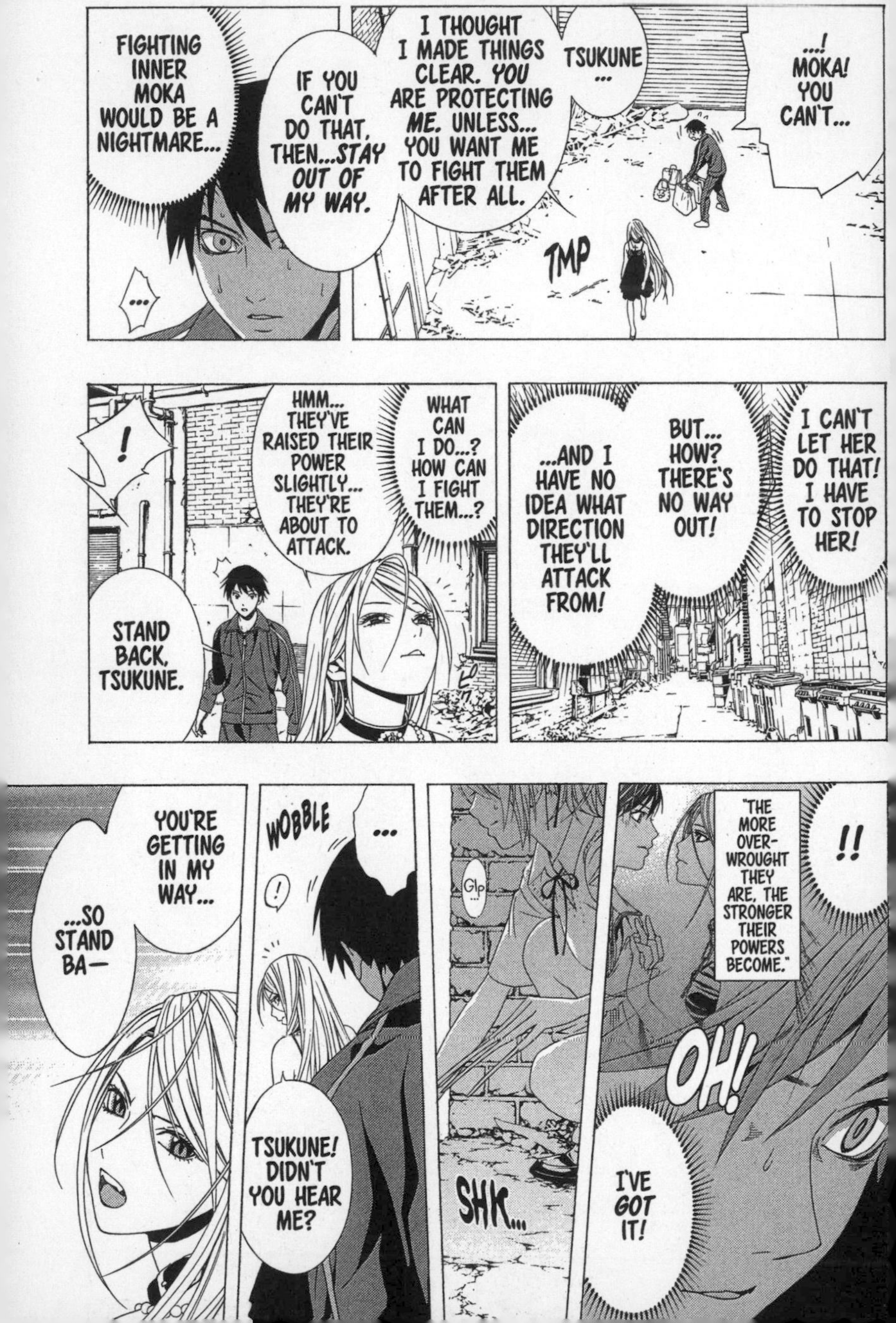
...! MOKA! YOU CAN'T...
TSUKUNE ...
I THOUGHT I MADE THINGS CLEAR. *YOU* ARE PROTECTING *ME*. UNLESS... YOU WANT ME TO FIGHT THEM AFTER ALL.
IF YOU CAN'T DO THAT, THEN...*STAY OUT OF MY WAY.*
TMP
FIGHTING INNER MOKA WOULD BE A NIGHTMARE...
...
I CAN'T LET HER DO THAT! I HAVE TO STOP HER!
BUT... HOW? THERE'S NO WAY OUT!
...AND I HAVE NO IDEA WHAT DIRECTION THEY'LL ATTACK FROM!
WHAT CAN I DO...? HOW CAN I FIGHT THEM...?
HMM... THEY'VE RAISED THEIR POWER SLIGHTLY... THEY'RE ABOUT TO ATTACK.
!
STAND BACK, TSUKUNE.
!!
"THE MORE OVER-WROUGHT THEY ARE, THE STRONGER THEIR POWERS BECOME."
OH!
I'VE GOT IT!
Glp...
SHK...
...
WOBBLE
!
TSUKUNE! DIDN'T YOU HEAR ME?
YOU'RE GETTING IN MY WAY...
...SO STAND BA—

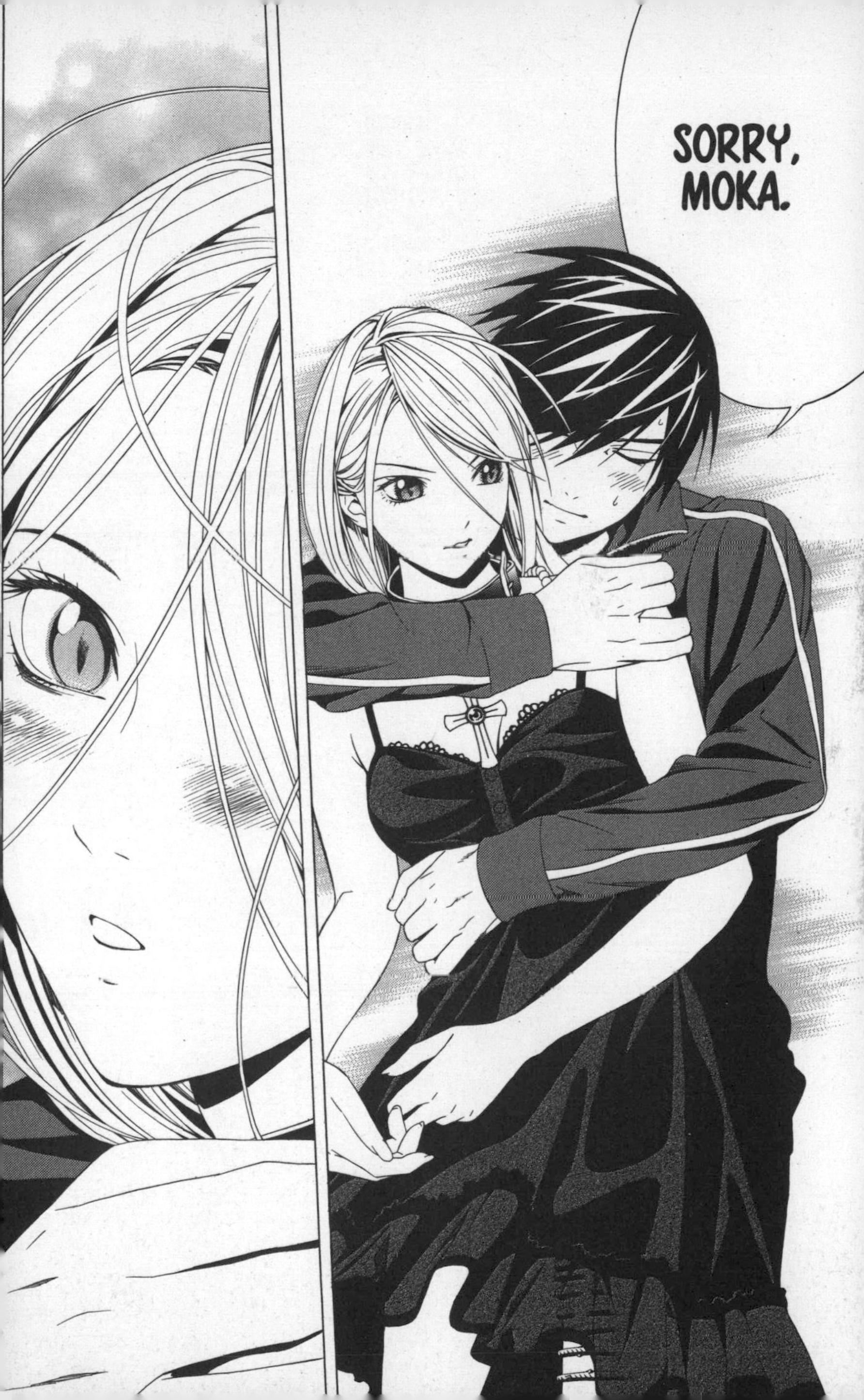
SORRY, MOKA.

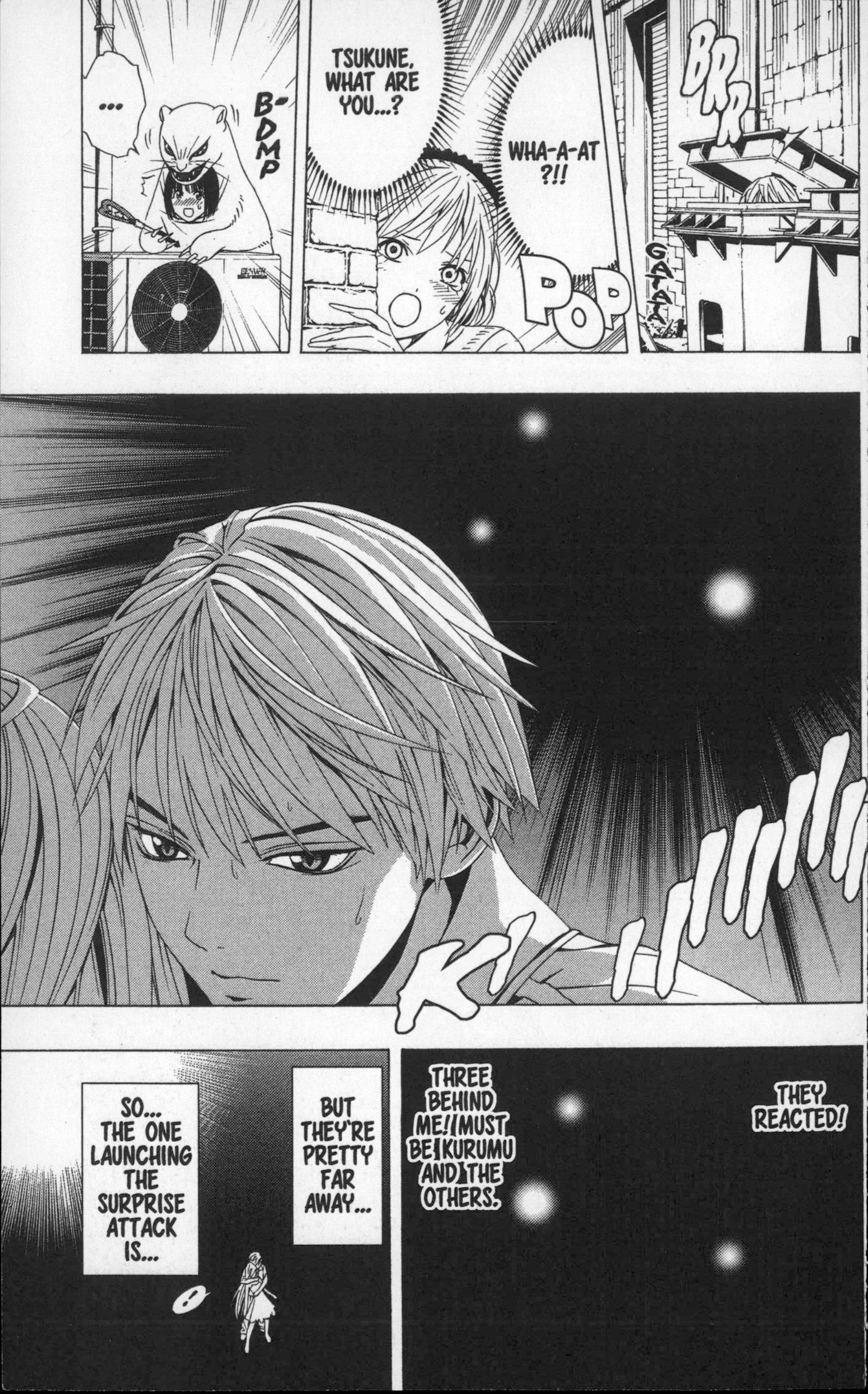
BRR
GATATA
WHA-A-AT?!!
TSUKUNE, WHAT ARE YOU...?
POP
B-DMP
...
KI
THEY REACTED!
THREE BEHIND ME!! MUST BE KURUMU AND THE OTHERS.
BUT THEY'RE PRETTY FAR AWAY...
SO... THE ONE LAUNCHING THE SURPRISE ATTACK IS...
!

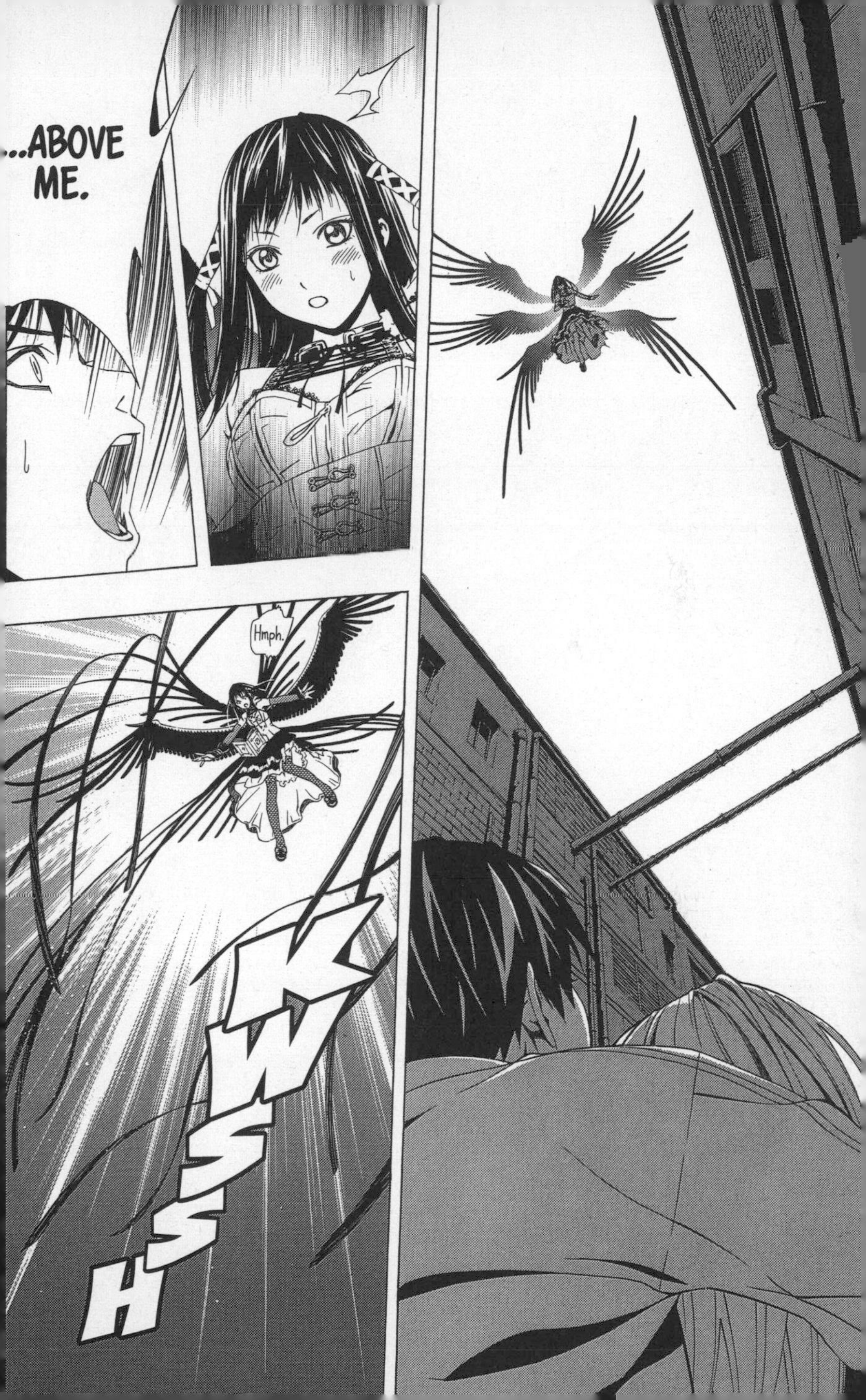
...ABOVE ME.
Hmph.
HSSWK

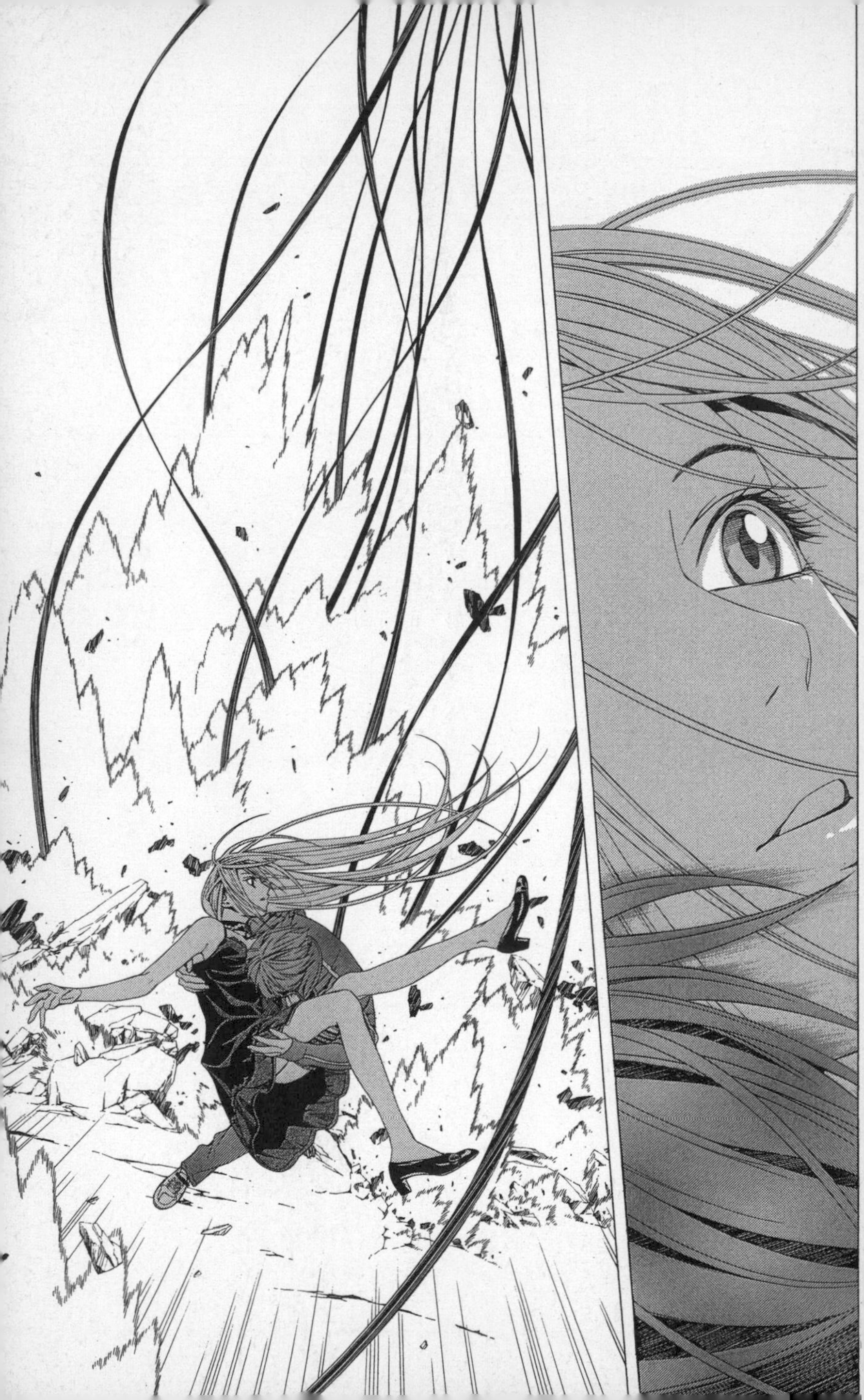

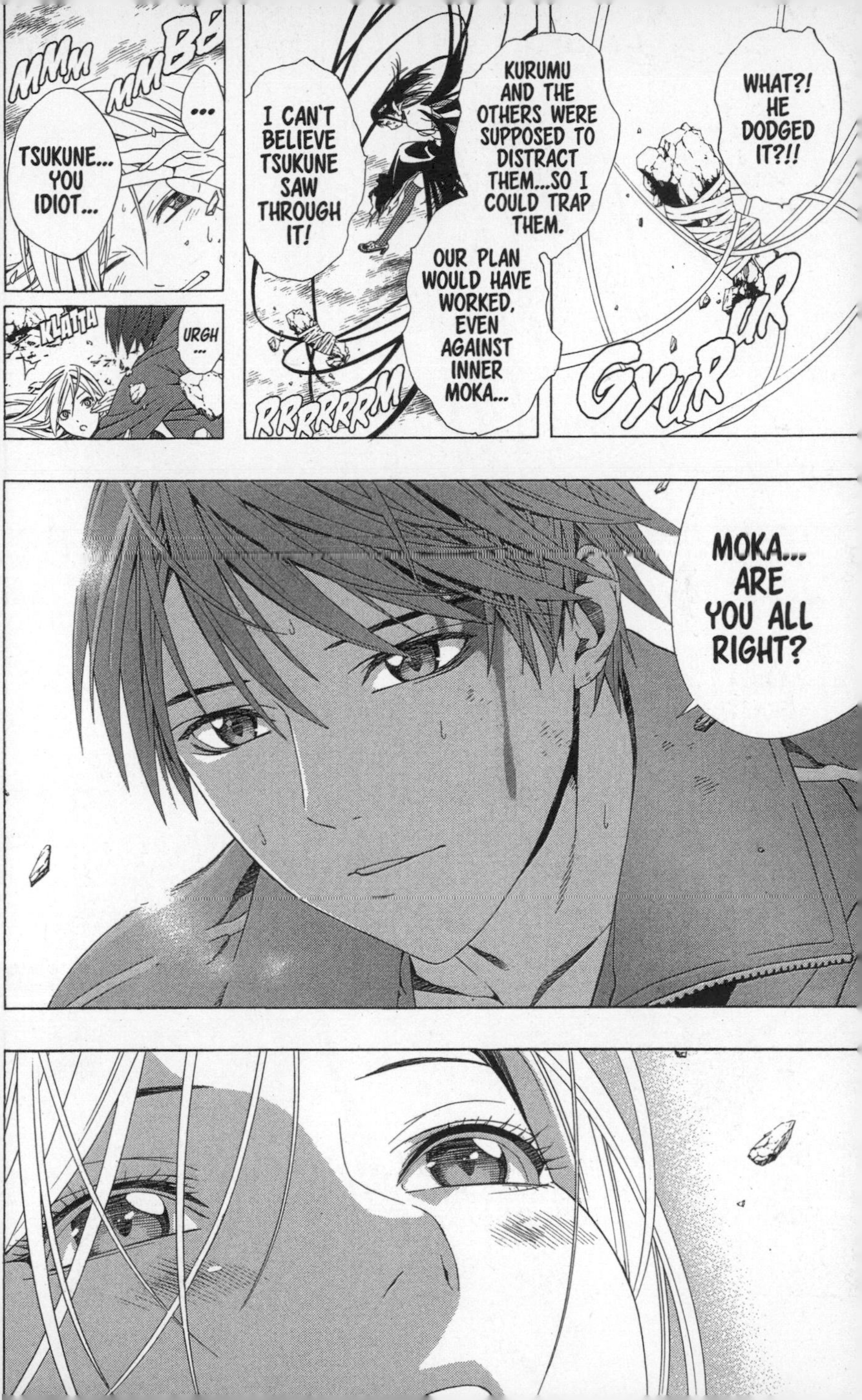
WHAT?! HE DODGED IT?!!
GYURUR
KURUMU AND THE OTHERS WERE SUPPOSED TO DISTRACT THEM...SO I COULD TRAP THEM.
I CAN'T BELIEVE TSUKUNE SAW THROUGH IT!
OUR PLAN WOULD HAVE WORKED, EVEN AGAINST INNER MOKA...
RRRRRRM
MMM MMBB
...
TSUKUNE... YOU IDIOT...
URGH...
KLATTA
MOKA... ARE YOU ALL RIGHT?

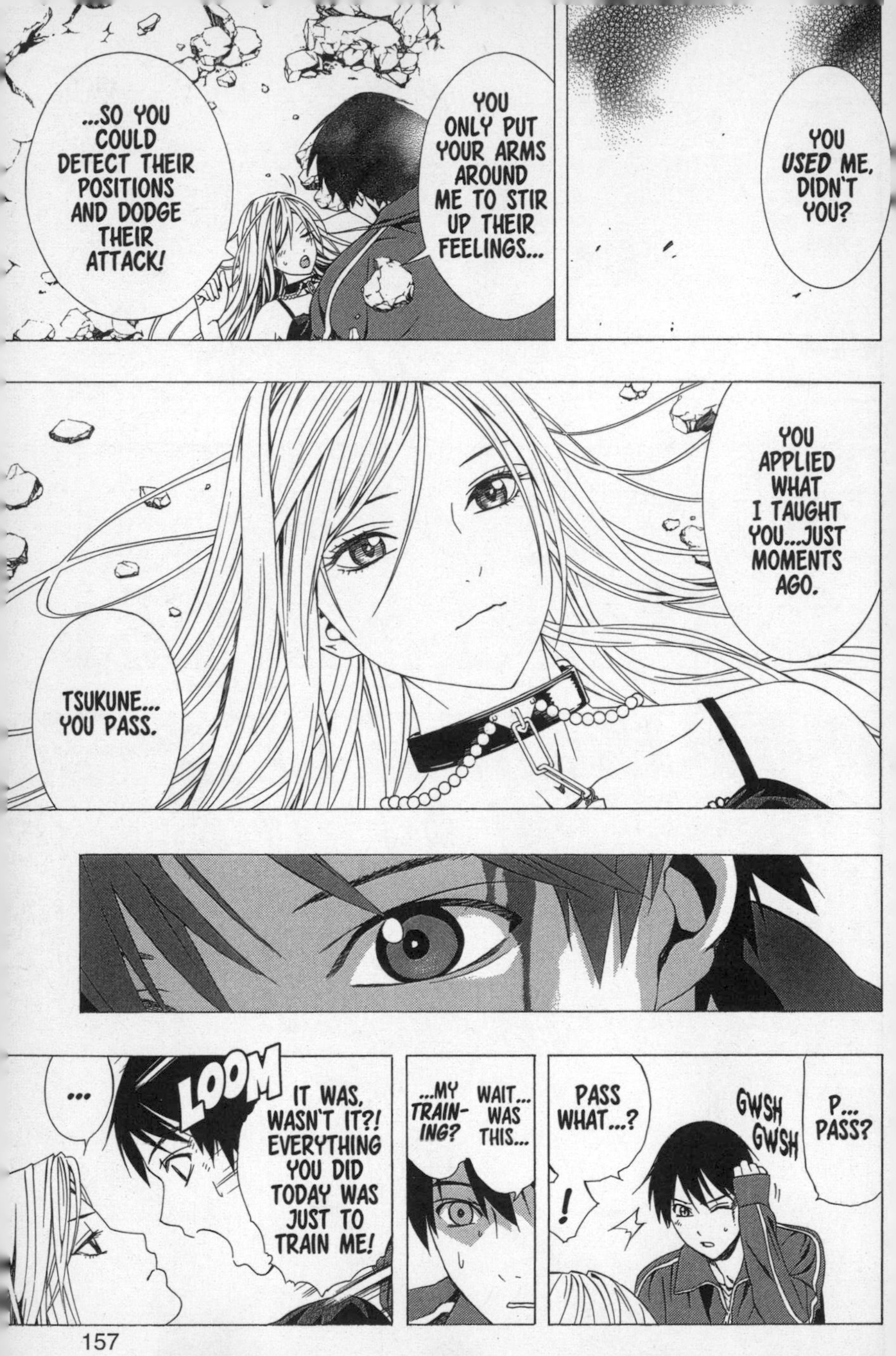
YOU USED ME, DIDN'T YOU?
YOU ONLY PUT YOUR ARMS AROUND ME TO STIR UP THEIR FEELINGS...
...SO YOU COULD DETECT THEIR POSITIONS AND DODGE THEIR ATTACK!
YOU APPLIED WHAT I TAUGHT YOU...JUST MOMENTS AGO.
TSUKUNE... YOU PASS.
P... PASS?
GWSH GWSH
PASS WHAT...?
!
WAIT... WAS THIS...
...MY TRAINING?
IT WAS, WASN'T IT?! EVERYTHING YOU DID TODAY WAS JUST TO TRAIN ME!
LOOM
...

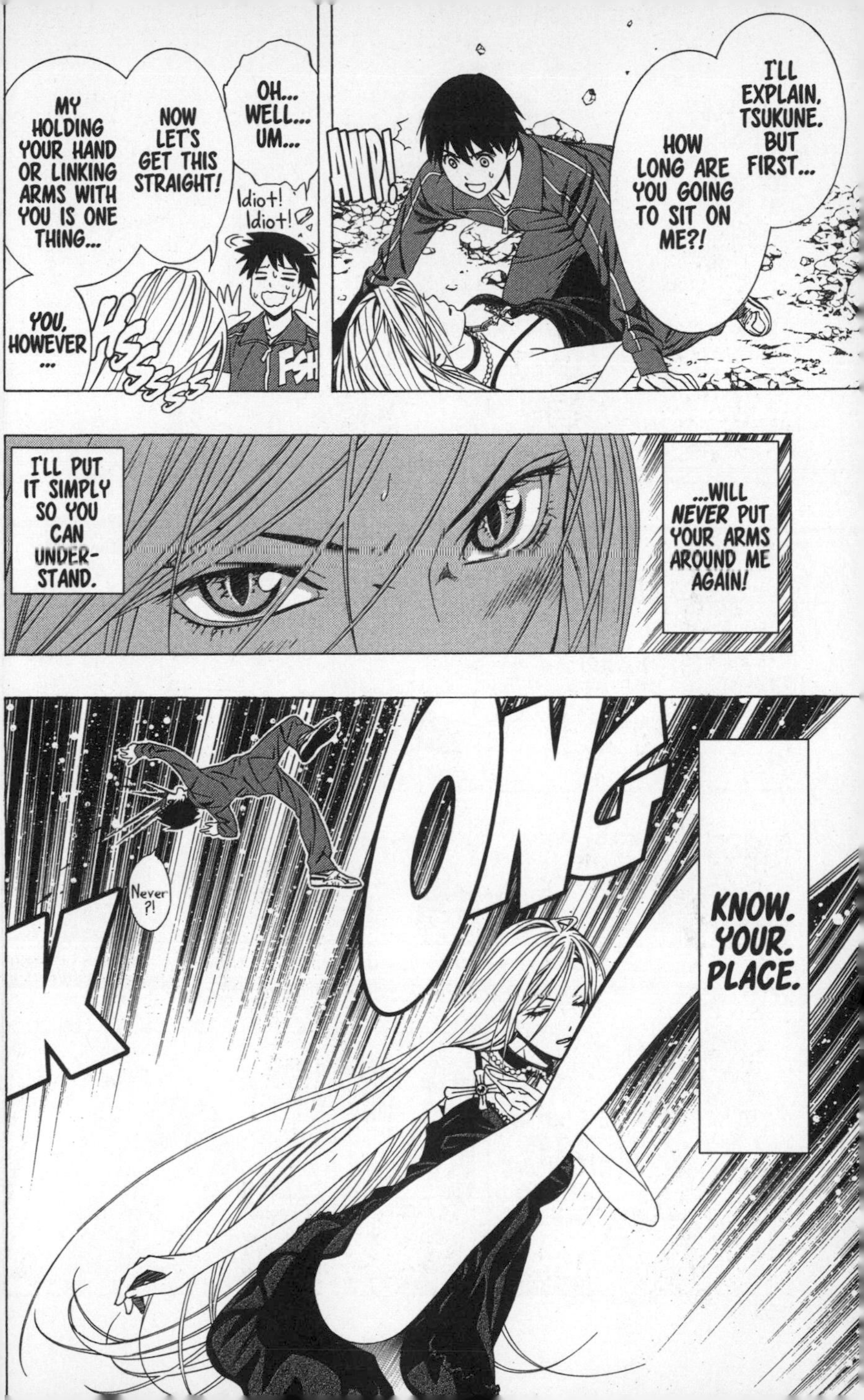
I'LL EXPLAIN, TSUKUNE. BUT FIRST...
HOW LONG ARE YOU GOING TO SIT ON ME?!
AWP!
OH... WELL... UM...
NOW LET'S GET THIS STRAIGHT!
MY HOLDING YOUR HAND OR LINKING ARMS WITH YOU IS ONE THING...
Idiot! Idiot!
YOU, HOWEVER ...
HSSSSS
...WILL NEVER PUT YOUR ARMS AROUND ME AGAIN!
I'LL PUT IT SIMPLY SO YOU CAN UNDER-STAND.
KNOW. YOUR. PLACE.
KONG!
Never ?!

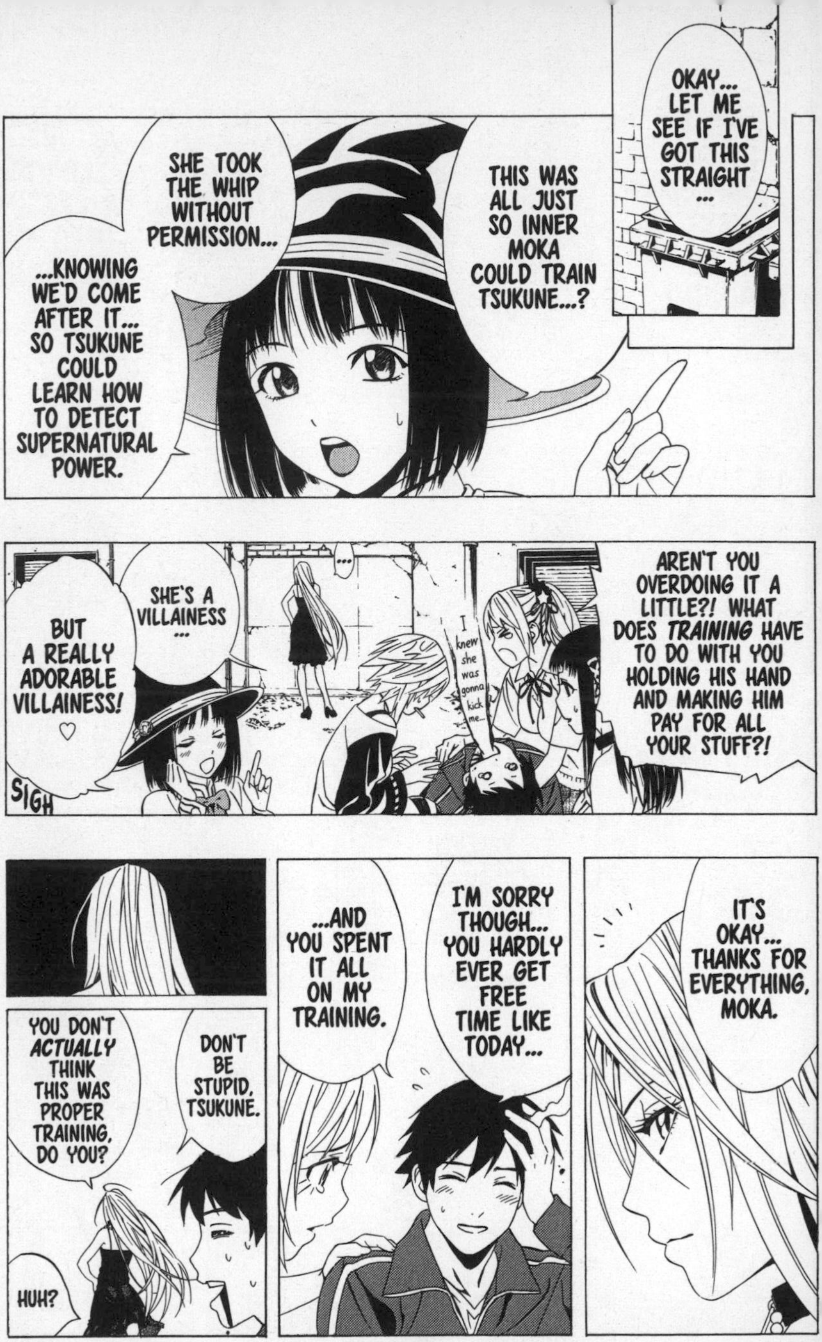
OKAY... LET ME SEE IF I'VE GOT THIS STRAIGHT...
THIS WAS ALL JUST SO INNER MOKA COULD TRAIN TSUKUNE...?
SHE TOOK THE WHIP WITHOUT PERMISSION...
...KNOWING WE'D COME AFTER IT... SO TSUKUNE COULD LEARN HOW TO DETECT SUPERNATURAL POWER.
AREN'T YOU OVERDOING IT A LITTLE?! WHAT DOES *TRAINING* HAVE TO DO WITH YOU HOLDING HIS HAND AND MAKING HIM PAY FOR ALL YOUR STUFF?!
I knew she was gonna kick me...
...
SHE'S A VILLAINESS...
BUT A REALLY ADORABLE VILLAINESS! ♡
SIGH
IT'S OKAY... THANKS FOR EVERYTHING, MOKA.
I'M SORRY THOUGH... YOU HARDLY EVER GET FREE TIME LIKE TODAY...
...AND YOU SPENT IT ALL ON MY TRAINING.
DON'T BE STUPID, TSUKUNE.
YOU DON'T *ACTUALLY* THINK THIS WAS PROPER TRAINING, DO YOU?
HUH?

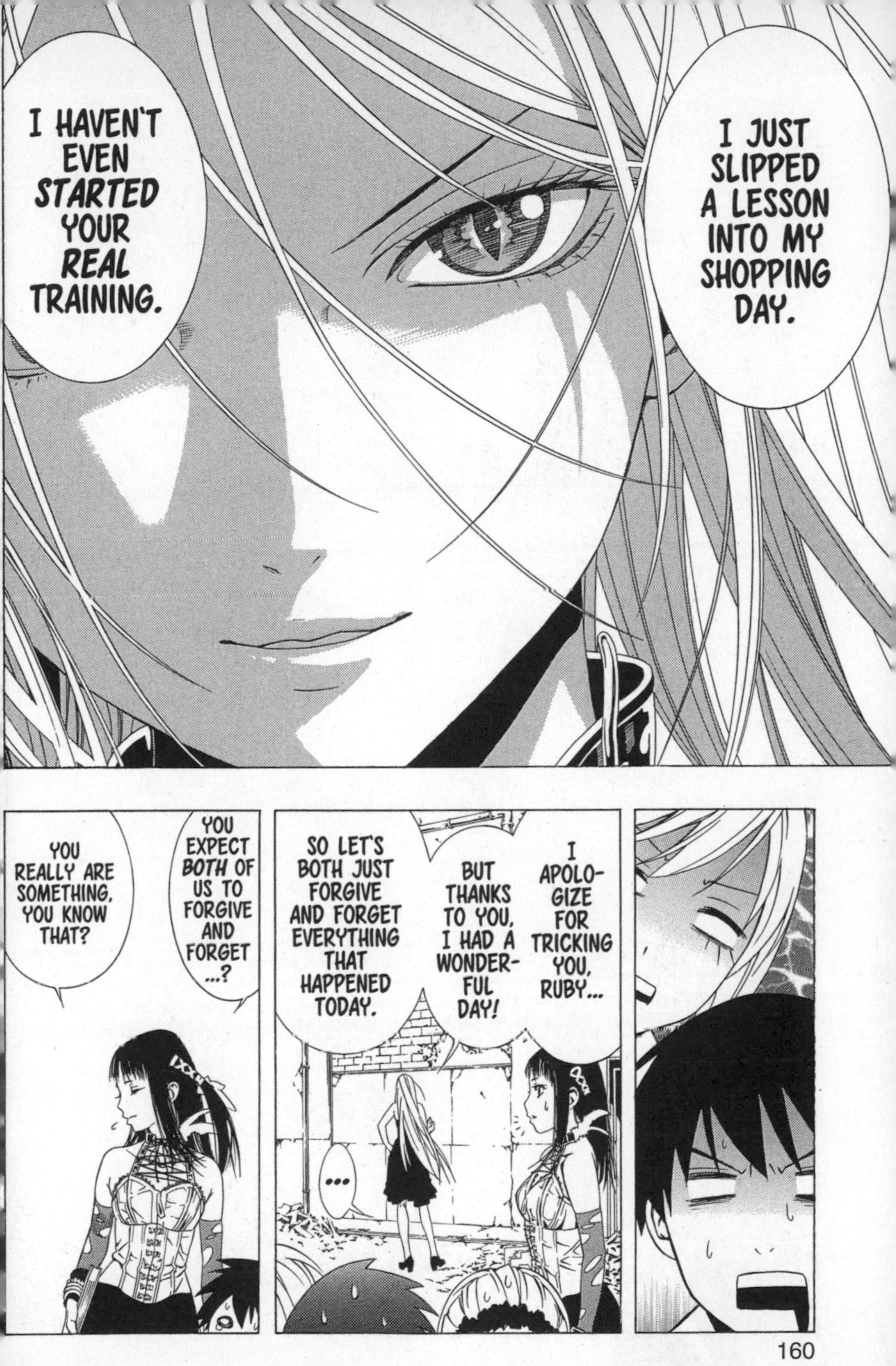
I JUST SLIPPED A LESSON INTO MY SHOPPING DAY.
I HAVEN'T EVEN STARTED YOUR REAL TRAINING.
I APOLO-GIZE FOR TRICKING YOU, RUBY...
BUT THANKS TO YOU, I HAD A WONDER-FUL DAY!
SO LET'S BOTH JUST FORGIVE AND FORGET EVERYTHING THAT HAPPENED TODAY.
...
YOU EXPECT BOTH OF US TO FORGIVE AND FORGET...?
YOU REALLY ARE SOMETHING, YOU KNOW THAT?

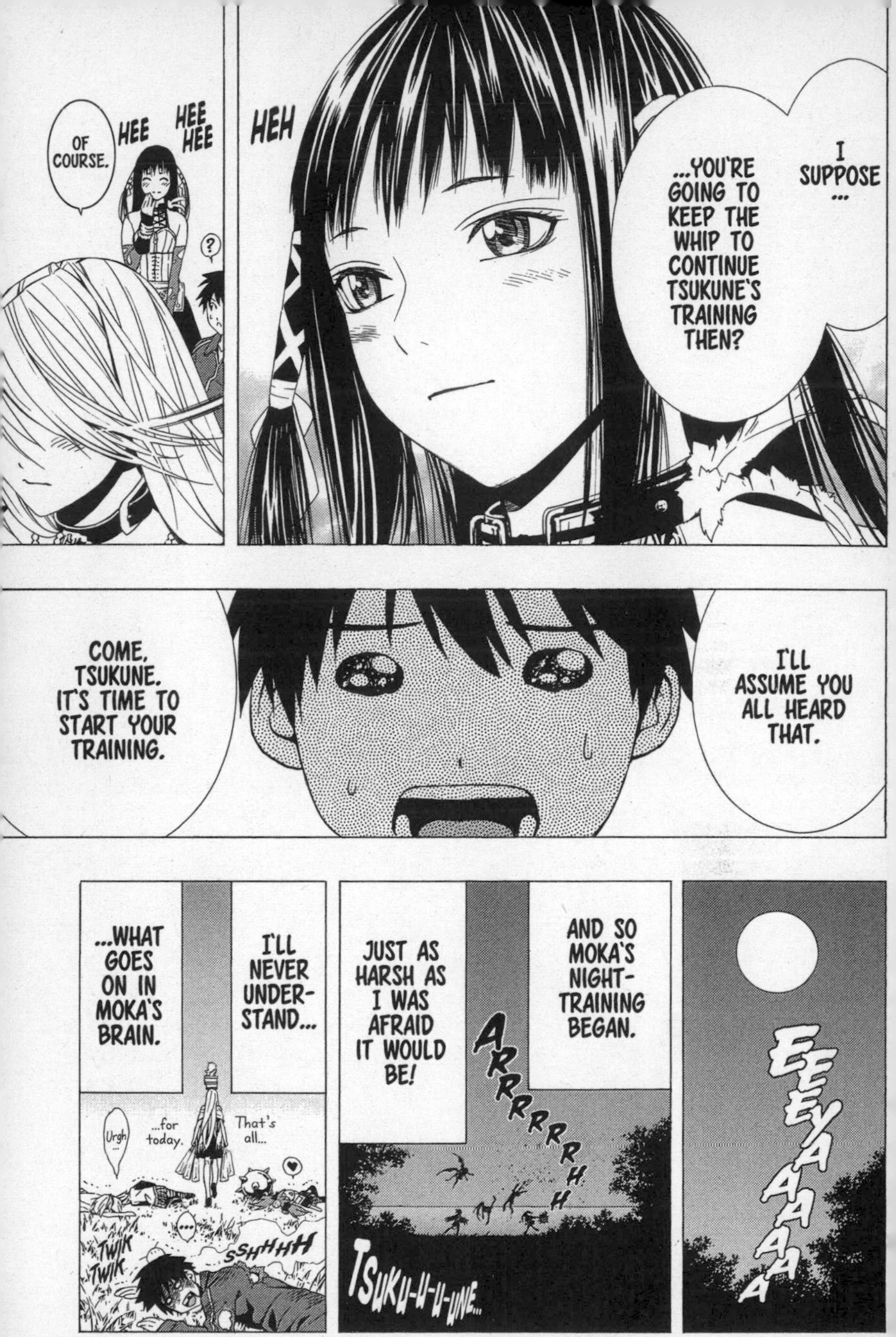
I SUPPOSE...
...YOU'RE GOING TO KEEP THE WHIP TO CONTINUE TSUKUNE'S TRAINING THEN?
HEH
HEE HEE
HEE
OF COURSE.
?
I'LL ASSUME YOU ALL HEARD THAT.
COME, TSUKUNE. IT'S TIME TO START YOUR TRAINING.
EEEYAAAAAA
AND SO MOKA'S NIGHT-TRAINING BEGAN.
ARRRRRRHH
JUST AS HARSH AS I WAS AFRAID IT WOULD BE!
TSUKU-U-U-UNE...
I'LL NEVER UNDER-STAND...
...WHAT GOES ON IN MOKA'S BRAIN.
That's all...
...for today.
Urgh...
...
SSHHHHH
TWIK TWIK

17: Dream of a Butterfly

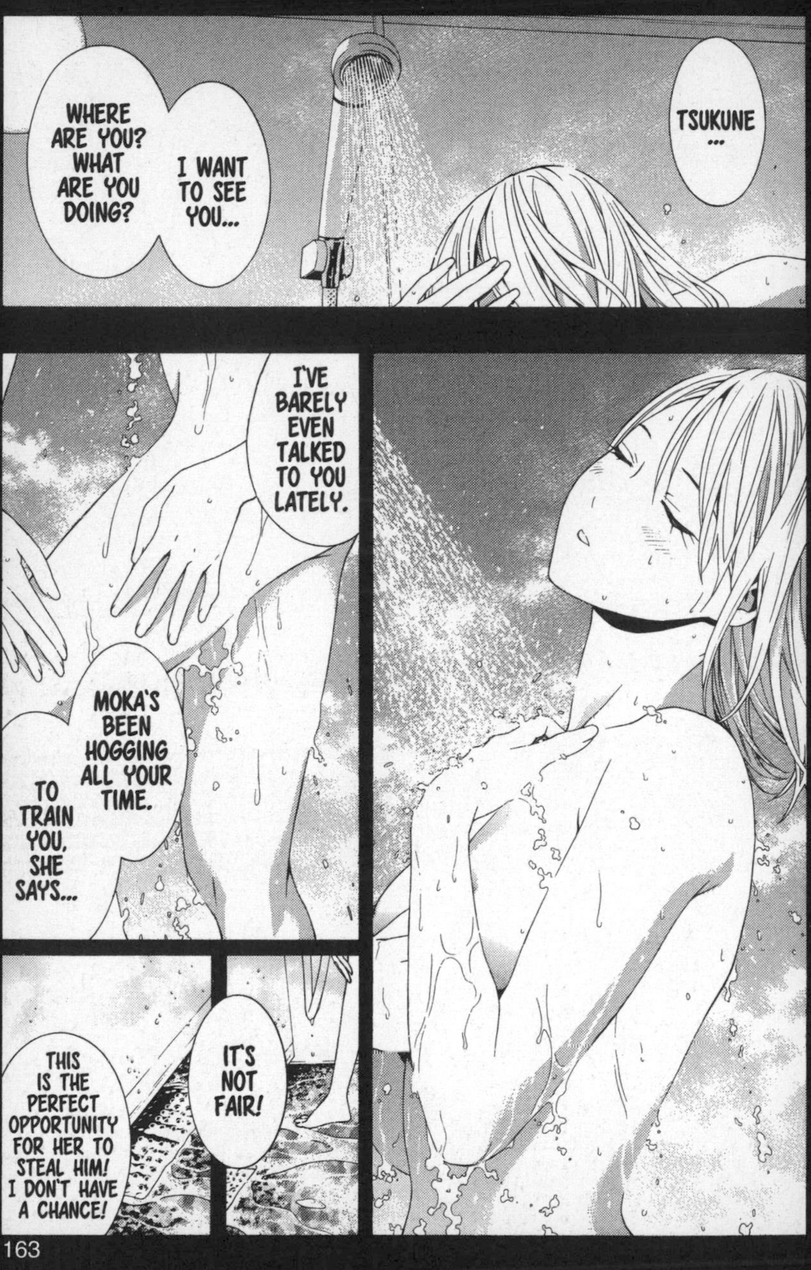
TSUKUNE ...
WHERE ARE YOU? WHAT ARE YOU DOING?
I WANT TO SEE YOU...
I'VE BARELY EVEN TALKED TO YOU LATELY.
MOKA'S BEEN HOGGING ALL YOUR TIME.
TO TRAIN YOU, SHE SAYS...
IT'S NOT FAIR!
THIS IS THE PERFECT OPPORTUNITY FOR HER TO STEAL HIM! I DON'T HAVE A CHANCE!

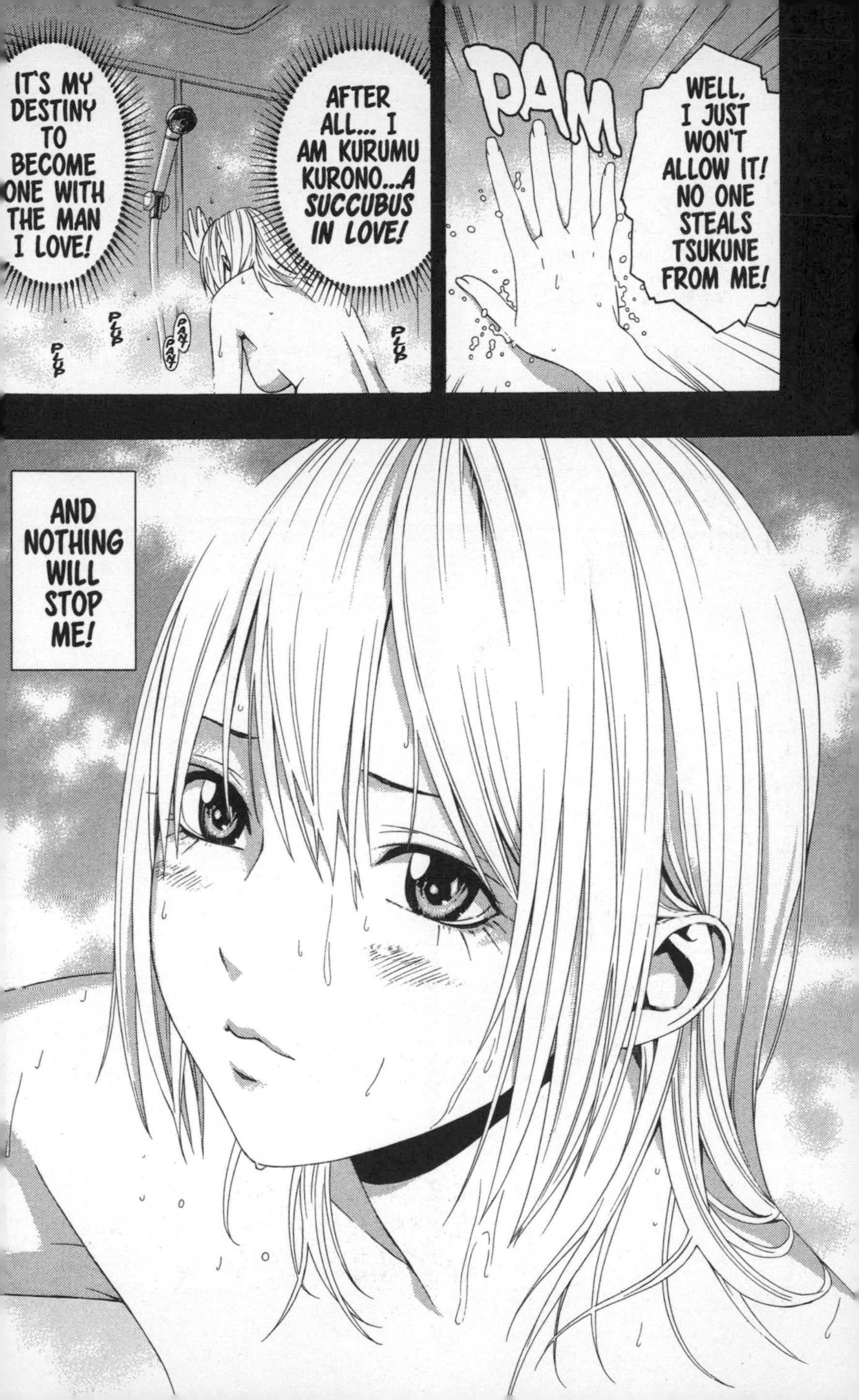
PAM
WELL, I JUST WON'T ALLOW IT! NO ONE STEALS TSUKUNE FROM ME!
PLUP
AFTER ALL... I AM KURUMU KURONO...A SUCCUBUS IN LOVE!
IT'S MY DESTINY TO BECOME ONE WITH THE MAN I LOVE!
PANT PANT
PLUP
PLUP
AND NOTHING WILL STOP ME!

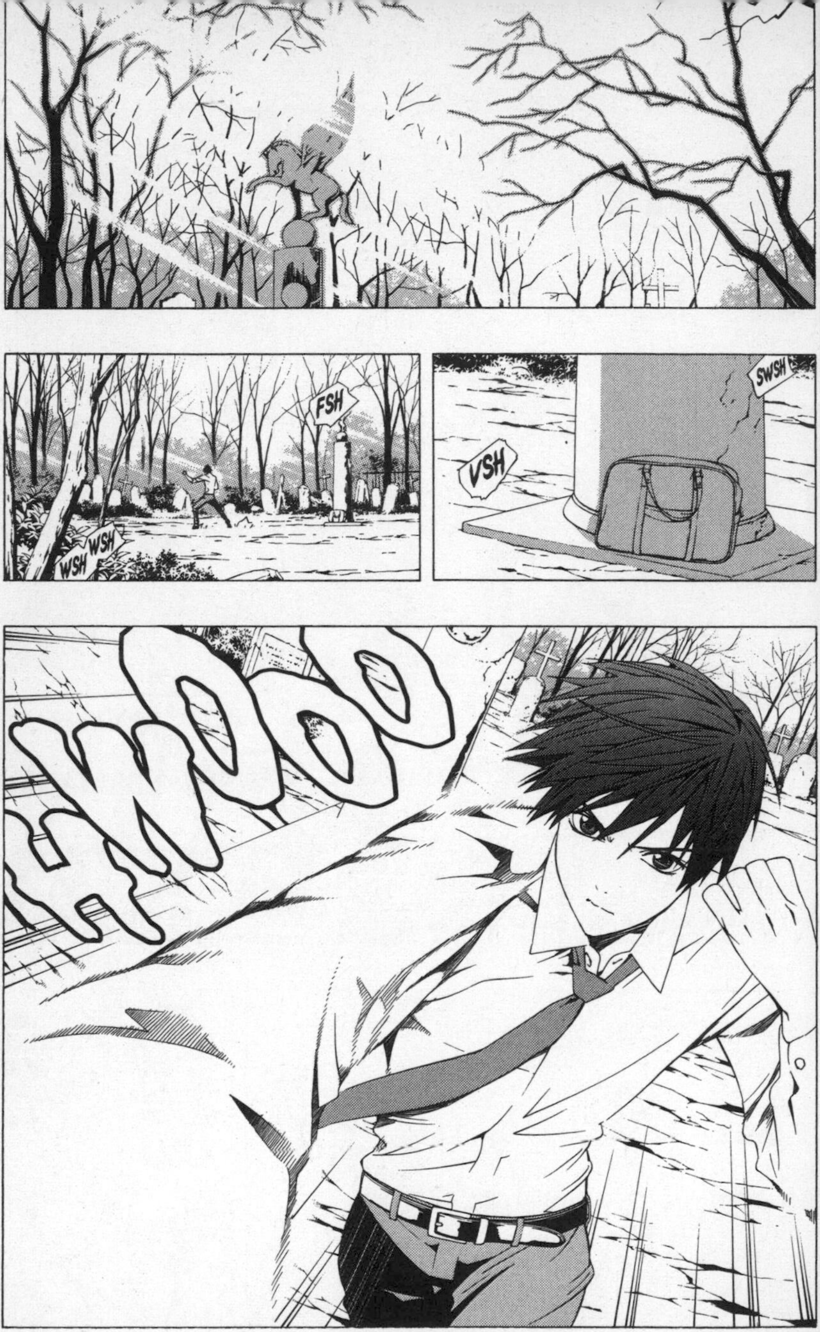
SWSH
VSH
FSH
WSH
WSH

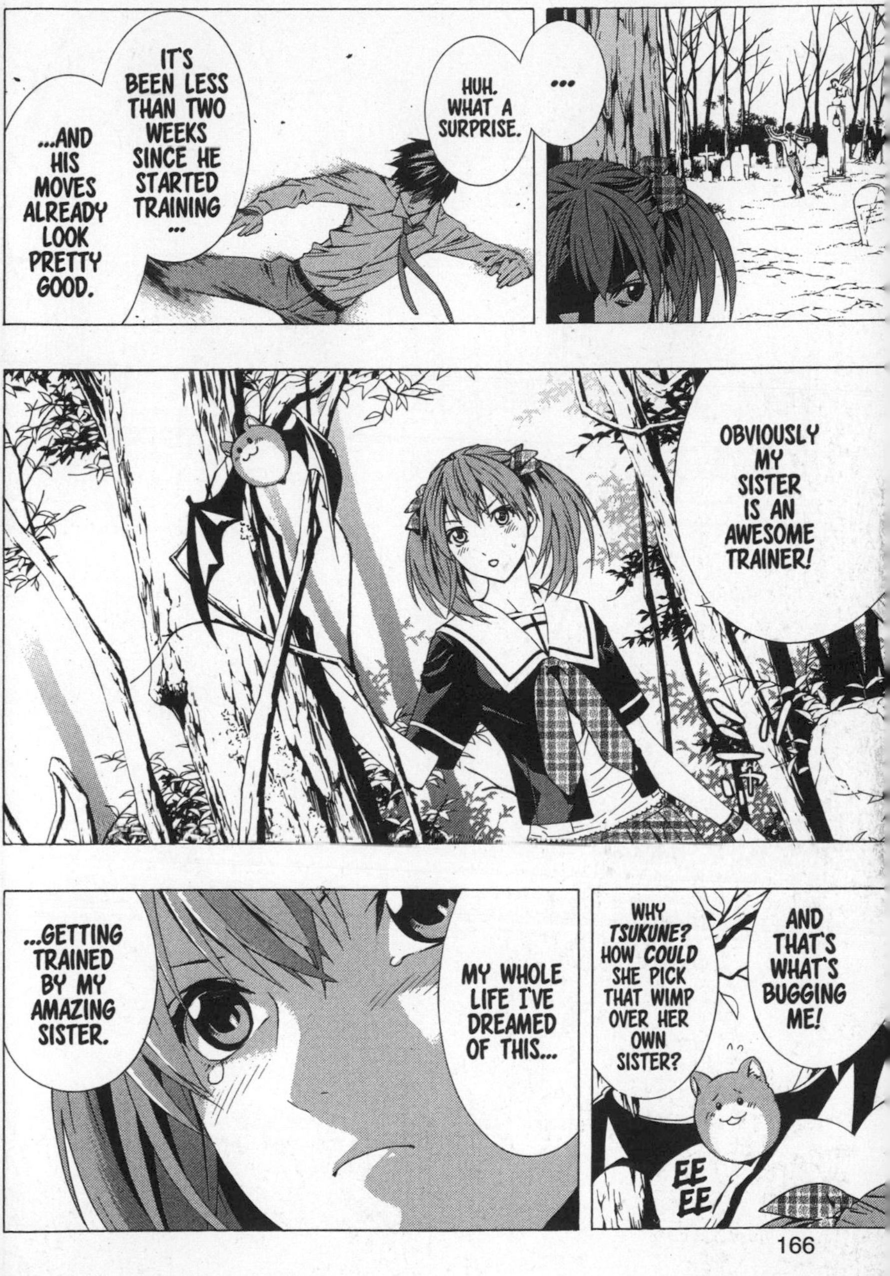
...
HUH. WHAT A SURPRISE.
IT'S BEEN LESS THAN TWO WEEKS SINCE HE STARTED TRAINING...
...AND HIS MOVES ALREADY LOOK PRETTY GOOD.
OBVIOUSLY MY SISTER IS AN AWESOME TRAINER!
AND THAT'S WHAT'S BUGGING ME!
WHY *TSUKUNE*? HOW *COULD* SHE PICK THAT WIMP OVER HER OWN SISTER?
EE EE
MY WHOLE LIFE I'VE DREAMED OF THIS...
...GETTING TRAINED BY MY AMAZING SISTER.

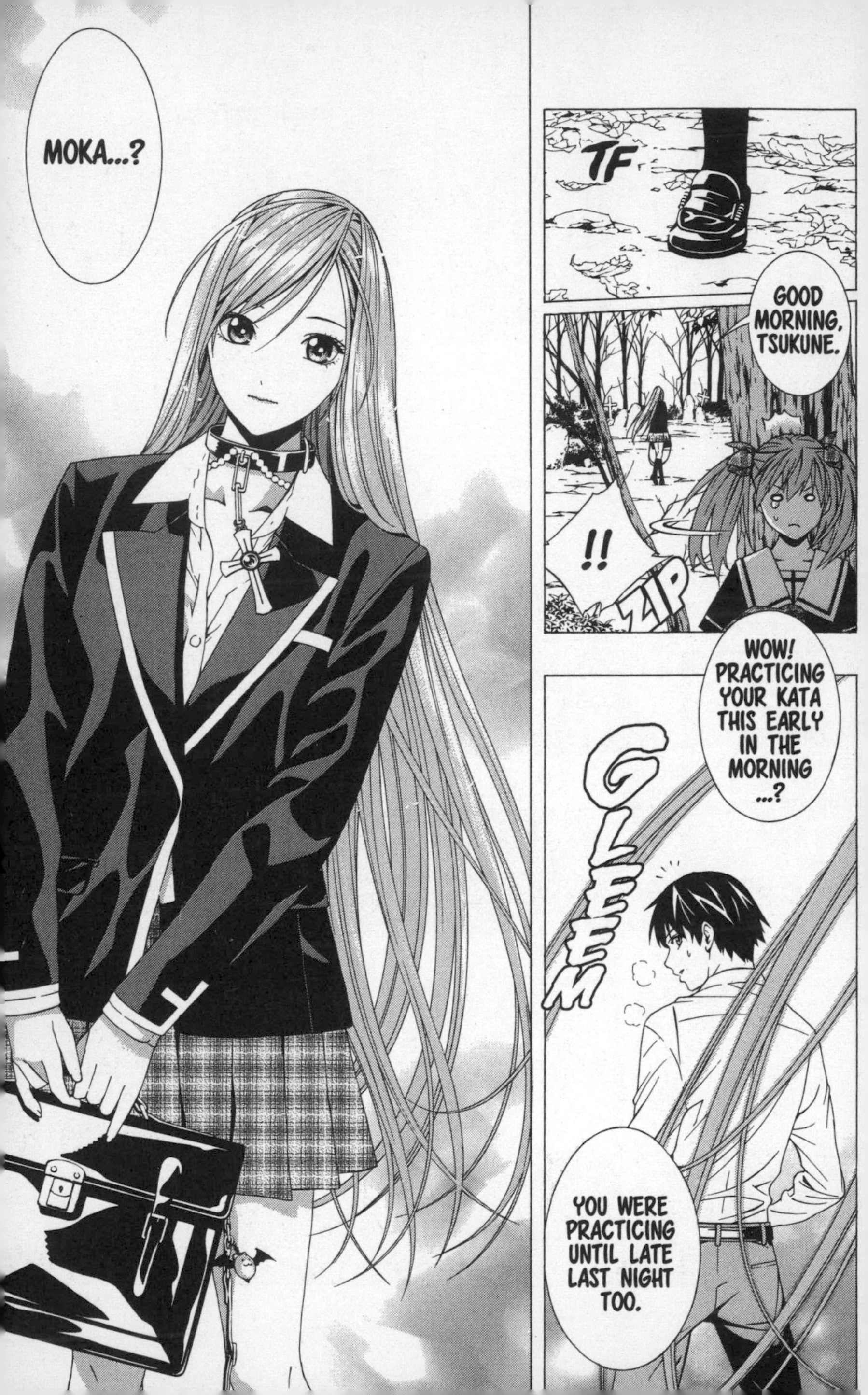
TF
GOOD MORNING, TSUKUNE.
!!
ZIP
WOW! PRACTICING YOUR KATA THIS EARLY IN THE MORNING ...?
GLEEM
YOU WERE PRACTICING UNTIL LATE LAST NIGHT TOO.
MOKA...?

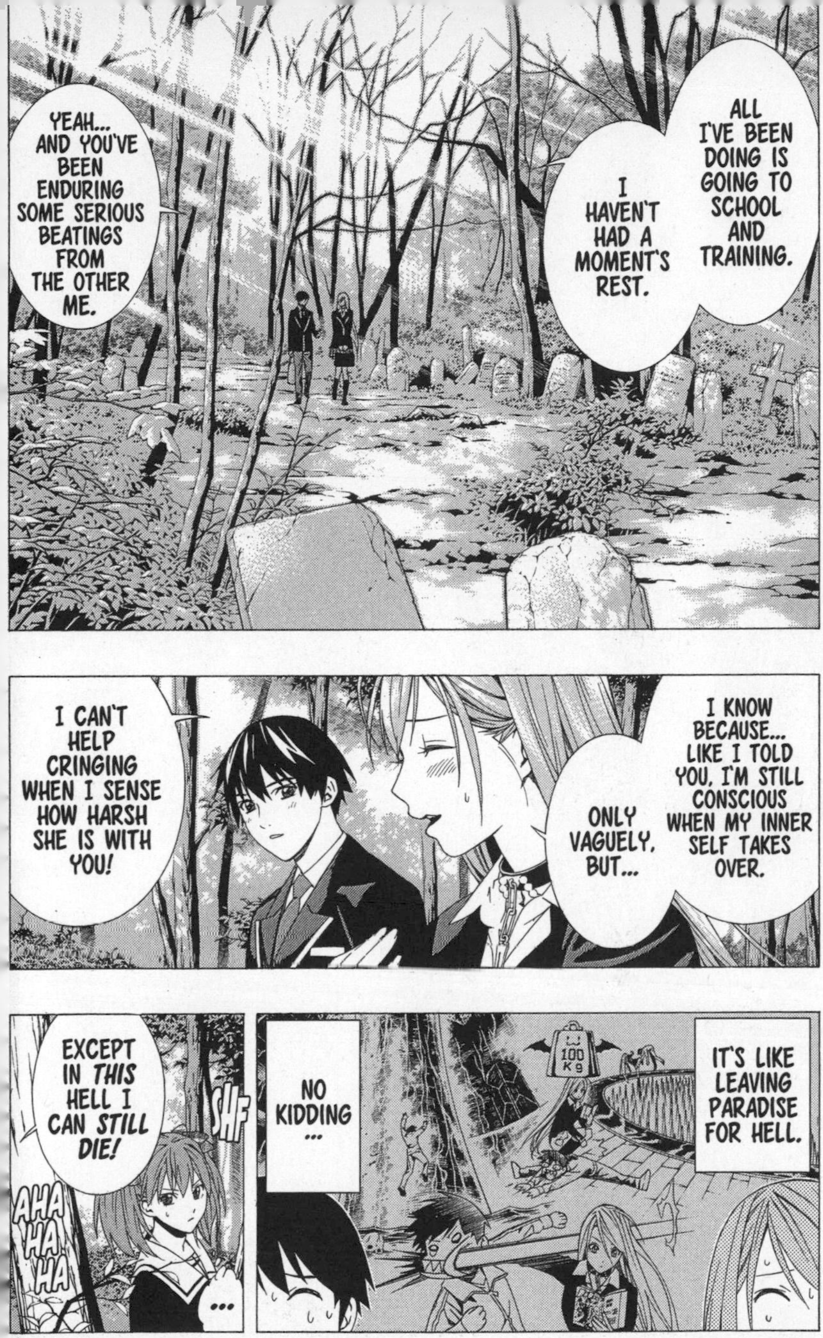
ALL I'VE BEEN DOING IS GOING TO SCHOOL AND TRAINING.
I HAVEN'T HAD A MOMENT'S REST.
YEAH... AND YOU'VE BEEN ENDURING SOME SERIOUS BEATINGS FROM THE OTHER ME.
I KNOW BECAUSE... LIKE I TOLD YOU, I'M STILL CONSCIOUS WHEN MY INNER SELF TAKES OVER.
ONLY VAGUELY, BUT...
I CAN'T HELP CRINGING WHEN I SENSE HOW HARSH SHE IS WITH YOU!
IT'S LIKE LEAVING PARADISE FOR HELL.
100 Kg
NO KIDDING...
EXCEPT IN *THIS* HELL I CAN *STILL* DIE!
SHF
AHA HA HA
...

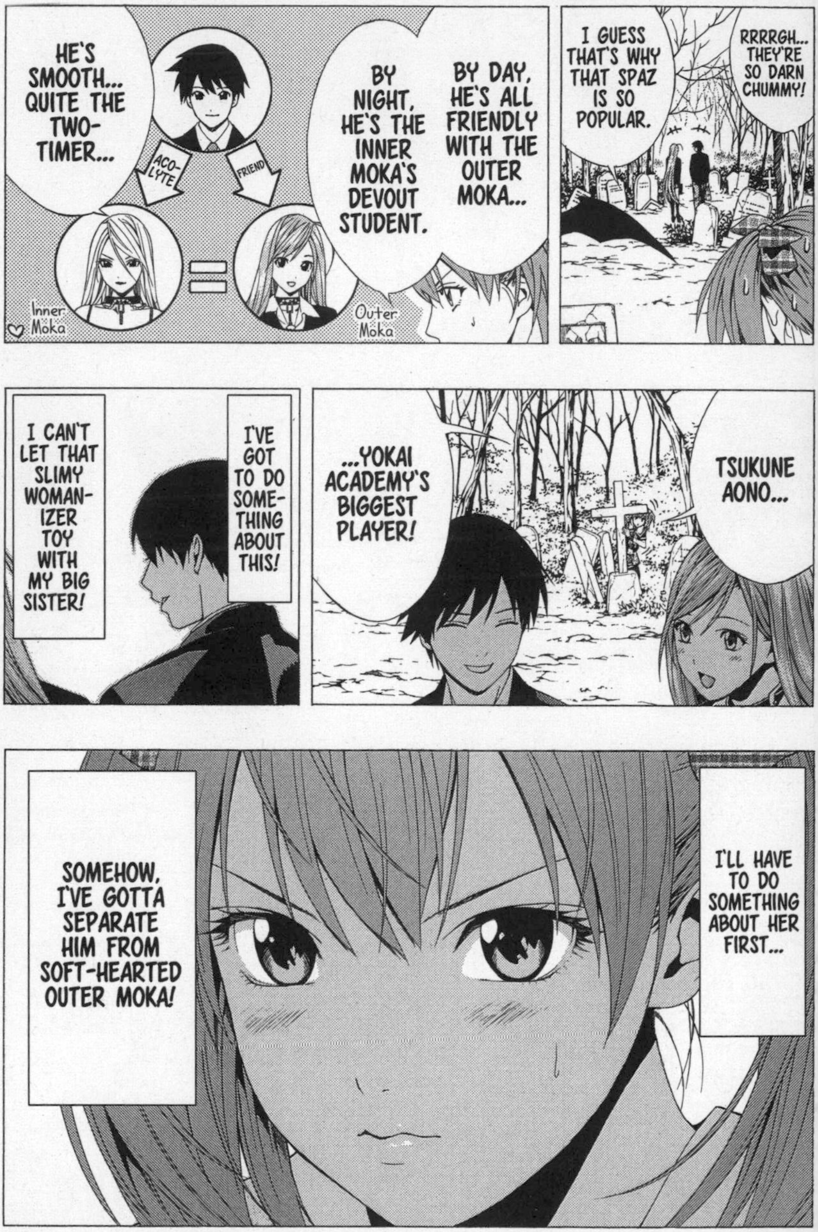
RRRRGH... THEY'RE SO DARN CHUMMY!
I GUESS THAT'S WHY THAT SPAZ IS SO POPULAR.
BY DAY, HE'S ALL FRIENDLY WITH THE OUTER MOKA...
BY NIGHT, HE'S THE INNER MOKA'S DEVOUT STUDENT.
HE'S SMOOTH... QUITE THE TWO-TIMER...
FRIEND
ACOLYTE
Outer Moka
Inner Moka
TSUKUNE AONO...
...YOKAI ACADEMY'S BIGGEST PLAYER!
I'VE GOT TO DO SOMETHING ABOUT THIS!
I CAN'T LET THAT SLIMY WOMANIZER TOY WITH MY BIG SISTER!
I'LL HAVE TO DO SOMETHING ABOUT HER FIRST...
SOMEHOW, I'VE GOTTA SEPARATE HIM FROM SOFT-HEARTED OUTER MOKA!

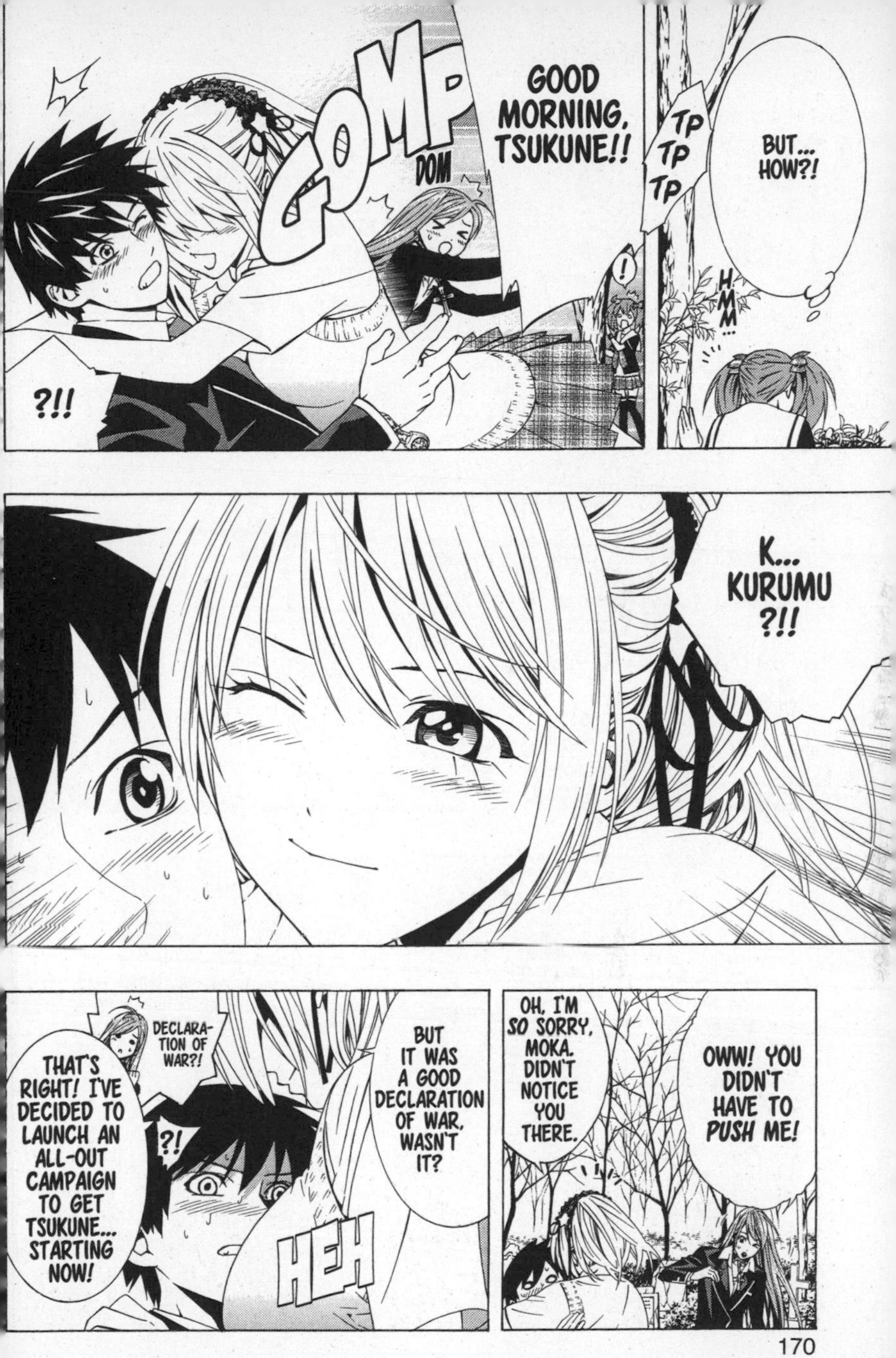
BUT... HOW?!
TP TP TP
HMM...
GOOD MORNING, TSUKUNE!!
COMP
DOM
?!!
K... KURUMU ?!!
OWW! YOU DIDN'T HAVE TO PUSH ME!
OH, I'M SO SORRY, MOKA. DIDN'T NOTICE YOU THERE.
BUT IT WAS A GOOD DECLARATION OF WAR, WASN'T IT?
HEH
DECLARATION OF WAR?!
?!
THAT'S RIGHT! I'VE DECIDED TO LAUNCH AN ALL-OUT CAMPAIGN TO GET TSUKUNE... STARTING NOW!

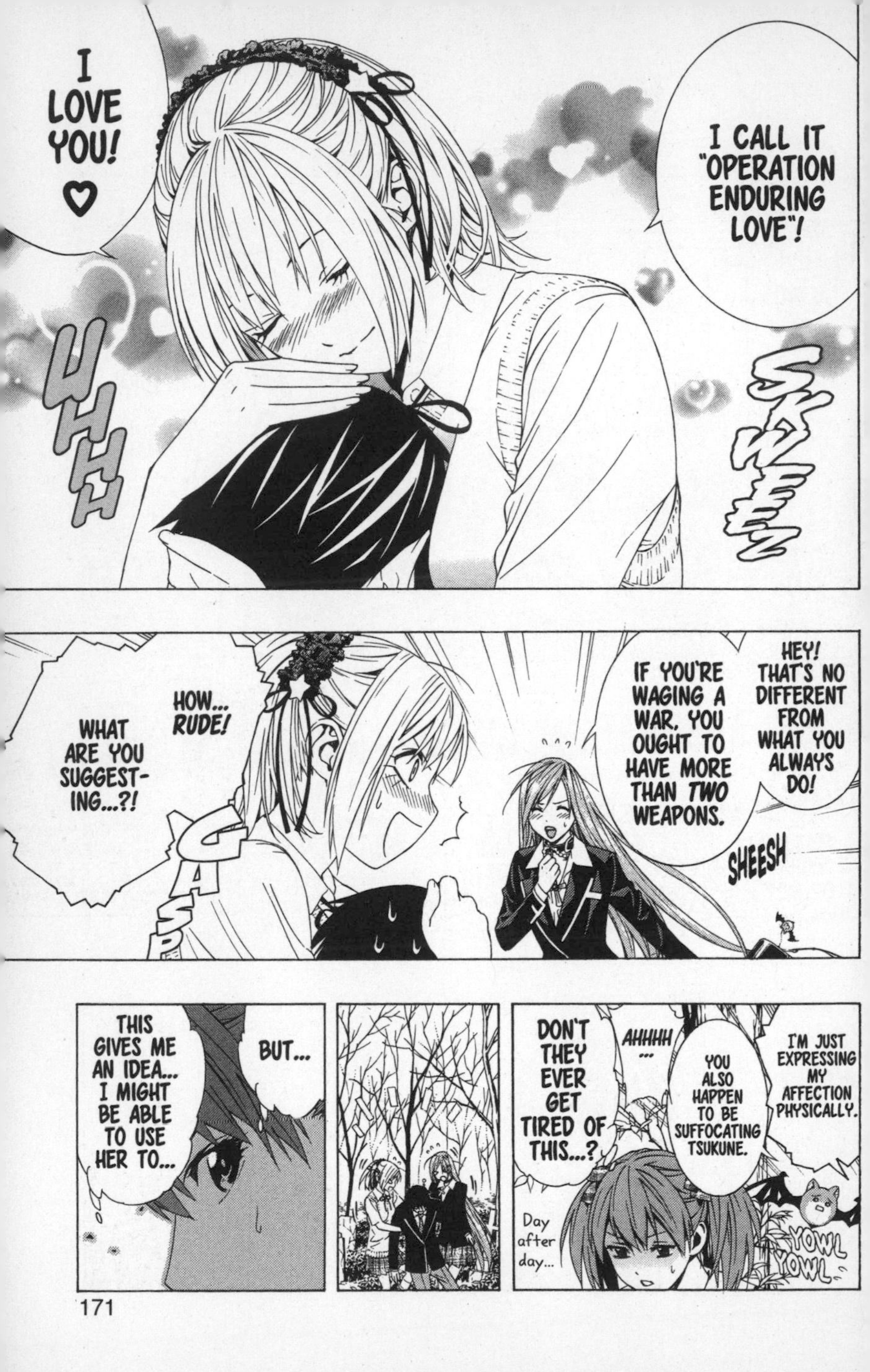
I CALL IT "OPERATION ENDURING LOVE"!
SKWEEZ
I LOVE YOU! ♥
UHHH
HEY! THAT'S NO DIFFERENT FROM WHAT YOU ALWAYS DO!
IF YOU'RE WAGING A WAR, YOU OUGHT TO HAVE MORE THAN *TWO* WEAPONS.
SHEESH
HOW... RUDE!
WHAT ARE YOU SUGGEST-ING...?!
GASP
I'M JUST EXPRESSING MY AFFECTION PHYSICALLY.
YOU ALSO HAPPEN TO BE SUFFOCATING TSUKUNE.
AHHHH...
DON'T THEY EVER GET TIRED OF THIS...?
YOWL YOWL
Day after day...
BUT...
THIS GIVES ME AN IDEA... I MIGHT BE ABLE TO USE HER TO...

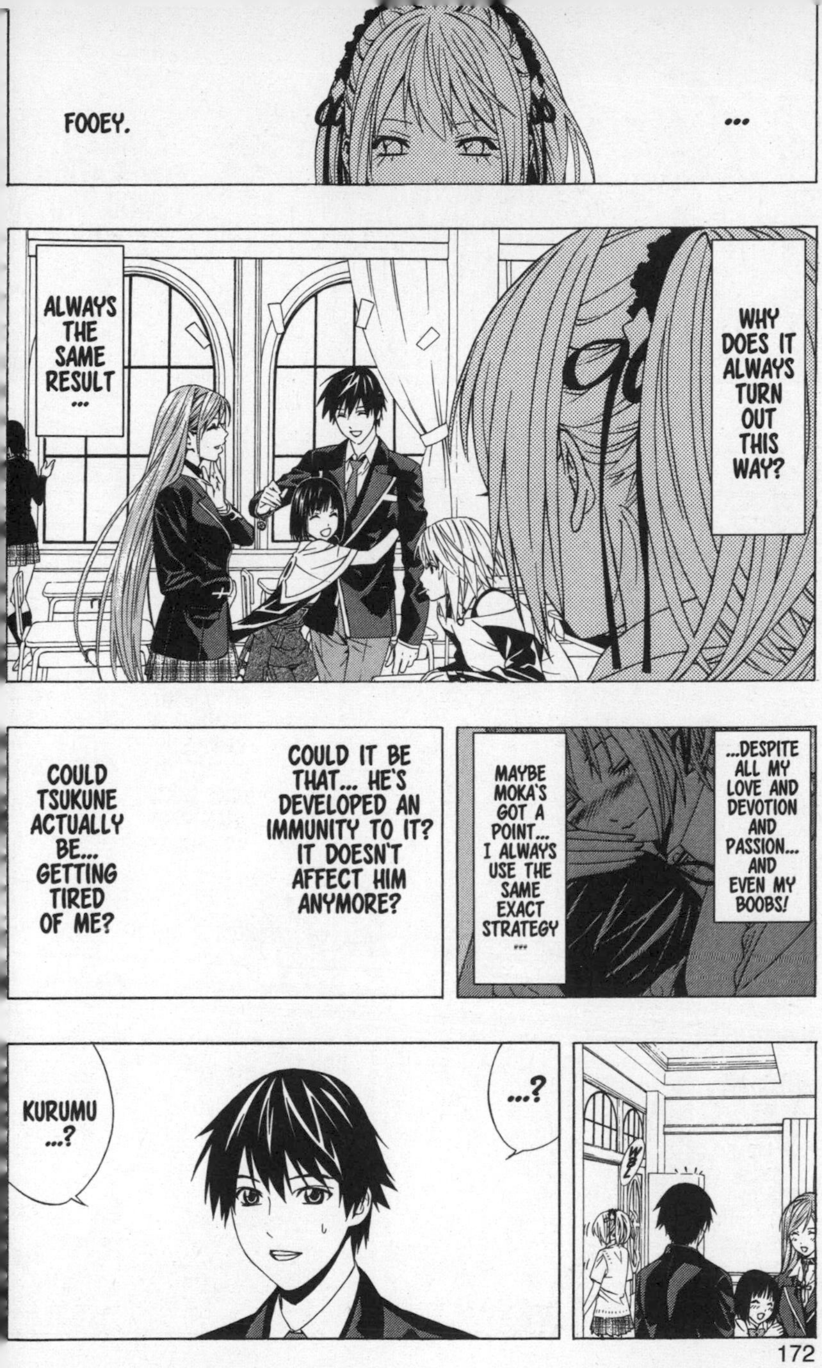
...
FOOEY.
WHY DOES IT ALWAYS TURN OUT THIS WAY?
ALWAYS THE SAME RESULT...
...DESPITE ALL MY LOVE AND DEVOTION AND PASSION... AND EVEN MY BOOBS!
MAYBE MOKA'S GOT A POINT... I ALWAYS USE THE SAME EXACT STRATEGY...
COULD IT BE THAT... HE'S DEVELOPED AN IMMUNITY TO IT? IT DOESN'T AFFECT HIM ANYMORE?
COULD TSUKUNE ACTUALLY BE... GETTING TIRED OF ME?
...?
KURUMU...?

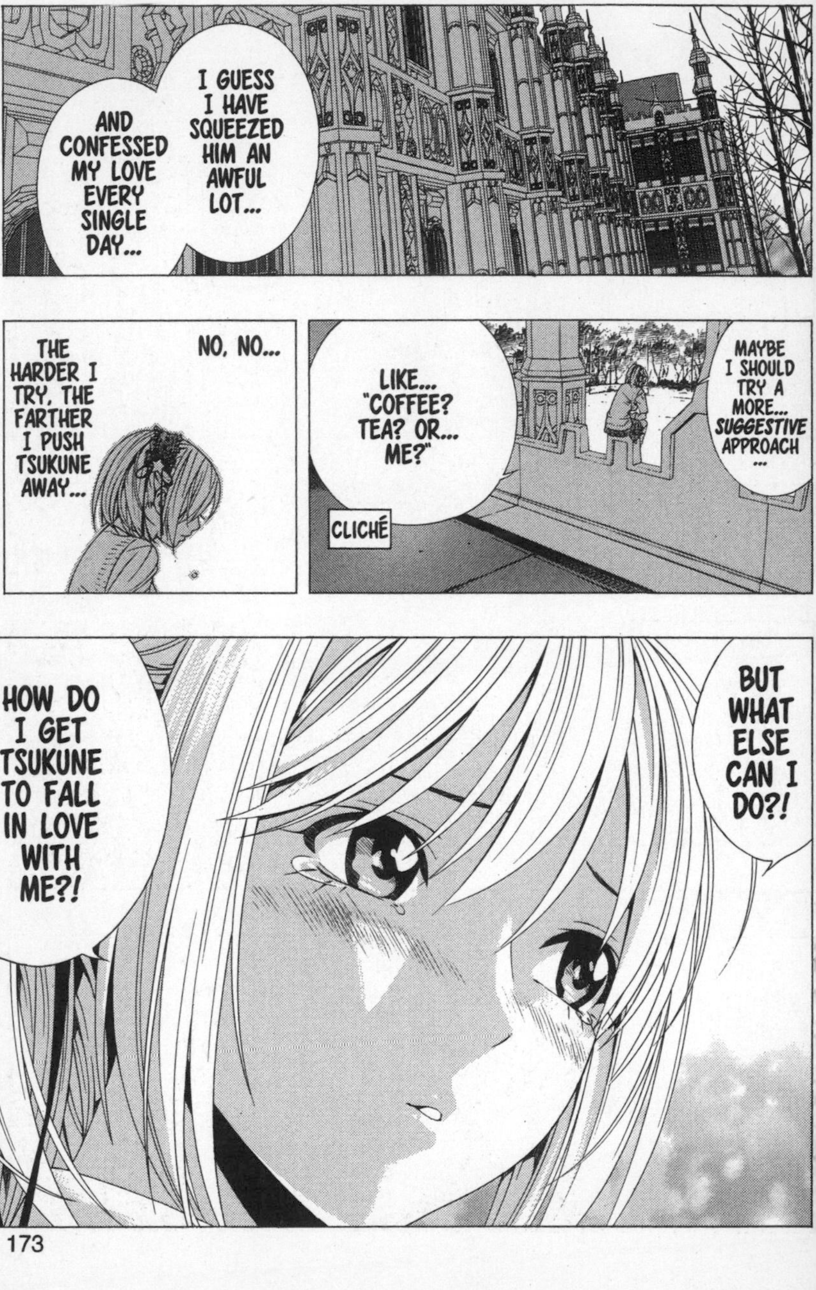
I GUESS I HAVE SQUEEZED HIM AN AWFUL LOT...
AND CONFESSED MY LOVE EVERY SINGLE DAY...
MAYBE I SHOULD TRY A MORE... *SUGGESTIVE* APPROACH...
LIKE... "COFFEE? TEA? OR... ME?"
CLICHÉ
NO, NO...
THE HARDER I TRY, THE FARTHER I PUSH TSUKUNE AWAY...
BUT WHAT ELSE CAN I DO?!
HOW DO I GET TSUKUNE TO FALL IN LOVE WITH ME?!

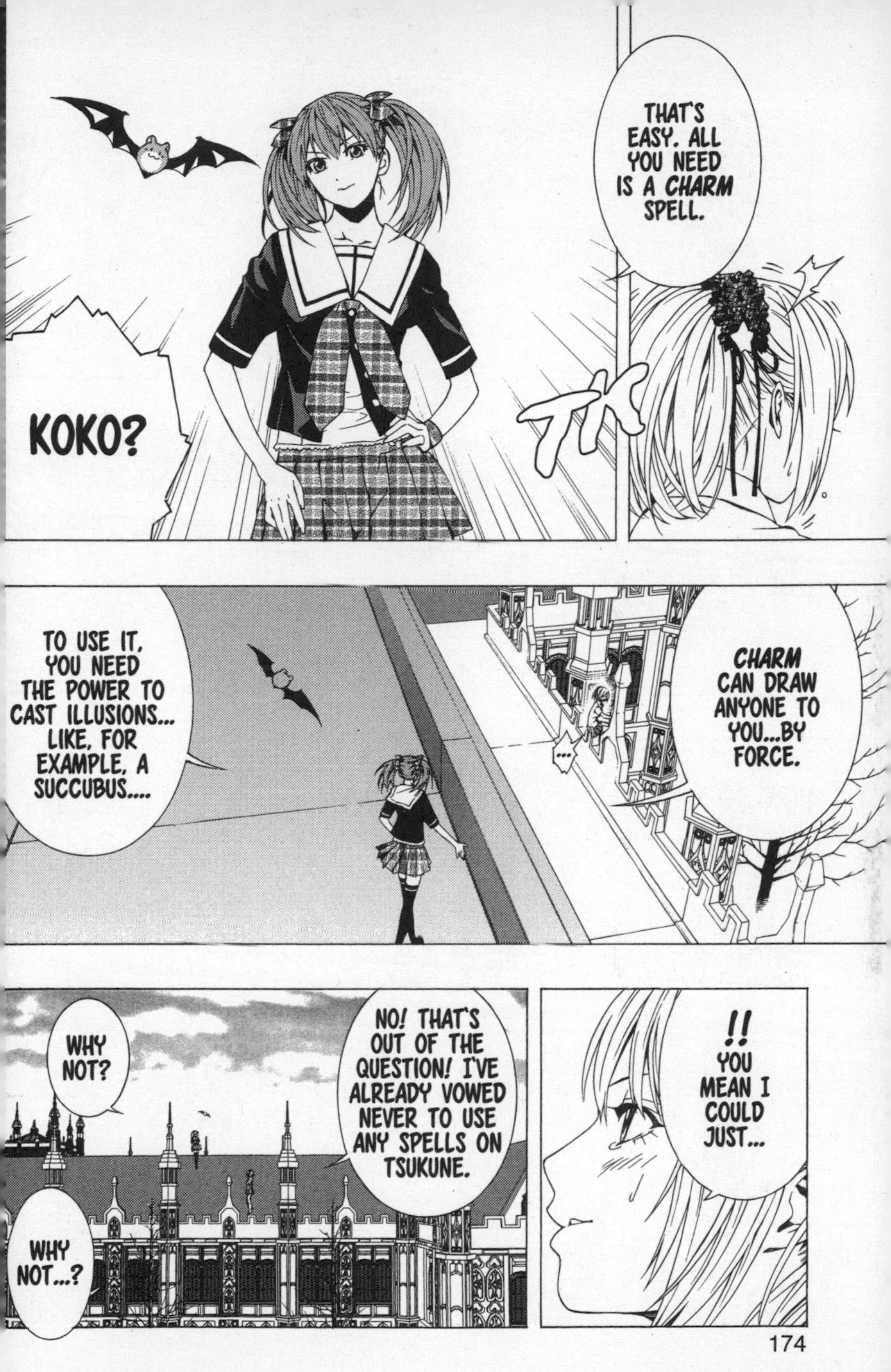
THAT'S EASY. ALL YOU NEED IS A *CHARM* SPELL.
TK
KOKO?
CHARM CAN DRAW ANYONE TO YOU...BY FORCE.
...
TO USE IT, YOU NEED THE POWER TO CAST ILLUSIONS... LIKE, FOR EXAMPLE, A SUCCUBUS....
!! YOU MEAN I COULD JUST...
NO! THAT'S OUT OF THE QUESTION! I'VE ALREADY VOWED NEVER TO USE ANY SPELLS ON TSUKUNE.
WHY NOT?
WHY NOT...?

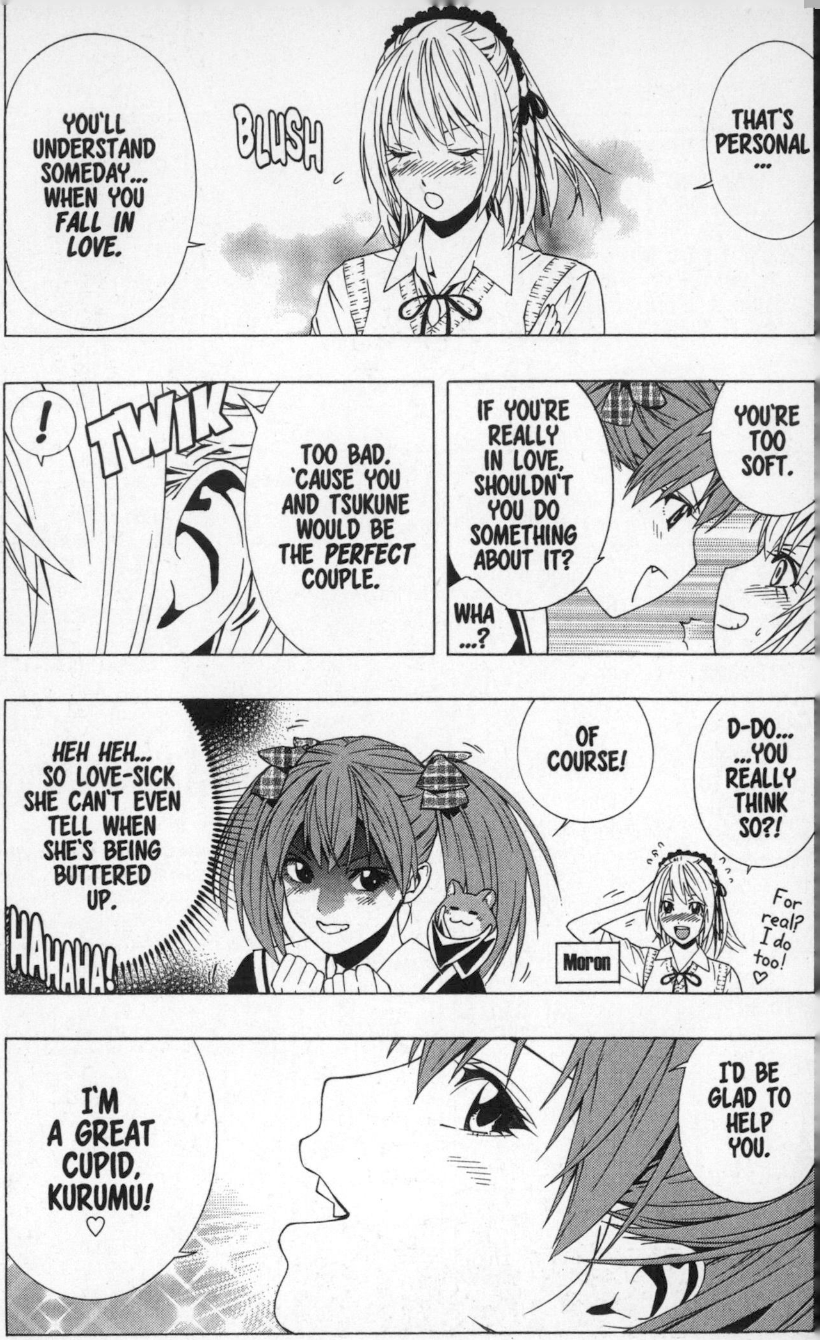

THAT'S PERSONAL ...
BLUSH
YOU'LL UNDERSTAND SOMEDAY... WHEN YOU *FALL IN LOVE.*
YOU'RE TOO SOFT.
IF YOU'RE REALLY IN LOVE, SHOULDN'T YOU DO SOMETHING ABOUT IT?
WHA ...?
TOO BAD. 'CAUSE YOU AND TSUKUNE WOULD BE THE *PERFECT* COUPLE.
TWIK
!
D-DO... ...YOU REALLY THINK SO?!
For real? I do too! ♡
OF COURSE!
Moron
HEH HEH... SO LOVE-SICK SHE CAN'T EVEN TELL WHEN SHE'S BEING BUTTERED UP.
HAHAHA!
I'D BE GLAD TO HELP YOU.
I'M A GREAT CUPID, KURUMU! ♡

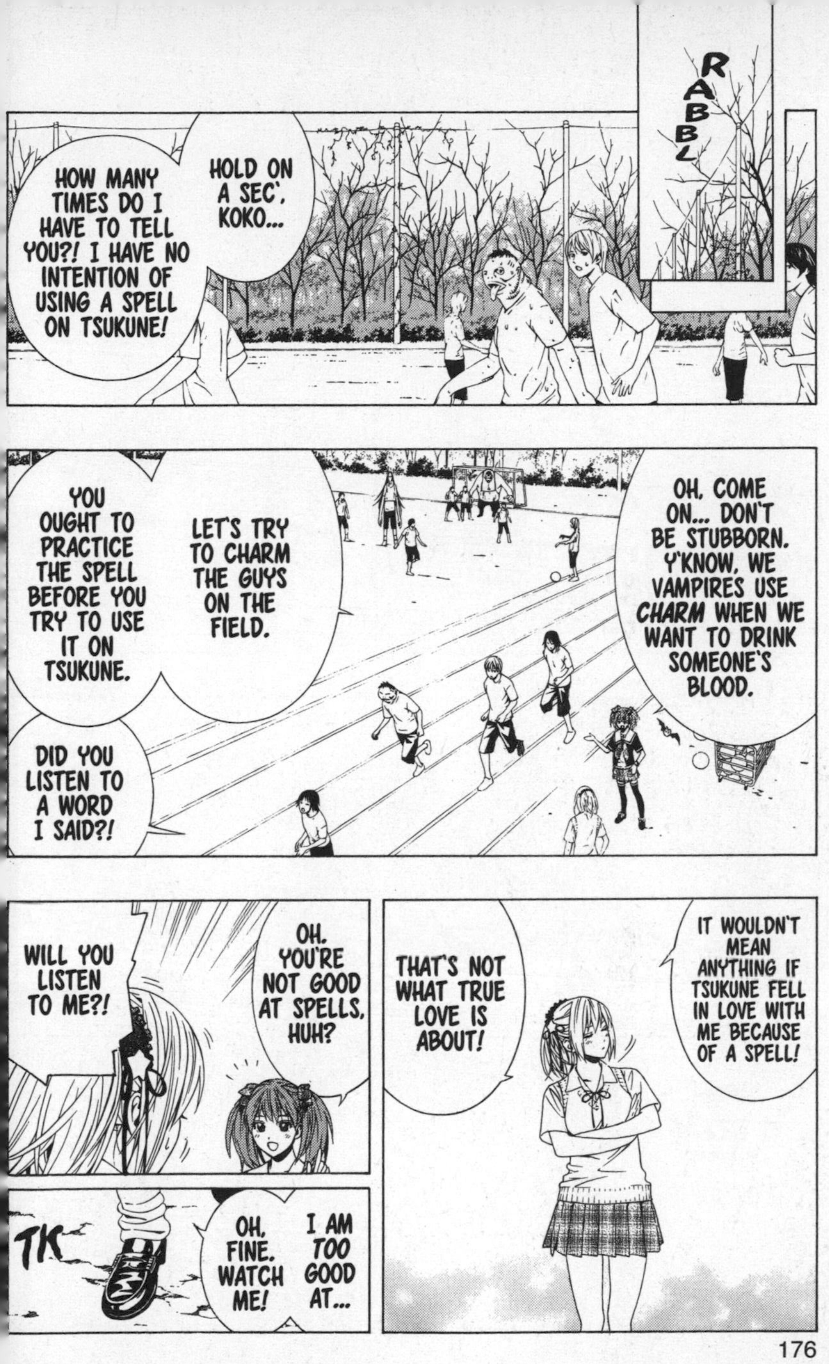
RABBL
HOLD ON A SEC', KOKO...
HOW MANY TIMES DO I HAVE TO TELL YOU?! I HAVE NO INTENTION OF USING A SPELL ON TSUKUNE!
OH, COME ON... DON'T BE STUBBORN. Y'KNOW, WE VAMPIRES USE *CHARM* WHEN WE WANT TO DRINK SOMEONE'S BLOOD.
LET'S TRY TO CHARM THE GUYS ON THE FIELD.
YOU OUGHT TO PRACTICE THE SPELL BEFORE YOU TRY TO USE IT ON TSUKUNE.
DID YOU LISTEN TO A WORD I SAID?!
IT WOULDN'T MEAN ANYTHING IF TSUKUNE FELL IN LOVE WITH ME BECAUSE OF A SPELL!
THAT'S NOT WHAT TRUE LOVE IS ABOUT!
OH. YOU'RE NOT GOOD AT SPELLS, HUH?
WILL YOU LISTEN TO ME?!
I AM *TOO* GOOD AT...
OH, FINE. WATCH ME!
TK

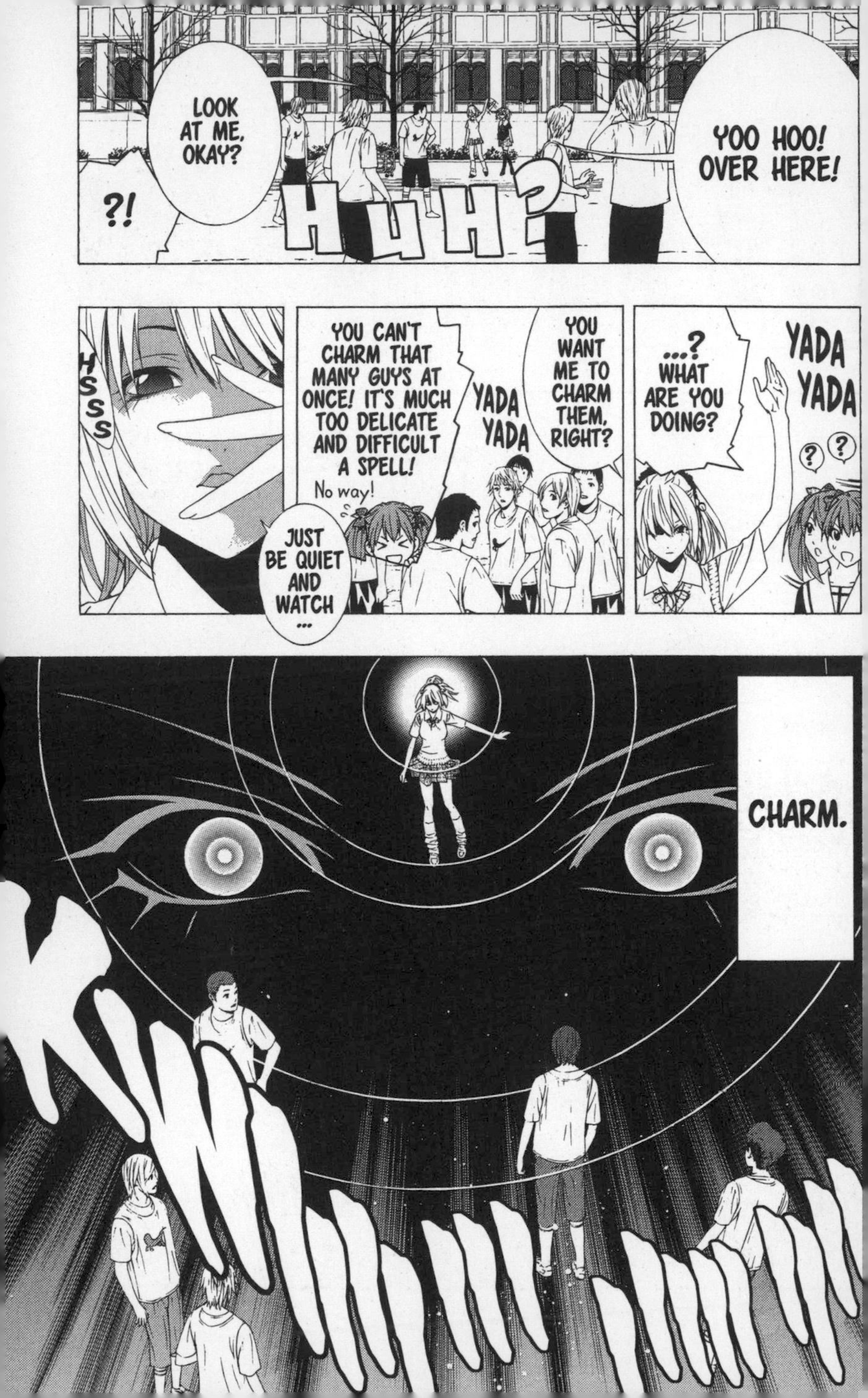
YOO HOO! OVER HERE!
HUH?
LOOK AT ME, OKAY?
?!
YADA YADA
...? WHAT ARE YOU DOING?
? ?
YOU WANT ME TO CHARM THEM, RIGHT?
YADA YADA
YOU CAN'T CHARM THAT MANY GUYS AT ONCE! IT'S MUCH TOO DELICATE AND DIFFICULT A SPELL!
No way!
JUST BE QUIET AND WATCH ...
HSSS
CHARM.

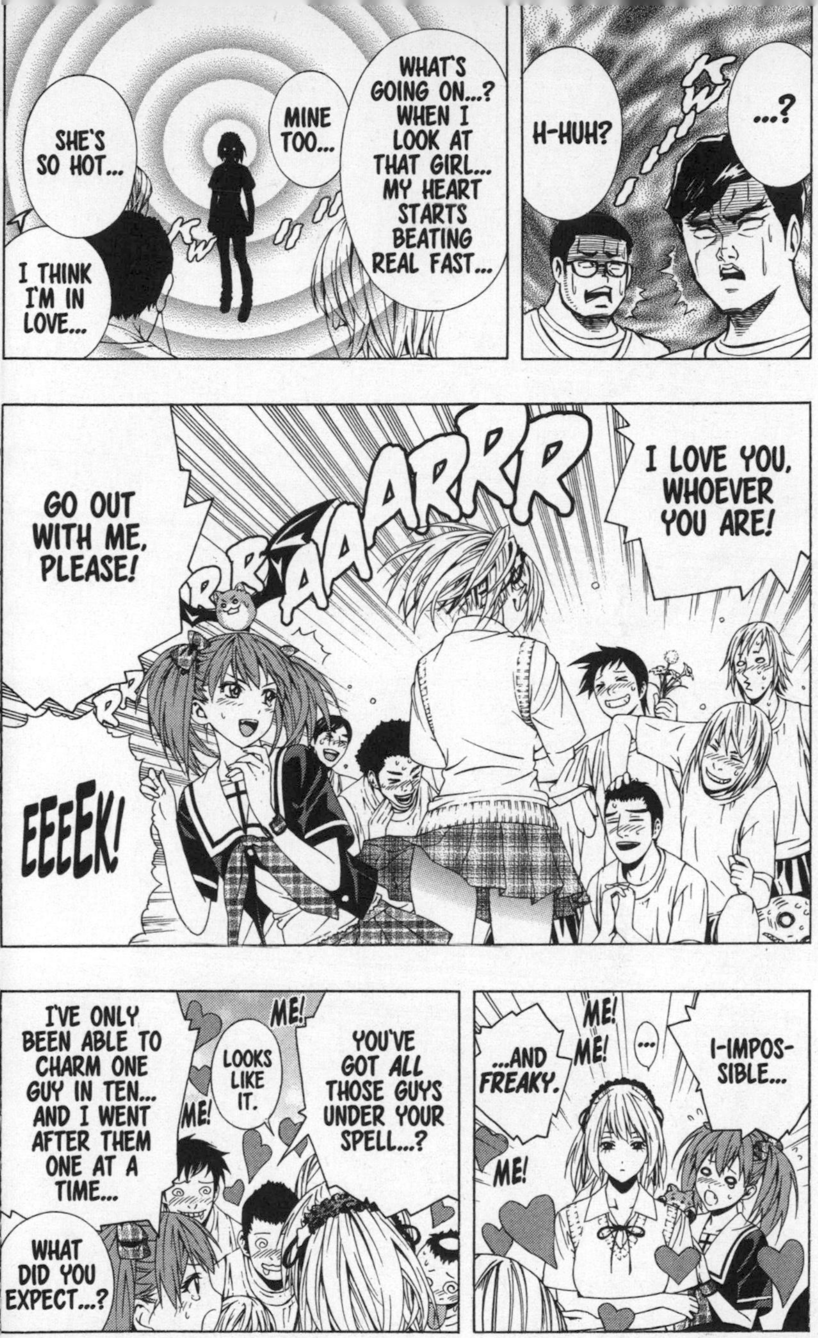
...?
H-HUH?
KW-I-I-I-I
WHAT'S GOING ON...? WHEN I LOOK AT THAT GIRL... MY HEART STARTS BEATING REAL FAST...
MINE TOO...
SHE'S SO HOT...
I THINK I'M IN LOVE...
I LOVE YOU, WHOEVER YOU ARE!
RRAAARRR
GO OUT WITH ME, PLEASE!
EEEEK!
I-IMPOS-SIBLE...
...
ME! ME!
...AND *FREAKY*.
ME!
YOU'VE GOT *ALL* THOSE GUYS UNDER YOUR SPELL...?
ME!
LOOKS LIKE IT.
I'VE ONLY BEEN ABLE TO CHARM ONE GUY IN TEN... AND I WENT AFTER THEM ONE AT A TIME...
ME!
WHAT DID YOU EXPECT...?

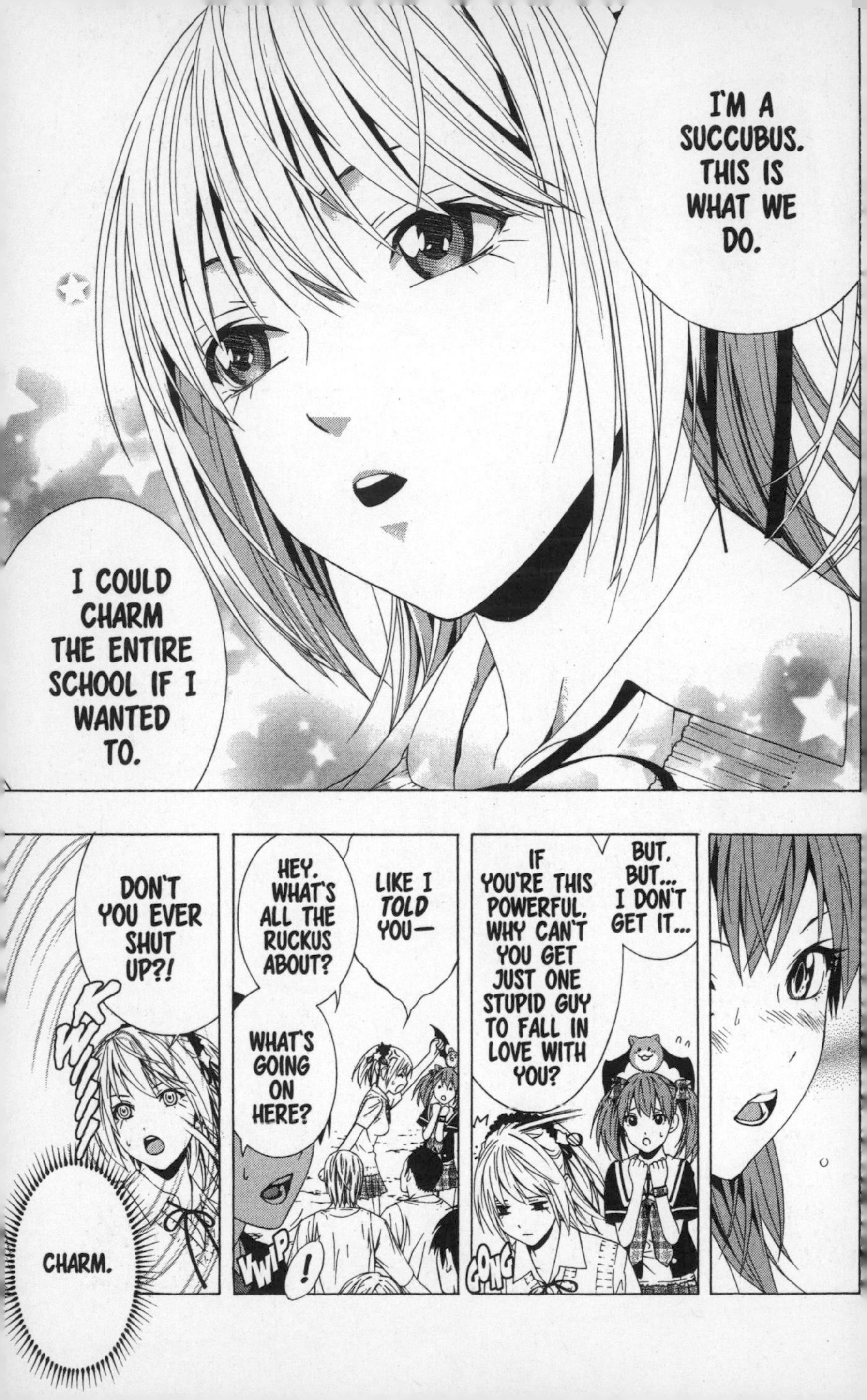
I'M A SUCCUBUS. THIS IS WHAT WE DO.
I COULD CHARM THE ENTIRE SCHOOL IF I WANTED TO.
BUT, BUT... I DON'T GET IT...
IF YOU'RE THIS POWERFUL, WHY CAN'T YOU GET JUST ONE STUPID GUY TO FALL IN LOVE WITH YOU?
GONG
LIKE I *TOLD* YOU—
HEY. WHAT'S ALL THE RUCKUS ABOUT?
WHAT'S GOING ON HERE?
VWIP
!
DON'T YOU EVER SHUT UP?!
CHARM.

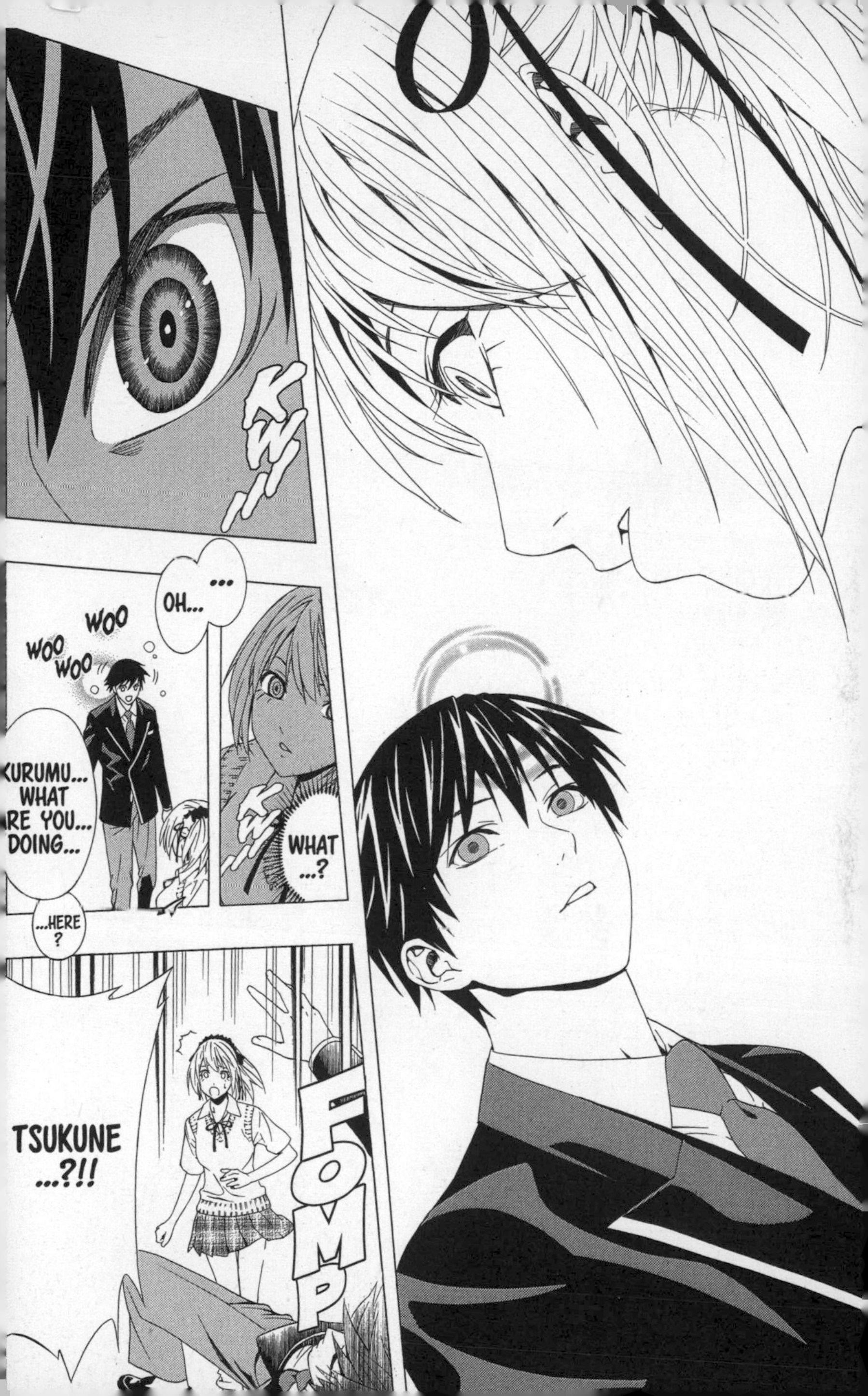

WHAT
...?
WOO
WOO
WOO
... OH...
KURUMU...
WHAT
RE YOU...
DOING...
...HERE
?
FOMP
TSUKUNE
...?!!

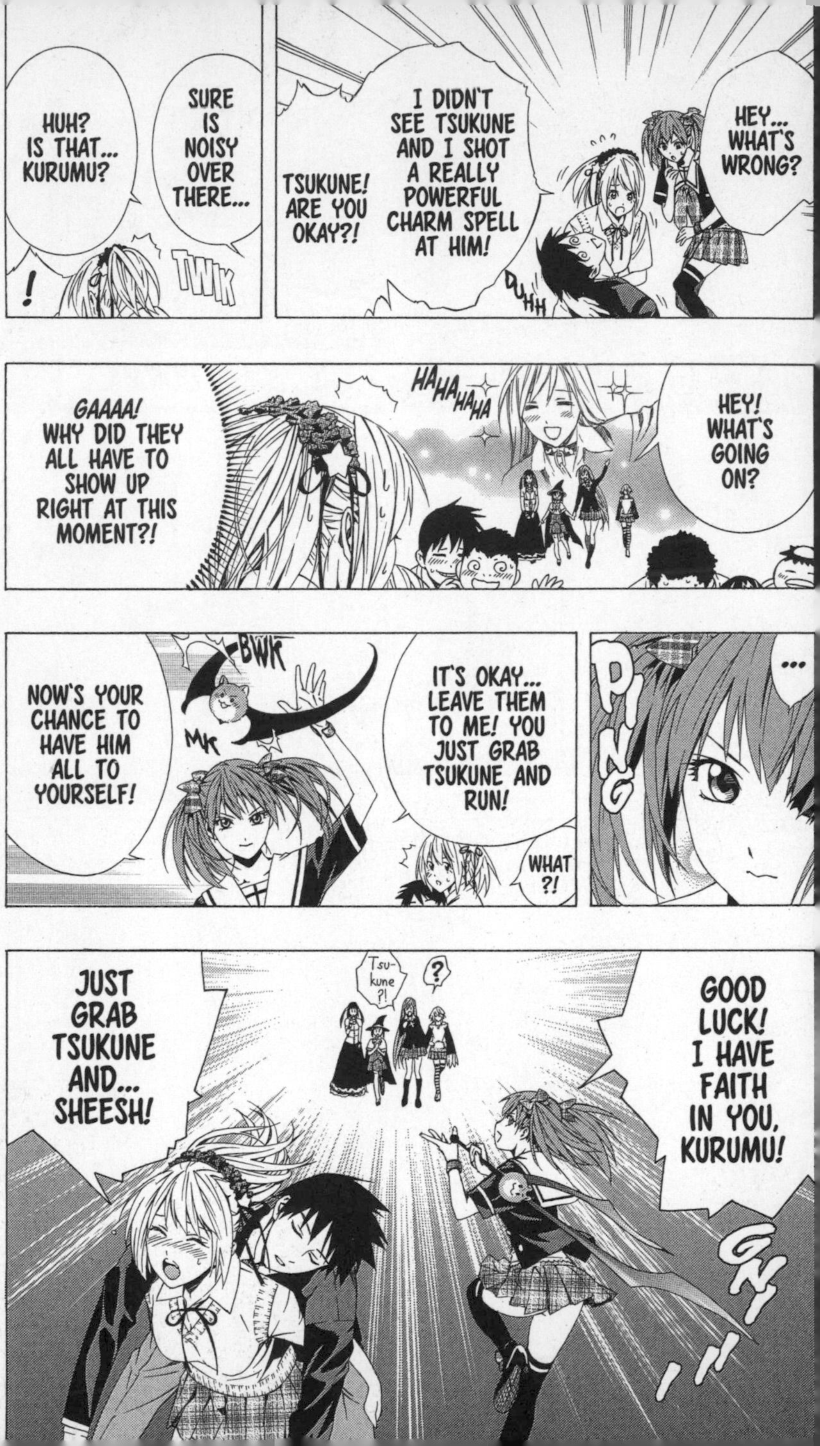
HEY... WHAT'S WRONG?
I DIDN'T SEE TSUKUNE AND I SHOT A REALLY POWERFUL CHARM SPELL AT HIM!
TSUKUNE! ARE YOU OKAY?!
DUHH
SURE IS NOISY OVER THERE...
HUH? IS THAT... KURUMU?
TWIK
!
HEY! WHAT'S GOING ON?
HAHAHAHA
GAAAA! WHY DID THEY ALL HAVE TO SHOW UP RIGHT AT THIS MOMENT?!
...
PING
IT'S OKAY... LEAVE THEM TO ME! YOU JUST GRAB TSUKUNE AND RUN!
WHAT?!
BWK
NOW'S YOUR CHANCE TO HAVE HIM ALL TO YOURSELF!
MK
GOOD LUCK! I HAVE FAITH IN YOU, KURUMU!
?
Tsu-kune?!
JUST GRAB TSUKUNE AND... SHEESH!
GNY

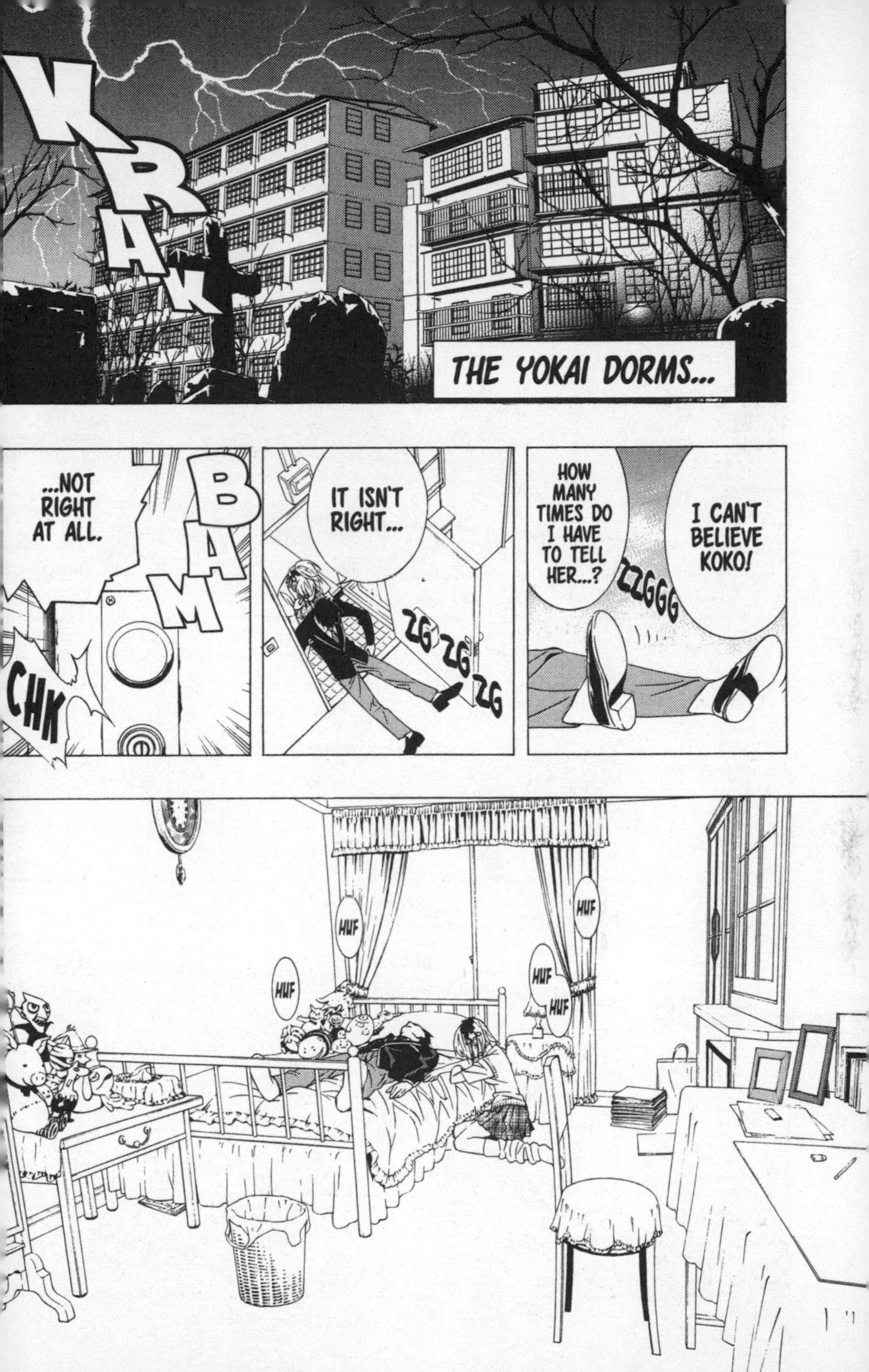
KRAK
THE YOKAI DORMS...
I CAN'T BELIEVE KOKO!
HOW MANY TIMES DO I HAVE TO TELL HER...?
ZZGGG
IT ISN'T RIGHT...
ZG ZG ZG
BAM
...NOT RIGHT AT ALL.
CHK
HUF
HUF
HUF
HUF
HUF

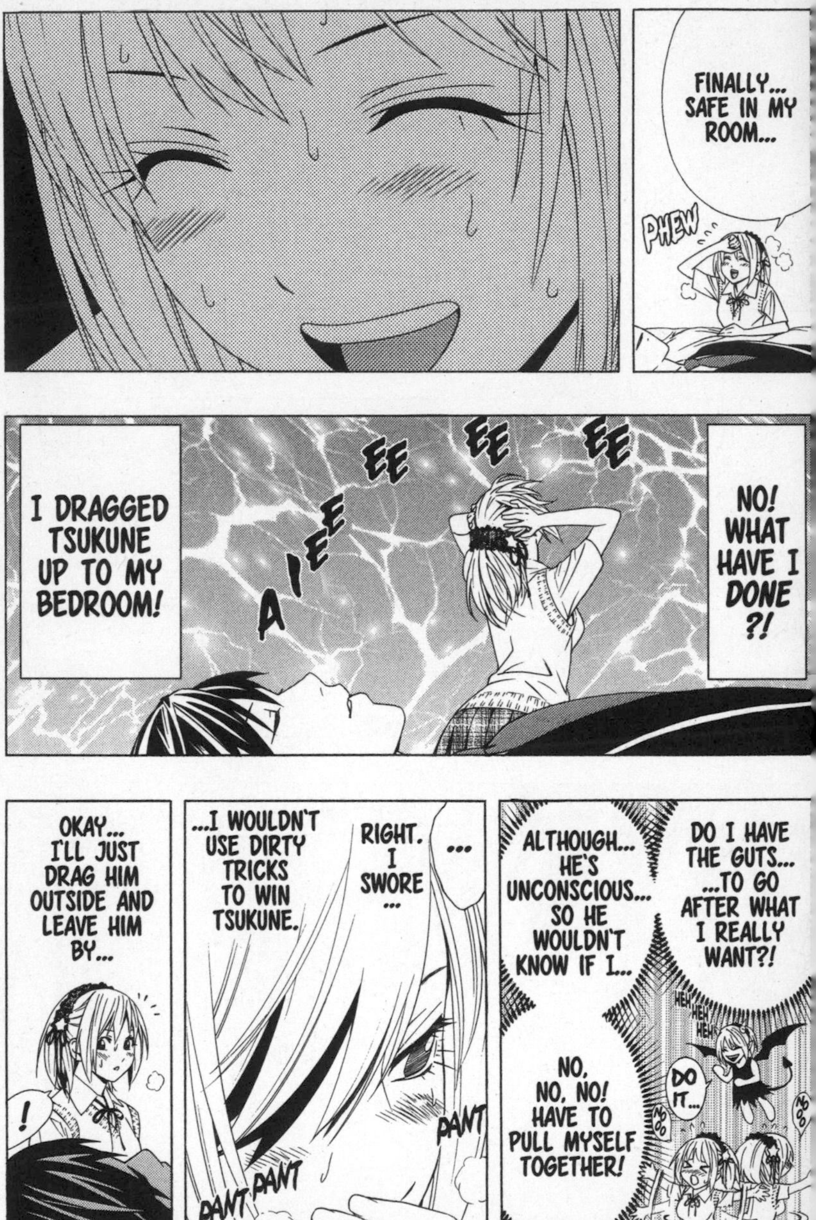

FINALLY... SAFE IN MY ROOM...
PHEW
NO! WHAT HAVE I DONE?!
AIEEEEEEEE
I DRAGGED TSUKUNE UP TO MY BEDROOM!
DO I HAVE THE GUTS... ...TO GO AFTER WHAT I REALLY WANT?!
ALTHOUGH... HE'S UNCONSCIOUS... SO HE WOULDN'T KNOW IF I...
HEH HEH HEH
DO IT...
NO, NO, NO! HAVE TO PULL MYSELF TOGETHER!
...
RIGHT. I SWORE...
...I WOULDN'T USE DIRTY TRICKS TO WIN TSUKUNE.
PANT
PANT PANT
PANT
OKAY... I'LL JUST DRAG HIM OUTSIDE AND LEAVE HIM BY...
!

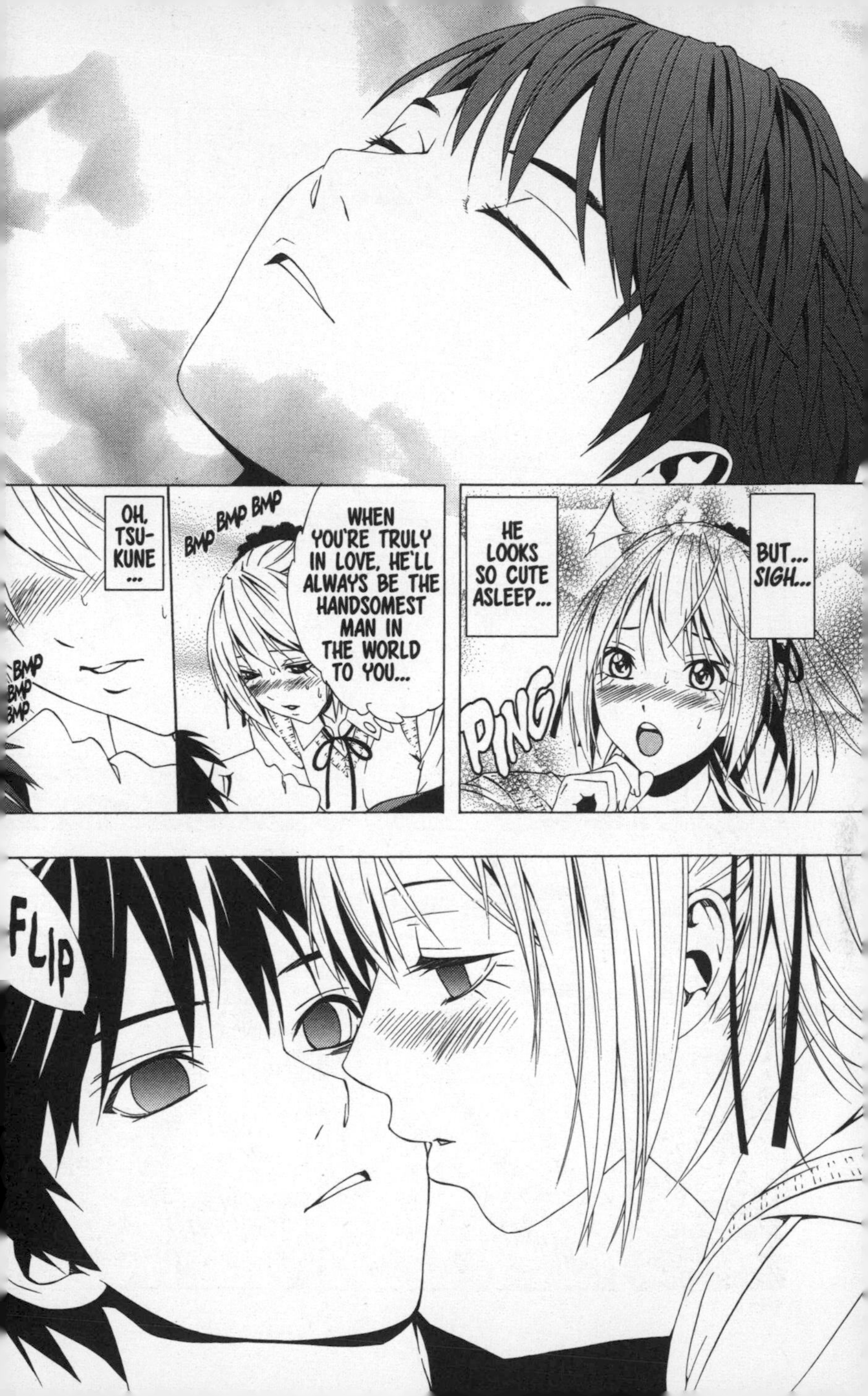
BUT... SIGH...
HE LOOKS SO CUTE ASLEEP...
PING
BMP BMP BMP
WHEN YOU'RE TRULY IN LOVE, HE'LL ALWAYS BE THE HANDSOMEST MAN IN THE WORLD TO YOU...
OH, TSU-KUNE...
BMP BMP BMP
FLIP

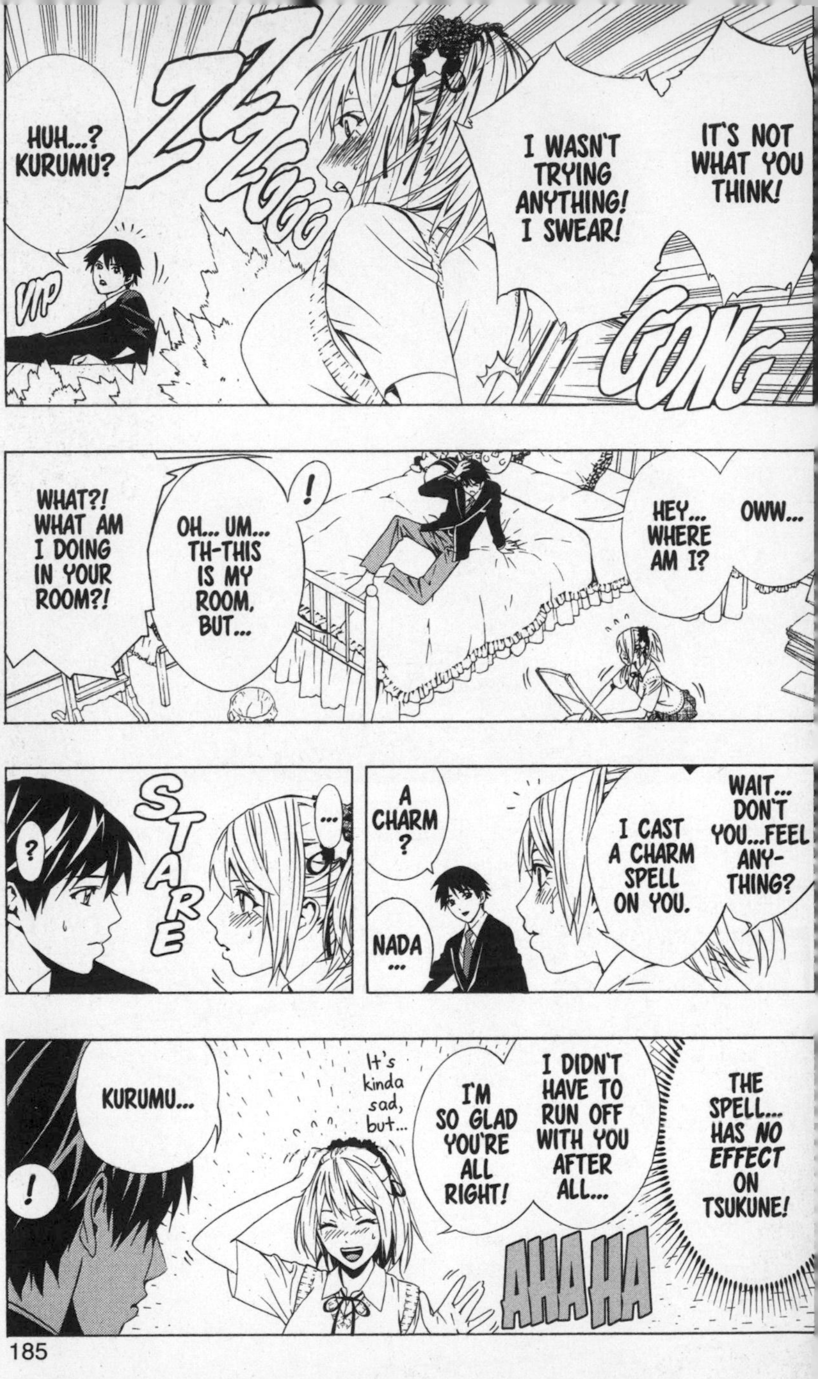

IT'S NOT WHAT YOU THINK!
I WASN'T TRYING ANYTHING! I SWEAR!
GONG
HUH...? KURUMU?
OWW...
HEY... WHERE AM I?
!
OH... UM... TH-THIS IS MY ROOM, BUT...
WHAT?! WHAT AM I DOING IN YOUR ROOM?!
WAIT... DON'T YOU...FEEL ANYTHING?
I CAST A CHARM SPELL ON YOU.
A CHARM?
NADA...
...
STARE
?
THE SPELL... HAS NO EFFECT ON TSUKUNE!
I DIDN'T HAVE TO RUN OFF WITH YOU AFTER ALL...
I'M SO GLAD YOU'RE ALL RIGHT!
It's kinda sad, but...
AHAHA
KURUMU...
!

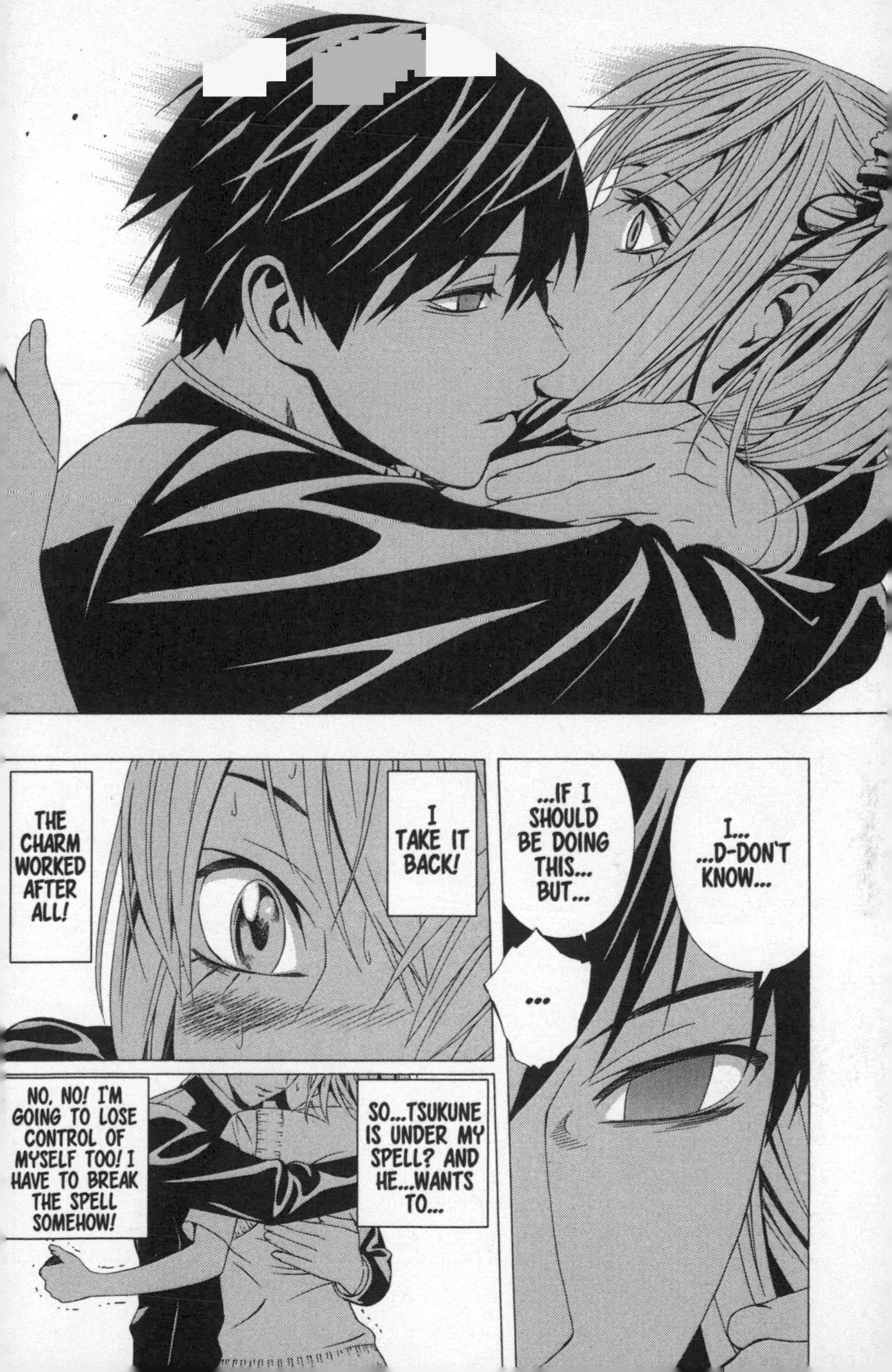
I... ...D-DON'T KNOW...
...IF I SHOULD BE DOING THIS... BUT...
...
I TAKE IT BACK!
THE CHARM WORKED AFTER ALL!
SO...TSUKUNE IS UNDER MY SPELL? AND HE...WANTS TO...
NO, NO! I'M GOING TO LOSE CONTROL OF MYSELF TOO! I HAVE TO BREAK THE SPELL SOMEHOW!

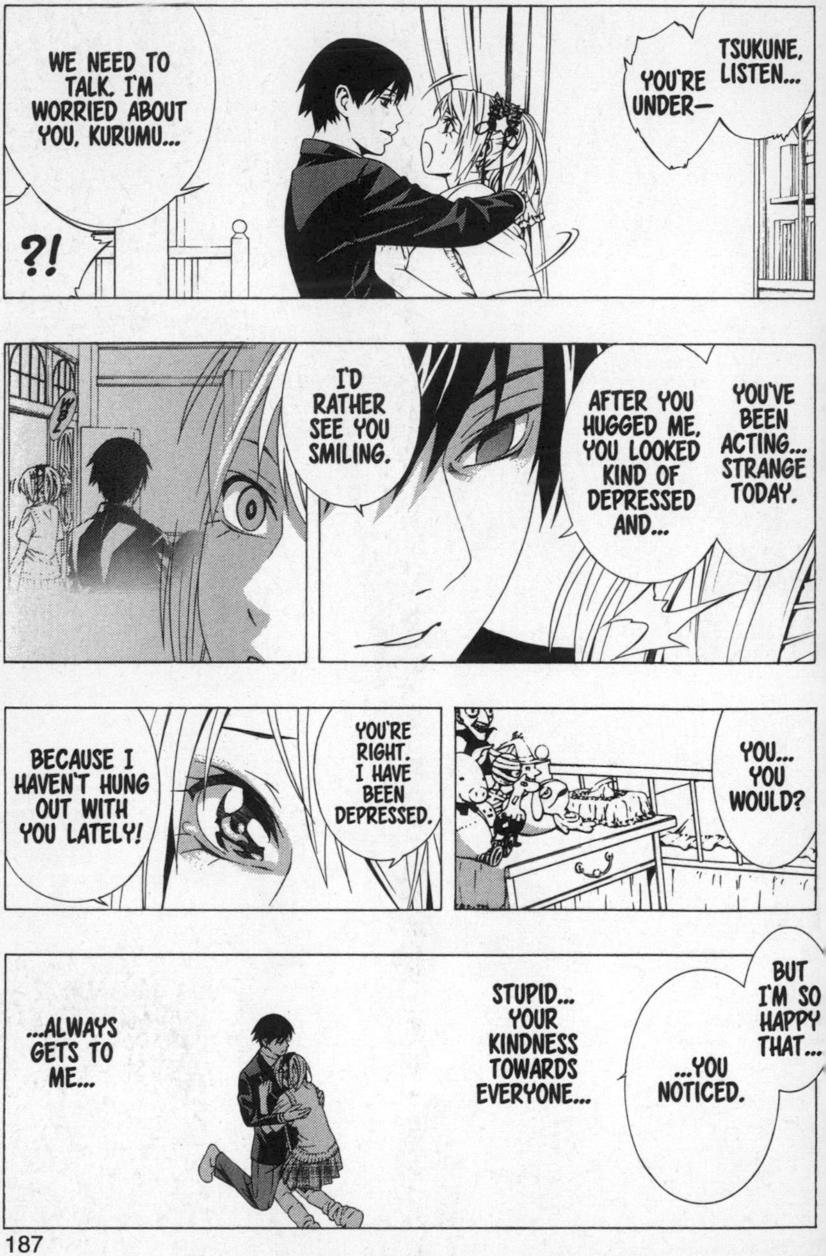
TSUKUNE, LISTEN...
YOU'RE UNDER—
WE NEED TO TALK. I'M WORRIED ABOUT YOU, KURUMU...
?!
YOU'VE BEEN ACTING... STRANGE TODAY.
AFTER YOU HUGGED ME, YOU LOOKED KIND OF DEPRESSED AND...
I'D RATHER SEE YOU SMILING.
YOU... YOU WOULD?
YOU'RE RIGHT. I HAVE BEEN DEPRESSED.
BECAUSE I HAVEN'T HUNG OUT WITH YOU LATELY!
BUT I'M SO HAPPY THAT...
...YOU NOTICED.
STUPID... YOUR KINDNESS TOWARDS EVERYONE...
...ALWAYS GETS TO ME...

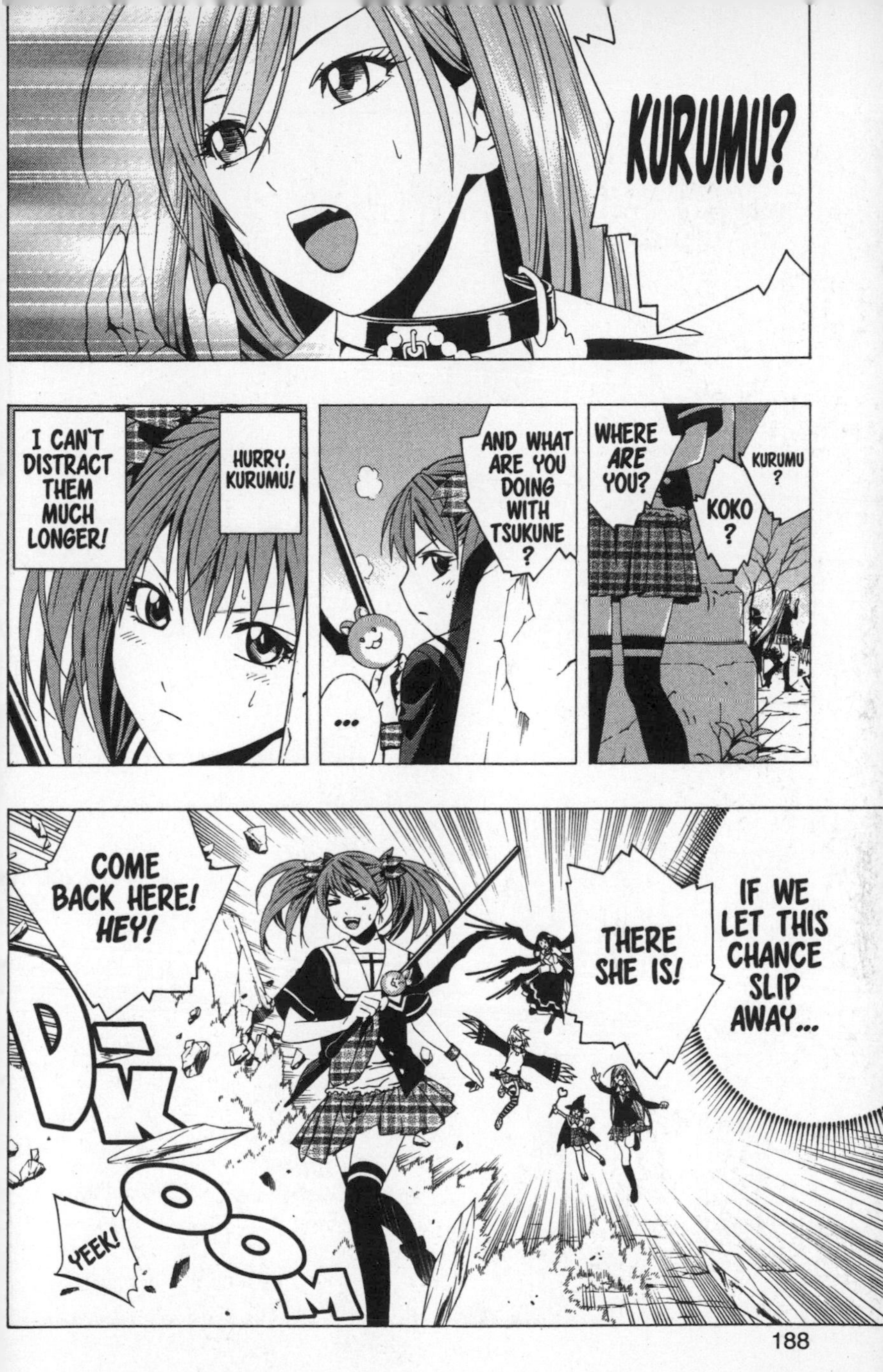
KURUMU?
KURUMU?
WHERE ARE YOU?
KOKO?
AND WHAT ARE YOU DOING WITH TSUKUNE?
...
HURRY, KURUMU!
I CAN'T DISTRACT THEM MUCH LONGER!
IF WE LET THIS CHANCE SLIP AWAY...
THERE SHE IS!
COME BACK HERE! HEY!
D-KOOOOM
YEEK!

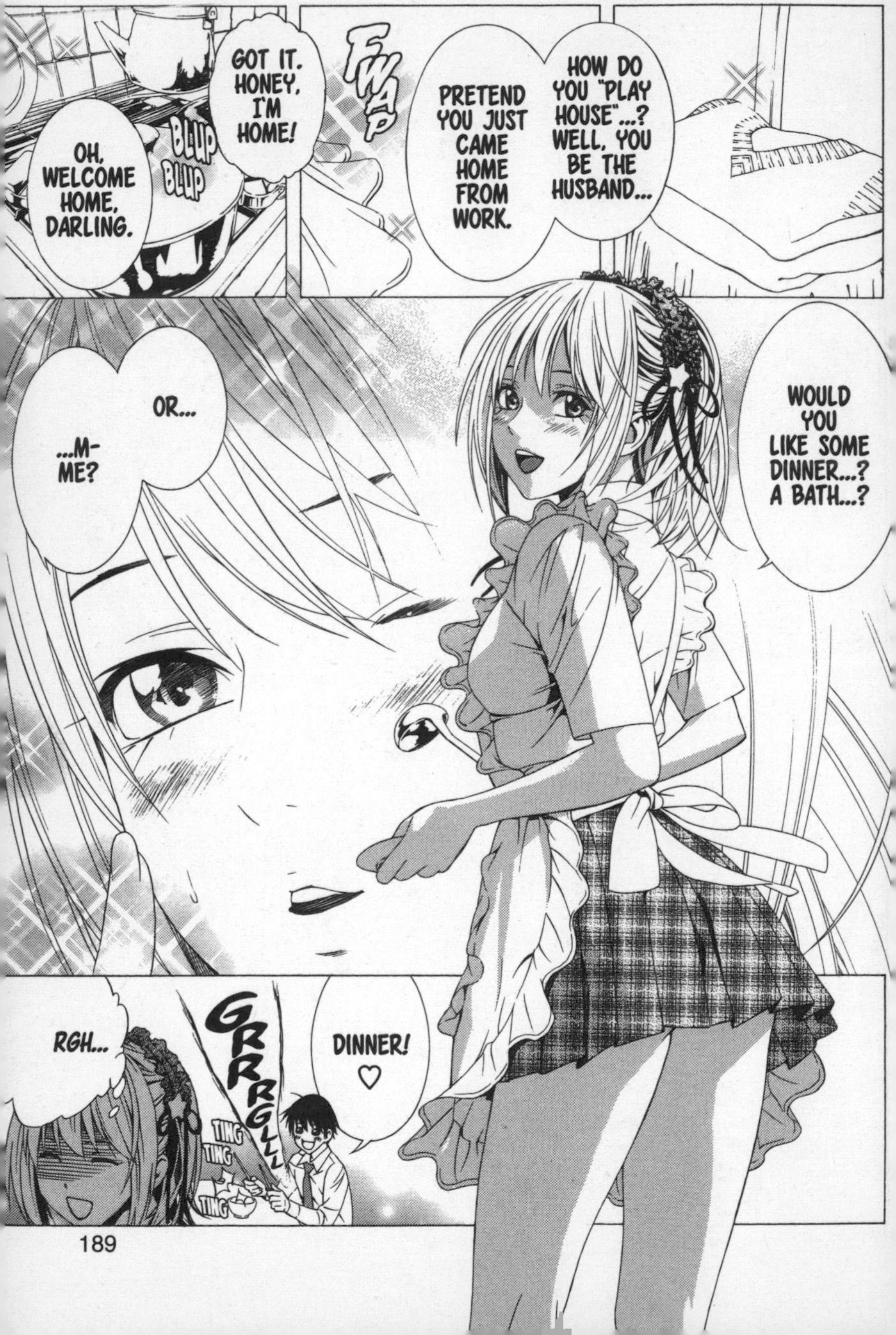
HOW DO YOU "PLAY HOUSE"...? WELL, YOU BE THE HUSBAND...
PRETEND YOU JUST CAME HOME FROM WORK.
FWAP
GOT IT. HONEY, I'M HOME!
BLUP BLUP
OH, WELCOME HOME, DARLING.
WOULD YOU LIKE SOME DINNER...? A BATH...?
OR...
...M-ME?
DINNER! ♡
GRRRGLLL
TING TING
TING
RGH...

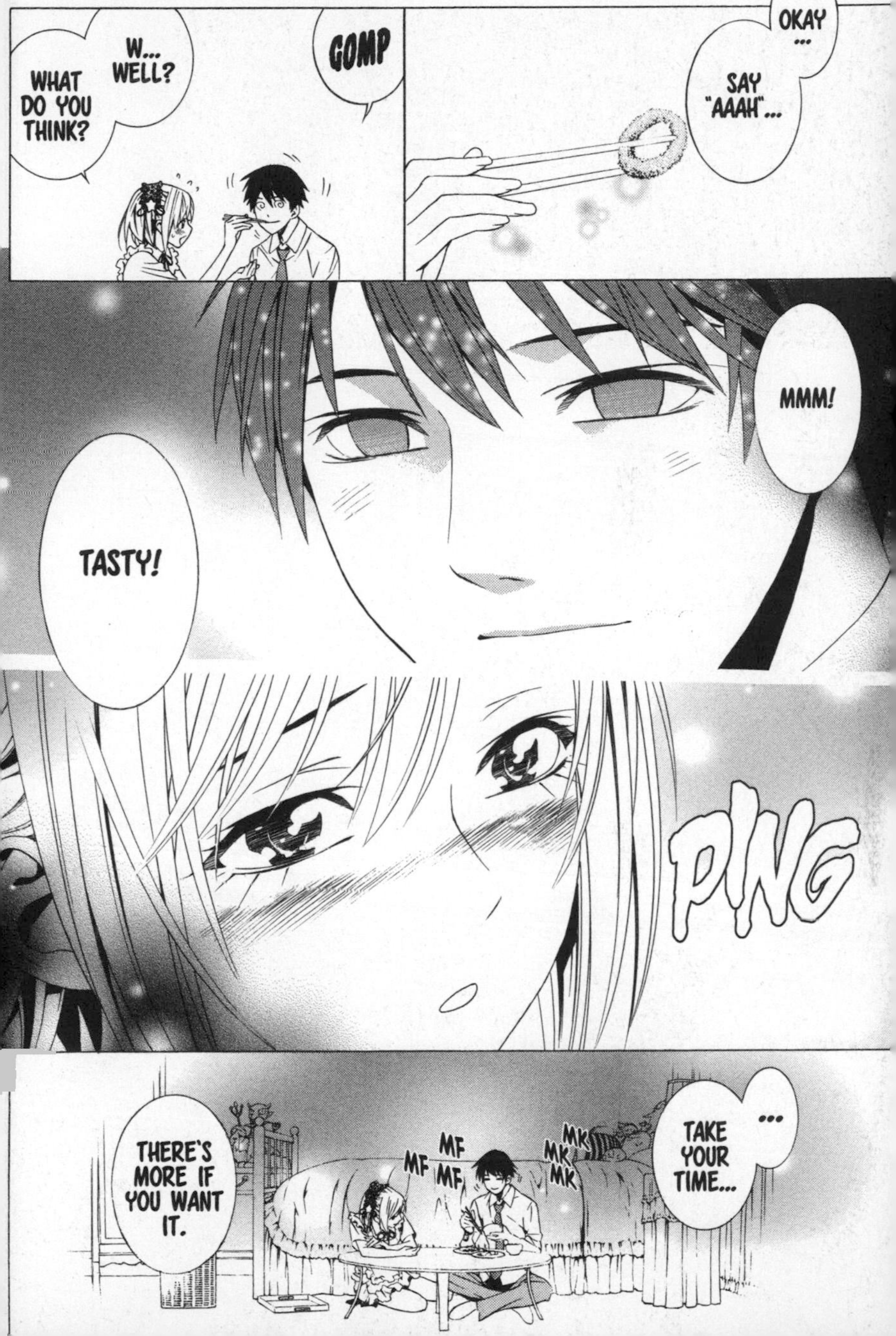
OKAY...
SAY "AAAH"...
GOMP
W... WELL?
WHAT DO YOU THINK?
MMM!
TASTY!
PING
...
TAKE YOUR TIME...
MK MK MK
MF MF MF
THERE'S MORE IF YOU WANT IT.

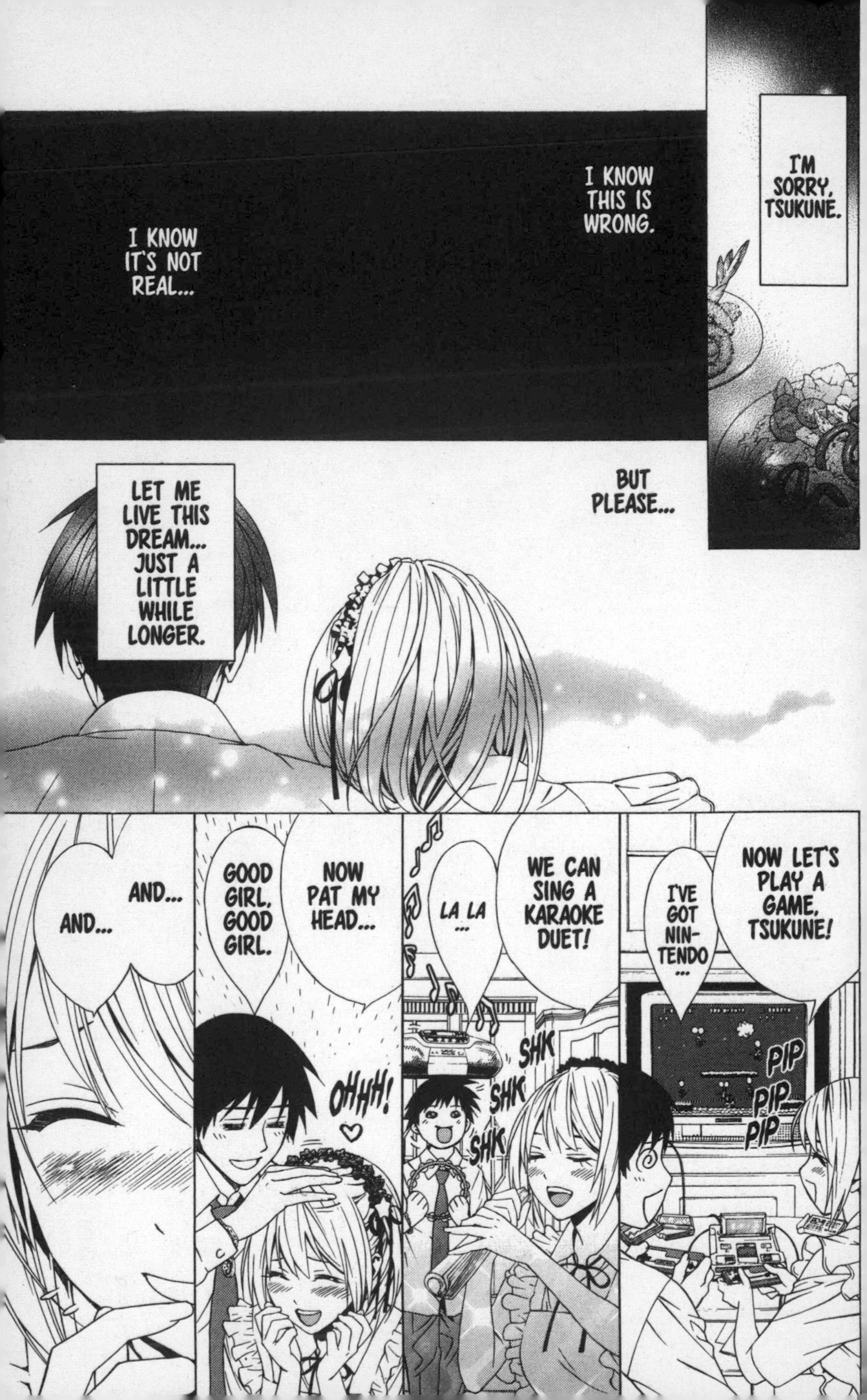
I'M SORRY, TSUKUNE.
I KNOW THIS IS WRONG.
I KNOW IT'S NOT REAL...
BUT PLEASE...
LET ME LIVE THIS DREAM... JUST A LITTLE WHILE LONGER.
NOW LET'S PLAY A GAME, TSUKUNE!
I'VE GOT NIN-TENDO...
PIP PIP... PIP
WE CAN SING A KARAOKE DUET!
LA LA ...
SHK SHK SHK
NOW PAT MY HEAD...
GOOD GIRL, GOOD GIRL.
OHHH!
AND...
AND...

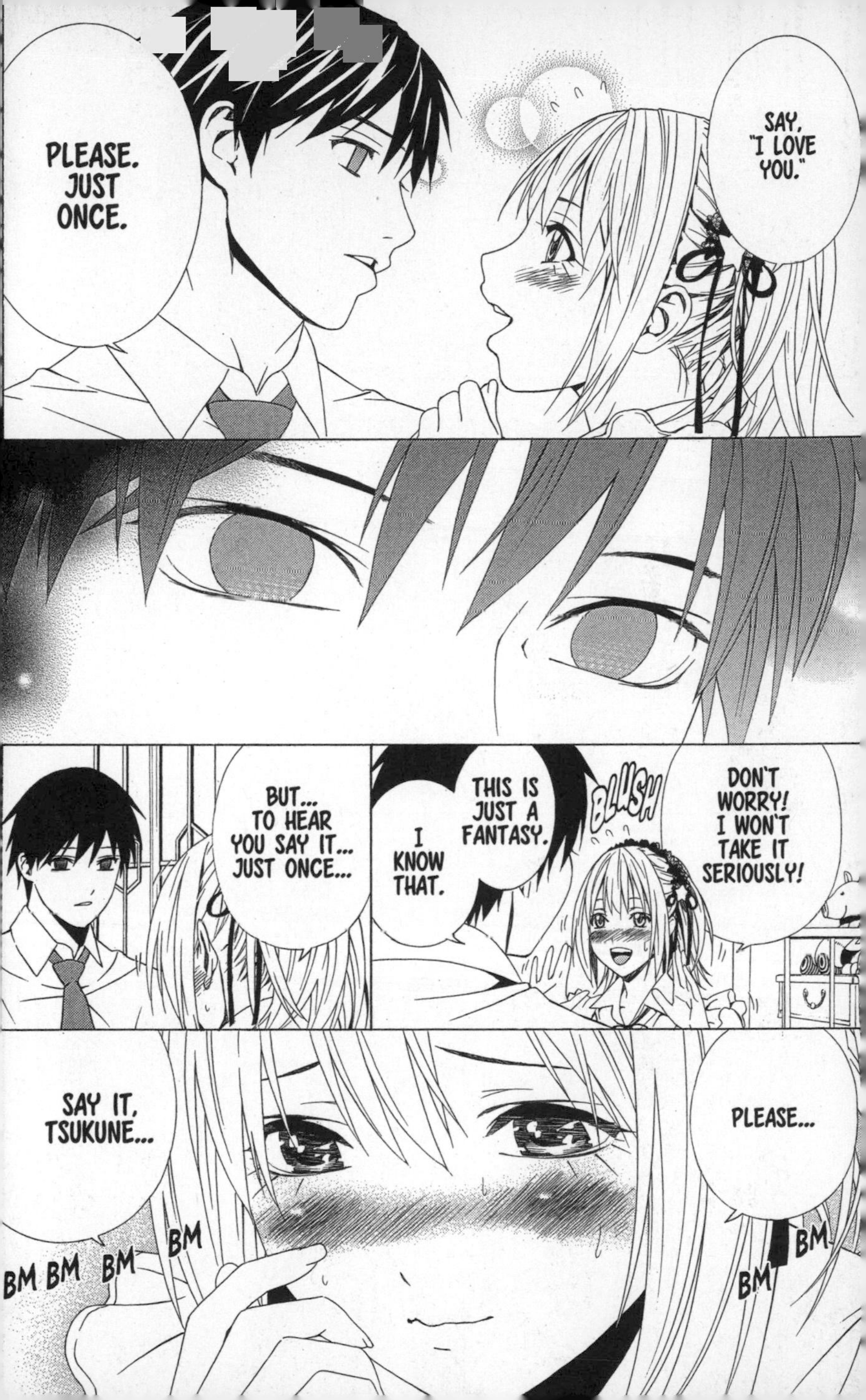
SAY, "I LOVE YOU."
PLEASE. JUST ONCE.
BLUSH
DON'T WORRY! I WON'T TAKE IT SERIOUSLY!
THIS IS JUST A FANTASY.
I KNOW THAT.
BUT... TO HEAR YOU SAY IT... JUST ONCE...
PLEASE...
BM
BM
SAY IT, TSUKUNE...
BM
BM
BM BM

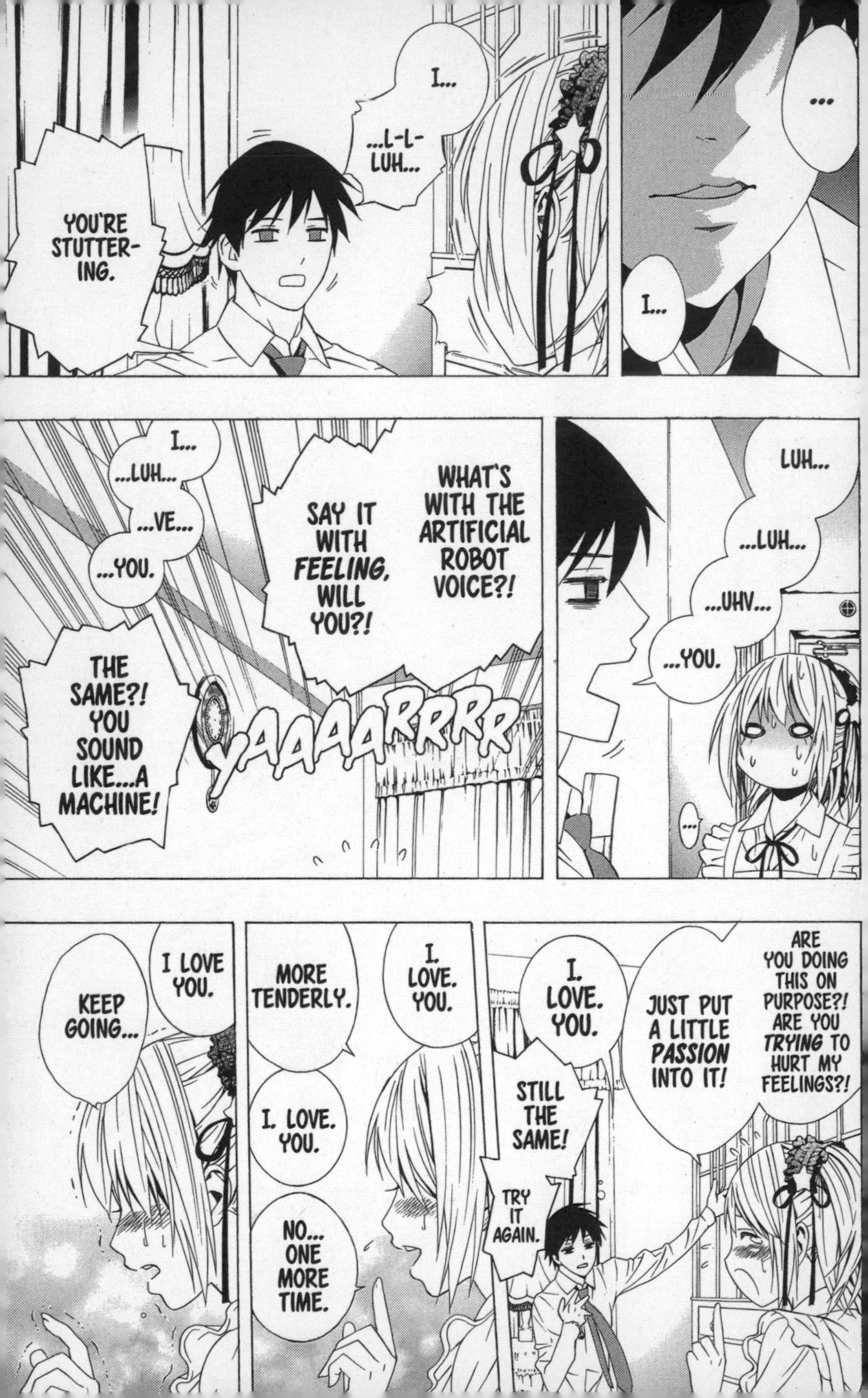
...
I...
I...
...L-L-
LUH...
YOU'RE STUTTER-ING.
LUH...
...LUH...
...UHV...
...YOU.
...
WHAT'S WITH THE ARTIFICIAL ROBOT VOICE?!
SAY IT WITH *FEELING*, WILL YOU?!
I...
...LUH...
...VE...
...YOU.
YAAAARRRR
THE SAME?! YOU SOUND LIKE...A MACHINE!
ARE YOU DOING THIS ON PURPOSE?! ARE YOU *TRYING* TO HURT MY FEELINGS?!
JUST PUT A LITTLE *PASSION* INTO IT!
I. LOVE. YOU.
STILL THE SAME!
TRY IT AGAIN.
I. LOVE. YOU.
MORE TENDERLY.
I. LOVE. YOU.
NO... ONE MORE TIME.
I LOVE YOU.
KEEP GOING...

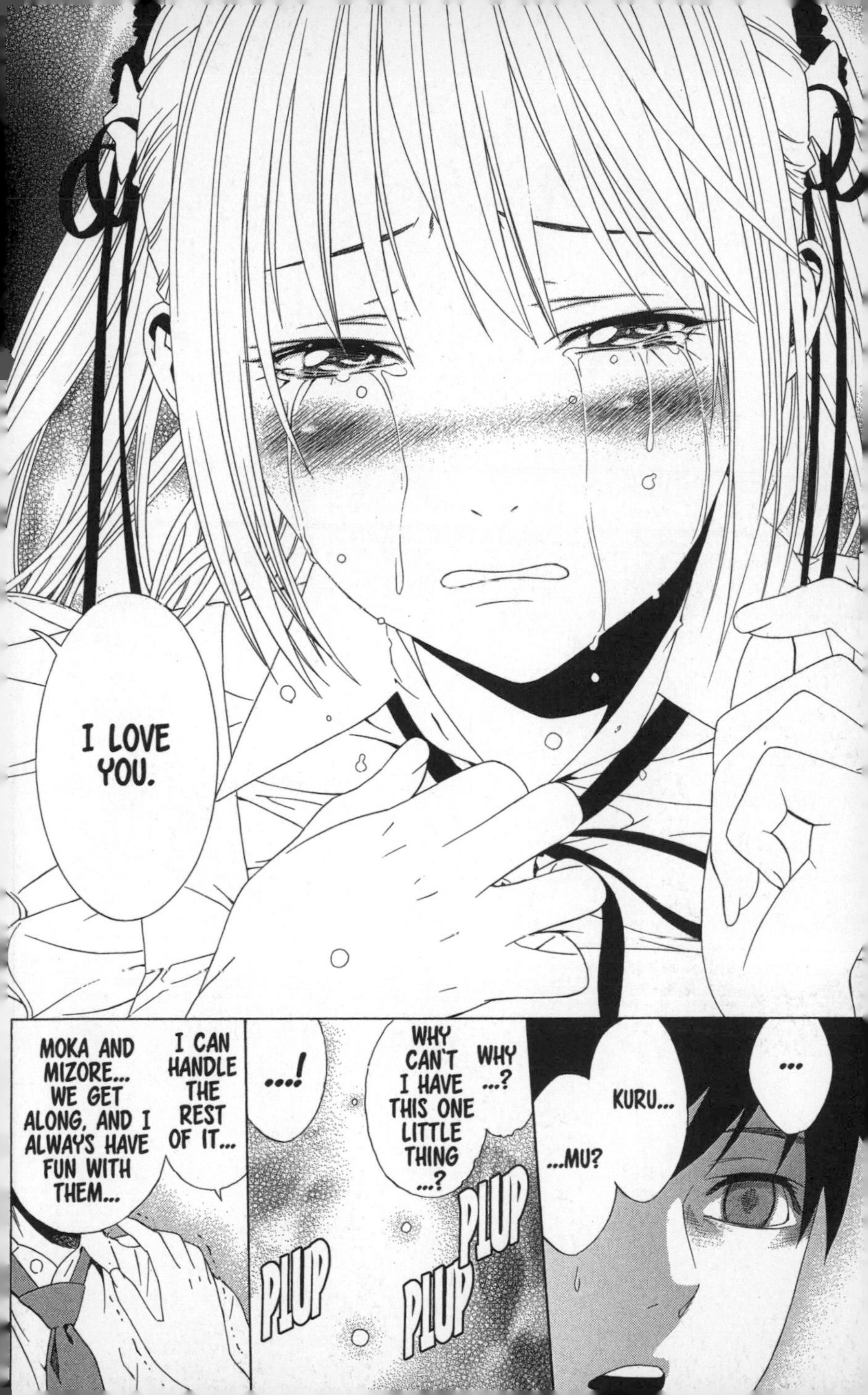
I LOVE YOU.
...
KURU...
...MU?
WHY ...?
WHY CAN'T I HAVE THIS ONE LITTLE THING ...?
...!
PLUP
PLUP
PLUP
I CAN HANDLE THE REST OF IT...
MOKA AND MIZORE... WE GET ALONG, AND I ALWAYS HAVE FUN WITH THEM...

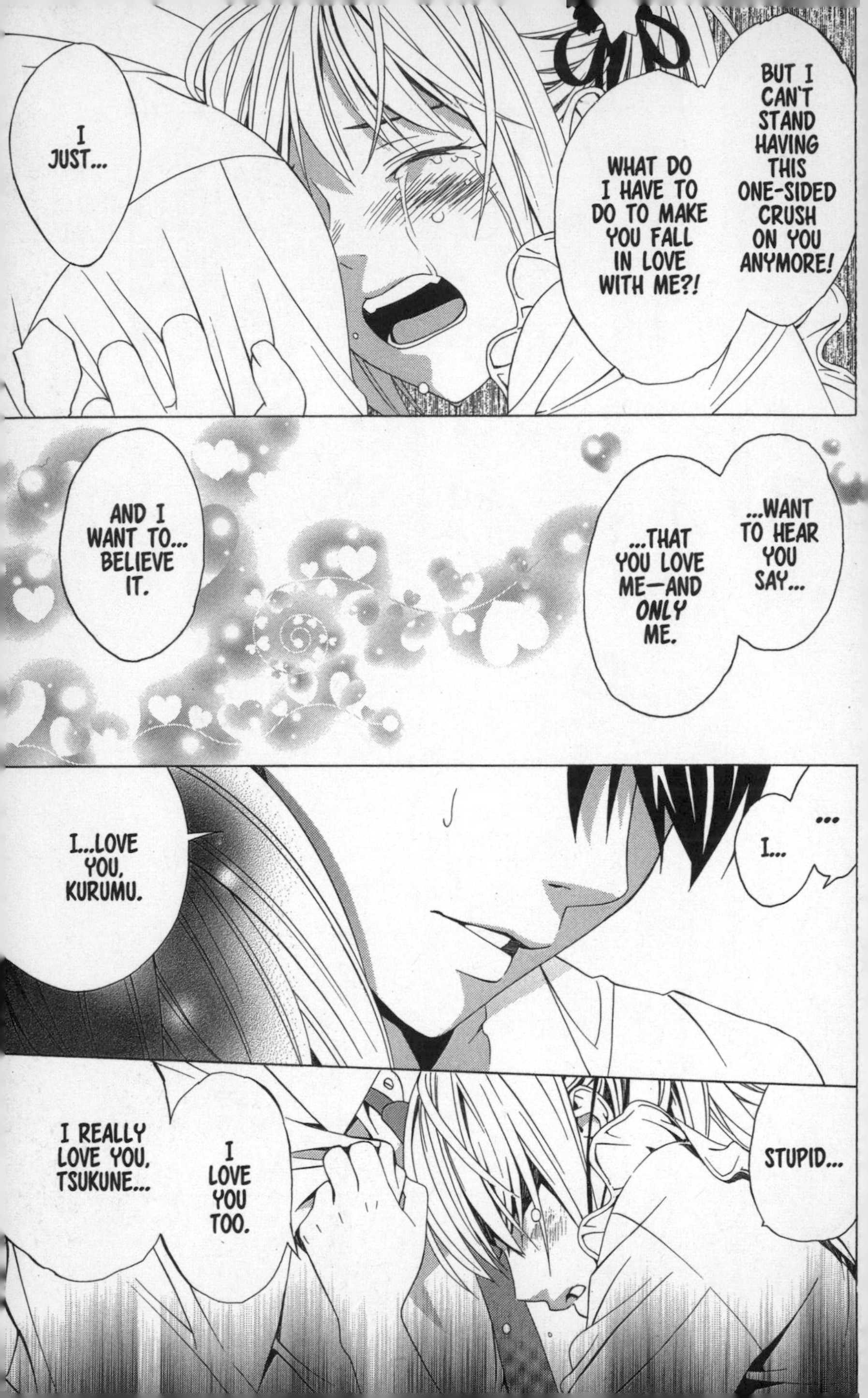
BUT I CAN'T STAND HAVING THIS ONE-SIDED CRUSH ON YOU ANYMORE!
WHAT DO I HAVE TO DO TO MAKE YOU FALL IN LOVE WITH ME?!
I JUST...
...WANT TO HEAR YOU SAY...
...THAT YOU LOVE ME—AND ONLY ME.
AND I WANT TO... BELIEVE IT.
... I...
I...LOVE YOU, KURUMU.
STUPID...
I LOVE YOU TOO.
I REALLY LOVE YOU, TSUKUNE...

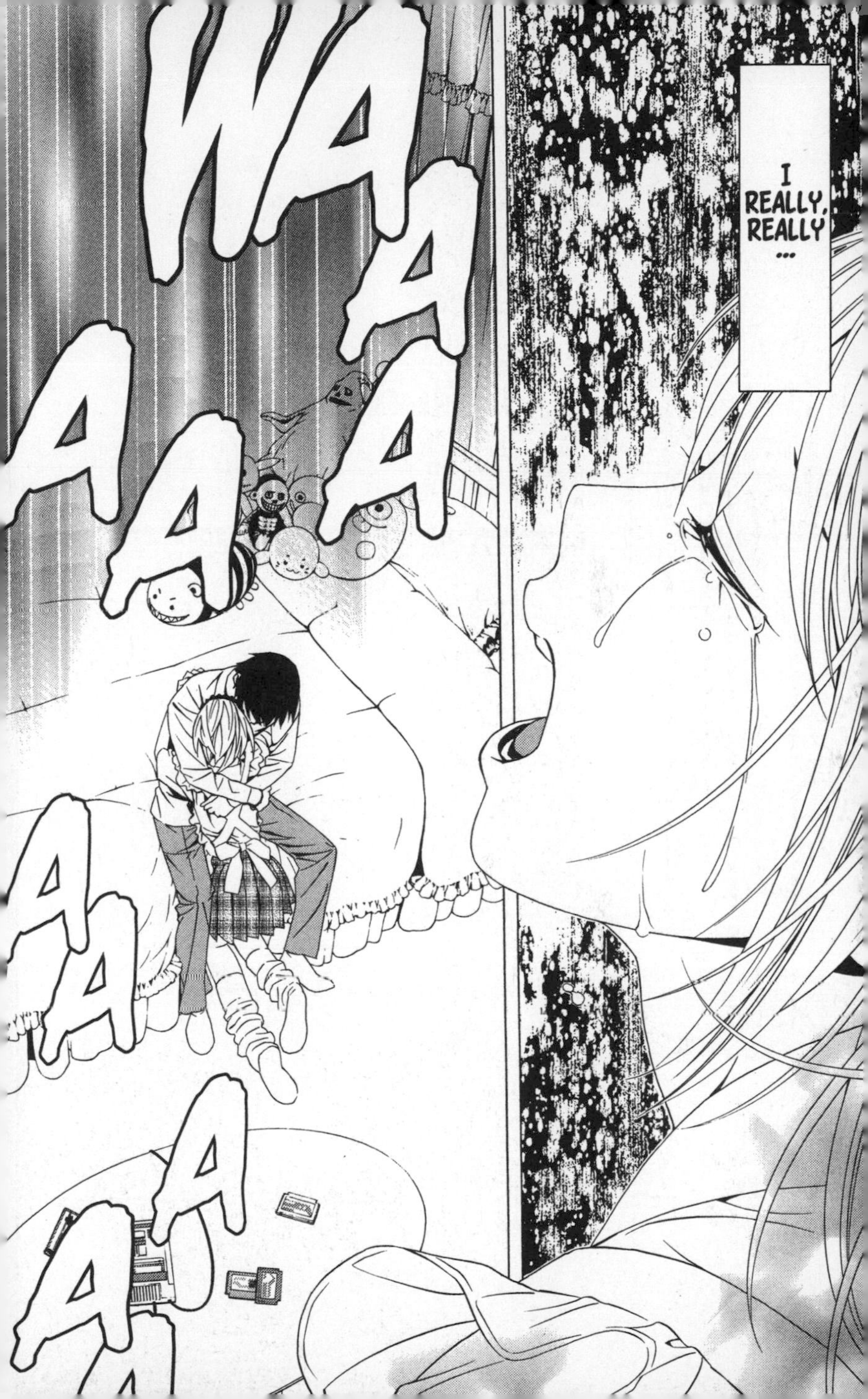
I REALLY, REALLY ...
WAAAAA
AA
AAA

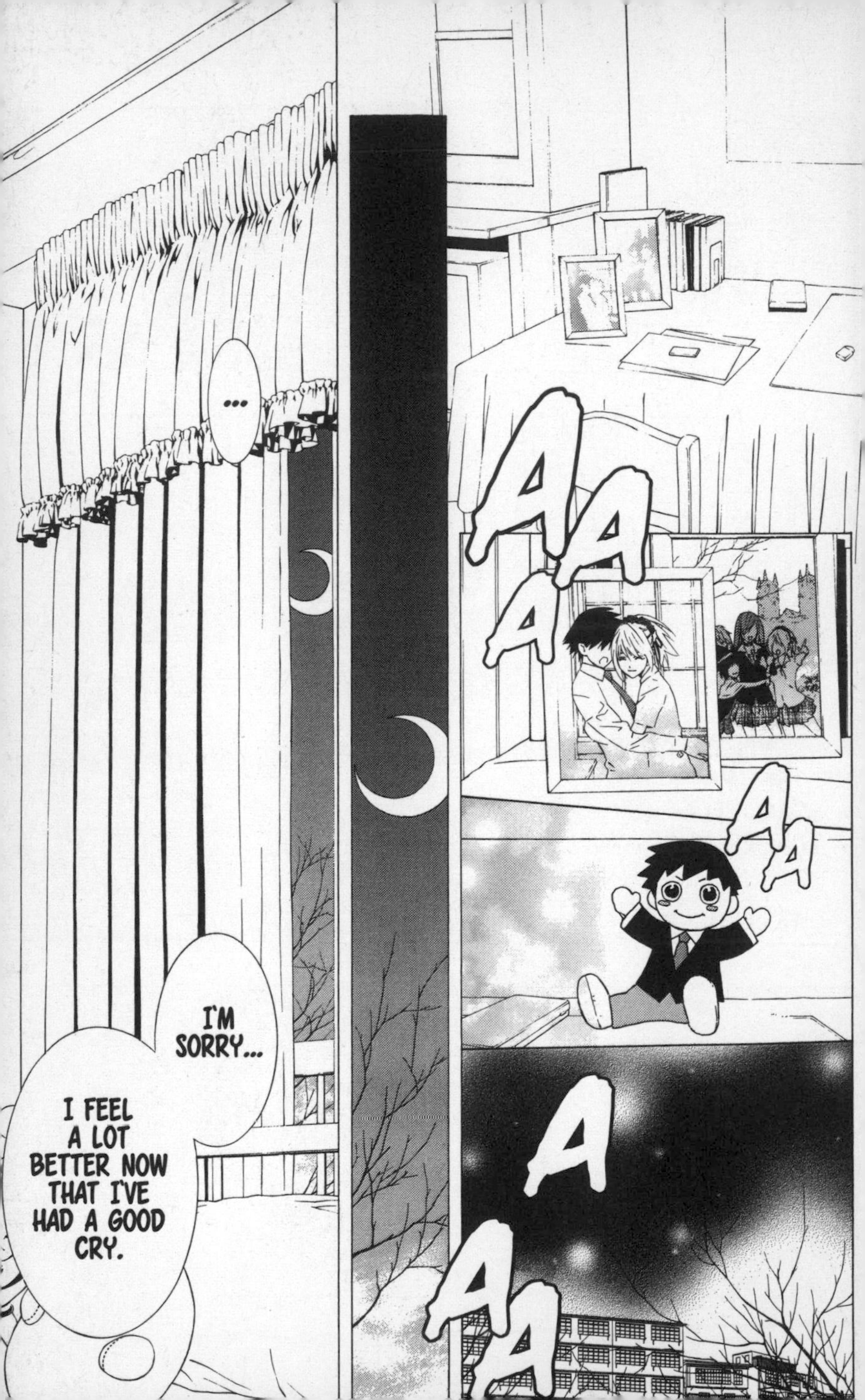
AAA
AA
A
AA
...
I'M SORRY...
I FEEL A LOT BETTER NOW THAT I'VE HAD A GOOD CRY.

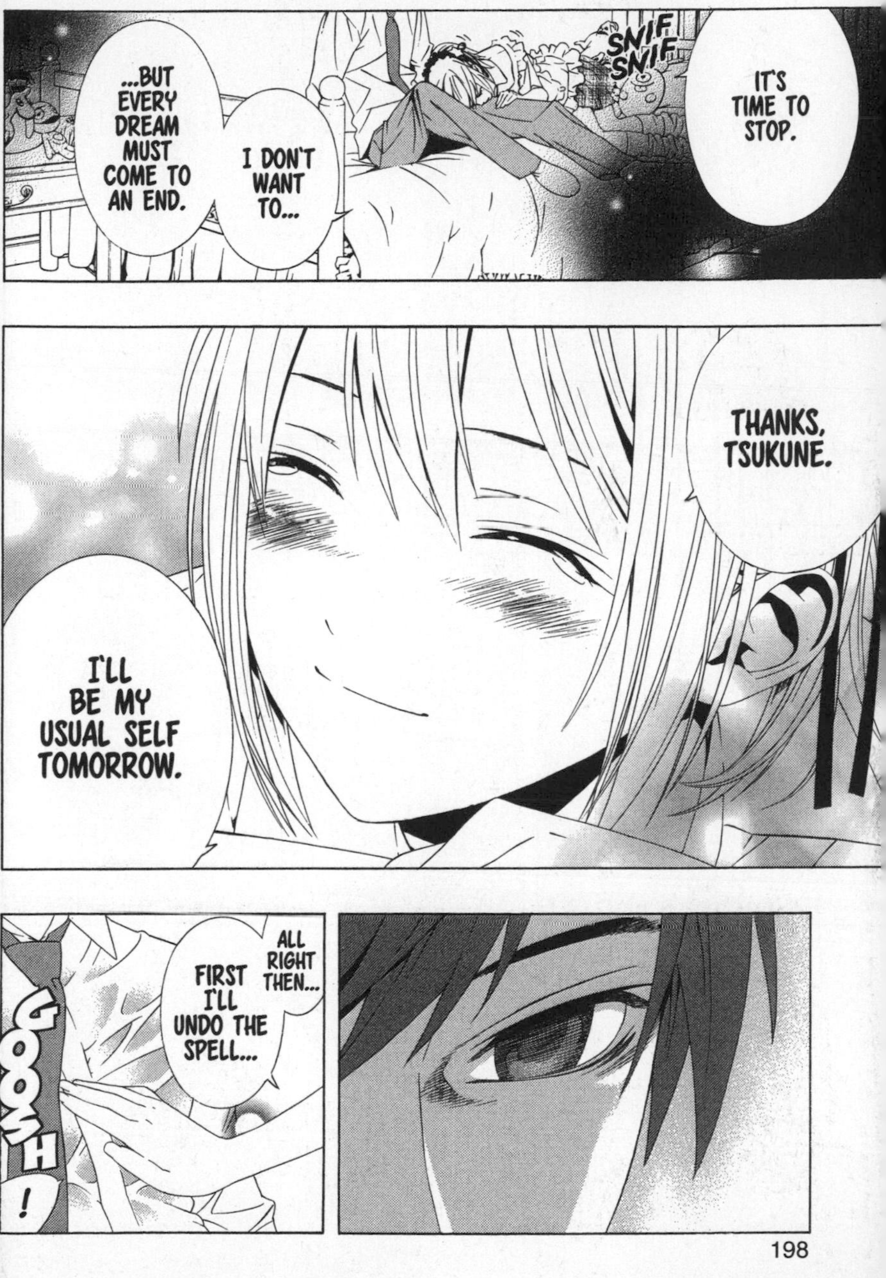
IT'S TIME TO STOP.
SNIF SNIF
I DON'T WANT TO...
...BUT EVERY DREAM MUST COME TO AN END.
THANKS, TSUKUNE.
I'LL BE MY USUAL SELF TOMORROW.
ALL RIGHT THEN...
FIRST I'LL UNDO THE SPELL...
GOOSH!

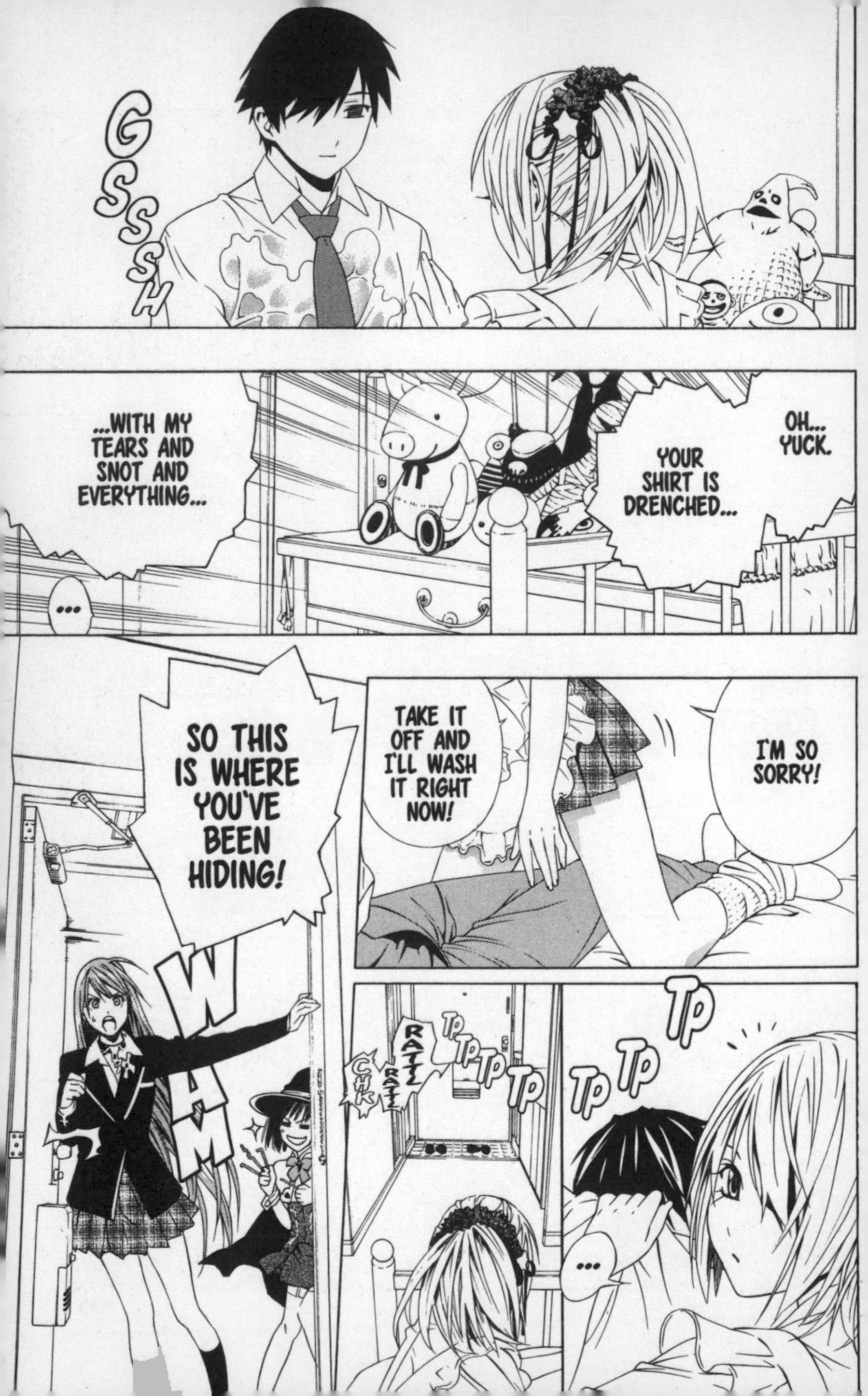
GSSSH
OH... YUCK.
YOUR SHIRT IS DRENCHED...
...WITH MY TEARS AND SNOT AND EVERYTHING...
...
I'M SO SORRY!
TAKE IT OFF AND I'LL WASH IT RIGHT NOW!
Tp Tp Tp
...
Tp Tp Tp Tp
RATTZ RATTZ
CHK
SO THIS IS WHERE YOU'VE BEEN HIDING!
WHAM

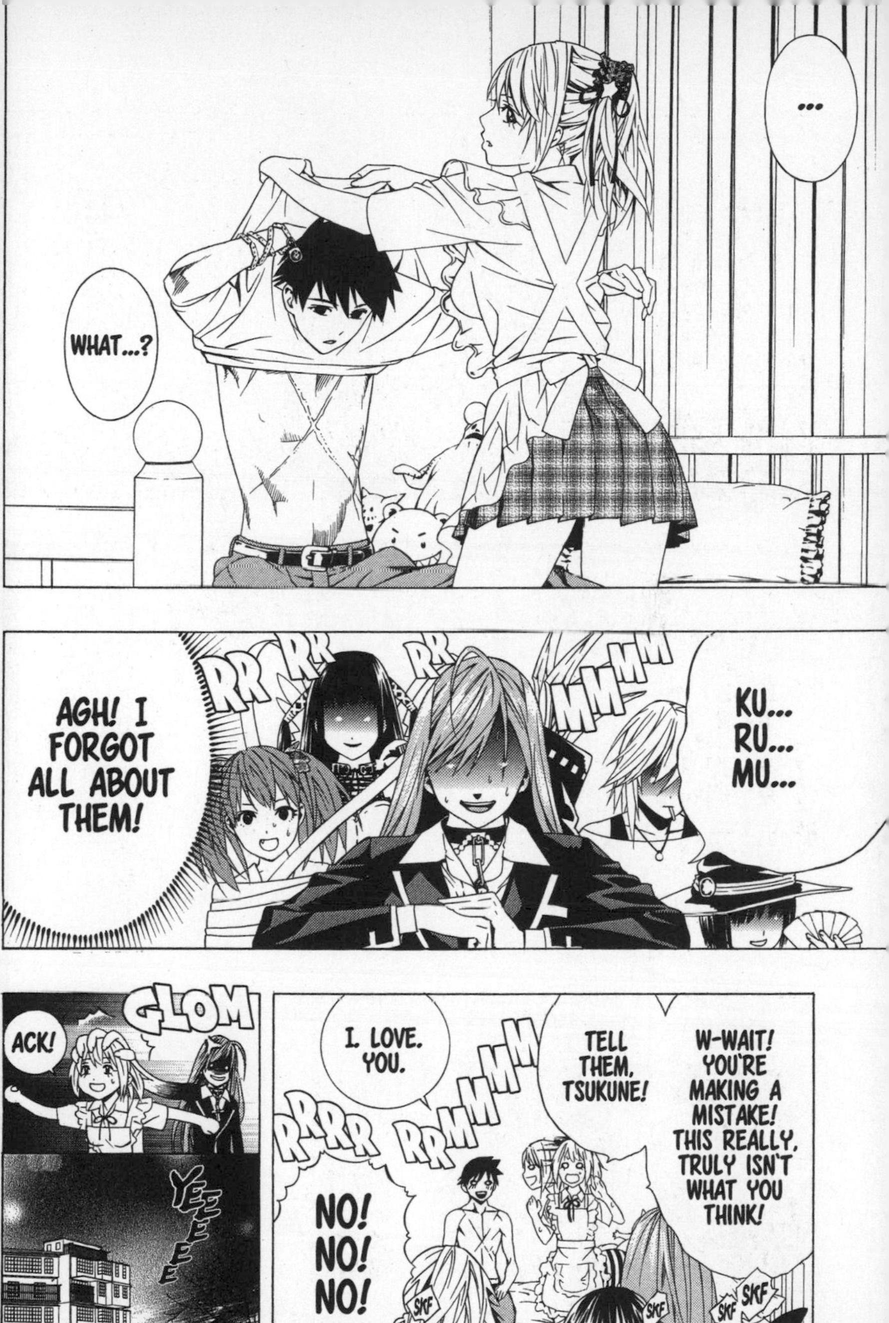
...
WHAT...?
KU... RU... MU...
RRRR MMMMM
AGH! I FORGOT ALL ABOUT THEM!
W-WAIT! YOU'RE MAKING A MISTAKE! THIS REALLY, TRULY ISN'T WHAT YOU THINK!
TELL THEM, TSUKUNE!
I. LOVE. YOU.
RRRR RRMMMMM
NO! NO! NO!
SKF SKF SKF SKF
GLOM
ACK!
YEEEEE

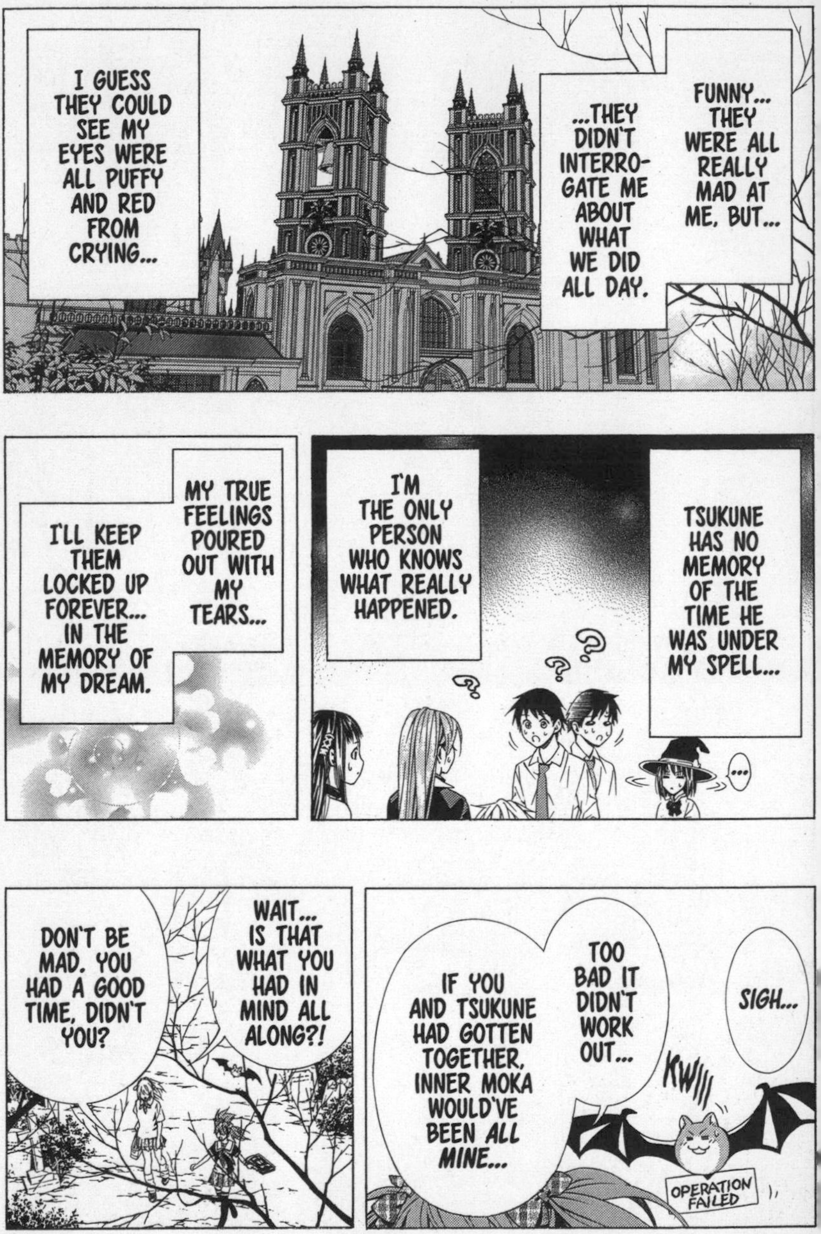
FUNNY... THEY WERE ALL REALLY MAD AT ME, BUT...
...THEY DIDN'T INTERROGATE ME ABOUT WHAT WE DID ALL DAY.
I GUESS THEY COULD SEE MY EYES WERE ALL PUFFY AND RED FROM CRYING...
TSUKUNE HAS NO MEMORY OF THE TIME HE WAS UNDER MY SPELL...
...
I'M THE ONLY PERSON WHO KNOWS WHAT REALLY HAPPENED.
MY TRUE FEELINGS POURED OUT WITH MY TEARS...
I'LL KEEP THEM LOCKED UP FOREVER... IN THE MEMORY OF MY DREAM.
SIGH...
TOO BAD IT DIDN'T WORK OUT...
IF YOU AND TSUKUNE HAD GOTTEN TOGETHER, INNER MOKA WOULD'VE BEEN ALL MINE...
KWIIII
OPERATION FAILED
WAIT... IS THAT WHAT YOU HAD IN MIND ALL ALONG?!
DON'T BE MAD. YOU HAD A GOOD TIME, DIDN'T YOU?

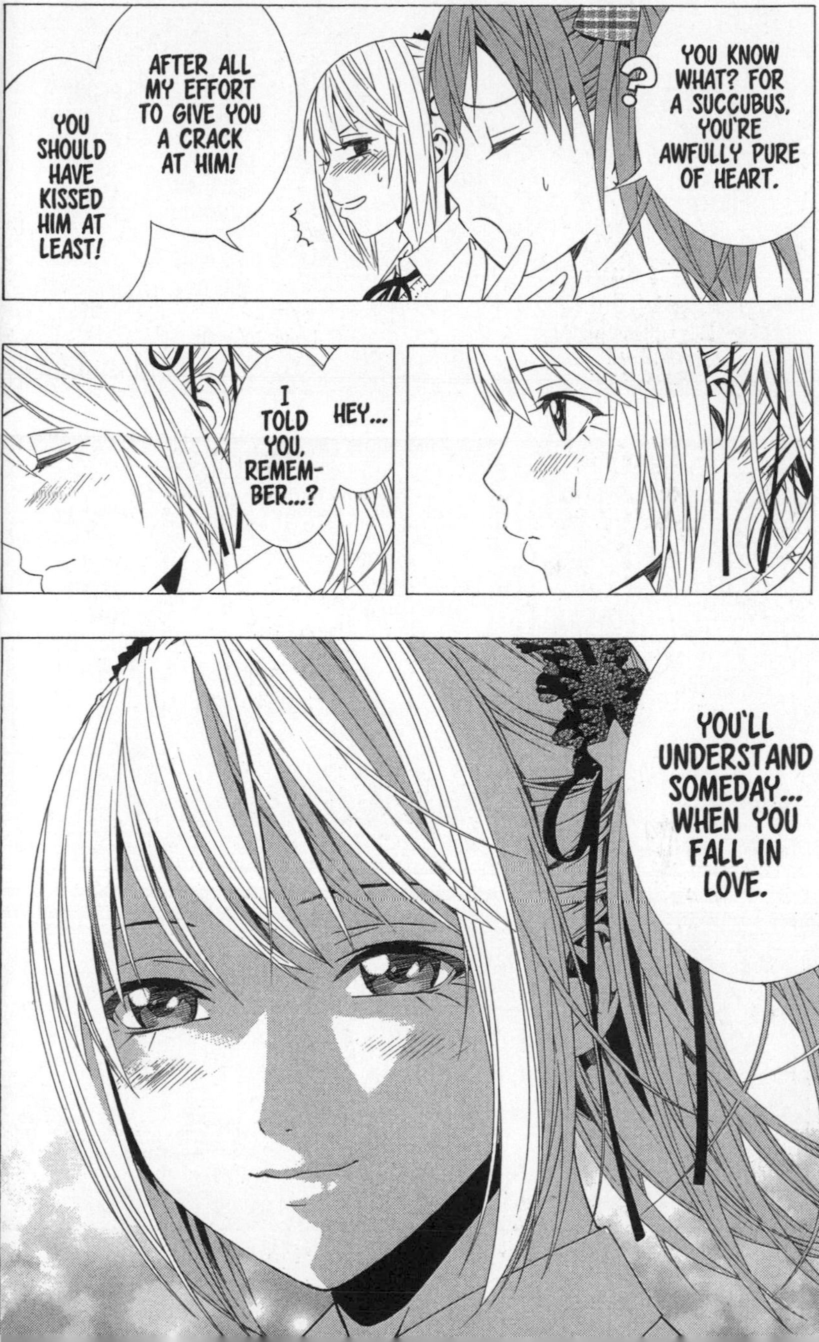
YOU KNOW WHAT? FOR A SUCCUBUS, YOU'RE AWFULLY PURE OF HEART.
AFTER ALL MY EFFORT TO GIVE YOU A CRACK AT HIM!
YOU SHOULD HAVE KISSED HIM AT LEAST!
HEY...
I TOLD YOU, REMEMBER...?
YOU'LL UNDERSTAND SOMEDAY... WHEN YOU FALL IN LOVE.

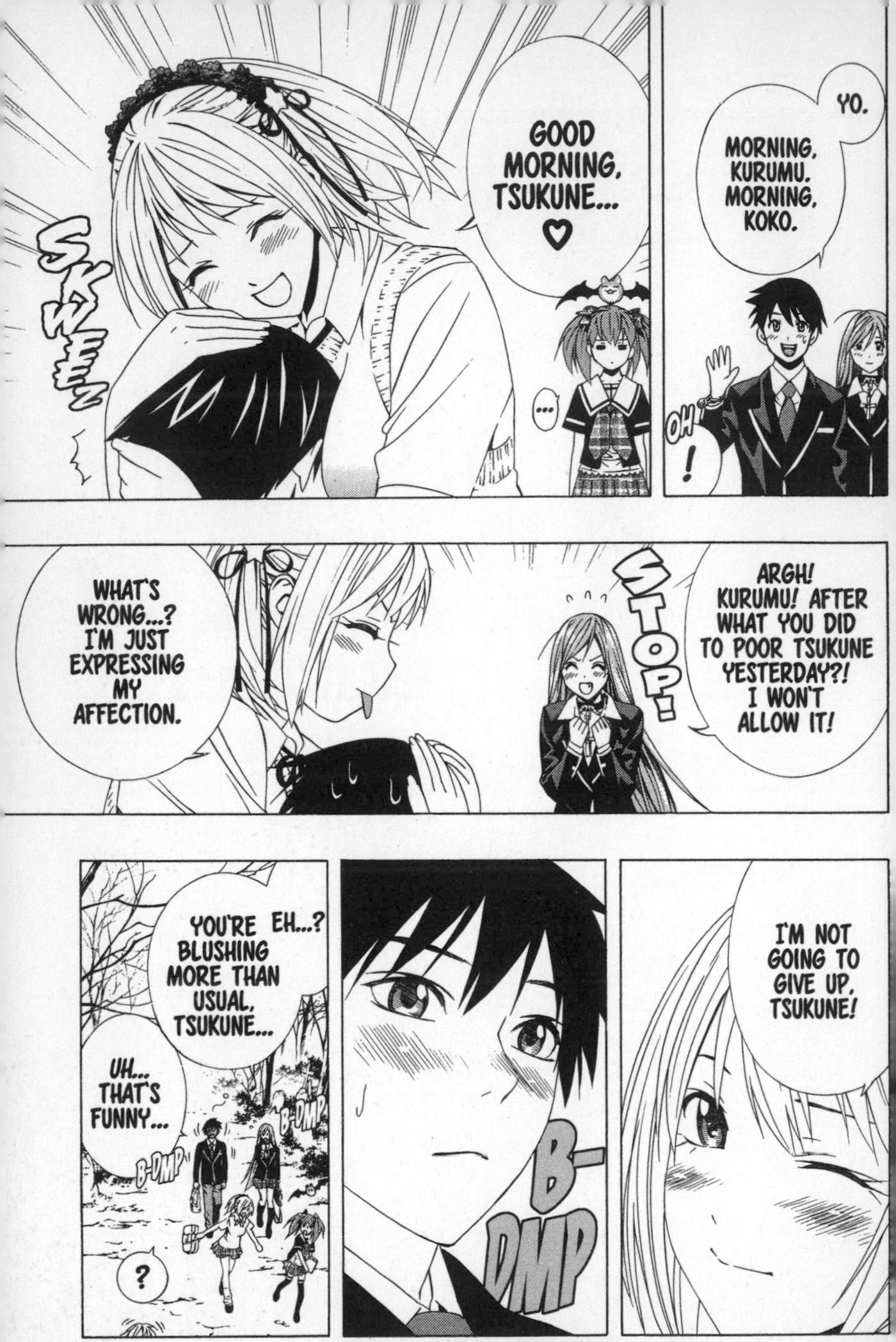
YO.
MORNING, KURUMU. MORNING, KOKO.
OH!
GOOD MORNING, TSUKUNE... ♡
...
SKWEEZ
ARGH! KURUMU! AFTER WHAT YOU DID TO POOR TSUKUNE YESTERDAY?! I WON'T ALLOW IT!
STOP!
WHAT'S WRONG...? I'M JUST EXPRESSING MY AFFECTION.
I'M NOT GOING TO GIVE UP, TSUKUNE!
B-DMP
EH...?
YOU'RE BLUSHING MORE THAN USUAL, TSUKUNE...
UH... THAT'S FUNNY...
B-DMP
B-DMP
?

INNER GHOUL (THE END)

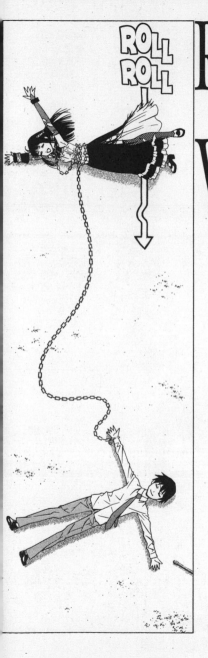

ROSARIO + VAMPIRE

Season II

Meaningless End-of-Volume Theater

ROLL ROLL

IV

· Training for What? ·

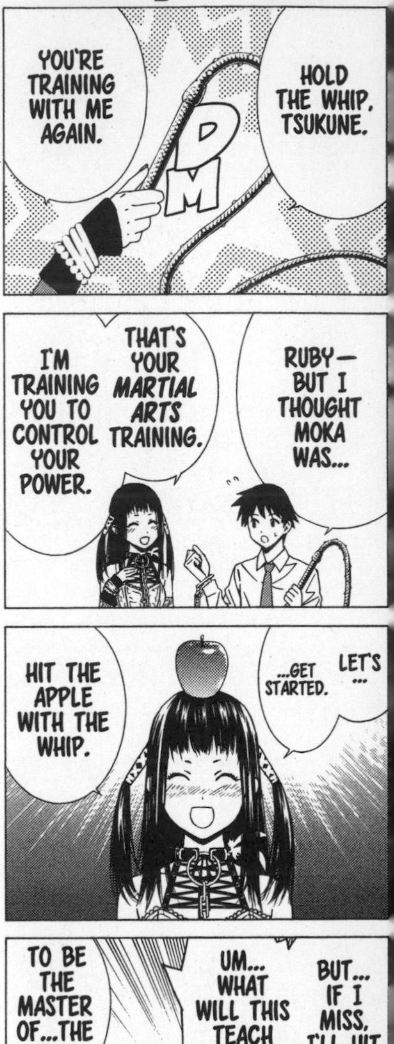
HOLD THE WHIP, TSUKUNE.
YOU'RE TRAINING WITH ME AGAIN.
DM
RUBY— BUT I THOUGHT MOKA WAS...
THAT'S YOUR MARTIAL ARTS TRAINING.
I'M TRAINING YOU TO CONTROL YOUR POWER.
LET'S ...
...GET STARTED.
HIT THE APPLE WITH THE WHIP.
BUT... IF I MISS, I'LL HIT YOU!
UM... WHAT WILL THIS TEACH ME...?
TO BE THE MASTER OF...THE WHIP.
PANT PANT PANT
It's okay if you miss. Really, it is.
BMP BMP BMP BMP

· A New Game ·

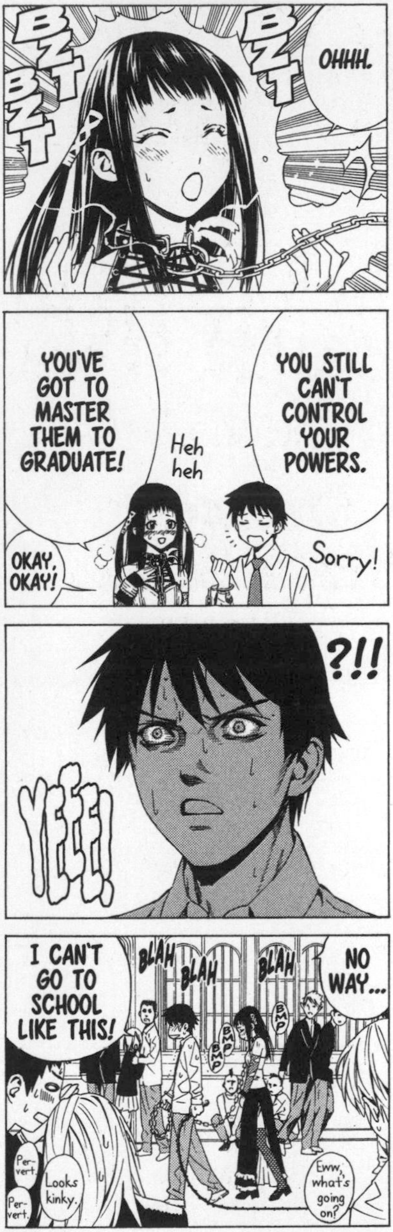
OHHH.
BZT BZT BZT
YOU STILL CAN'T CONTROL YOUR POWERS.
Heh heh
YOU'VE GOT TO MASTER THEM TO GRADUATE!
Sorry!
OKAY, OKAY!
?!!
YEEE!
NO WAY...
BLAH BLAH BLAH
I CAN'T GO TO SCHOOL LIKE THIS!
BMP BMP BMP
Eww, what's going on?
Looks kinky.
Pervert.
Pervert.

• Putting on the Dog •

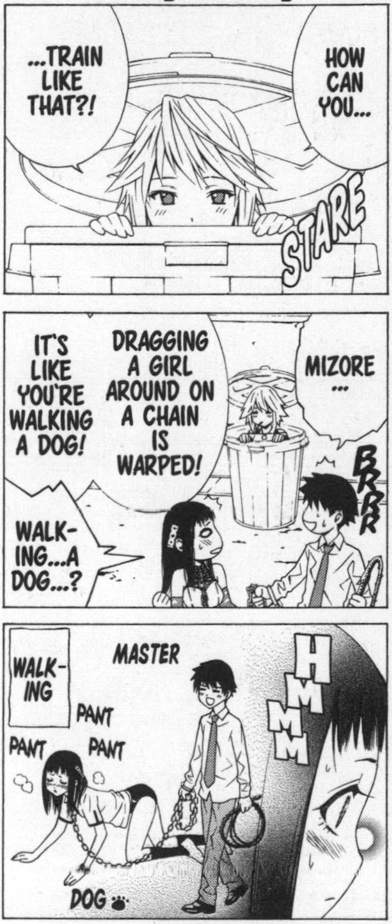
HOW CAN YOU...
...TRAIN LIKE THAT?!
STARE
MIZORE ...
BRRR
DRAGGING A GIRL AROUND ON A CHAIN IS WARPED!
IT'S LIKE YOU'RE WALKING A DOG!
WALK-ING...A DOG...?
HMMMM
MASTER
WALK-ING
PANT
PANT
PANT
DOG
IF I'M THE DOG...
OO!
...I OUGHTA BE ON ALL FOURS!

• To Each Her Own •

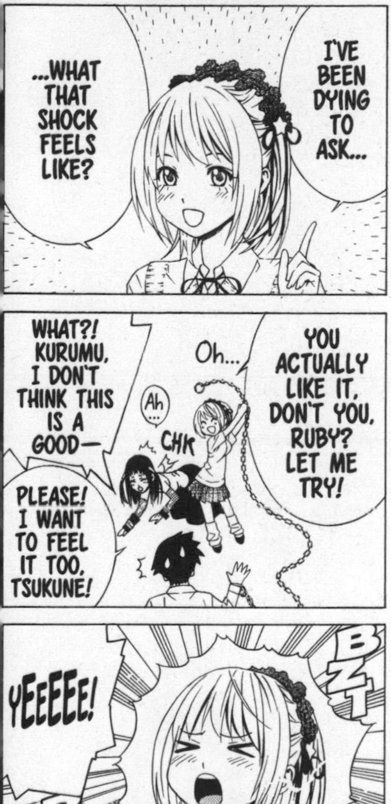
I'VE BEEN DYING TO ASK...
...WHAT THAT SHOCK FEELS LIKE?
YOU ACTUALLY LIKE IT, DON'T YOU, RUBY? LET ME TRY!
Oh...
WHAT?! KURUMU, I DON'T THINK THIS IS A GOOD—
Ah ...
CHK
PLEASE! I WANT TO FEEL IT TOO, TSUKUNE!
BZZT
YEEEEE!
BZZT
BZZT
THAT'S STUPID! IT DOESN'T FEEL GOOD AT ALL, IT HURTS!
REALLY? LET ME TRY! MY TURN!
ME NEXT!
HEY! YO! WHAT ABOUT MY TRAINING ...?!
BMP BMP
BMP BMP
I'm numb all over!
...

Please send questions and fan letters to ➡ Rosario+Vampire Fan Mail, VIZ Media, P.O. Box 77010, San Francisco, CA 94107

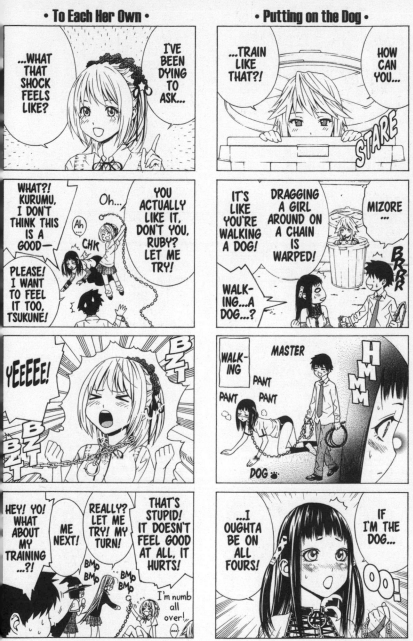

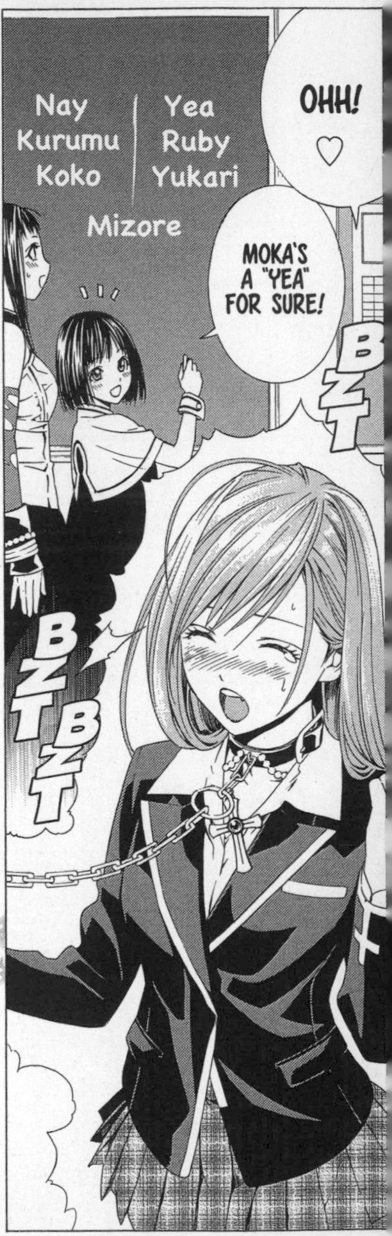
OHH! ♡
MOKA'S A "YEA" FOR SURE!
Yea
Ruby
Yukari
Nay
Kurumu
Koko
Mizore
BZT
BZT
BZT

Rosario+Vampire

Akihisa Ikeda

• Staff •
Makoto Saito
Kenji Tashiro
Nobuyuki Hayashi

• Help •
Hajime Maeda
Shinichi Miyashita
Hiroki Inoue

• 3DCG •
Takaharu Yoshizawa

• Editing •
Makoto Watanabe

• Comic •
Kenju Noro

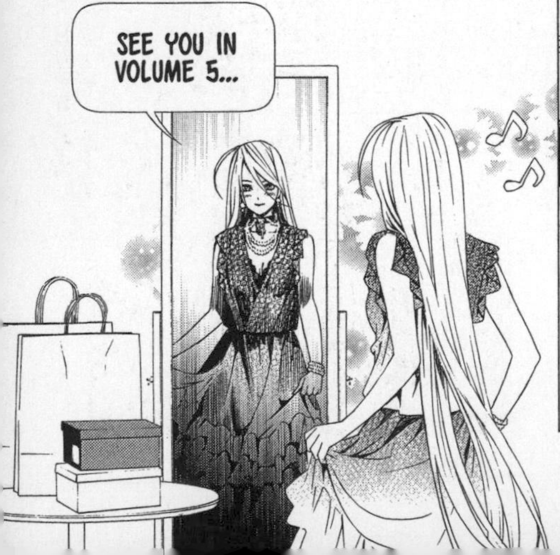
SEE YOU IN VOLUME 5...

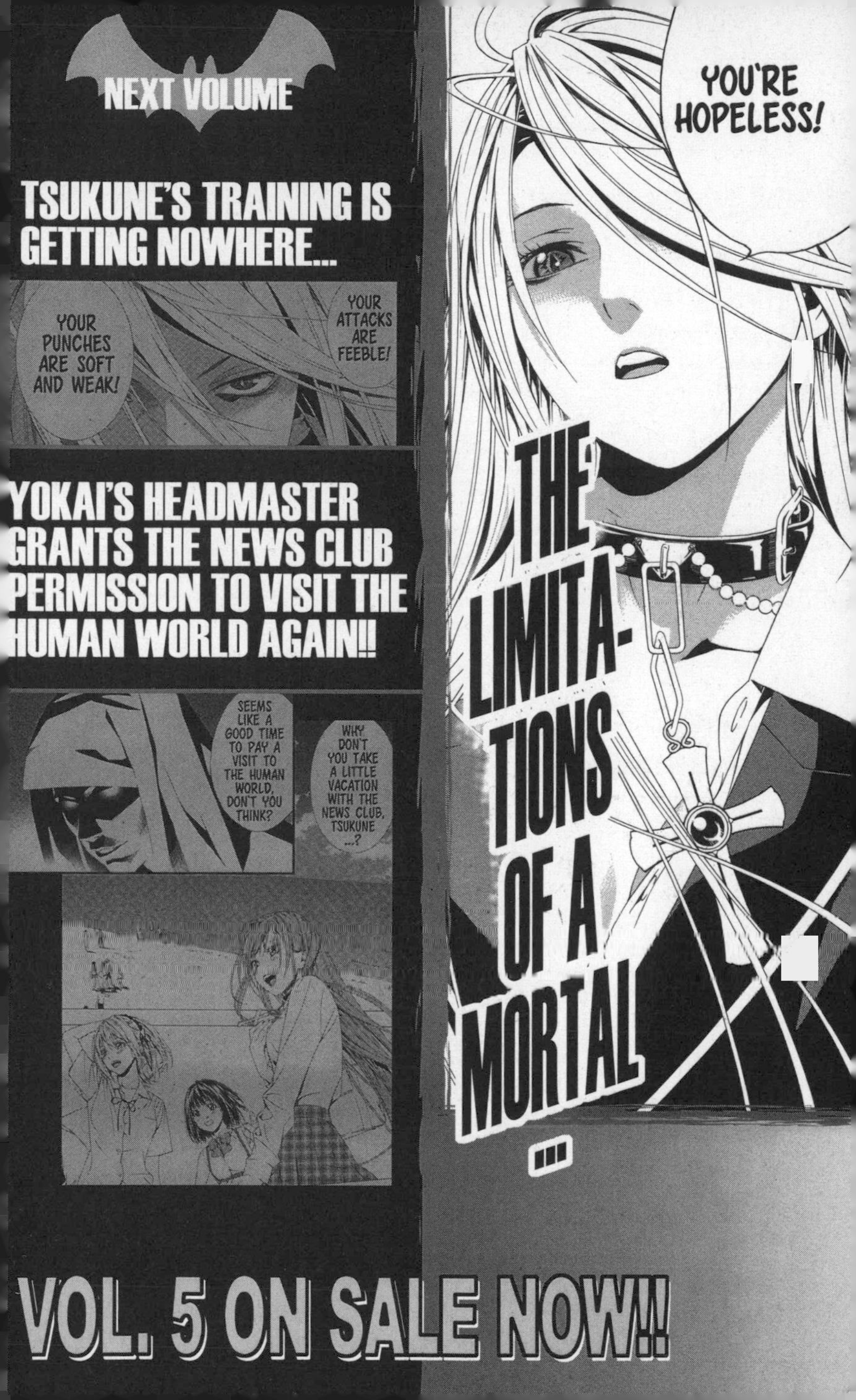
NEXT VOLUME
TSUKUNE'S TRAINING IS GETTING NOWHERE...
YOUR ATTACKS ARE FEEBLE!
YOUR PUNCHES ARE SOFT AND WEAK!
YOKAI'S HEADMASTER GRANTS THE NEWS CLUB PERMISSION TO VISIT THE HUMAN WORLD AGAIN!!
SEEMS LIKE A GOOD TIME TO PAY A VISIT TO THE HUMAN WORLD, DON'T YOU THINK?
WHY DON'T YOU TAKE A LITTLE VACATION WITH THE NEWS CLUB, TSUKUNE ...?
YOU'RE HOPELESS!
THE LIMITA-TIONS OF A MORTAL...
VOL. 5 ON SALE NOW!!

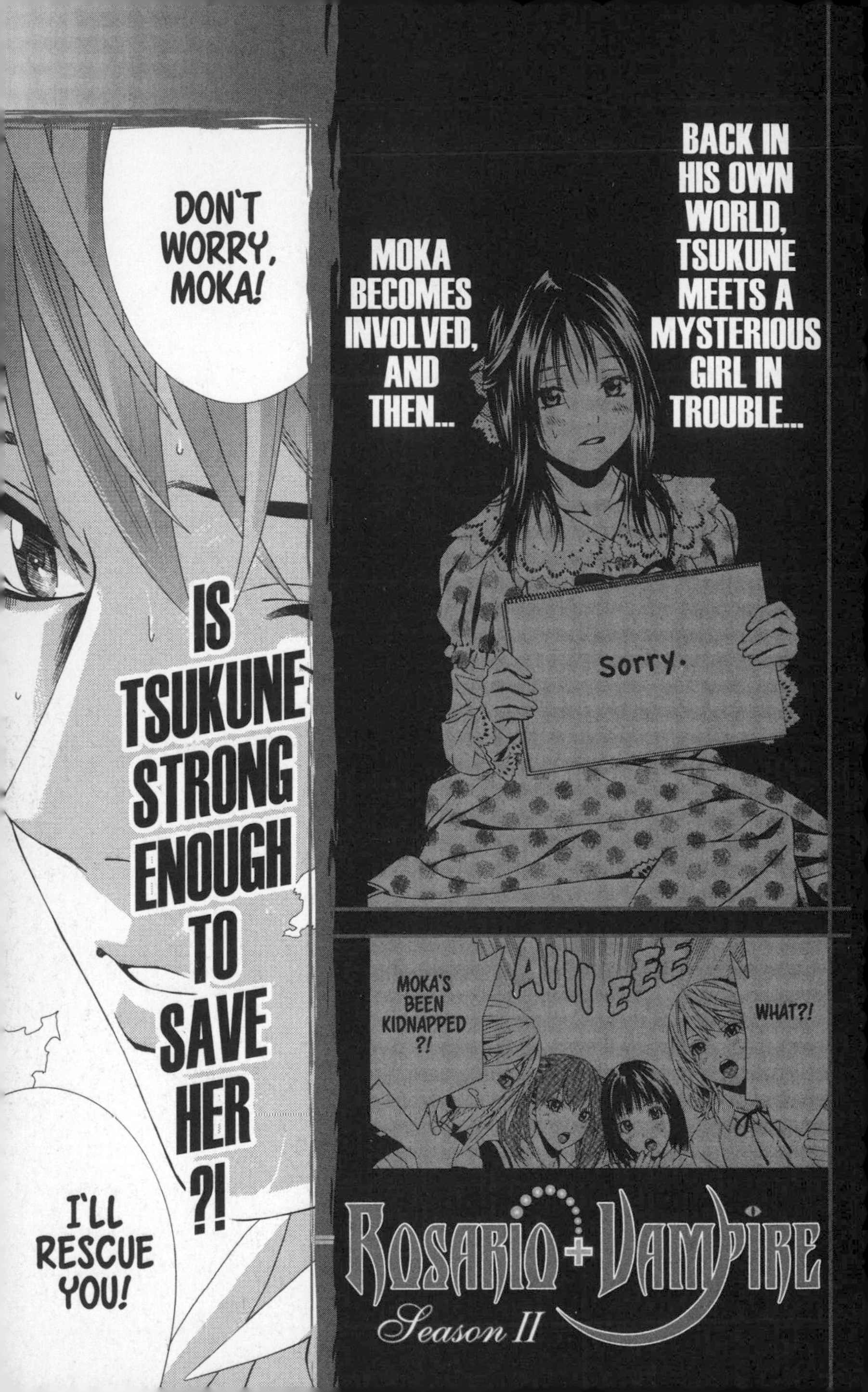
BACK IN HIS OWN WORLD, TSUKUNE MEETS A MYSTERIOUS GIRL IN TROUBLE...
MOKA BECOMES INVOLVED, AND THEN...
Sorry.
WHAT?!
AIIIEEE
MOKA'S BEEN KIDNAPPED?!
ROSARIO+VAMPIRE
Season II
DON'T WORRY, MOKA!
IS TSUKUNE STRONG ENOUGH TO SAVE HER?!
I'LL RESCUE YOU!

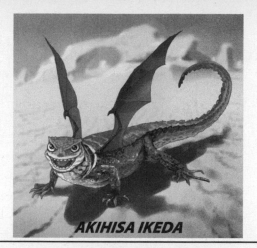

AKIHISA IKEDA

Every now and then I'm asked the question, "How much of the story have you planned out so far?" This is the fourth volume of Season II. I guess I'm about a third of the way into the "Whole Plot."

But...the characters and story don't always follow my plan exactly, so this "Whole Plot" is pretty flexible. Also, the "Whole Plot" inside my head is kind of like a movie trailer...one fragment of a scene after another. In this volume, Ruby was running all over the place. That was unexpected... (LOL) But I think the fun of creating a story is that things don't always go according to plan...

Akihisa Ikeda was born in 1976 in Miyazaki. He debuted as a mangaka with the four-volume magical warrior fantasy series *Kiruto* in 2002, which was serialized in *Monthly Shonen Jump*. *Rosario+Vampire* debuted in *Monthly Shonen Jump* in March of 2004 and is continuing in the magazine *Jump Square (Jump SQ)* as *Rosario+Vampire: Season II*. In Japan, *Rosario+Vampire* is also available as a drama CD. In 2008, the story was released as an anime. Season II is also available as an anime now. And in Japan, there is a Nintendo DS game based on the series.

Ikeda has been a huge fan of vampires and monsters since he was a little kid. He says one of the perks of being a manga artist is being able to go for walks during the day when everybody else is stuck in the office.

ROSARIO+VAMPIRE: Season II
4
SHONEN JUMP ADVANCED Manga Edition

STORY & ART BY **AKIHISA IKEDA**

Translation/Tetsuichiro Miyaki
English Adaptation/Gerard Jones
Touch-up Art & Lettering/Stephen Dutro
Cover Design/Hidemi Sahara
Interior Design/Ronnie Casson
Editor/Annette Roman

Printed in the U.S.A.

Published by VIZ Media, LLC
P.O. Box 77010
San Francisco, CA 94107

10 9 8 7 6 5 4
First printing, April 2011
Fourth printing, September 2015

www.viz.com

www.shonenjump.com

CRYPT SHEET FOR

ROSARIO+VAMPIRE: SEASON II, VOL. 5

SIREN SONG

TEST 5

WHEN YOUR EARS ARE ASSAULTED BY THE SONG OF A SIREN...

a. press shuffle

b. tie yourself to a mast

c. have a sing-off

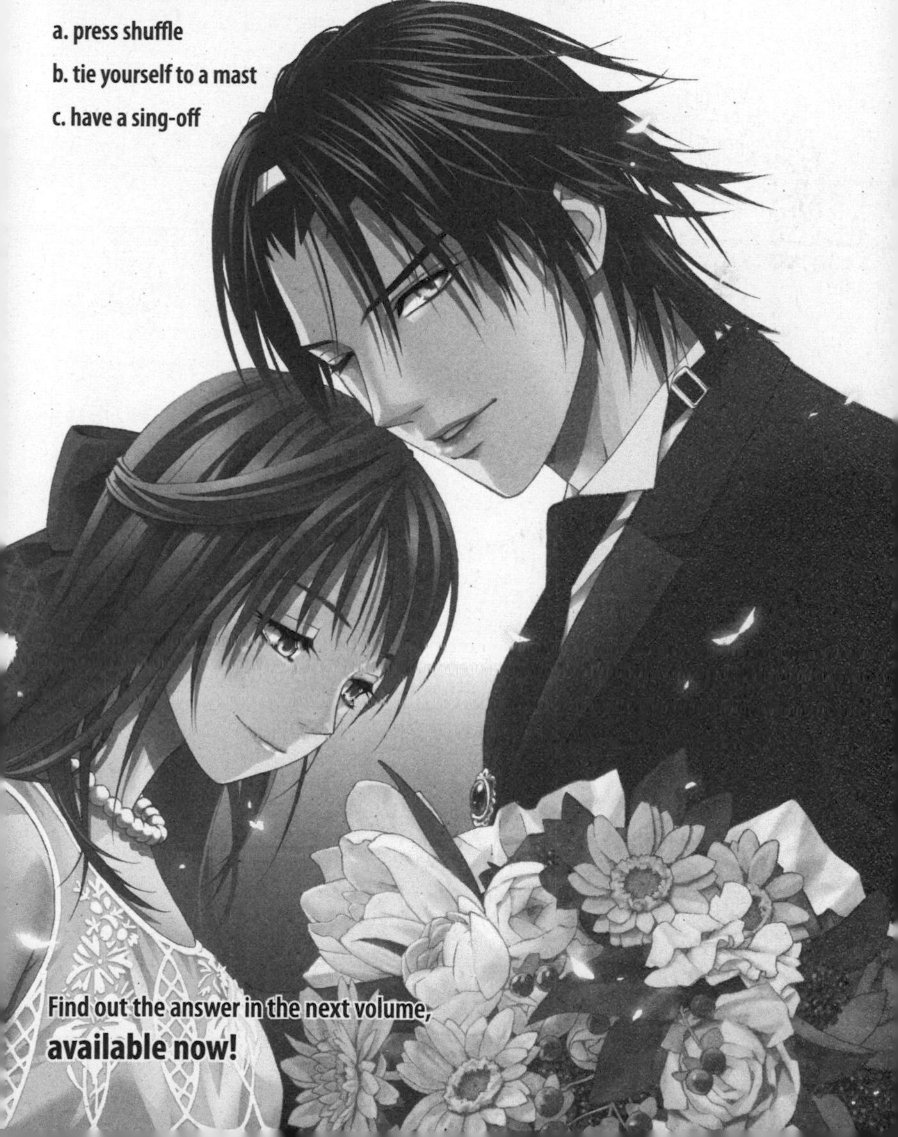

Find out the answer in the next volume,
available now!

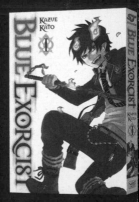

Seraph of the End

VAMPIRE REIGN

STORY BY Takaya Kagami ART BY Yamato Yamamoto
STORYBOARDS BY Daisuke Furuya

**Vampires reign—
humans revolt!**

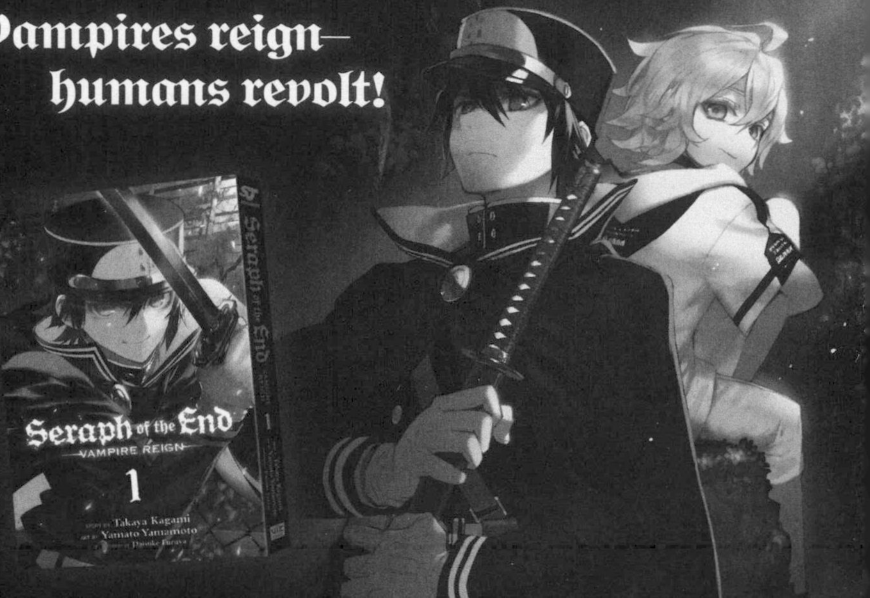
Seraph of the End
VAMPIRE REIGN
1
Takaya Kagami
Yamato Yamamoto
Daisuke Furuya

Yuichiro's dream of killing every vampire is near-impossible, given that vampires are seven times stronger than humans, and the only way to kill them is by mastering Cursed Gear, advanced demon-possessed weaponry. Not to mention that humanity's most elite Vampire Extermination Unit, the Moon Demon Company, wants nothing to do with Yuichiro unless he can prove he's willing to work in a team—which is the last thing he wants!

THE LATEST CHAPTERS SERIALIZED IN WEEKLY SHONEN JUMP

RATED T+ FOR OLDER TEEN ratings.viz.com

SHONEN JUMP ADVANCED www.shonenjump.com

VIZ media www.viz.com

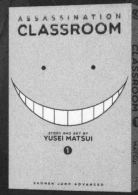

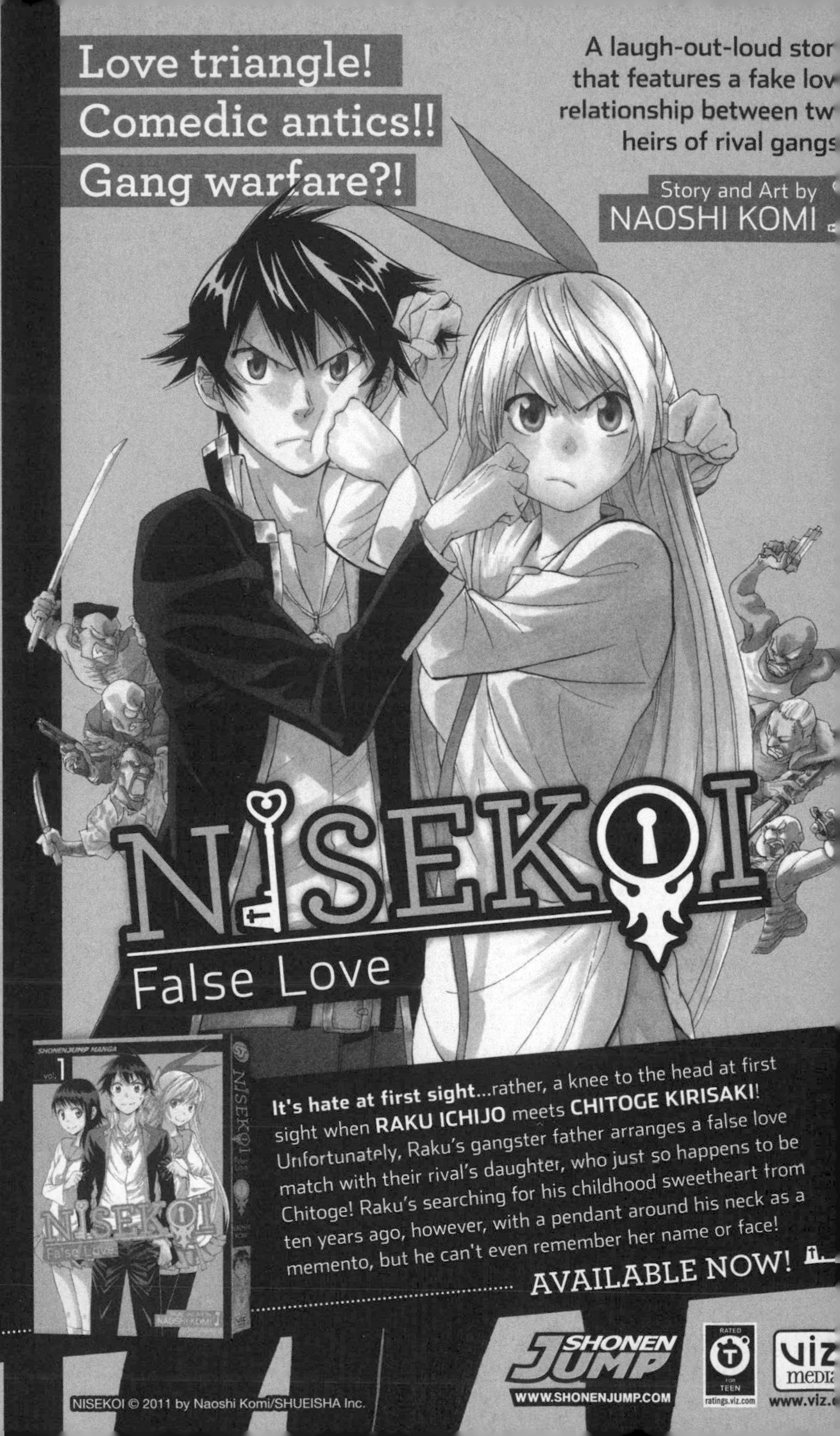

Love triangle!
Comedic antics!!
Gang warfare?!
A laugh-out-loud stor
that features a fake lov
relationship between tw
heirs of rival gangs
Story and Art by
NAOSHI KOMI
NISEKOI
False Love
SHONEN JUMP MANGA
vol. 1
It's hate at first sight...rather, a knee to the head at first sight when RAKU ICHIJO meets CHITOGE KIRISAKI! Unfortunately, Raku's gangster father arranges a false love match with their rival's daughter, who just so happens to be Chitoge! Raku's searching for his childhood sweetheart from ten years ago, however, with a pendant around his neck as a memento, but he can't even remember her name or face!
AVAILABLE NOW!
SHONEN JUMP
WWW.SHONENJUMP.COM
RATED T FOR TEEN
ratings.viz.com
viz media
www.viz.
NISEKOI © 2011 by Naoshi Komi/SHUEISHA Inc.

Yo[illegible]g in the Wrong Direction!!

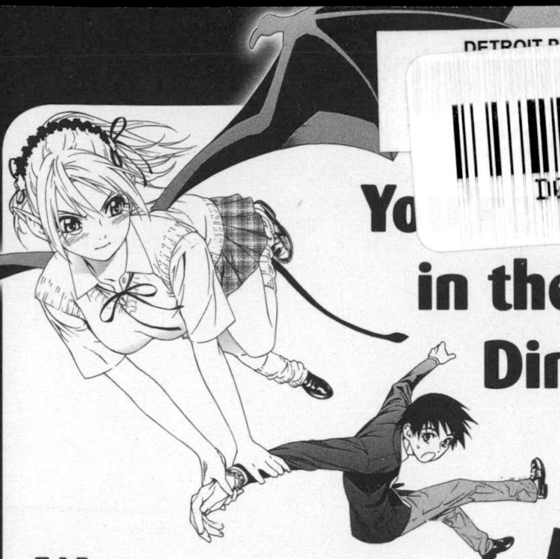

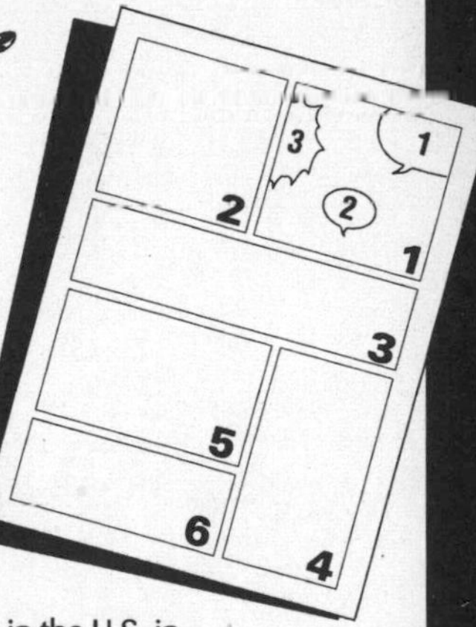
1
2
3
1
2
3
4
5
6

Whoops! Guess what? You're starting at the wrong end of the comic!

...It's true! In keeping with the original Japanese format, **Rosario+Vampire** is meant to be read from right to left, starting in the upper-right corner.

Unlike English, which is read from left to right, Japanese is read from right to left, meaning action, sound effects and word-balloon order are completely reversed... something which can make readers unfamiliar with Japanese feel pretty backwards themselves. For this reason, manga or Japanese comics published in the U.S. in English have sometimes been published "flopped"—that is, printed in exact reverse order, as though seen from the other side of a mirror.

By flopping pages, U.S. publishers can avoid confusing readers, but the compromise is not without its downside. For one thing, a character in a flopped manga series who once wore in the original Japanese version a T-shirt emblazoned with "M A Y" (as in "the merry month of") now wears one which reads "Y A M"! Additionally, many manga creators in Japan are themselves unhappy with the process, as some feel the mirror-imaging of their art skews their original intentions.

We are proud to bring you Akihisa Ikeda's **Rosario+Vampire** in the original unflopped format. For now, though, turn to the other side of the book and let the haunting begin...!

–Editor